To the memory of Eugène Vinaver

AMS Studies in the Seventeenth Century: No. 1

International Standard Serials Number: 0731-2342

Also in this series:

No. 2 Stephen K. Land. *The Philosophy of Language in Britain: Major Theories from Hobbes to Thomas Reid.* 1986.

No. 3 William Frost. *John Dryden: Dramatist, Satirist, Translator.* 1986.

THE FRENCH STAGE AND PLAYHOUSE
IN THE SEVENTEENTH CENTURY

T. E. LAWRENSON, 1918–1982

THE FRENCH STAGE
AND PLAYHOUSE
IN THE XVIIth CENTURY

A STUDY IN THE ADVENT OF
THE ITALIAN ORDER

SECOND EDITION
Revised and Enlarged

T. E. Lawrenson

AMS PRESS
New York

LIBRARY OF CONGRESS CATALOGING IN PUBLICATION DATA

Lawrenson, T. E. (Thomas Edward), 1918–1982.
  The French stage and playhouse in the XVIIth
century.

  (AMS studies in the seventeenth century,
ISSN 0731-2342 ; no. 1)
  Rev. ed. of: The French stage in the XVIIth
century. 1957.
  Bibliography: p.
  Includes index.
  1. Theaters—Stage-setting and scenery.
2. Theaters—France. 3. Theaters—Italy. 4. Theater—
France—History—17th century. I. Lawrenson, T. E.
(Thomas Edward), 1918–1982. French stage in the
XVIIth century. II. Title. III. Series.
PN2091.S8L3   1986   792'.025   79-3697
ISBN 0-404-61721-2

MANUFACTURED IN THE UNITED STATES OF AMERICA

CONTENTS

LIST OF ILLUSTRATIONS

* Photo. Bibliothèque Nationale Imprimés
† Photo. Bibliothèque Nationale Estampes

ix

FOREWORD

THE PUBLICATION OF the first edition of this work in 1957 was both a breakthrough in theater research and the stimulus for much further research. The discoveries it prompted, together with Professor Lawrenson's own subsequent work, have in turn helped to shape this second edition. The present volume is, therefore, not merely a revised version of the original work but a new and timely *mise au point*. Sadly, however, because of the author's death, it must also serve as a memorial volume: hence the inclusion of ancillary matter compiled by Professor Lawrenson's friends and colleagues in homage to the author. My excuse for adding to it with this foreword is not to justify the publication of a work whose importance is self-evident but to place on record how the volume came to be assembled in its present form and seen through the press.

Professor Lawrenson had completed the manuscript of this book shortly before he died. The Lawrenson Memorial Committee which was set up after his death agreed that its efforts should be directed towards helping the publication of his work, and that this should be done by subscription. Subscription sales were organized by Dr. L. M. Newman, Professor H. W. Wardman and Dr. M. H. Merriman. On their behalf, I must thank the International Federation for Theatre Research, the Society for Theatre Research and the Société d'Histoire du Théâtre for their help in distributing prospectuses. Dr. Newman also assembled the details of Professor Lawrenson's publications and theatrical activities, compiled the list of illustrations for the main body of the text, and attended to the many queries which arose during the normal editorial process. I myself must take responsibility for checking the proofs. Our aim throughout has been to ensure that the book conforms as nearly as possible in matters of accuracy and detail to the author's intentions.

I should like to thank Mrs. P. Lawrenson for supplying the photograph that accompanies Professor Wardman's appreciation of the author. Finally, all the members of the Lawrenson Memorial Committee are indebted to the many individuals who by donations and subscriptions gave their support and guaranteed the successful, if belated, publication of this work.

DAVID WHITTON

T. E. LAWRENSON

THOMAS EDWARD LAWRENSON was born on September 19, 1918. A Yorkshireman by birth, he was educated at Castleford and Skipton Grammar Schools. Then he forsook the county of his birth and crossed the Pennines to become a student under Eugène Vinaver at the University of Manchester in 1934. He took a very good first in French Honors there in 1939.

In the Second World War he served in West Africa and Burma. After the war he held academic appointments at Manchester, the University College of the Gold Coast (now the University of Ghana), as Senior Lecturer and Head of Department, then as Lecturer at Glasgow and Aberdeen. Finally, in 1964 he became one of the University of Lancaster's foundation professors as Professor and Head of the Department of French Studies. He held this post until 1979 when he became Professor of Theatre Studies in the same university.

French was, for him, as he used to call it, a "second classic," in the sense that it was Latin and Greek which had given to modern and contemporary French drama some of its most potent and enduring themes. His imagination was also fired by the Greek theater itself, the amphitheater. This, for him, was almost the theater as it should be, without the proscenium arch. He had ambitious plans for using the Greek amphitheater in a revival of African drama with which he was closely associated in Ghana. On the top of Legon Hill, a few miles outside Accra, where the University of Ghana stands, there still exists an open-air amphitheater where plays were produced and in which he performed.

French was also for him "French Studies," that is, a study in depth, not only of language and literature, but also of French culture, including history, art, music, ideas, law, and geography. The theater was certainly studied too, but, to use his expression, "on the hoof" in the Nuffield Theater Studio, the setting-up of which owed much to his efforts. Plays were not just "books," as students were apt to be gently reminded, but dramatic performances. Thus acting was an active force in the department long before he became Professor of Theatre Studies.

With his pioneering energies he had brought one new department into being in Ghana. When appointed to Lancaster he began to use the same energies to create another. Nineteen sixty-four, the beginning of the Robbins expansion, gave him a great opportunity. He embodied his conception of French Studies in an exacting first-year course, which taxed staff and students alike. Courses had to be linked at some point, whether Major with Major or Major with Minor. He was a firm upholder of the original "ethos" of this university. He believed in the university as an academic community.

With him, this was no empty expression. To some extent, he stood for tradition and formality between staff and students. He believed that gowns should be worn at formal lectures and in the virtues of this form of teaching. But while his lectures may have been formal, they were also often lively dramatic performances. As to his audience, the student in his eyes was essentially a human being and an equal, who should therefore take part in university life as a whole. This explains the importance which he attached to residence, not, of course, in "hostels," but in colleges governed by staff and students and integrated into the whole university. At Aberdeen he was one of the first to be head of a mixed college. At Lancaster, he was one of the first principals of Lonsdale College. All of this was to be expected from his witty and lively book, *Hall of Residence* (M.U.P., 1957).

In the field of theater research he did distinguished work, with numerous articles and editions of plays, but above all, with the publication of his revised doctoral thesis, the important *The French Stage in the Seventeenth Century* (M.U.P., 1959). It is this work which is now being published in a completely revised form under the title, *The French Stage and Playhouse in the Seventeenth Century*. The value of his work was recognized internationally: the French Government made him a *Chevalier de l'Ordre National du Mérite*; he became Secretary-General of the International Federation for Theatre Research and, shortly before his death, he was appointed adviser to the B.B.C. in connection with its television series, *All the World's a Stage*.

He did not confine himself to the academic study of the theater. He produced plays himself and was a gifted comic actor. On the top of Legon Hill he played an exuberant Sir Toby Belch and took part in Giraudoux's *Amphitryon 38*; comic roles in Giraudoux and Anouilh suited his talents. But Molière was for him the supreme dramatist, so that what he may well be most remembered for is his Madame Pernelle in *Tartuffe*, and above all, his interpretation of the role of Arnolphe in *L'Ecole des femmes* which brought out all the pathetic absurdity of that unfortunate man.

He was something of an actor in life itself. With his wit and talent for repartee he could enliven meetings of Senate, and, in his capacity as University Orator, such solemn occasions as Convocation. He was a "character" in the best sense of the word who mixed freely and on equal terms with all members of the university.

He was active in the local community. He established a local branch of the *Alliance Française* and brought his department into contact with schools. He believed that universities should put down roots in the regions where they exist and which they should therefore serve. He died after a short illness on April 4, 1982. May the publication of this book help to perpetuate the memory of one who was an intensely human individual and a scholar of the first rank.

H. W. W.

PUBLICATIONS

1950

"The 'Théâtre Étagé' in the seventeenth century." *French Studies* 4: 55–58.

"Three final curtains and an act-drop." *Modern Languages* (November): 3–12.

1954

"The idea of a National Theatre." *Universitas* [Accra] (June): 6–10.

1956

"Ville imaginaire, décor théatral et fête: autour d'un recueil de Geofroy Tory," 425–30 & 1 plate in Jean Jacquot, ed. *Les fêtes de la Renaissance, 1* [Paris: CNRS].

"La mise en scène dans *L'Arimène* de Nicolas de Montreux." *Bibliothèque d'Humanisme et Renaissance* 18: 286–90.

1957

The French stage in the XVIIth century: a study in the advent of the Italian order. Manchester University Press, in conjunction with the Publications Board of the University College of the Gold Coast. xxvi, 209 pp. 45 plates.

Hall of residence: Saint Anselm Hall in the University of Manchester, 1907–1957. Manchester University Press. x, 147 pp.

1961

Alain-René Lesage. *Crispin rival de son maître: comédie.* Edited with an introduction by T. E. Lawrenson. (Textes Français Classiques et Modernes) University of London Press. 109 pp.

1964

"Les éditions illustrées de Térence dans l'histoire du théâtre: spectacles dans un fauteuil?" Par T. E. Lawrenson et Helen Purkis, 1—23 & 8 plates in Jean Jacquot, ed. *Le lieu théâtral à la Renaissance.* [Paris: CNRS]

"Le *Mémoire* de Mahelot et L'*Agarite* de Durval: vers une reconstitution pratique." Par T. E. Lawrenson, Donald Roy, et Richard Southern, 363–76 & 3 plates in Jean Jacquot, ed. *Le lieu théâtral à la Renaissance.* [Paris: CNRS]

"Voltaire and Shakespeare: ordeal by translation," 58–75 in G. I. Duthie, ed. *Papers, mainly Shakespearian.* [(Aberdeen University Studies 14) Edinburgh: published for the University of Aberdeen [by] Oliver & Boyd].

[Review of Leo Schrade. *La représentation d'Edipo au Teatro Olimpico (Vicence 1585).* Paris: CNRS, 1960] *Modern Language Review* 59: 150–1.

1965

"The shape of the eighteenth-century French theatre and the drawing-board renaissance [1]." *Theatre Research/Recherches Théâtrales* 7: 7–25 & 6 plates.

"A theatre research laboratory." *Prospects* [Lancaster] (December): 15–20.

1966

"The shape of the eighteenth-century French theatre and the drawing-board renaissance [2]." *Theatre Research/Recherches Théâtrales* 7: 99–109 & 6 plates.

1967

"The place of the theatre in the modern humanities," 63–79 in The University of Lancaster *Inaugural lectures, 1965-1967.* [University of Lancaster. Delivered on June 16, 1965]

1968

"The comic theatre: Marivaux and Beaumarchais," 117–33 in John Cruickshank, ed. *French literature and its background*, Vol. 3. [Oxford University Press]

1969

Alain-René Lesage. *Turcaret.* Edited with an introduction by T. E. Lawrenson. University of London Press. vii, 128 pp.

Modern miscellany presented to Eugène Vinaver by pupils, colleagues and friends. Edited by T. E. Lawrenson, F. E. Sutcliffe and G. F. A. Gadoffre. Manchester University Press/New York: Barnes & Noble. xiii, 314 pp. 2 plates.

"The contemporary staging of Théophile's *Pyrame et Thisbé:* the open stage imprisoned," 167–79 & 1 plate in *Modern Miscellany.*

[Review of Jacques Morel, *La tragédie* [and] Pierre Voltz, *La comédie.* Paris: Colin, 1964] *French Studies* 23: 205–7.

1970

"Voltaire, translator of Shakespeare." *Western Canadian Studies in Modern Languages & Literature* 2: 28–32.

1971

[Review of Marvin Carlson. *The theatre of the French Revolution.* Ithaca: Cornell University Press, 1966] *Theatre Research/Recherches Théâtrales* 11: 179–81.

"Madame Bovary: essai de reconstitution. Avant-Propos." *Cahiers Gaston Baty* 8: 15–16. [Reprinted in *Theatre Research/Recherches Théâtrales* 13 (1974): 155].

Gustave Flaubert. *Madame Bovary: tableaux 14 et 15 de l'adaptation et mise en scène de Gaston Baty au Théâtre Montparnasse, Paris, 1936.* [Postgraduate reconstruction, supervised by T. E. Lawrenson, presented in the Nuffield Theatre Studio in May 1971. University of Lancaster. Videotape. Black & white, 23 minutes]

1972

[Review of Frances A. Yates. *Theatre of the world.* London: Routledge, 1969] *Modern Language Review* 67: 614–6.

The open stage imprisoned. Researched and narrated by T. E. Lawrenson. [University of Lancaster. Videotape. Black & white. Part 1: The theatrical convention of the 'décor simultané'. 29 minutes. Part 2: Walk through of *Pyrame et Thisbé* in a reconstruction of Mahelot's set. 34 minutes]

1973

"The wearing o' the Green: yet another look at 'l'homme aux rubans verts,' " 163-9 in W. D. Howarth and Merlin Thomas, eds. *Molière: stage and study: essays in honour of W. G. Moore.* [Oxford: Clarendon Press]

[Review of Anna Raitière. *L'art de l'acteur selon Dorst et Samson (1766-1863/65)* (Etudes de Philologie et d'Histoire 8) Genève: Droz, 1969] *French Studies* 27:457-8.

1974

"Madame Bovary: essai de reconstitution. Avant-Propos." *Theatre Research/Recherches Théâtrales* 13:155. [Reprinted from *Cahiers Gaston Baty* 8 (1971): 15-16]

[Review of T. J. Reiss. *Toward a dramatic illusion: theatrical technique and meaning from Hardy to "Horace."* New Haven & London: Yale University Press, 1971] *Modern Language Review* 69: 637-9.

Maurice Maeterlinck. *La mort de Tintagiles.* [Postgraduate project supervised by T. E. Lawrenson, performed by puppets at the Lancaster Girls Grammar School on May 25 1974. University of Lancaster. Videotape. Black & white, 27 minutes]

1975

"The Lancaster University Nuffield Theatre Studio and Workshop: conception, form and function," 60-61 in Margret Dietrich, ed. *Regie in Dokumentation, Forschung und Lehre: Festschrift für Heinz Kindermann zum 80. Geburtstag.* [Salzburg: Müller]

1976

"Les *Noces de Pélée* et la guerre des bouffons," 121-9 in Maria Teresa Muraro, ed. *Venezia e il melodramma nel Seicento.* [(Studi di musica veneta 5) Firenze: Olschki]

"Timon of Athens, Alceste of Paris, and Old Manly of the Sea: *Le Misanthrope* and the *Plain Dealer." Comparison* 4 (Winter): 47-70.

[Review of H. W. Lawton. *Térence en France au seizième siècle.* 2 vols. Genève: Slatkine, 1970-72] *Modern Language Review* 71: 915-6.

Ionesco: areas of non-communication. [Postgraduate project, supervised and narrated by T. E. Lawrenson, with acted excerpts. University of Lancaster. Videotape. Black & white, 39½ minutes]

[Molière]. *L'École des Femmes* [as produced by Louis Jouvet at the Athénée, Paris, in May 1936. Excerpts from postgraduate reconstruction, supervised by T. E. Lawrenson, who also played Arnolphe, presented in the Nuffield Theatre Studio in May 1976. University of Lancaster. Videotape. Black & white, 45 minutes]

1977

[Molière]. *Tartuffe* prepared for the Course Team by Tom Lawrenson, 79-99 in *The Open University, Arts: a third level course: drama* [(A307 Units 7-11 Study 5 *Comedy*) Milton Keynes: The Open University Press]

1978

[Review of Nicola Mangini. *I teatri di Venezia.* Milan: Mursia, 1974] *Revue de la Société d'Histoire du Théâtre* 30: 91-94.

1979

[Review of Henri Lagrave. *Le théâtre et le public à Paris de 1715 à 1750*. Paris: Klinck-sieck, 1972] *Modern Language Review* 74: 458–61.

1980

"The ideal theatre in the eighteenth century: Paris and Venice," 51–64 in James Redmond, ed. *Drama and mimesis*. [(Themes in drama 2) Cambridge University Press]

"Holsboer and after: the French stage and auditorium in the seventeenth century. *Newsletter of the Society for Seventeenth-Century French Studies* [Norwich] 2: 65–71.

1981

"The lessons of the reconstructed performance." By C. M. Fogarty and Tom Lawrenson. *Theatre Survey* 22: 141–59.

1983

[Unsigned contributions] in Phyllis Hartnoll, ed. *The Oxford Companion to the Theatre*, fourth edition. [Oxford University Press]

THEATRICAL ACTIVITY

1948
Jean Anouilh. *Le bal des voleurs*. Whitworth Gallery Theatre, Manchester. Directed and played Peterbono.

1949
Jean Giraudoux. *La guerre de Troie n'aura pas lieu*. Arthur Worthington Hall, University of Manchester. Directed and played Demokos.

1950
Jean Anouilh. *The burglars' ball;* translated from the French by T. E. Lawrenson. Saint Anselm Hall, University of Manchester. Directed and played Peterbono.
William Shakespeare. *The taming of the shrew*. Library Theatre, Manchester. Played Grumio.

1951
Founded the Curtain Club of the University College of the Gold Coast. Collaborated in the planning and construction of the Garden Theatre, Accra.

1952
Oscar Wilde. *The importance of being earnest*. The Community Centre, Accra. Directed and played Algernon Moncrieff.
George Bernard Shaw. *Arms and the man*. The Community Centre, Accra. Played Bluntschli.

1953
William Shakespeare. *Twelfth Night*. The Garden Theatre, Accra. Played Sir Toby Belch.
Collaborated in planning a stone Greco-Roman open-air theater for the new university campus at Legon.

1954
Jean Giraudoux. *The Apollo of Bellac;* translated from the French by T. E. Lawrenson. The Garden Theatre, Accra, Directed.

1955
Aristophanes. *The frogs*. The Garden Theatre, Accra. Directed.

1956
William Shakespeare. *The taming of the shrew*. Greco-Roman Theatre at Legon. Played Grumio.

1957
Work in progress. Gold Coast Film Unit independence film. Played Brother Gregory.

1958
Jean Giraudoux. *Intermezzo*. Athenaeum Theatre, Glasgow, and Edinburgh Festival. Directed and played Le Maire.

1959

Thomas Corneille. *Mélite*. A dramatized play reading. Queen Margaret Hall, University of Glasgow. Directed.

1960

Molière. *George Dandin*. University of Aberdeen. Supervised the student director.

1966

Molière. *La jalousie de Barbouillé*. Nuffield Theatre Studio, University of Lancaster. Directed and played Le Docteur.

1969

Sir John Vanbrugh. *The provoked wife*. Nuffield Theatre Studio, University of Lancaster. Played the Justice of the Peace.

1970

Eugène Ionesco. *Jacques ou la soumission*. University of Saskatchewan at Regina. Supervised the direction.

1971

William Shakespeare. *Othello*. Nuffield Theatre Studio, University of Lancaster. Played the Duke of Venice.

1972

Molière. *Tartuffe*. Nuffield Theatre Studio, University of Lancaster. Played Mme Pernelle.
The open stage imprisoned. Researched and narrated by T. E. Lawrenson. University of Lancaster. Videotape. Black & white. 63 minutes.

1973

Molière. *L'Ecole des femmes*, Act II, scene 5. Gardens of the Fondazione Cini, Venice. Played Arnolphe.

1976

Molière. *L'Ecole des femmes*. Nuffield Theatre Studio, University of Lancaster. Played Arnolphe. [Excerpts have been recorded on videotape. Black & white. 45 minutes.]
Oscar Wilde. *The importance of being earnest*. Original 4-act version. Nuffield Theatre Studio, University of Lancaster. Played Mr. Gribsby.
Ionesco: areas of communication. Postgraduate project, supervised and narrated by T. E. Lawrenson. University of Lancaster. Videotape. Black & white. 39½ minutes.

1977

Jean Giraudoux. *Intermezzo*. Nuffield Theatre Studio, University of Lancaster. Played L'Inspecteur.

1979

Alfred Jarry. *Ubu Roi*. Nuffield Theatre Studio, University of Lancaster. Played Père Ubu.

Niccolò Machiavelli. *The mandrake*. Nuffield Theatre Studio, University of Lancaster. Played Messer Nicia.

Jean Anouilh. *Le bal des voleurs*. Nuffield Theatre Studio, University of Lancaster. Played Peterbono.

1980

William Shakespeare. *Romeo and Juliet*. Nuffield Theatre Studio, University of Lancaster. Played Escalus.

Georges Feydeau. *A stitch in time*. Nuffield Theatre Studio, University of Lancaster, Directed.

1981

William Shakespeare. *The merchant of Venice*. Nuffield Theatre Studio, University of Lancaster. Played Old Gobbo.

Eugène Ionesco. *La leçon*. Nuffield Theatre Studio, University of Lancaster. Directed.

1982

William Shakespeare. *A midsummer night's dream*. Nuffield Theatre Studio, University of Lancaster. Played Philostrate.

PREFACE TO THE SECOND EDITION

AS THE INTRODUCTION to the first edition of this volume has been left virtually intact, a word of explanation is perhaps necessary regarding the general historical basis against which is set this study of the arrival of the Italianate proscenium arch theater in France.

That basis is postulated in the introduction as being a progression from the (relative) actor-audience, stage-auditorium cohesion of the ancient theater, to the polarized modern form. Now, that basis continues in my opinion to be valid, but two reservations must be made. First, one can no longer say with quite the confidence that I appear to employ on p. 2 of the introduction, "The Dionysian ceremony became the play," and this since Gerald Else, in a series of four lectures published in 1965, tore through the Dionysian origins as though they were fustian.[1] One's only consolation is that the spirit of Nietzsche has a little more re-writing to do than the present author, and we must even re-read our Artaud with a difference, if not with a pinch of Attic salt. The new dating in the 460s of what had hitherto been thought of as Aeschylus' first extant play, *The Suppliants*, permits Else to attack the choral origins of tragedy, and the other conclusions that concern us are as follows:

1. There is no solid evidence for tragedy ever having been Dionysiac in any sense except that it was originally and regularly presented at the City Dionysia in Athens.
2. There is no reason to believe that tragedy grew out of any kind of possession or ecstasy (*Ergriffenheit*), Dionysiac or otherwise.[2]

Secondly, we are now even less justified in assuming that the evolving shape of the European theater moves in any regular way from the circular lay-out of the ancient performance through a segment of circle to the rectangular house. Elizabeth R. Gebhard[3] had unearthed at Isthmia a three-sided auditorium with wings diverging towards the skené, and is able to point out straight rows of seating at Rhamnous, Ikaria, Tegea, and Morgantina.

Yet I still think the concept of "polarization" of stage and auditorium is a sensible and useful one when it comes to viewing the growth of the proscenium arch theater, although that concept met with a mixed reception from reviewers of the first edition. The use of an historical base at all drew fire from the Sorbonne in the person of the late Raymond Picard: ". . . the author all but goes back to the Ark before which David danced."[4] In Oxford, the late Dr. W. G. Moore took what I take to be an opposite point of view: "the chief merit of Dr. Lawrenson's research is to my mind the search for meaning and pattern in the evidence."[5] Clearly, no man can serve two masters.

1. Gerald Else, *The Origin and Early Form of Greek Tragedy*, Cambridge, Mass., 1967.
2. Pp. 6, 7.
3. Elizabeth K. Gebhard, *The Theater at Isthmia*, Chicago, 1973.
4. *Revue des Sciences Humaines*, April–June, 1958. I have translated from the French.
5. *Modern Language Review*, vol. LIII, 1958, 260-1.

I should perhaps repeat what I say in the introduction regarding the term "baroque." I think it now generally accepted by theater historians that the theatrical baroque is not necessarily coincidental with literary baroque, that the defining features of three-dimensional baroque on the stage determine its essential arrival in Paris as 1645, in the production of the *Finta Pazza* with sets by Torelli. Bjurström's work seems conclusive here.[6] The literary historian could, on the other hand—and has—described Théophile's *Pyrame et Thisbé* as the best French baroque tragedy, although it is dated more than two decades earlier than the *Finta Pazza*, and its Hôtel de Bourgogne setting is not theatrical baroque. As before, I shall use the term purely in its theatrical sense.

> "In my youth," Father William replied to his son,
> "I feared it might injure the brain;
> But now I am perfectly sure I have none,
> Why, I do it again and again."

Our knowledge of the Parisian theaters of the seventeenth century has been advanced considerably during the two decades that have elapsed since the publication of the first edition. In particular, the dimensions of the Hôtel de Bourgogne have been ascertained with virtual exactitude by Roy, Illingworth, Wiley and others. Mme Deierkauf-Holsboer has published her two volumes on that theater, the second volume of her history of the Marais, and another volume on Parisian staging from 1600 to 1673. Védier has examined the problem of the curtain in great detail.[7] I have tried to take account of all these, and many other, labors in the present edition.

The appendix on eighteenth-century theaters I have ventured to suppress, the material, in the interim, having received scholarly treatment elsewhere.

TOM LAWRENSON

Lancaster, England
October, 1978

6. Per Bjurström, *Giacomo Torelli and Baroque Stage Design*, Stockholm, 1961.
7. Georges Védier, *Origine et évolution de la dramaturgie néo-classique*, Paris, 1955.

ABBREVIATIONS

Est. BN.—Bibliothèque Nationale, Département des Estampes.
MSS. BN.—Bibliothèque Nationale, Département des Manuscrits.
Arch. Nat.—Archives Nationales.

RHT—Revue d'Histoire du Théâtre.
RHLF—Revue d'Histoire Littéraire de la France.

Celler, *Décors*.—Celler, Ludovic (pseud. Leclerc). Les décors, les costumes et la mise en scène au XVIIe siècle. 1615–80.
Cohen, *Théâtre religieux*.— Histoire de la mise en scène dans le théâtre religieux français du moyen âge.
D'Aubignac, *Pratique*.—La pratique du théâtre.
Holsboer, *Mise en scène*.—Histoire de la mise en scène dans le théâtre français de 1600 à 1657.
Lancaster, *History*.—A History of French Dramatic Literature in the Seventeenth Century.
———*Mémoire*.—(ed). Le mémoire de Mahelot, Laurent, et d'autres décorateurs de l'Hôtel de Bourgogne et de la Comédie Française au XVIIe siècle.
Leclerc, *Origines*.—Les origines italiennes de l'architecture théâtrale moderne. L'évolution des formes en Italie de la Renaissance à la fin du XVIIe siècle.
Pickard-Cambridge, *Dionysus*.—The Theater of Dionysus in Athens.
Prunières, *Ballet de cour*.—Le ballet de cour en France avant Benserade et Lulli.
———*L'Opéra italien*.—L'Opéra italien en France avant Lulli.
Rigal, *Théâtre français*.—Le théâtre français avant la période classique.
Rouchès, *Inventaire*.—Inventaire des lettres et des papiers manuscrits de Gaspare, Carlo et Lodovico Vigarani . . .
Sabbattini, *Pratica*.—La pratica di fabricar scene e macchine ne'teatri.
Sauval, *Antiquités*.—Histoire et recherches des antiquités de la ville de Paris.

INTRODUCTION

THE LACK OF cohesion, of effective communion, in our own century, between actor and audience, stage and auditorium, is a commonplace notion to the lowliest amateur producer, let alone the professional director, or theorist of the drama. Variously ascribed, rarely defined, it is in fact felt by the great majority of men of the theater, and in an acute form.

A considerable body of opinion sees the root of the evil in the increasing heterogeneity of theater publics; others see its cause in the shape of the theater alone. Monolithic conventions of the past are brought forth as criteria against which the present-day stage is found wanting: in the Greek theater, the Medieval theater, and others, we are told, there was a unity of purpose between stage and auditorium which is no longer to be discerned.

Can we ascertain what was in fact the collective nature of the ancient Greek and Christian mystery theaters? In what way are they more homogeneous spectacles—if spectacle is the right word—than any we can experience today?

Excluding those primitive manifestations of the drama, the mimetic song and dance sequences which lead up to the dithyramb, Aeschylean tragedy, and Old Comedy; delimiting our drama by postulating a text, conscious and pre-invented, we can say with justification that the fifth-century Greek theatrical performance exhibited a degree of psychological cohesion between spectator, chorus, and the (at first) embryonic actor such as we have not witnessed since, at least in Western Europe. But that is a statement susceptible of many reservations not always accorded it. Professor George Thomson has suggested the manner in which Aeschylean tragedy is the outcome of a developing social superstructure, of differentiations commencing in earliest times.[1] He has examined the crystallization of early collective fertility rites into myth, into the secret societies of the Dionysian cult, bifurcating through Phallic hymns to Old Comedy and through primitive dithyrambic choruses to Tragedy and the mature dithyramb, with, along each channel, a process whereby priest becomes successively leader of the chorus, then actor, while the initiates become the chorus itself.

Looking at Thomson's view of the historical basis to this cultural superstructure,[2] certain limitations spring to the mind before we assume any absolute unity of purpose: tragedy, comedy, and dithyramb as we first meet them are the immediate products of political and economic changes in the seventh and sixth centuries B.C.—the growth of trade, the invention of money, facilitating the expropriation of the landed aristocracy by the *nouveaux riches*, the necessity for a political freedom which would enable the middle classes to increase trade: all these lead to the installation in 540 B.C. of the second of the aristocratic-commercial tyrants, Peisistratos. He it was who revived the Dionysian cult, which had passed down to the peasantry, to

---

1. *Aeschylus and Athens*, 2nd edn., 1945, Pt. III, Origin of Drama.
2. Ibid., ch. VI.

strengthen his hand against the landed aristocracy. "The aim underlying all these cultural innovations was to reinforce the commercial expansion of the new city-state *by fostering a spirit of national self-consciousness.*"[3] Peisistratos' reorganization, on a vast municipal scale, of the City Dionysia was as much a political act as the division of confiscated estates amongst the peasantry, the development of coinage and the export trade, or the program of public works.

Here perhaps we are approaching a definition of the limited unity of this theater. Between the tyrant's reconstitution of the festival of Dionysos, and Aeschylus' first extant play, little is known of tragedy. Yet, presumably working backwards from the extant plays, Thomson assumes that before Aeschylus they had normally begun and ended with a recitation by the chorus as it entered or left the orchestra. He sees in this the last traces of the "pompé" or ritual "going out" procession of the Bacchants, and the "kômos," or ceremonial return. This, if it is true, brings home the nearness of Aeschylean tragedy to the direct religious ritual, its nearness to, but not its identity with, direct participation in a religious ceremony in which, broadly speaking, it may be said that the lower strata of society believed and to which the class of state-promoters at least paid lip service. The Dionysian ceremony became the play, and though the memory of its religious implications died the "Church" continued to be its home. Altar and theater remained in the same place. There was no parallel development of the two.

Throughout the period of Aeschylus, Sophocles, and Euripides it has frequently been supposed then that the memory of the central part of the Dionysian secret remained with audience, choreutae, and actors. Such, according to this view, was the religious cohesion of the theatrical ceremony.

The landed aristocracy were out of the theater. They had never had much interest in Dionysos and in any case the majority of them were in exile. The City Dionysia brought together in common interest the merchant classes (at first through their tyrant representative) and the peasantry, however fallacious the "common interest" turned out to be for these latter. The festival sanctified in a resurrected cult the alliance of two classes against a third. Such was its political cohesion.

Jeanmaire has adopted a different standpoint.[4] For him the Dionysian roots of the dithyramb, of comedy and the satyr play, are well enough established for us to understand why Dionysos should be known as the god of the theater. Tragedy, on the other hand, developed admittedly in the theater of Dionysos but was not for that primarily Dionysian.

These two recent positions regarding the origin of the theater have seemed to me worthy of a restatement, however baldly, because in the considerable heart-searching that has gone on over theatrical problems in the nineteenth and twentieth

---

3. *Aeschylus and Athens*, p. 91. The italics are ours.
4. Henri Jeanmaire, *Dionysos*, Paris, 1951, pp. 312 et seq. Sir William Ridgeway, *The Origin of Tragedy*, 1910, and *Dramas and Dramatic Dances of Non-European Races in Special Reference to the Origin of Greek Tragedy*, 1915, has previously questioned the Dionysian origin of Greek tragedy.

centuries, two distinct myths have arisen amongst men of the theater, who are busy people and have not always time to peruse the recent publications of classicists and anthropologists. Firstly, that the ancient Greek theater represents an initial summit of theatrical achievement, and that the subsequent history of the European theater is a steady falling off, with diminishing peaks here and there. Secondly, that the City Dionysia in the fifth century B.C. exhibited some savage singleness of purpose utterly transcending division between spectator, chorus and actor, the audience in this case being roughly analogous to the crowd at a football match from which the supporters of one team have been excluded.

Basically, this latter attitude rests upon the identification of two stages in society a long way apart: Aeschylean tragedy is virtually identified with primitive ritual. This, in its turn, seems to imply that actors at least, probably chorus, and possibly spectators, are "possessed," and for that matter the phenomenon of possession is never far from primitive ritual. There is no reason to resist the idea that the collective exaltation of the Bacchants even as late as the fifth century B.C. exhibited the clinical symptoms of possession: in 187 dancing scenes on vases, almost entirely of the classical period, studied by Miss Lilian B. Lawler, about a third of the women would appear to be in an inspired or ecstatic condition;[5] indeed, the cult may well have undergone a renaissance in the latter part of the century; but what we really require to know is what went on in the theater itself throughout the period. That Dionysos and Bacchic dances are present in Greek tragedy is of course beyond refutation. In Euripides' *Bacchants* the chorus goes into a prophetic trance as it dances, but it is playing, not being, the Bacchant, and it seems probable that this obtained in the Aeschylean period too.[6] The idea that there was a greater measure of sophistication in tragedy of the Aeschylean period than is sometimes supposed is naturally reinforced by the possibility that tragedy is not primarily Dionysian in origin. Nietzsche tells us that the dithyrambic chorus is a chorus of metamorphosed people who have completely lost the memory of their family past, of their civic status: they have become the serfs of their god. In connecting this with fifth-century tragedy the philosopher fails to ask himself how, since this loss of memory is typical of Bacchic possession, the theatrical Bacchants contrived to remember their lines, since lines they certainly had by this time. His numerous descendants might ask themselves the same question.

There has been an accretion of comparable attitudes around the Christian mystery play, at least in France. "Comment parler," says M. Gouhier, "de spectacle et de jeu en présence de cet ouvrier tourneur qui, dans la *Passion* d'Auxerre, ressuscite en lui le Christ avant de le figurer?"[7] He asks us to remember Oberammergau, the actor's communion and prayer before and during acting. The hege-

---

5. *The Maenads: a contribution to the study of the dance in Ancient Greece*, Memoirs of the American Academy in Rome, vol. VI, 1927.
6. It is unfortunate that we have no extant play of Aeschylus treating the same theme. See Jeanmaire, op. cit., in particular pp. 79-80, 89, 106, 149, 162-64. But the absence itself may be significant for Else's thesis, q.v.
7. Henri Gouhier, *L'essence du théâtre*, 1943, p. 210.

mony of the *régisseur* in the French mystery over actor and crowd is well known, as is the crowd's sharing in a Te Deum at the end of the ceremony, and the occasionally alarming naturalism of the production: a function no doubt of the sincerity and fervor of the participants. Nevertheless reservations similar to those which hold good for the Greek theater may be made. The play had left the Church, and though there is no doubt as to its religious origin, there is equally none as to the fact that it was being rapidly secularized.

Dramatists and producers today, turning around these central myths of an initial summit of excellence and more particularly of a ritual transcendent unity, repair variously for their evidence to the ancient theater, the Christian mystery, and primitive manifestations of the dance-drama amongst other races. A common corollary to over-simplified views of these dramas is a sort of nostalgic atavism: a desire to take the theater back to primitivism,[8] or, where the pagan implications of the situation cannot be accepted, a more short-term desire for historical regression, an implied longing for the social system of the Middle Ages as a basis for the play, for a return to the collective Christian mystery. The late French producer Gaston Baty is a good case in point. In his treatment of the problem he is occasionally almost possessed rather than self-possessed:

> Vous, Jean Michel, Guillaume Flamang, Eustache Mercadé, bons facteurs de mistères, subtils sonneurs de rimes redoublées, batelées, couronnées; vous, les deux Gréban, que le coeur populaire garda si longtemps sur le manteau des cheminées entre la Bible des Pauvres et le Calendrier des Bergers; vous, superintendants, maîtres du jeu, charpentiers des échafauds et des secrets, peintres des mansions, musiciens des ménéstrandies et chanteurs des chanteries; et vous aussi, les bons joueurs, Jean de Missey, qui fûtes un Judas trop bien pendu, Nicolle de Neufchastel, curé de Metz, qui faillîtes mourir en l'arbre de la croix, Madame de Latour, notre première actrice; et vous encore, commissaires qui faisiez faire silence; vous tous qui êtes à votre tour spectateurs chez le Bon Dieu, priez pour nous.[9]

There is no doubt that this *cri de coeur* typifies a profound pessimism about society as expressed in the theater public: Baty sees it as moving on the one hand towards a diluted mass spectacle, and on the other towards a *théâtre d'élite*:

> Le théâtre actuel est sous le signe du chaos. De celui de demain, nous ne savons rien. Il n'y a place, là, que pour des voeux platoniques. Je serais tenté de penser que le théâtre se divisera de plus en plus en deux formules: l'une pour les masses dans les constructions qui viseront à fondre les spectateurs entre eux et avec l'action présentée—l'autre pour une élite de plus en plus restreinte, avec des salles intimes, dont l'ambition sera, tout au contraire, de permettre à chaque spectateur de *rêver comme s'il était seul*.[10]

8. Cf. Antonin Artaud, *Le théâtre et son double*, ch. IV, "Sur le théâtre balinais," pp. 56 et seq.

9. *Rideau baissé*, 1949, p. 73. With this attitude it is useful to compare Konigson's account of the business angle of the mystery play in *La passion de Valenciennes en 1547*, Paris, 1969, pp. 15–22.

10. The italics are mine. Cf. also Jean Hytier, *L'esthétique du drame*, quoted by Gouhier, *L'essence du théâtre*, pp. 93–94. Hytier notes a fractionalization of theater publics since Greek antiquity, and equates this with progress: it culminates in a "passage du public uniforme au spectateur original"; the new theatrical experience will be based on

Elsewhere, he tells us that "des individus rassemblés, mais restés isolés les uns des autres, séparés qu'ils sont par leur culture, leurs convictions, leurs habitudes, voire par leurs passions et leurs haines, ce n'est pas un public, c'est une foule."[11]

The difficulty is potentially solved for those who claim that any common human idea or feeling can form the basis of a mass theatrical experience: for M. Gouhier, for instance, who thinks that the communion, the hierarchy of participation "se retrouve toutes les fois qu'une oeuvre et un public se rejoignent dans une même glorification." What Henri Ghéon had esteemed held good for a Catholic theater applies, he says, to any religiously inspired theater "et la question reste la même lorsque l'homme ou la nation ou la classe tiennent la place de Dieu."[12] Firmin Gémier in his turn thinks that a "lay religion" can crystallize in the audience around such concepts as justice, liberty, and so on, and adds that the performance itself can create "une âme collective."[13]

Unfortunately the abstractions adduced as unifying forces are equivocal: justice for one is injustice for another, liberty for one class, bondage for another, unless the genius, poetic or otherwise, of an author can persuade a haphazard collection of individuals to the contrary. Only as the most bloodless generalities could these things now "sell" to a heterogeneous audience. There is neither the room, money, nor indulgence in any one country for a Christian theater, class theater, and all the other possible theaters. There is an undoubted nostalgia for the mass experience in our theater publics: the success of the French Théâtre National Populaire should be sufficient proof of that; yet such incipient collective reactions as occur in our theaters, varying, certainly, with the prowess of the dramatic author, when compared with the European theater in its cradle (reservations included) and the medieval mystery, remain strictly vestigial.

The shape of the theater has not unnaturally expressed progressively this growing distance between actor and public: the stage has developed a barrier against the auditorium. Ensconced behind the panoply of a proscenium arch, the actor is normally, by convention, "supposed" to be in a different place from his audience, or at least, he is not "in the same place" in anything like the sense in which the expression can be understood for the ancient theater. The *front de contact* has dramatically diminished. The terms used to characterize the modern type of theater

"une multiplicité d'admirations particulières." See also Valéry, "Mes théâtres" in *Vues*, 1948. Rousset's pages on "L'Ile enchantée: la Scène et la Salle" in *L'Intérieur et l'Extérieur*, Paris, 1968, pp. 165–82 are an application of this illusion to the baroque themes of magic, madness, water, and the enchanted island itself, showing it to be well under way in the seventeenth century.

11. *Rideau baissé*, p. 224. (*Finale en mineur.*)
12. Op. cit., pp. 207 et seq.
13. Curiously enough, Gaston Baty, apparently contradicting his other statements, agrees that there is common theatrical ground in any human group: "Aussi bien qu'un caractère personnel les communautés sont des entités dramatiques: le métier, la cité, la classe, la nation, la race. Non point réunion de plusieurs êtres—chaque fois un être nouveau, polycéphale, existant en soi." (*Témoignage* to Gouhier's *Essence*).

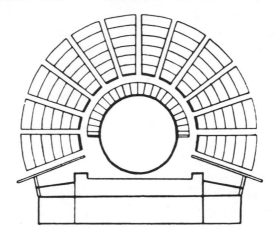

lay-out are well known. The commonest English phrase is perhaps "picture-frame stage." The French say "scène encadrée" or "scène-tableau." Louis Jouvet found a less courteous and typically ironical formula: "boîte à illusions." Its architectural features can, in their *ensemble*, be described as "the Italian Order."

The rebels against such a state of affairs are many. A certain form of expressionism, exemplified by the Thornton Wilder of *Our Town*, would solve the problem by ignoring it, and Pirandello's six characters, let us remember, are really as much in search of a theater as they are of an author. Theatrical literature too is rich in projected cures for the ill-defined malady: a Congress on Theatrical Architecture in 1950 produced a spate of them.[14] Theater-in-the-round—an arena stage surrounded by audience—has for many years been popular with small companies in the U.S.A.: Glenn Hughes's Penthouse theater was opened in 1932, and there are earlier examples. Easier to administer, cheaper to finance than the traditional house, the majority of them have remained small. English student groups have experimented in the same direction, and more recently the Théâtre National Belge, while permanent theaters-in-the-round have been opened in Milan (by Carlo Lari in October 1953) and by Mme. Paquita Claude in Montmartre (September 1954). It is in origin the destruction of the barrier between "salle" and "scène" that is claimed for such a theater by its exponents: thus, Carlo Lari:

14. The International Theatre Institute's Conference on Modern Theater Architecture, Paris, 19–21 June 1950 (typescript verbatim report), and see especially two publications of the Centre d'Etudes Philosophiques et Techniques du Théâtre: (i) *Architecture et dramaturgie*, 1950 ("notes sténographiques de la première session du Centre . . . tenue à la Sorbonne en décembre 1948 et consacrée aux rapports du lieu théâtral avec la dramaturgie présente et à venir"). (ii) *Théâtre et collectivité*, 1951 ("sténogrammes des secondes et troisièmes sessions du Centre . . ."). See also Rousset, op. cit., pp. 166 et seq.

> Le spectateur est jeté d'emblée dans l'action; il est arraché à lui-même pour s'identifier au spectacle. Il ne voit que ce qu'il doit voir, il ne perd pas une syllabe du texte; il s'oublie vraiment lui-même pour le drame.[15]

The ancient example is the obvious inspiration of these ventures, and it is thus paradoxical that by a considerable consensus of opinion, these theaters should serve most suitably as vessels for intimate, domestic-interior plays, even of the type that seems to demand a *scène à l'italienne*: Mme. Paquita Claude opened her theater with Wilde's *Importance of Being Earnest*: a deliberately artificial comedy lent itself to the intimate connivance of a small encircling public. The success of this "intimité salonnière" is noted by Villiers,[16] but it carries with it serious inconveniences: even with a minor, contemporary kitchen-comedy sort of complicity the absence of a distance, an architectural and conventional threshold, is difficult for the contemporary public to accept:

> Je me souviens encore [says Villiers] de ces spectateurs d'en face, aussi éclairés que l'acteur qui les touche presque, et dont l'expression me contrarie; et de ceux-là du premier rang qui, lorsque les comédiens se rapprochent, se sentant inclus dans le champ de l'action, mis eux-mêmes en évidence, baissent pudiquement les yeux.

Most objective critics agree that such a form will not suitably contain all types of drama, and those that they think unsuitable, those that in their estimation still require a distance between actor and public, are almost confined to high tragedy, the ancients, Racine, Corneille, Shakespeare. There is further, it would appear, a tendency for some sort of barrier to creep back into arena productions: the masonry of the fourth wall is more durable than had been thought; lighting is so arranged as to leave the spectator opposite in darkness, the stage itself is raised in relation to the first circle of seats, or these are raised themselves. Gauze veils, wire frames representing windows and doors through which the spectator sees the interior of a house, are beginning to make their appearance.

This prompts the reflection that whatever the interest and brilliance of these experiments, they are essentially formalistic: they assume the matter to be one of aesthetics, of form, and while they do not altogether ignore the social nature of the problem they fail of necessity to cope with its most important aspect: the existence of profound social divisions. There are still those who assume that having changed the art form and the shape of the theater, by legislation, invention, incantation or what you will, society will follow. They might choose as their device a remark made by Gide in his lecture on the evolution of the theater in 1910: "On ne peut pas changer les moeurs avant le théâtre; mais si on change le théâtre, les moeurs suivront."

We have seen many theatrical changes since 1910; but the "changement de moeurs" will not occur through such intermediaries.

---

15. "La querelle du Rond en Europe," *Revue Théâtrale*, No. 29, 9e année, p. 32.
16. "Théâtre en rond aux U.S.A.," *Revue Théâtrale*, No. 20, 7e année.

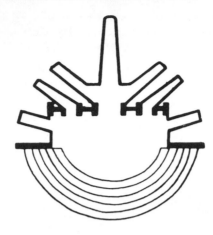

It is against this historical background of growing cleavage between stage and auditorium expressed architecturally in the lines of the theater, in the existence of a proscenium arch and the use of a proscenium arch curtain, that I have attempted to place the study that follows. If the play of the past is to live

> . . . plus que le jeu des acteurs, que la masse et l'âme du public, il importe à qui veut la ressusciter d'évoquer l'aire où se cristallisa la forme de son impulsion, où ces deux pôles sensibles que sont la scène et l'auditoire se disputèrent la place, refluèrent l'un vers l'autre, cherchant instinctivement la forme qui convenait le mieux à leur mutuelle pénétration.
>
> Cela nous invite à replacer les formes dramatiques dans l'ordre des faits naturels, et à créer une sorte de *biologie théâtrale*, destinée à éclairer les lois qui régissent leur économie.
>
> Dans la "ressuscitation" d'une esthétique dramatique, le verbe peut nous égarer, non l'édifice.[17]

Jouvet attributes to the shape of the theater somewhat wider evocative powers than appear to be justified, for although it is of course valuable in fixating for us the social hierarchy, the points of contact and division stemming from a given convention of dramatic writing, there is only a limited repertoire of possible forms: they do not necessarily reflect either fully or immediately the perfect physical organization of that convention. Nevertheless, my own study is largely "formalistic," and is meant as a modest contribution to our understanding of the *impasse* of modern scenography that I have described, viewed at a particular moment of its growth.

The advent of the Italian Order, accomplished, for France, in the seventeenth century, is a long process having its source in the ancient Greek and Roman theaters. In the former, there is a progression in the shape of the auditorium from circle to segment, and the solidity of the back wall of the stage, the *skené*, tends to diminish in favor of real or represented space through and behind the wall. There is in short

---

17. Louis Jouvet, *Témoignage* to Gouhier's *Essence du théâtre*, p. vi.

INTRODUCTION   9

an incipient polarization of the spectacle which increases in Roman times, militating against the original conventional oneness of place as between audience and actor. The shape of both theaters is recorded by Vitruvius, in the fifth book (chiefly) of his *De Architectura*, the illustrations to which have never been discovered.

The scenographers of the Italian Renaissance, in their interpretations of the Vitruvian precepts, and in their reconstitutions of the ancient theater, accentuate just these processes. They find in *De Architectura* case law, as it were, from among the ancients, for all the tricks which are to make up the baroque theater: machinery, stage marvel and change, and the perspective set infinitely prolonging the space behind what had been the solid back wall of the stage. The theater house, meanwhile, has become rectangular, though some form of ellipse lingers in the lines of its seating arrangements.

The arrival of these forms in France is not a simple importation. There is an indigenous stream of staging habits which mingles inextricably with the Italian, and which has never been completely admitted or chronicled: the street theater and *tableau-vivant* of the Royal Entry borrow considerably from the French mystery play. Where the mystery proper came to an abrupt halt at the Hôtel de Bourgogne at the end of the sixteenth century, its methods, fused with those of the Italian Renaissance, are preserved, developed, and carried through to the seventeenth century in France in the shows prepared for the entry of the Prince into a town, and in the decorations of all other courtly occasions. I have felt the need of some general term to apply to such phenomena in their relationship to the theater, and have accordingly coined the expression "para-theatrical."

Where the Italian Renaissance, in the process of extracting what it wanted from the ancient theater, attempted actual reconstruction, neither the French Renaissance nor the French seventeenth century does this. The Vitruvian tradition is diverted along a line of purely scholarly, not to say pedantic, attention, and only lessons of superficial decoration are drawn from it, none of these being consciously applied to the theater. As a result, the impact of the baroque is more immediate in France than in Italy.

"Baroque"—a mystical, elastic, cumulative, and regrettably inevitable category. Germinating in the plastic arts in Italy, the battle for its extension was fought out for France during the twenty-first "entretiens de Pontigny." Never was oyster more widely opened in the contemplation of a pearl. Eugenio d'Ors, on that occasion, summarizing the traditional views of baroque art the better to demolish them, finds that its birth, decadence, and death are situate, by general acceptance, in the seventeenth and eighteenth centuries, and confined to the western world; its proper domain is architecture, though it is permitted infrequent incursions into sculpture and painting; it is the product of some sort of decomposition of the classical style of the Renaissance. His own opinion is that the baroque is a repetitive historical constant, viable not only for the domain of art but for the whole of civilization. It does not originate in any classical style but is as fundamentally opposed to this as romanticism. The applications of such a view can result in a disconcerting *extensio ad absurdum*: for Eugenio d'Ors a whole gallery of figures, Robinson Crusoe, Jean-

Jacques Rousseau, Paul of *Paul et Virginie*, Mowgli, and the Sigismond of Calderon's *La vida es sueño*, are baroque.[18]

It was inevitable that "baroque" should, sooner or later, be made to comprehend literature. As d'Ors says, "Lorsque, vers la fin de la Décade, M. Paul Desjardins, M. Paul Fierens et le professeur de Liège, M. Sellix, se mirent à étudier quelle part de baroquisme l'on peut découvrir dans certains chapitres de la littérature française, dans l'art dramatique en particular, la bonne cause était déja engagée."

Focused upon literature it brought into unwonted prominence several figures written off by Lanson as "dissidents," "attardés," "égarés."[19] As an instrument of analysis, it has made discoveries. Yet the themes, the motifs, that had been seen to characterize the baroque of Borromini, della Porta, Cortone, Bernini, applied to the literature of France, seemed to limit the study, to arrest it somewhere around 1670, at precisely the moment when it is far less relevant in literature but has reached its highest point of significance in stage decoration with the opera.

If we take all those themes which purport to define the baroque—metamorphosis, magnificence, *trompe-l'oeil*, movement, flight, instability—it is clear that here is a tailor-made description of the French opera in the second half of the seventeenth century, and only the hypnosis habitually exercised by dramatic literature to the detriment of the play-in-performance could arrest the phenomenon before that time. The opera in France, and to a lesser extent Molière's comédie-ballet and the court fête, drain the spectacular from French dramatic literature.[20] Yet their decoration can be viewed, without the intervention of literature at all, as a simple (not necessarily competent or great) extension of the baroque style in terms of space and movement: real movement replacing its own figuration, a further stage in the wishful triumphing over the material world, an attempt at a more efficacious indiscipline. It is to this baroque and to that which prepares it outside dramatic literature that I shall essentially refer; it is to be found in genres (opera, pastoral, comédies-ballets, fêtes) for which, in contradistinction to classical comedy and tragedy of the seventeenth century, I have used the expression "illegitimate."

In one theater baroque magnificence, scene change and machinery are not allowed to suck at the life of the text, not allowed to rush towards their apotheosis as

---

18. *Du baroque* (version française de Mme. Agathe Rouardt-Valéry), Paris, 1936, pp. 100, 1, 41 et seq.

19. Lebègue, *Le théâtre baroque en France*, Bibliothèque d'Humanisme et Renaissance, Travaux et Documents, 1942, tome II, pp. 161–84. Cf. Rousset, *La littérature de l'âge baroque*, Introduction, p. viii: "moyen fécond . . . d'expliquer ou de réévaluer certains courants et certains poètes dont Lanson ne sait que faire."

20. Cf. Rousset, op. cit., p. 233:

> 1655 . . . Racine donne ses premières pièces: le Baroque est dépassé et surmonté; le Vau fait ses derniers travaux: le Baroque y est présent, mais dompté; Molière reprend le ballet et la pastorale, mais dans son théâtre de fête; il invente un genre nouveau, la comédie-ballet, où il draîne le baroque pour mieux l'éliminer de ses grandes comédies; l'opéra va s'épanouir: le Baroque s'y répand à flots, mais c'est un canal de dérivation; le Baroque n'est pas mort, mais au lieu d'agir partout comme à l'époque précédente, il se spécialise; il fera encore des poussées locales, dans la décoration ou par l'offensive rubéniste.

they do in other Parisian theaters. This is the Hôtel de Bourgogne. Here there is some search for spectacular effect in the dramatic pastoral especially while, during the first half of the century, a limited *décor simultané* survives. The development of regular tragedy and comedy halts this however, the set simplifies, and the baroque atrophies into the unchanging *palais à volonté* or the *chambre à quatre portes*, with the result that the theater is kept pure right up to the creation of the first Comédie Française, becoming, by comparison with the other houses, an oasis of dramatic poesy and dramatic entrance. It was granted to the least impressive theater edifice of the century, and to it alone, to catch some reflection of the cohesion, the oneness of place, of the ancient theater.

From 1640 onwards, the growth of stage perspective and the presence of the Italian *machiniste* accelerate the polarity of stage and auditorium. The stage decoration does not *set* the play as it does at the Hôtel de Bourgogne, but borrowing autonomous and repetitive elements which had already been developed in paratheatrical forms in the previous century, notably the Triumphal Arch, becomes a law unto itself, to be gazed at through a picture frame. The collective nature of the spectacle, apparent at the beginning of the century in the court ballet and paratheatricals generally, is lost in the process. The ultimate hypertrophy of this form, the completion of the ''carence du texte'' which accompanies its growth, is strikingly exemplified in the mute machine *féeries* of Servandoni at the beginning of the eighteenth century.

The perspective set, with a single optimum line of vision, demands a rectangular theater house and seats along that line. The economics of the public theater, on the other hand, demand the exploitation of wall space. The result is a tension between the form of the auditorium and the baroque staging convention. This tension grows with the century, and apart from timid attempts to solve the problem of *loges*, is bequeathed, along with the problem of theater acoustics (born in some degree of the opera), to the next century, which makes gallant and occasionally impressive attempts to grapple with its difficulties, blossoming in the process into a minor renaissance of theater structure.

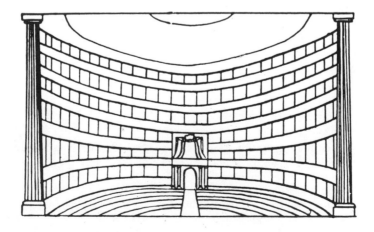

CHAPTER ONE

ORIGINS ANCIENT AND MODERN

BOOK FIVE OF Vitruvius' *De Architectura* is the tenuous bridge over which the ancient theater, shedding much of itself on the journey, crosses to the modern world. The proper approach to our study is then to be found in that crossing, and in what came over at the other side. It is no easy matter to find solid ground in the morass of controversy that has grown around the discoveries and conjectures of Dörpfeld touching the Greek stage, yet fortunately there does emerge a rough order of events in the evolution of the ancient theater which is of some significance to us, for matters of actual precedence are not often in doubt.[1]

Beyond this, our initial concern is not archaeological veracity (and we may be thankful for it), but the theater that Vitruvius described or thought he was describing, whether it was exact, prototypical, or confused. And the same may be said, in lesser measure, of the remarks of Pollux upon the same subject. For in the Renaissance treatments of these two writers lies the basis of the Italian Order in scenography. The Renaissance scholar, architect, scenographer, or what was frequently the Renaissance combination of all three, was interested in what Vitruvius meant, and with putting this into practice with suitable modifications for contemporary taste. The care and conscience that he brought to his archaeology varied with the individual, but as we shall see it was not the practice of the best archaeologist which prevailed in the theater.[2]

The development of the drama from Aeschylus onward may be held to consist in the progressive atrophy of the chorus, in the broadest terms. We may no longer claim, it is true, that Aeschylus' *Suppliants,* with its extensive choral role, constitutes his first extant play, but it seems undeniable that the function of the chorus declined progressively, and that decline is balanced by the growing importance of the actor. This had its effect (with reasonable delay, since dramatic form can change more easily than architecture or even earthworks) upon the shape of the theater. The audience can be viewed as a mute prolongation of the chorus; the chorus is the most immediate expression of the crowd's religious sentiments, and the chorus gives off the actor, upon whom interest gradually centers. And we may see that such a process is roughly matched by the development of the shape of the theater, however slight our knowledge of this may be.

THE GREEK AND ROMAN THEATERS

The Auditorium

It requires little imagination to visualize the crowd as originally surrounding the orchestra. The size of the municipal audience, the elevation of Dionysian cult under

1. Dörpfeld and Reisch, *Das griechische Theater*, 1896.
2. The same fructifying blend of enthusiasm and misinterpretation underlies not only Aristotelian exegesis and the growth of classical dramatic poetry in France, but music

the Athenian tyrants, the growth of statement and response between chorus leader and chorus culminating in the introduction of the first actor and the *skené*, tent or booth at the back of the orchestra, in which he is assumed to have changed his costume, all militate in favor of a breaking down of the orchestra shape.[3] This is the first differentiation of the play, in the case of the theater of Dionysos in Athens; later, wooden benches and supports are replaced by earthworks, the Periclean reconstruction (about 443 B.C.) results in a steeper auditorium and supporting walls to the south, east, and west, fixing the extent to which the audience may encroach upon the chorus. At the same time the orchestra is shifted slightly northward,[4] leaving at the southern extremity a space most suitable for the scenery demanded by Sophoclean and Euripidean performances.

In delimiting architecturally the extent to which the audience may enclose the orchestra, this reconstruction facilitates yet a further differentiation in the spectacle, a consolidation of the actor's newly won ground in the plays of Sophocles, by providing him and no doubt his contemporaries with a solid, though probably not at this stage permanent, background. The theater of Dionysos was perhaps an exemplar to other theaters in that the new curved section of its auditorium was no more than a semi-circle, foreshadowing the Roman pattern; the two ends however are prolonged in parallel lines until they touch the still circular orchestra at a tangent. The normal development in other theaters was an extension of the inner lines of the auditorium towards a completion of the semi-circle, forming something in the region of two-thirds of a circle. Historically, the poles of the auditorium are retreating "northward" (assuming for the purposes of argument an auditorium with a north–south orientation). While, in theaters other than that of Dionysos, the "southernmost" sections of the audience face away from the *skené*, those spectators in Athens who are seated on the two parallel poles of the auditorium do not. There is the beginning of an orientation of vision, of attention, upon the *skené*.

The collective nature of the spectacle however, in terms of audience accommodation and the shape of the auditorium, suffers little disintegration in the Greek period. Though it would be impossible to claim that social differences were not at any time observed in the seating,[5] yet it is correct to say that with the exception of the first two rows of seats, they rarely influenced the shape of the auditorium. Their proximity to the orchestra could hardly be identified with the best view-point, es-

and the Italian opera through Aristoxenes and Aristotle. (Cf. Hélène Leclerc, *Origines*, p. 123.)

3. In view of recent research, it is increasingly difficult to speak of a perfect circle as being either the chronological or indeed the architectural starting point of the ancient theater building. Professor Michael J. Osborne, of the University of Melbourne, points out that the shape of orchestra seems to be pretty varied. Trapezoidal and oblong ones are attested, and Carlo Anti, in his *Teatri Greci Arcaici* of 1947 even suggested the trapezoidal form as the original one. I am indebted to Professor Osborne for much advice here.
4. Pickard-Cambridge, *Dionysus*, p. 15.
5. See Haigh, *The Attic Theatre*, p. 337, and Pickard-Cambridge, p. 19.

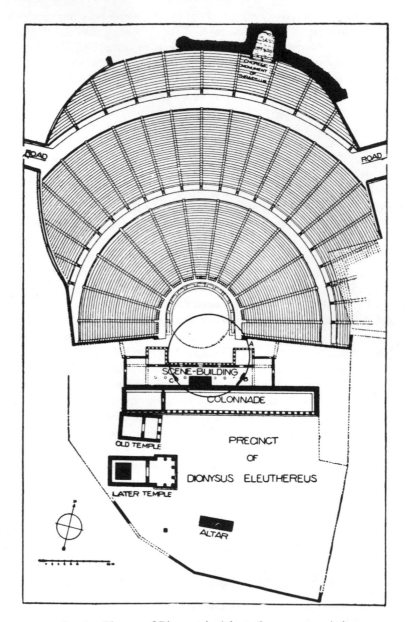

Fig. 1.—Theater of Dionysos in Athens (Lycurgean period).

pecially if there was no raised stage in the fifth century B.C.[6]—the higher seats must have afforded a better view of the actor behind the chorus. The original distinction was of course a religious one—the priest of Dionysos understandably occupied the seat nearest the altar, which was always in the center of the orchestra, the later addition of more stone seats being a prolongation of this priestly privilege. Even irrespective of the lines of the auditorium, there is little trace of economic differentiation in the seating: civic distinction is the only discernible criterion of privilege.

At the point where the Roman theater begins to borrow from the Hellenistic, it perpetuates chiefly those features which, conventionally, were removing the play from the spectator. The disappearance of the chorus link between audience and actor is expressed in a bisected orchestra. An exactly semi-circular auditorium soon develops, and to a greater extent than its Greek counterpart its form is a man-made choice: it is far from the casual, natural growth of the Greek amphitheater from a circle, from the "arena"; it had not grown from the orchestra outwards, and not being a spontaneous growth it did not automatically find its way to a hillside, as did the Greek auditorium. This necessitated substructures in order to provide a slope, and thus it was comparatively easy to introduce new entrances. It rapidly acquired exits and entrances other than the *parodoi* entrances on either side of the Greek theater which provided access to the orchestra, and thence to the seating.[7]

The very existence of a deliberate substructure providing a slope for the Roman auditorium increases its autonomy as a single element in the whole theater building, and its outside wall now becomes of importance architecturally, a highly "conscious" feature, providing a vast area for the play of vaulted arcades and engaged columns,[8] frequently imitated in the Roman Empire, recorded by Serlio and Peruzzi in the late Renaissance, surviving often where the interior of the theater did not. It was essentially this which filtered through to the consciousness of the seventeenth-century French architect. The covered colonnade at the top of the Roman auditorium, exactly on a level with the top of the wall of the stage building, or *frons scaenae*, for acoustic reasons given by Vitruvius,[9] completes, by comparison with the Greek, the cleanness of its line. The disappearance of the chorus permits further concentration of the line of vision, and the retreat of the poles of the auditorium "northward" is carried a stage further, the elliptical auditoria of some of the later

---

6. Pickard-Cambridge, preface, p.v. The same author claims however (p. 70) that at a performance of the *Rhesus* in the gardens of New College, Oxford, without a raised stage, the chorus in no way interfered with the public's view of the actors. There are examples of the "best" seats being placed elsewhere. Epidauros is a case in point.
7. The movement away from the hillside of the Roman theater does not of course apply where these are simply remodellings of Hellenistic theaters. Similarly the Greeks did not necessarily utilize hillsides. Eretreia and Isthmia are cases in point. See Gebhard, op. cit.
8. See Bieber, *The History of the Greek and Roman Theater*, 1939, p. 343, and her Fig. 453, for a description of the theater of Marcellus, the outer wall of which was to attract repeatedly the interest of the Renaissance architect.
9. Bk. V, ch. vi.

Roman theaters occasionally approaching that of the Olympic Theater at Vicenza[10] (e.g. Ostia, Arles, Orange, Timgad, Dugga).

The Orchestra

It is the orchestra which remains the hard core of the Greek theatrical lay-out. Until possibly some time between Nero and Phaedrus a circular orchestra was maintained,[11] that is to say that it retained its original form long after the justification for it had died, long after the chorus had waned in importance. Its presence hinders the growth and encroachment of the stage, and it is not until, under the Romans, the chorus has completely disappeared that it is bisected.

The chorus was originally the womb of the drama, and the orchestra was accordingly the focus of attention. It was at the center of a round formed by the crowd; thus, the original differentiation away from the unity of the spectacle corresponds (though roughly, and in no unbroken manner) to an architectural development from circle to segment, born, on the one hand, of the physical necessity for terracing on a slope, and on the other, of the actor's growth reflected in that of the *skené*. For a while, certainly at the time of Aeschylus, the orchestra serves as a psychological stepping stone between audience and actors; it fixates the spectator *in the same place* as itself and the actors. Yet it continues to hinder any architectural change reflecting the growth of the actor's importance, even for a long period when it is fulfilling its original function to an infinitely lesser extent. The stage had "caught up" the auditorium in its movement "northward," its edges joining the two corners of the latter.[12] The new semi-circle orchestra, filled with the seats of the Roman senators, may be regarded as a filling-in of the auditorium: the orchestra had become the orchestra stalls. The process towards a one-way line of vision, irrevocably set in motion when the chorus, which had previously surrounded its leader, ranged itself in lines facing the actor, was now fully under way.

The *parodoi* also outlive the dramatic form which justified them, in which they admitted chorus, public, and occasionally actors *to the same place*. They persist in the Roman building, but they now admit spectators ônly to the "orchestra stalls," and are lavishly supplemented by other entrances as they no doubt were in the late Greek theater.[13]

The Skené

The chorus leader, leaving the altar or table in the center of the orchestra, eventually moved to his booth at the "southernmost" edge of the orchestra, shifting thereby the focus of attention and creating a new place for entrance: the two are

10. Bieber, pp. 356 et seq.
11. But see Pickard-Cambridge, pp. 257–8.
12. Haigh, *The Attic Theatre*, p. 102.
13. Ibid., p. 111.

linked from the start. The rudimentary *skené* is at some time replaced by a wooden structure which probably persisted into the middle of the fourth century B.C.[14]

Thus, the tragedies of Aeschylus would seem to have been played before such an erection. The actor made his entrance through it, stood immediately in the orchestra, on the same level as the chorus, and thereby, we must repeat, in the same place as the crowd. It is true that the plays of Aeschylus are set in places far apart, so that we may not affirm that the spectator was to suppose himself actually in the precinct of Dionysos, as well as in the same place as actor and chorus. Yet doubtless at the birth of the form of spectacle that he was attending, his conventional and physical positions coincided, and the temple was ever present to remind him of the fact. Given too the paucity of decorative definition of place in Aeschylus' plays it is surely not rash to conclude that not only was the representation of place not uppermost in his mind, but that the audience itself maintained a lively consciousness that all was being enacted in the precinct of the god. This religiously inspired realization was as much a part of the dramatic phenomenon as any "suspension of disbelief."[15]

As the *skené* grows in importance, in solidity, the possibilities of dramatic entrance through the wall increase. To the surviving conventional oneness of place is added the sudden appearance of the actor in that place. It is precisely this which is lost when in the Hellenic, Romanic, and Renaissance elaborations of the entrances, that solidity diminishes.

By the time of Euripides the play seems to demand a *skené* pierced by three doors, with possibly an extra two in the *paraskenia*, or jutting sidewings, if these yet existed. The act of entrance defined the character as well as allowing him access to the play, a new function which grew in complexity, for while it is not necessary to assume that the accuracy of Vitruvius and Pollux reaches back to Euripides,[16] we still assume that at some time or other there came to be partial truth in their further details of this hierarchy: occasionally one door would lead out from a guest chamber, the other from a slave's prison.[17]

"Secundum ea loca versurae sunt procurrentes, quae efficiunt una a foro, altera a peregre, aditus in scaenam."[18] Thus says Vitruvius. When an actor entered by the (English) stage-left *paraskenion* entrance, he was held to be coming either from

---

14. Bieber (op. cit., p. 121) disagrees.
15. The Aeschylean theater set must have allowed for a central door at least; witness the notorious occasion when he startled the audience by having the chorus enter through it rather than through the customary *parodoi*. As regards the representation of place, Professor Osborne points out the highly rhetorical nature of Greek drama, in a world dominated by the spoken word which would naturally be the chief setter of scenes. The need for scenic illusion would be correspondingly less.
16. "The country, city, and marketplace have no organic connection with the plots of the fifth-century tragedies." Rees, "The Significance of the Parodoi in the Greek Theater." *American Journal of Philology*, vol. XXXII, 1911, pp. 377 et seq.
17. *Onomasticon,* Basle edn. of 1541, pp. 198–9.
18. *De Architectura,* Bk. V, ch. vi.

the city or the harbor. If however he used the eastern, stage-right entrance, then he was held to be coming from a distant land. In short, these directions corresponding roughly to the topography of Athens, the stage buildings were held conventionally to be in, and refer to, Athens. It would be interesting to know to what extent this operated across the instructions and stage setting of the dramatic poet, who more often than not set the play elsewhere; but in any case it is a fascinating survival of the original oneness of conventional and physical place.

The front face of the stage itself is known to have had, in the Hellenistic period, a row of columns or half-columns interrupted in the middle to form a space in which a door is assumed to have existed; decorative panels, or *pinakes*, may have been placed between them. Scholars cannot agree as to whether they were nothing more than a support for the stage, or whether they formed part of the stage background, on the same vertical plane as the *skené* but farther forward.[19] In the latter case the stage background in the Hellenistic period, as we can see, is already riddled with concavities. Whether this theory is true or not, large openings in the *skené* proper, above the stage, are known to have existed in the Hellenistic theater at Priene.

In the Roman theater, the original representation of space on what was to begin with a wooden *frons scaenae* is largely pictorial, but within this limitation it is considerable, increasing by at least the first century B.C., and followed by a rapid flowering of architectural decoration. The final form of the larger theater at Pompeii shows the spatial irruption in what was for the Roman period its culmination: the center door is now in a large curved niche, while the *hospitalia*, or guest doors, are in rectangular niches (Fig. 2).

From our point of view of conventional oneness of actor and public, of stage and auditorium, the main break has not yet taken place. The places thus represented in painting invite the audience vaguely to suppose themselves somewhere else, but in a body, and that tentatively. The spectator has not yet access to ''that which is within,'' but the nature of the dramatic entry, as inroads are made in the *frons scaenae*, is beginning to change, to lose something of its suddenness.

That bogey of the modern theater house, the rectangle, with its inevitable stage at one end and audience at the other, has not precisely reared its head, but its approach is heralded by certain features: the top edge of the auditorium wall and that of the *frons scaenae*, being of equal height, could theoretically have been roofed;[20] indeed, the whole building, when necessary, is covered to a far greater extent by awnings than was the Greek theater. Most interesting too in the Roman theater is the new wooden roof over the stage building, rising towards the spectator to give, acoustically, a megaphone. For us this consecrates the ''line of voice,'' if one may use such an expression, the complement of the line of sight, for now there is no chorus to turn its back upon the audience and apostrophize the actors. One need

19. Bieber, op. cit., p. 222: ''The Hellenistic proskenion building was meant to reproduce a house and its forebuilding with a terraced roof. The forebuilding has the form of a colonnade attached as a porch to the main building.''
20. Ibid., p. 345.

FIG. 2.—Reconstruction of a Roman Theater.

scarcely add that visually it completes a "picture-frame" which is finally closed from the audience (mostly, one assumes, before the commencement of the play) by the new curtain. The polarization of which we are speaking has progressed considerably.

Machines

Of the various devices and machines which have at one time or other been postulated as belonging to the Greek stage, only the *periaktoi* are specifically mentioned by the ancient Greek writers. Haigh views them as triangular prisms placed at either end of the stage, coinciding with the scene painting on the back wall and harmonizing with the topography of the theater in that the *periaktos* on the English stage right would represent the neighborhood of the city while that on the left would depict a more remote country.

The interpretation of the authors upon whom these remarks are based is in considerable doubt, and in particular any matching of scene painting and *periaktos*.[21] More probable is the thesis of Gardner which suggests that the wooden *skené* of the time of Aeschylus or Sophocles might be permanently painted to represent a palace for tragedy, easily acceptable as a street of houses for comedy, while the satyr play, with its rustic setting, relied perhaps entirely on the *periaktoi* for its decoration, as-

21. *De Architectura*, Bk. V, ch. viii, Servius on Vergil, *Georgics*, iii, 24, and Pollux, *Onomasticon*, p. 199 of the Basle edn. of 1541.

suming that these latter were in use in the classical period.[22] Yet at whatever moment we place the arrival of painted scenery and the use of revolving machines, they can only signify an increasing preoccupation with represented place on the stage, and as, originally, any conscious figuration of place would be foreign to the climate of a dramatic performance which, in its earliest form, is enacted in the place of worship itself, both scenery and *periaktoi* may be said to be a function of the breaking up of the spectacle.

So little is known of the Greek theater machines that their chief interest for us must be the lively manner in which the mere suggestion of them by the ancient writers touches off rich explosions of activity among the Renaissance and baroque scenographers. The *periaktoi* are just such a releasing influence, for two reasons. Firstly, as machines, they were imitated and developed, and secondly, they provided case law, as it were from among the ancients, for the legality of the *changement à vue d'oeil*. The complement to the *scena versatilis*, as the *periaktoi* came to be called, the *scena ductilis*, is an even richer source. This "machine" is assumed to have consisted of painted scenes placed one behind the other in the back wall, the removal of the first revealing the one behind, and so on. The *ekkyklema* in its turn may have been something rolled out suddenly through the *skené* to reveal a scene inside the house or palace, or (another theory) a semi-circular platform on a pivot, which, placed in the doorway, turned at the dramatic moment, carrying the slain victim or some other moving sight into full view of the audience. In either case there is a clear aesthetic connection with the solidity of the *skené* and the dramatic value of the actor's entrance. The device is the mechanized reverse of the entry itself considered as a dramatic phenomenon: it is, conventionally, the spectator's passage through the wall to the horrors within.[23]

The *mechane* is the obvious ancestor of the *gloire*, and appears to have been required by the plays of Aeschylus. We know that the actor hung from the machine by a hook and ropes. The *theologeion*, some form of superstructure above the roof of the *skené*, presumably to take gods who were not flying by means of the *mechane*, interests us again chiefly in the measure in which it "recurs" in the Renaissance. Sophocles was certainly shy of machinery; Aristophanes makes fun of the *mechane* in the *Peace*, where the machine-man is addressed directly, and in the *Daedalus*; its use as a mechanized *dénouement* for authors in a fix earns it a sneer from Plato which echoes into the French seventeenth century.[24] It seems in fact that the taste for the spectacular was severely restricted in classical times, and this is ignored by the majority of Renaissance theorists and theater craftsmen.

22. Gardner, *Journal of Hellenic Studies*, 1899, pp. 260 et seq., Octave Navarre, *Le théâtre grec*, 1925, p. 83, and Bieber, op. cit., p. 144, believe that the machines were in use during the classical period. Pickard-Cambridge (*Dionysus*, p. 126), does not.
23. Except, of course, when used comically! Aristophanes has Euripides brought out on the *ekkyklema*, presumably implying that Euripides was fond of this piece of equipment in his own productions.
24. Pickard-Cambridge, *Dionysus*, pp. 127-8. Cf. D'Aubignac, *Pratique du théâtre*, Bk. III, ch. ix; also Horace, *Ars Poetica*, ll. 191-2.

Whatever they really were, and whether or not they existed in the classical period, the *periaktoi* and the *pinakes*, backdrops, curtains, tablets, or what you will, gave to the Renaissance the fertile concepts of *scena versatilis* and *scena ductilis*. The *mechane* gave it the *gloire*, the *theologeion* possibly the *théâtre supérieur*.[25]

The development of the theater under the Roman Empire is accompanied by a plethora of architectural and plastic magnificence, and of spectacle. If tragedy and comedy were still popular under Nero, it is doubtful whether Seneca was ever acted: mime, pantomime, and Atellan farce gain rapid ground. The theater which, outliving Roman dramatic literature, housed the spectacular excesses of that age, was to be rediscovered, as far as the meager guidance of Vitruvius and the archaeological prowess of the Renaissance permitted. And the very lacunae in the theater form which grew up eventually served the intensification of internal, decorative, and architectural magnificence which was the baroque theater.

VITRUVIUS AND THE RENAISSANCE THEATERS IN ITALY

Polarization, decoration: both are spontaneously accentuated by those architects and scenographers who thought to interpret the ancient theater with more or less accuracy through Vitruvius.

This latter, in his description of the Greek theater, is almost certainly speaking of the late Hellenistic theater which he himself knew,[26] while his remarks on the three scenes, tragic, comic, and satyric, all of them having specific characteristics which reappear in the Renaissance, leave us in doubt as to how they were applied to the stage of his time.[27]

The considerable spread of the Vitruvian manuscripts before the Renaissance is attested by Choisy, who affirms that more than twelve copies go back to the period between the end of the ninth century and the end of the twelfth century, and are to be found in London, Paris, Berlin, the Escurial, the Vatican, Leyden, Brussels, Leeuwarden, Wolfenbüttel, and Sélestat.[28] For the period between the thirteenth century and the invention of printing, copies are to be found in Florence, Rome, Venice, Milan, Paris, Breslau, Frankfurt, Leyden, Bologna, Cesena, and Modena. Copies were undoubtedly numerous: one may mention at random in the Bibliothèque Nationale in Paris, a tenth-century manuscript, a manuscript in a fifteenth-century hand and, evidence no doubt of a plentiful supply, the remains of an elev-

---

25. Though the mystery play is most probably its original source in France. See p. 57.
26. Bieber, op. cit., pp. 255 et seq.
27. Bk. V, ch. viii:

> There are three kinds of scene, one called tragic, another comic, and a third satyric. Their decorations are different and unlike each other, for the tragic scenes are shown with columns, pediments, statues, and other royal appurtenances; the comic scenes show private houses with views of windows after the manner of ordinary dwellings; the satyric scenes are decorated with caves, mountains, and other rustic objects delineated in landscape style.

Translated by Allardyce Nicoll, *Development of the Theatre,* 3rd. edn., 1948, p. 84.
28. Choisy, *Vitruve,* 1909, introduction to vol. II.

enth-century manuscript constituting the front fly-leaf of a twelfth-century anti-phonary belonging to the church of Nevers.[29]

Given the comparative absence of divergence amongst the copyists, and since we are trying to examine what the Renaissance made of Vitruvius on the theater, the unillustrated *editio princeps* of 1486 is of no great interest to us.[30] The year before, Alberti's *De Re Aedificatoria*[31] had been published, the eighth book of which is a summary of the ancient theater according to Vitruvius. One remark by Alberti will be of use to us in our consideration of the Jocundus edition: "expeditus sinus areae medianae sub diualis . . ."[32]—"the unencumbered curve of the central space open and roofless." He accepts Vitruvius' explanation of the round form of the theater: that it was deliberately so for acoustic reasons, the ancients being aware of the acoustic properties of such a design, though along with Vitruvius he passes over the obvious and simple historical explanation: the gathering of a crowd in a circle round an altar. Let us however simply retain from the above remark that Alberti was perfectly aware that the ancient auditorium was not roofed. Of the *pulpitum*, or stage proper, he says merely "et pro faucibus exaggeratum opus pulpiti, ubi quae ad fabulam pertineant coaptentur." There is here in embryo the spirit of Renais-sance treatment of ancient theatrical precept, a vagueness of detail which is to justify an abundance of decorative elements. Later, he betrays for the first time the natural choice by the Italians of the Roman as opposed to the Greek formula: "Sed theatra Graeca a Latinis differebant ea re, quod illi choros et scaenicos saltatores media in area producentes pulpito indigebant minore, nostrique totis ludionibus fabulam agerent in pulpito. Id ea de re habere laxius uoluere." Speaking of the Roman *pulpitum*, Alberti, like Vitruvius himself, says "ours." Thus is the architectonic distance between Greek and Roman instinctively confirmed by the Renaissance humanist: he has a sense of unity with the *Roman* past, whose theater appeared to offer more excuses for elaboration.

This brings us to the Jocundus illustrated edition of *De Architectura*, which con-stitutes the first of two families of Vitruvian iconography.[33] The edition of 1511 is in Latin, as is the pocket Florence edition of 1513, and the Florence edition of 1522. Italian versions are printed in 1521, 1524, and 1535. Of the success of the work there is no doubt, nor is there any doubt of its infidelity: Jocundus has not hesitated to alter where the text appeared obscure to him. It was misinterpretation of Vitru-vius that was being propagated. Yet Jocundus has perhaps been accused of prop-

---

29. MSS. BN fonds latin, 10277; nouvelles acquisitions latines 1422, 1236.
30. Lucii Vitruvii Pollionis, *De Architectura Libri Decem.* Detta anche Sulpiciana da Giov. SULPICIO DA VEROLI che un union a Pomponion Leto . . . Roma, 1486, fo.
31. Albertus, Leo Baptista, *De Re Aedificatoria Libri Decem.* Florentiae, 1485, fo.
32. Bk. VIII, ch. vii, fo. 123 v°, of the Strasburg (Argentorati) edn. of 1541. Sub diualis = subdialis, an edifice without a roof.
33. *M. Vitruvius per JOCUNDUM solito castigatior factus cum Figuris et Tabula ut, iam, legi et intelligi possit,* Venetiis, 1511. On the subject of illustration, see Pierre Colombier, "Jean Goujon et le Vitruve de 1547," *Gazette des Beaux Arts,* tome V, 1931.

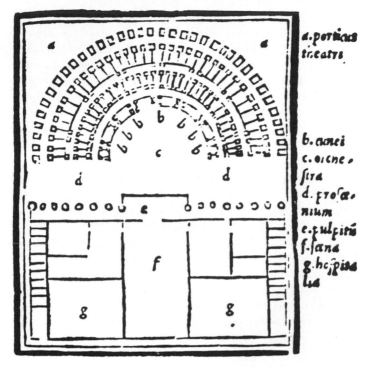

FIG. 3.—The Greek Theater according to Vitruvius.

agating misinterpretations which in fact he did not. We have seen that before the
appearance of the *editio princeps* Alberti had stated that the ancient theater was an
open-air affair, and had accepted without question what is abundantly clear from
Vitruvius' text, namely that the building was round.[34] It is probable that Jocundus
had read Alberti's most important work on the same subject as his own, and most
likely too that he had read the text he himself was editing! With this in mind, let
us now examine what has come to be almost a "classical" misinterpretation attributed to Jocundus. Allardyce Nicoll asks what a humanist at the end of the fifteenth century would be likely to seize upon first in Vitruvius, and in deciding that
it would unquestionably be the arrangement of the auditorium, adds that perhaps
the humanist would not at once realize that the theaters were open-air structures.
Thus, he notes, the 1513 Florence edition showed a rectangular building for both
the Greek and Roman theaters. Hélène Leclerc repeats the assumption: "ne réal-
isant pas bien la forme extérieure du théâtre antique, à ciel ouvert, on enferme
l'hémicycle dans un bâtiment rectangulaire." The theory is earlier voiced by Lily
B. Campbell[35] (Fig. 3).

34. Eg., Bk. V, ch. iii, "sol enim cum implet eius rotunditatem."
35. Allardyce Nicoll, 3rd edn., pp. 84–85. The matter is omitted from later editions.
Leclerc, *Origines*, p. 56; Lily B. Campbell, *Scenes and Machines on the English Stage*,
1923, p. 20.

There seems to be only one piece of evidence to support the suggestion that Jocundus thought the Roman and Greek theaters were rectangular and roofed, or that he was in any doubt about the matter. This is the existence of two rectangular outlines, one thick and one thin, to the pictures. But Jocundus' illustrations are all woodcuts. It would be normal for the rectangular outline of the block to be reproduced: and so it is. Similar outlines, double and treble, surround for instance the initial working out of the plans for the two theaters, where triangles or rectangles are inscribed in a circle, and, more conclusively, illustrations other than plans of buildings are framed in the same manner. The Renaissance theater, enclosed in a roofed rectangular building, was so for reasons other than these.

The Renaissance plays—Terence, Plautus or the *sacre rappresentazioni*—were played both in and out of doors. The first theaters constructed under the ancient influence were of wood and, it seems, were put up in courtyards as much as anywhere else. The movement indoors is, as elsewhere, not the outcome of a transmitted mistake, but the breaking up of a collective popular art form, and a seeking not merely after show, for the pageants already had that, but after *trompe-l'oeil*, in an enclosed space, and even in a darkened room, before an elite which, being elite, occupied less space and could be so accommodated.

Hélène Leclerc summarizes well the contribution of Jocundus when she suggests that his theater building is a mixture of the medieval stage, with its compartments, the ancient theater, and the hypotheses of the author.[36]

The same is apparent in the second of the illustrated editions of Vitruvius, that of Cesariano (Figs. 4 and 5), which also forms the basis of Caporali's.[37] The illustrator was aware of Jocundus' work, but his own is quite original.[38]

Like Jocundus, Cesariano is well aware that the theater is not roofed or rectangular: his elevation shows a round building and the *velaria* or awnings which protect from the sun are plainly visible. The five doors of the scene building are falsely shown in the plan as lying flat, no doubt to show off their decoration. The Royal Door, marked B, is in the center, flanked by two entrances to the *hospitalia* marked L and M. At the two extremes he has placed two doors giving access to the *proscaenium* along the side wings or *versurae*, one from the forum, the other from abroad.[39]

The doors, then, are situated in the rear of a deep building, the actor going through a portico and traversing the entire scene building to reach the *proscaenium*

---

36. *Origines*, p. 56.

37. Cesariano, *Di Lucio Vitruvio Pollione de Architectura Libri Dece*, Milano, 1521; Caporali, *Architettura con il suo commento e figure Vitruvio*, Perugia, 1536.

38. Colombier, op. cit., p. 157, and see Leclerc, *Origines*, p. 56.

39.   Ma doue sono li cinqui Cunei quali componeno la Scaena nel medio e signato B. Ma contra se ha le ualue seu porte Regie. li altri dui: che sono da la dextra e sinistra parte: Signati. L.M. Sono li hospitaliti loci de la Scaena: con le sue scale dentro: in li dui Cunei doue sono le littere. I.K. e le littere che dirigeno le extense lineae. C.D. Indicano lo adito dilatato per potere andare da le uersure signate ε, procurrente con il porto Theatrale: Queste hano la effectione perueniente una dal foro: laltra da la peragrante itinerationc pergendo lo adito in la scaena . . . [fo. LXXXII]

FIG. 4.—Elevation of the Roman Theater according to Cesariano.

which is separated from the *scaena* by the line I–K,[40] a method of access apparently confirmed by an alternative (schematic) plan which appears elsewhere in the same work.[41] The *periaktoi*, if we are to believe Cesariano's elaborate legend, are marked

40. "La linea che desiunge la portica: e la Scaena: dal proscaenio: signata in le sue extremitate conle littere I.K.", fo. LXXXI v°.
41. Bk. V, ch. iii, fo. LXXV v°.

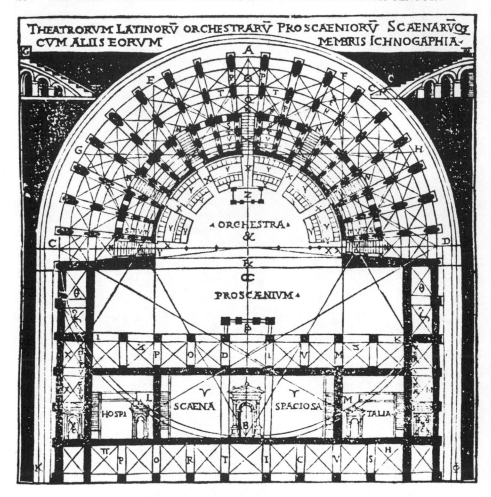

FIG. 5.—Plan of the Roman Theater according to Cesariano.

χ, but are only to be found in the left side-wing, while the writer reads the *pulpitum* (which he marks β) as a raised place in front of the scene wall, for preaching.[42]

Thus, in Cesariano's imagination, a deep stage, with compartments again reminiscent of those of the mystery play, is pierced by three deep passages going back to impressive doorways. Another curiously premature interpretation is the treatment of the auditorium, in which, above the main body of spectators, are to be seen porticoes in two stories, sectioning off the remaining audience almost into loggias.

42. "Pulpito, idest loco alto da orare in publico spectaculo al populo commune uel particulare," fo. LXXXI.

The tendency to pierce the space of the scene building is even farther advanced in a projected edition by San Gallo, mentioned by Hélène Leclerc (Fig. 6). The depth of the *aula regia* or Royal Palace is striking, and it is to be noted that it is not framed in any sense by a doorway, but has all the appearance of a perspective set. In the main sketch there is a jutting apron which does not figure in the rough plan, and this looks very much like the flat "acting" portion of Serlio's stage.[43] An obvious point about the drawing is that San Gallo has confused the function of the *mechane* and the *periaktoi*, and has in fact run them together. The key to the San Gallo design reads thus: "Triangular machine which turns according to the effects of the comedy, because on each side it has different effects: that is in one the apparition of the gods, in the other another act, in the other another act." Much depends upon our interpretation of "effects" and on how we read "in one the apparition of the gods." It could be argued that this merely means that when the gods were to appear, the *periaktoi* turned: that is what Vitruvius meant. But it might more cogently be affirmed that San Gallo was lumping together *periaktoi* and *mechane* so that when the *periaktos* on one side turned, it actually turned into view of the audience a god: this accords admirably with their raised position above the *hospitalia*. The very rough large sketch of the "machine" at the top of the original drawing might plausibly be interpreted as a god, either on clouds or on Olympus, while the lower, small reproduction above the *hospitalia* appears to be recessed to contain a figure: it is in short a synthesis of *mechane, periaktoi*, and even *ekkyklema*. There is also the later authority of Barbaro's gloss on the *periaktoi*: "Da queste machine parlavono i Dei"; and perhaps the commentator Philander had the same idea.[44]

The synthesis of old and new apparent in these formulae does not follow a line of increasing fusion, as might be expected. This is especially the case with Serlio (Figs. 7-11) for here the breakdown of the face wall is obviously far advanced: the elements of decoration are now constructed and there is no question of flat painted perspective; they stretch back into space, though by reason of the sharpness of the constructed perspective the space represented is much greater than the physical space covered: a fact which was to strike the eye, unfavorably, of more than one critic when actors began to use this back region, since it made the actor look unreasonably tall. Later reconstructions in Italy however were to restore in some measure the *frons scaenae*, as Vitruvian interpretation became more competent.

Space has been gained at the back of the stage, though probably only for decoration: it seems unlikely that the actors were ever present to any serious extent on the inclined portion:

> Et pour l'aisance des étranges figures de personnages qui se devaient entremettre du jeu (il s'agit de masques) même pour ce qu'il était besoin qu'il y eût des chars de triomphe, des éléphants et des morisques de beaucoup de sortes, je voulus qu'il y eût

43. See Fig. 8.
44. Barbaro, *I dieci libri dell'Architettura di M. Vitruvio tradutti et commentati . . .*, In Vinegio . . . MDLVI, p. 155. Philander, *In decem libros M. Vitruuii Pollionis "De Architectura" annotationes*, Paris, 1545.

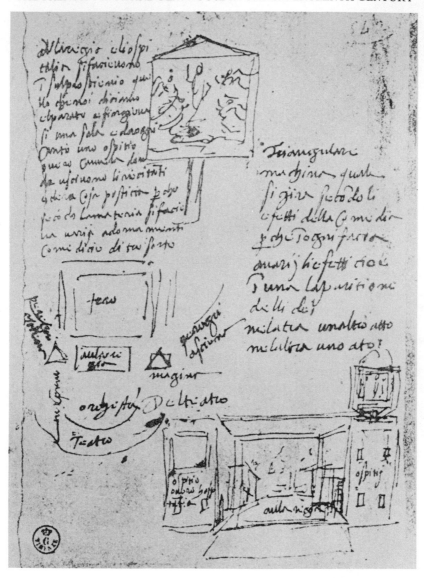

FIG. 6.—The San Gallo drawings.

devant la scène une plate-forme large de douze pieds et longue de soixante, laquelle fut certes bien commode et d'une fort belle présence.[45]

The passage suggests that, practically, Serlio invented the inclined stage to make room for the decoration, thus leaving room on the flat part for the triumphal cars,

45. Serlio, *Premier livre d'architecture*, translated by Jean Martin, quoted by Leclerc, *Origines*, p. 77, fn. 3.

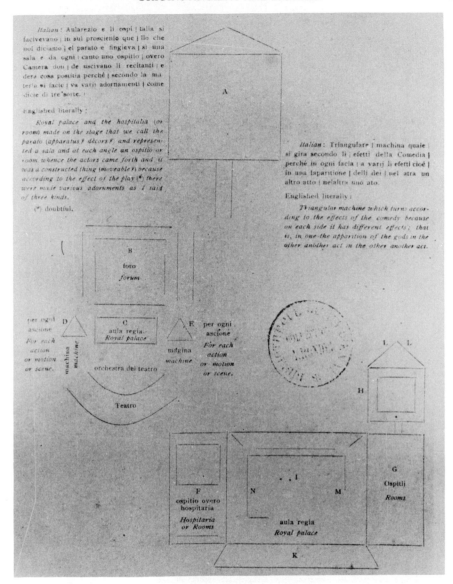

Italian: Aularezio e li ospi | talia si facivevano | in sul proscienio que | llo che noi diciamo | el parato e fingieva | si una sala e da ogni | canto uno ospitio | overo Camera don | de uscivano li recitanti | e dera cosa positia perché | secondo la ma teria si facie | va varii adornamenti | come dicie di tre 'sorte. |

Englished literally;

Royal palace and the hospitalia (or room) made on the stage that we call the parato (apparatus) and represented a sala and at each angle an ospitio or room whence the actors came forth and it was a constructed thing (moveable) because according to the effect of the play (*) there were made various adornments as I said of three kinds.

(*) doubtful.

Italian: Triangulare | machina quale | si gira secondo li | efetti della Comedia | perché in ogni facia | a varij li efetti cioè | in una laparitione | delli dei | nel atra un altro | nelaltro uno ato.

Englished literally:

Triangular machine which turns according to the effects of the comedy because on each side it has different effects; that is, in one the apparition of the gods in the other another act in the other another act.

B
foro
forum

per ogni
ascione
*For each
action
or motion
or scene.*

D machina *machine*

C
aula regia
Royal palace

orchestra del teatro

E matgina machine

per ogni
ascione
*For each
action
or motion
or scene.*

Teatro

L L

H

F
ospitio overo
hospitaria
*Hospitaria
or Rooms*

N

I

M

aula regia
Royal palace

G
Ospitlj
Rooms

K

FIG. 6.—The San Gallo drawings.

the elephants, and the dancers. It is one of the more obvious functions of the theaters we are considering, and it may owe this to vestiges of a medieval disposition.

In 1548 the *Accademia della Virtù* was founded in Rome for the study of the Vitruvian text. This may be taken as the turning point in the practical attitudes of the Renaissance humanist to reconstruction. The writers and architects we have so far examined had a much freer hand than their successors, such as Barbaro or

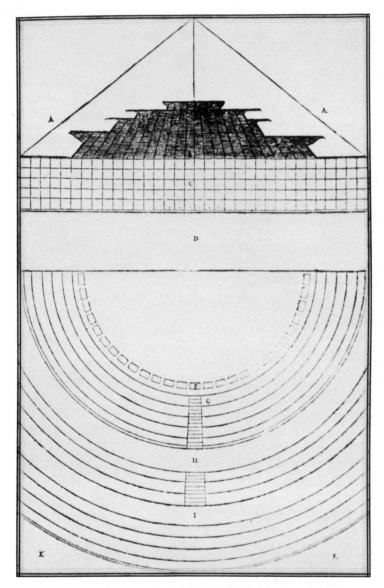

FIG. 7.—Plan of Serlio's Theater.

Palladio. Increasing archaeological competence momentarily arrests the spate of ancient-modern fusion. Both the drawings of Barbaro and the Olympic theater at Vicenza by Palladio (and Scamozzi) are nearer to Vitruvius than anything so far dealt with. Barbaro reproduces the plan of the Roman theater with more fidelity than his predecessors (Fig. 12). The three entrances of the *frons scaenae* are at the

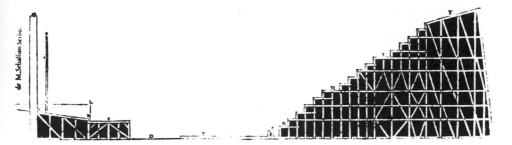

FIG. 8.—Section of Serlio's Theater.

back of three concave recesses, but in these entrances Barbaro has placed the turning machines.

The implications of this move are far-reaching. The origin of the misinterpretation is clear: Vitruvius says "dextra . . . ac sinistra hospitalia, secundum autem ea, spatia ad ornatus comparata, quae loca Graeci periactes dicunt." As Magagnato

FIG. 9.—The tragic scene according to Serlio.

FIG. 10.—The comic scene according to Serlio.

has pointed out, Barbaro, collaborating with Palladio in this work, has simply read "secundum" as meaning "behind" rather than "and then."[46] This is clear from Barbaro's own Italian commentary: "There were other doors, one on the right and the other on the left, so that the face of the scene had three great recesses, as is to be seen on the plan, in which were erected three triangular machines."[47]

46. "The Genesis of the Teatro Olimpico," *Journal of the Warburg and Courtauld Institutes*, vol. XIV, July–Dec., 1951, p. 217.

47. "Eranui altre porte una dalla destra, e l'altra dalla sinistra di modo, che la fronte della Scena haveva tre gran Nichi, come si vede nella pianta, in quelli erano drizzate tre machine triangulari," op. cit., p. 255. The explanation of this error has in any case been given in much greater detail by Galiani, who sweeps the *periaktoi* to either side of the stage (like Vignola and Furttenbach before him: see pp. 39, 40):

En effet, on voit que Vitruve commence par le milieu et continue ensuite à décrire, l'un après l'autre, les objets qui se suivent sur les côtés, à droite et à gauche. "Mediae valvae ornatus habeant aulae regiae," dit-il: "La Porte du Milieu aura la magnificence de celle d'un palais royal." Il continue ensuite en disant: "Dextra ac sinistra hospitalia." Voilà

FIG. 11.—The satyric scene according to Serlio.

The solution "behind" is neat and tempting, in spite of its evasion of the problem of entrance. So much so that it is repeated by Perrault as late as 1673.[48] Thus, the most responsible of the Renaissance reconstitutions, as is patent from a glance at Barbaro's plan, restored at one blow the solidity of what was now termed the

> donc qu'il parle immédiatement après des deux objets qui étaient aux deux côtés de celle-ci: "à droite et à gauche sont les portes des étrangers." Il continue toujours, et dit: "SE-CUNDUM EA," c'est à dire "ENSUITE DE celles-ci: A COTE DE celles-ci; spatia ad ornatus comparata, se trouvent les espaces où l'on place les décorations." Il continue encore en disant "SECUNDUM EA," c'est à dire "APRES ces espaces"; ou bien, "en suivant toujours la même ligne; sur les côtés à droite et à gauche. Versurae sunt procurrentes, etc., sont les deux galeries qui conduisent en dehors," et qui forment deux chemins pour les acteurs, l'un qu'on suppose venir de la ville, et l'autre de la campagne.

(Quoted by Tardieu and Coussin in their edition of Perrault's *Vitruvius*, Paris, 1836, vol. I, p. 278)

48. *Vitruve*, Bk. V, ch. vii, p. 168.

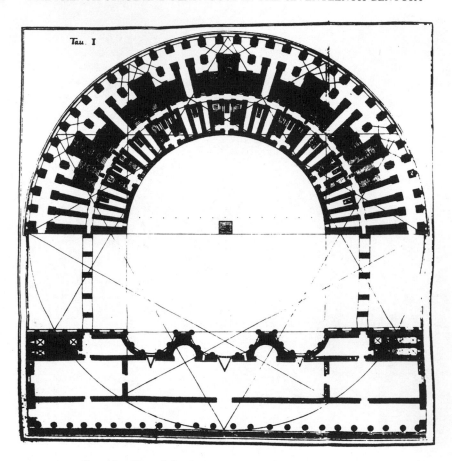

FIG. 12.—Plan of the Roman Theater according to Barbaro.

proscenio, and in fact took it one stage further by blocking such "holes" as the *frons scaenae* originally possessed.

The close relationship between Barbaro's work and the *proscenio* of the Olympic theater has enjoyed some attention of recent years (Figs. 13 and 14). It is the scholastic prowess of the *Accademia della Virtù*, of Barbaro's edition, of Palladio's examination of ancient monuments, that goes into the *Olimpico*. The face is a magnificent solid background in the Roman manner. *Proscenio* and *versurae* embrace the stage and are open to the auditorium. The ellipse of this latter is partly a memory of those slightly truncated Roman auditoria that Palladio had himself inspected. (Pola, Berga and Aosta are examples.) The fact that Barbaro and Palladio had placed revolving machines in the doors of their Vitruvian illustration does not necessarily signify that originally Palladio meant his theater face in the *Olimpico* to be thus, although if we ignore the difference between real and represented space the two are

FIG. 13.—Stage and auditorium of the Olympic Theater today.

FIG. 14.—The façade of the Olympic Theater today.

extraordinarily similar (Figs. 15 and 16).[49] However this may be, Scamozzi's final constructed perspectives (for it was he who finished the theater) are what subsist.

The situation of this building in the general evolution of the stage has been widely discussed. Lily B. Campbell says of it: "In the latter part of the sixteenth century there was built . . . a theatre which was, to some extent at least, to standardize the ideas of theatrical construction. . . ."[50] This gives little credit to the really exceptional nature of the Olympic design: it is curious, if it standardized anything, that it should be so little imitated.

There is the temptation to regard it as the beginning of the modern stage, standing at the significant crossroads of ancient and modern: the streets in perspective are seen as an explosion through the solid, ancient *frons scaenae*, winning space for all the new elements of the baroque. This is accompanied by the theory that the Royal Door of the theater face becomes gradually enlarged by subsequent architects in other theaters until it is actually the modern proscenium arch.[51] The theory is rejected by Kernodle and Magagnato, and indeed seems nicely disposed of by the fact that the proscenium arch was in use before the Olimpico was built.[52]

In this impasse of theories Magagnato's monograph is a valuable carminative. He argues convincingly that archaeological reconstitution is Palladio's primary motive. He sees the Olympic theater as standing not at a significant crossroad, but in a side street as it were: "The new scene, worked out in the fifteenth century, from Alberti on, dominates the whole of the sixteenth, and from this, and this alone, derives modern theatrical architecture and stage design."[53] In this way Palladio's theater is revealed as an "anachronistic experiment" for "it is only in the Olimpico that an attempt is made to confront the true problems of the theater—and the problems of the theater all turn in this central and essential question of the relation of actors to spectators—as architectural problems, and find an organic and unitary solution to them in terms proper to this art and no other."[54]

The Olympic theater, wherever with more or less fidelity it reproduced the Roman theater (of necessity in miniature), was appealing, architectonically, to social

49. See Leclerc, *Origines*, p. 90, and Magagnato, op. cit., p. 217; also *Teatri italiani del Cinquecento*, pp. 60 and 66–72.
50. *Scenes and Machines*, p. 54. Cf. Magagnato, *Teatri italiani del Cinquecento*, p. 62.
51. Leclerc, *Origines*, p. 91, states that the *Porta Regia* contains in embryo the modern proscenium arch; this contrasts with her earlier remark (p. 84): "Dernier théâtre romain . . . plutôt que premier théâtre moderne." Barsacq, "Lois scéniques," *Revue Théâtrale*, No. 5, April–May 1947, p. 150, and Sheldon Cheney, *Stage Decoration*, 1928, quoted by Kernodle, *From Art to Theatre*, 1944, p. 5.
52. Ibid., pp. 196 et seq. On the other hand, Kernodle's idea that without Vitruvius and the ancients the Olimpico would have been just the same will not bear serious examination (p. 171).
53. Op. cit., p. 209.
54. Op. cit, p. 214. Herein, of course, lies the absolute, as opposed to the historical, interest of this theater. In spite of the prolonged effect of entrance down the streets in perspective the effect of intimacy between actor and audience, between stage proper (*palco scenico*) and auditorium, is very great.

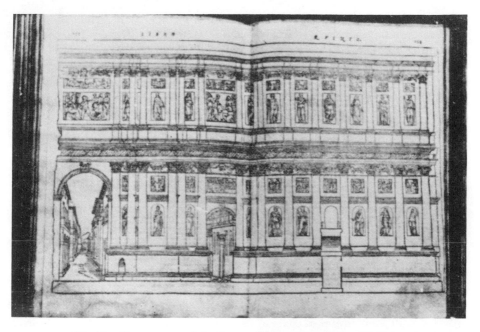

FIG. 15.—*Frons scaenae* of the Roman Theater according to Barbaro.

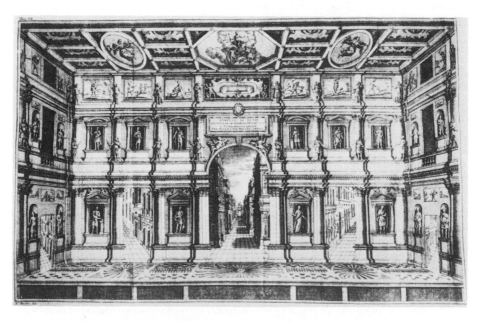

FIG. 16.—The façade of the Olympic Theater, set for a play.

conditions which no longer existed. In reconstructing an archaic architectural form, its architect built something which reflected a dead society. It solved no theatrical problem of the time, whatever absolute architectural merit it may be held to possess.[55] The audience which attended the contemporary performance in a "reconstituted" theater was, considered as a social unit, an élite, interested possibly in the reconstruction of the classical drama, but always provided that it should fulfill the purpose of supplying that audience with proof of its own identity with the glories of the Roman past: a process it could best achieve by seizing upon those elements of the Roman theatrical performance most susceptible of development in that direction: marvel, magnificence, metamorphosis. Of such a spectacle the proscenium arch was an inevitable appendage: it was natural that the Renaissance élite should look at itself through a Triumphal Arch.

As Magagnato tells us, "against all this, Palladio reacts." For the audience as a unit (whatever the sincerity of the scholarly instigators of the reconstituted performance) the appeal to the classical past was a bluff; and the trouble with the Olimpico was that it went far enough along the road towards a genuine reconstruction to call that bluff. That is why the line of development from Alberti to Serlio, through Perruzzi, thrives.[56]

This famous theater represents a maximum, for the period, of archaeological prowess, with a minimum of concession to the taste of the time. It was a brilliant and final demonstration of the impracticability of a compromise between the baroque and the ancient theater rebuilt. It was essentially an unworkable theater. Historically, and in detail, its function has been to prove the necessity for the proscenium arch; and in this it has had an immense negative significance. Magagnato has shown that Palladio's *proscenio* rendered difficult what was being demanded—"framing": the isolation of audience from actors, the use of the curtain (although a Romanized, i.e. falling, curtain was used for *Oedipus Rex*). He suggests that the three descendants of the Olimpico took up again the problem of the proscenium arch. The inference is that Palladio had shown them, by negative example, that it was not possible for them to produce the required effects otherwise. Ingegneri, who knew that stage better than anyone, felt that its disposition limited it to tragedy: "è un Apparato più Tragico, che Comico, e in niuna guisa Pastorale"; and yet the

55. For a general evaluation of the Olimpico transcending the limits imposed by a mere study of the perspective scene and proscenium arch, see Magagnato, *Teatri italiani del Cinquecento*, pp. 62–66.

56. The way in which the contemporary audience could reduce a classical tragedy to its own terms is admirably suggested in an account by Filippo Pigafetta of the *Oedipus Rex*, played in the Olimpico on 23rd March 1585, quoted by Kernodle, op. cit., p. 169. See in particular Leo Schrade, *La représentation d'Edipo Tiranno au Teatro Olimpico* (*Vicence 1585*), Paris, 1960, ch. IV. This has a section on Pigafetta's account which makes it quite clear that the choice of *Oedipus Rex* is a very deliberate attempt to reconstitute the ancient: "cosi nel più famoso Teatro del mondo è primieramente stata la più eccellente Tragedia del mondo rappresentata" (p. 48). A simple description of the employment of the perspective streets in a production is to be found in Angelo Ingegneri, *Della poesia rappresentativa. Parte seconda: Del modo di rappresentare le favole sceniche*, Ferrara, 1598.

importance of the pastoral genre in the development of baroque scenic effect is very considerable. Giovanni Montenari (*Del Teatro Olimpico*, 2nd edition, 1749) is of the same opinion: "La nostra scena serve solo per la favola tragica." The three "descendants" instanced, Scamozzi's theater at Sabbioneta, Aleotti's at Parma, and that drawn by Inigo Jones, all take up the problem again.[57] Two of these theaters have proscenium arches but "the most academic of the three architects returns to Serlio—*almost, one feels, by compulsion*. Scamozzi's Sabbioneta is a Serlian theater without a proscenium arch, and with an auditorium based on reminiscences of Palladio's."[58] All three, realizing that the Palladian formula is not viable, return to the living mode of stage design of their own day. Palladio had at his disposal the funds, such as they were, and the scholarly support of the Academy, while his successors realized that they could not serve two masters: the Prince and Vitruvius. A remark made by Patte will serve perhaps as a French epilogue to the Olimpico: "Aujourd'hui on y joue rarement, et il ne sert guère qu'à donner des bals, ou quelques représentations passagères de Tragédie, et qu'à tenir les assemblées publiques de l'Académie, dont les Salles sont contiguës."[59]

The Italian Baroque Theater

In their theaters, Scamozzi and Aleotti considerably augment the possibilities of scene change and to some extent they re-introduce a perspective with a single vanishing point. Sabbattini is in favor of the single perspective in 1637: "D'aucuns ont coutume de figurer en la perspective médiane plus d'une rue, tant avec un seul point comme aussi avec plusieurs. Chose, à dire le vrai, que je ne saurais approuver entièrement."[60] Vignola says that two vanishing points are impossible.[61] So that in a sense they not only set the stage for the whole gamut of baroque marvel, behind a picture frame,[62] but they also ensure that when, in mid-seventeenth century, the

57. See Leclerc, *Origines*, Pls. XXII, XXIII, and XXIII bis; also Nicoll, *The Development of the Theatre*, 3rd ed. 1948, Fig. 150, p. 134.
58. Magagnato, op. cit, p. 219. The italics are ours.
59. Patte, *Essai sur l'architecture théâtrale*, 1782, p. 57.
60. *Pratica di fabricar scene e machine ne' theatri*, 2nd edn., 1638, trans. by Mlles. M. and R. Carnavaggia in collaboration with Louis Jouvet, 1942, Bk. I, ch. 28, p. 46.
61. *Le Due Regole della Prospettiva pratica*, ed. Danti, 1583, p. 53.
62. The inevitability of the proscenium arch for the furtherance of stage illusion could not be better demonstrated at its moment of emergence than by Sabbattini (op. cit. Bk. II, ch. 3, p. 73):

> Encore que la façon dont il vient d'être parlé en ce précédant chapitre, à savoir de placer les deux premières maisons en tête du plancher de la scène, soit la plus pratique et la plus répandue elle semble néanmoins avoir ce défaut que les scènes avec maisons étant parfois changées en forêts, montagnes ou autres il ne semble alors ni très bon ni très vraisemblable que ces deux morceaux de maison restent seuls et sans se transformer eux aussi: or donc, pour remédier à pareil inconvénient, on pourra, en tête du plancher, faire un arc avec colonnades et statues et, en son dedans, fabriquer la scène car, outre que l'on sera ainsi bien assuré que les parties intérieures ne seront point en vue, la scène soi-même s'en trouvera magnifiquement ornée, y gagnera plus de fuyant et, au revers de l'arc que je dis, on pourra poser bon nombre de lumières lesquelles, non seulement illumineront les maisons de la scène, mais encore tout le ciel sans être vues et sans qu'on sache où elles sont placées.

hand of French classical doctrine in the drama arrests to some extent the effusion of spectacle, there shall be a well-established tradition of single-perspective décor to justify the hardly changing "palais à volonté" of the Hôtel de Bourgogne. Behind its frame, the further development of the Italian type of scene is to a great extent that of the *scena versatilis*, the *scena ductilis*, and those devices which may be held to have descended from the *mechane* and the *theologeion*. The auditorium in its turn is subjected to two main constraints: the rectangle, and the rupture, in terms of convention and hence of architecture, between stage and spectator.

Scena Versatilis

It is, we have claimed, a shrewder interpretation of the ancient theater which gives rebirth to the *periaktoi* in the theater of the Renaissance. Alberti, Jocundus, Cesariano knew of them, since they knew their Vitruvius. But the devices remained, with these writers, textual, theoretical. San Gallo, for instance, confused them with the *theologeion*. They have no place in Serlio's theater. Barbaro makes a serious attempt to place them: in the three doors of the *frons scaenae*, and in this form they have perhaps a fleeting existence in the Olimpico, but no more, disappearing with the introduction of streets constructed in perspective. They have no future in the hands of those architects who could not position them on the stage with a clear conscience. Conversely, their assimilation into the living entity of the baroque theater is due to the looseness with which they are interpreted by scenographers other than Barbaro and Palladio. Hélène Leclerc dates the first practical experiments with them between 1556 and 1585; Buontalenti (1536-1608), she feels, may have exploited them: his pupils, Giulio Parigi and Agostino Migliori certainly employed them and taught the German Furttenbach their use. The idea, in short, was in the air around 1580.[63]

Nevertheless, there is evidence of their practical use before 1547 at least. Danti, in his edition of Vignola's *Due Regole della Prospettiva Pratica*, warns the reader that while the *telari* are turning and changing, the eyes of the spectator must be occupied with some interval entertainment; he has heard tell of a scene with a two-sided revolving machine built in Castro by Aristotile da San Gallo.[64] Although he describes many of Aristotile's sets, Vasari, in his *Lives*, has nothing to say of this one, nor does he give the date of the scenographer's short stay in Castro, but it was

63. *Origines*, pp. 102–4. See also Fig. 3, p. 105, which shows their use by Furttenbach, *Architectura Civilis*, 1628.

64.   Et auuertiscasi, che mentre la scena si gira, sarà necessario di occupare gl'occhi de' riguardanti con qualche intermedio, acciò non vegghino girar le parti della scena mà solamente nello sparire dell'intermedio si vegga mutata. Così fattamente hò inteso io che già in Castro per il Duca Pierluigi Farnese fu fatta una scena, che si mutò due volte, da Aristotile da San Gallo.

Hélène Leclerc (p. 62) quotes Vignola as describing the functioning of the machines; in fact his work is purely theoretical, and it is his commentator Danti who describes them. See also Per Bjurström, *Giacomo Torelli and Baroque Stage Design*, Stockholm, 1961, p. 20, fn. 21.

certainly towards the end of his career, since the first dated event in his life given by Vasari after the journey is his arrival in Florence in 1547. We learn that it was Aristotile's cousin Antonio who sent him to Castro, and as the latter was the author of that version of the *periaktoi* which we have examined earlier, it may have been upon his suggestion that Aristotile used them in Castro.[65] Danti mentions a further instance of their use in 1569.[66]

Scena Ductilis

The first known mention of the *scena ductilis*, or double scene which parts in the middle, sliding to either side to reveal a further picture behind, is attributed to Philander.[67] His remarks bear considerable fruit: they are for example virtually a definition of the English Restoration shutter and certain usages of the French *ferme;* but we do well to remind ourselves that they have no direct Vitruvian backing. Philander bases himself upon Cassiodorus for the purpose of interpreting Vitruvius very widely. The device is thus one of the purest inventions of the Renaissance, for there is little evidence of anything resembling it in the medieval mysteries, or in the street scenes and *tableaux-vivants* so common on the occasion of Royal Entries and processions.

We may conveniently consider it under two heads, firstly its use down the sides of the stage, and secondly its use at the back. Now, the main entrance onto the presumed acting area of the Serlian stage, that is, its forestage, was from the sides. If no actor used the inclined stage, this would be natural.[68] In passing from Serlio's set to the Sabbattinian set, we pass then from three-dimensional houses partially obstructing wing entrance, to three-dimensional houses with wing entrance.[69]

Why did such a form not survive? In what manner did it prove inoperable? Firstly, the space left for entrance by these angle-wings must have been insufficient: indeed, this must be so as soon as actors pass onto that part of the stage which carries the decoration because the stage narrows as the perspective flees.[70] Yet there is no doubt of an increasing tendency for the play to go "backwards" with the perspective: it flees along the line of sight. Small wonder then that the stage designer, basing himself upon this principle of *scena ductilis*, hit upon the idea of representing the angle of his houses pictorially, thanks to the art of perspective, thus saving space

65. Vasari, *Le Vite*, ed. Milanesi, 1881, vol. VI, pp. 433–56.
66. Op. cit., p. 92. Kernodle, *From Art to Theatre*, p. 183, mentions Danti's second example only.
67. Bk. V, ch. vi, p. 156, Paris edn. of 1545: "Ea aut versilis fuit, quum subito tota machinis quibusdam verseretur et aliam picturae faciem ostenderet: aut ductilis, quum tractis tabulatis hac atque illac species picturae nudaretur interior."
68. Leclerc, *Origines*, p. 82, speaks of a lack of communication between the wings and the stage bearing the decoration, but there is an entrance on either side between the first (downstage) house and that behind it. Kernodle, op. cit., p. 192, claims that these entrances were used, and as they are there, he is probably right.
69. Leclerc, *Origines*, p. 108.
70. See Sabbattini, *Pratica*, Bk. II, ch. viii, p. 81.

for entrance where it was beginning to be needed. Ubaldus, Sabbattini's master, had thoroughly investigated the possibilities of reducing physically that face of the angle-wing (the "perspective" face) which ran upstage, by painted perspective falsely showing the angle of the house on the lateral face, an experiment continued by Sabbattini and Chiaramonti.[71]

This is a process rapidly extending to all the "houses" of the scene (only the downstage pair of houses resists), and its details are of interest to us, for we shall see it repeated, though with variations, in France. It is firstly then a winning of space for the actor, and, within our broader terms of reference, the handing to the actor of that physical space which had already been won for the stage decoration when this began to be constructed behind the doors of what had been a solid *frons scaenae*. The actor could not effectively act upon this area until he had easy access to it. The resultant wings retreat in symmetrical pairs upstage, in planes parallel to the front edge of the stage. And this hands over the set, or a much greater portion of it than he had exploited before, to the scene painter.

The superior overall convenience of this "flat" to the angle-wing needs no emphasis. One has only to cast an eye over the clumsy devices outlined by Sabbattini for the unconcealed changing of the angle-wing (justifiable so long as the main elements of change were confined to the *intermezzi* but surely glaring when the whole scene of a play was required to change, or when change of place appeared in the text), to be convinced of this. There could be little more naive or amusing than Sabbattini's recipe of placing a hireling at the back of the house to divert the view of the spectators at the moment of change by picking a quarrel, simulating the breaking of a rafter, blowing a trumpet or beating a drum, nor could anything appear more makeshift than that method of changing the angle-wings whereby the canvas covering bearing the initial scene is pulled aside by means of a stick manipulated from a platform offstage.

It is not surprising that the single surface flat, given the sanctity of Philander's comment on the *scena ductilis*, displaced such cumbersome exercises. Sabbattini himself seems to oscillate between a progressive and a retrogressive solution. On the one hand he prefers to all these methods a return to the *scena versatilis;* the best systems, he proclaims, are pivots placed beneath the stage with décors built in triangles (understandable in a theater in which wing entrance has not yet attained its maximum importance), and a form of *scena ductilis* but operating down the sides of the stage rather than across.

The *turning machines* had been swept to the sides of the stage by practical necessity, and from that position were once more swept away by the more practical *scena ductilis*, the elementary *coulisse*. The simplicity of changing these with a series of grooves one behind the other is apparent.

The *scena ductilis* at the back of the stage is nearer to the Philander text: "quum tractis tabulatis hac atque illac species picturae nudaretur interior." In our dis-

---

71. See Kernodle, op. cit., pp. 184–85. Guidibaldi e Marchionibus Montis, *Prospectivae Libri Sex*, 1600. Chiaramonti, *Delle scene e teatri*, 1675.

tinction between the back-scene and the flat side-wing, the operative word must be *interior*.

It is true that every scene, unless it be open to the landscape, must have some form of backing. We do not know when the painted back-cloth of continuing perspective replaced the wall with doors. Perhaps, indeed,the "picturatae scenae faciem" of Sulpicius' dedication to Cardinal Riario is the first backdrop.[72] Lily B. Campbell mentions further possibilities: Plautus' *Menaechmi* in 1486, or Nicolo del Cogo's painted scenery in 1491. The rough period seems clear enough. It would be quite natural that the painting of perspective on scenery should fasten first upon the back-wall since a flat surface facing the eye is the simplest experimental field for a would-be perspectivist, and in any case the development of complicated wing decorations for this period is highly unlikely. Kernodle instances the certain union of houses and painted background by 1508, with the production of Ariosto's *Cassaria* at Ferrara.[73]

The effect on the relationship between stage and auditorium is clear: much play has been made upon the Olympic Academy's purchase of fresh ground behind its stage back-wall for the purpose of extending a constructed perspective through such a wall, but spatially this cannot go on for ever in any theater. The point about painted perspective on the rear *scena ductilis* is that it permits the extension process (it is occasionally called an "extension" scene) to go on, if not for ever, at least for a very long way in pictured space, and combines with this a much greater possibility of scene change than the turning machines could do. The device could function just as well halfway upstage as at the back, and in fact often did, especially in the English Restoration and at the Hôtel de Bourgogne in France in the middle of the seventeenth century. Behind the incipient "proscenium arch" of each pair of side-wings, from front to back, the visual effect was an extension backward of the scenic space.[74] The stage ensemble was becoming a manifestation of competitive boasting seen through its obvious architectural motif: the triumphal arch.

Sheldon Cheney[75] has tended to see Palladio's dilation of the Porta Regia, and the manner in which he gives it the highly decorated appearance of a triumphal arch, as a first step in the development of the proscenium arch, further stages in the development being the theater at Sabbioneta and Aleotti's *Teatro Farnese*. This is now treated with general reserve, notably that of Elena Povoledo, who is more inclined to think that the proscenium arch in its very first form is no more than a simple wooden partition, not yet an architectonic structure, yet replacing already, with a logical, figuratively autonomous and independent solution, the elementary

---

72. His *Vitruvius* of 1486. Quoted by Nicoll, *Development of the Theatre*, 3rd edn., p. 81. See also Campbell, *Scenes and Machines*, pp. 12 et seq.
73. *From Art to Theatre*, p. 177. And see Franco Mancini, *La Scenografia Italiana dal Rinascimento all'età romantica*, Milan, 1966, pp. 17–18. He also draws attention to the possible contamination in these scenes, of medieval staging and *l'apparato festivo*.
74. Ibid., pp. 177 et seq.
75. Quoted by Mancini, op. cit. He also draws attention to the *torneo* as a possible factor in the development of the proscenium arch.

Serlian *cadre de scène* formed by a simple framing of the two houses of the *proscenio* by a decorative festoon.

The competitive element in baroque production is best seen in the growth of machinery and stage marvel. Lily B. Campbell considers at some length the influence of Pollux's *Onomasticon* on the use of machinery in the Renaissance. The number of early editions is for her *a priori* proof of its implementation in practice where it touches the matter of stage machines.[76] It is certainly evidence in that direction, and stronger evidence for Italy than for France, where the scholar-architect-scenographer is less frequent. One reservation however should perhaps be made. There are (as the writer points out) editions in Venice in 1502, Florence in 1520, and Basle in 1536; but it must be added that these contain merely the Greek text, and no Latin translation. It is fair comment that at the beginning of the sixteenth century this would somewhat restrict the spread of the work, and keep it at scholastic level. The first Latin edition is that of Tigurinus (Basle, 1541), followed by Seber's (Frankfurt) in 1608, and a century goes by before the next, that of Lederlin and Hemsterhuys (Amsterdam) in 1706. There is no Latin edition in Italy throughout the period of which we speak.

Philander quotes Pollux frequently, yet the only direct connection with Renaissance practice would appear to be through Barbaro, whose note to his own Book V, chapter vi, in which is to be discerned once more the familiar confusion between *theologeion* and *periaktoi*, does indeed seem to indicate familiarity with the author.[77] There is no doubt that textually Pollux completes Vitruvius with greater detail and it is equally clear that he has more to say about machines. Nevertheless, the real measure of his influence during the Renaissance must remain doubtful.

Stage appearance, disappearance, revelation, descent, flight, all flourish increasingly as the baroque theater develops. The most popular device, the *gloire*, has an obvious origin in Renaissance painting: the frame of radiant light around the body of a divine person, the clouds of glory, turn into a theater machine of cloud and sunlight in which gods descend from the heavens. It is one of the most striking pieces of evidence for Kernodle's thesis of "from art to theatre," for it is the painted picture given depth and movement. The descent upon a cloud (of glory) has a clear religious origin, occurring as it does in so many Church wall paintings; and here we may genuinely surmise that it would have passed into the theater without the help of Greeks and Romans—unlike the façade of the Olimpico! The textual consecration of the *mechane* was added to it however, chiefly one imagines through Barbaro, and the weight of Jupiter is in a manner of speaking added to that of Jehovah. It seems also to have an intermediate stage in the street theaters of the Royal Entries, where it is naturally and easily adapted to the game of monarch-pleasing.

To the descent from above corresponds the ascent from below. An analogy with the Heaven and Hell of the mystery play is justified here, although Heaven and

76. *Scenes and Machines*, pp. 61 et seq.
77. Ibid., p. 26.
78. The two acceptances rub shoulders in Littré.

Hell would doubtless have found machine expression even without their embodiment in the mystery décors. Forms of traps are described by Sabbattini, as are methods of getting men through them quickly.[79] Hell itself could be made to appear from below, as could mountains and other things. Sabbattini describes them all: the merest listing of some of the chapter headings of his second book forms a vertiginous repertory of possibilities at a time when the baroque was not completely developed. Demolitions, fires, blackouts, rocks into men and men into rocks, ships, marine monsters, rivers, mountains, skies, clouds, rainbows, oblique as well as vertical flights in the *gloire*, wind, thunder, lightning, paradise, dawn, ghosts . . . and, Parthian shot of baroque confidence, his final chapter, "De la facilité de la pratique"!

These machines have broken free of reference to the past, most especially of reference to classical antiquity; they are the baroque feeding upon itself alone.

Movement

Nevertheless, a significant development, of a purely technical nature, is necessary before the baroque is to reach its summit of the spectacular. The science of hydraulics was developed rapidly by the Italian engineers (frequently scenographers too) towards the end of the sixteenth century. The best known of the hydrologists is probably G.-B. Aleotti, whose *Idrologia overo Vaso delle Scienze et Arte delle Acque del ben regulare le acque* has remained in five manuscript volumes. In all senses of the term, techniques such as Aleotti's "accelerate" the baroque process. It is no accident that he should write the *Idrologia* and build the Teatro Farnese. From a date fixed by Mme. Horn-Monval[80] between 1588 and 1590 a period of great mechanical innovation gives an impetus of movement to the relatively static sets and machines of Perruzzi, San Gallo, Serlio, Palladio, Scamozzi and others. The stage machine effect becomes more complex, and nearer to the instantaneous in its execution. The techniques are taken over to France by Francini (first, and least chronicled) and then by Torelli and Vigarani.

The Auditorium

In the long and broken journey from *skené* to perspective set, the stage is cleared for the needs of scene change: it is left free to develop. The auditorium, on the other hand, can only change radically if the whole structure changes, the possibilities of modification within an existing form being limited.

The final shape of the ancient auditorium is semi-circular, focused upon a wide, solid wall. With its rediscovery, the principle of the semi-circle is accepted, but the social conditions underlying the existence of a mass, open-air theater are no longer there, and the social conditions of its rediscovery and reconstitution—the small courts

79. *Pratica*, Bk. II, ch. xvii, pp. 96 et seq.
80. For a very full treatment of this, see Madeleine Horn-Monval. "La grande machinerie théâtrale et ses origines," RHT, no. 4, 1957, pp. 291 et seq.

of the Italian Renaissance—are such as to make a mass audience impossible. It was not a theater form which answered the needs of the people. Consequently, the space it enjoys shrinks correspondingly to the size of its élite audience, and suffers the sporadic truncation of a roofed rectangular building, the indoor performance triumphing over the outdoor. The theaters we have looked at all evince some limitation of the hemicycle; meanwhile, the perspective set can best be seen from a position on its own line.

Thus, in spite of the comparatively slow evolution of the house as compared with the stage, it may be asked why the curved orchestra and auditorium survived for so long after the establishment of some sort of perspective set with a single line of vision? Sabbattini is at once entertaining and illuminating:

> Il convient d'accommoder les dames dans l'orchestre, autrement dit dans le tiers de la salle le plus voisin de la scène, en ayant soin de mettre aux premiers rangs, c'est-à-dire proche le parapet, les moins importantes et ainsi de suite, selon la qualité pour les autres rangs en prenant garde de mettre les plus belles au milieu afin que ceux qui oeuvrent et peinent, réjouis par ce beau point de vue, exécutent leur besogne plus allègrement avec plus de maîtrise et plus de coeur.[81]
>
> On placera aux derniers rangs les dames les plus âgées, en raison du voisinage des hommes, afin d'écarter toute cause d'ombrage . . . il faudra tâcher d'obtenir que les personnes obtuses et du commun soient installées sur les gradins et de côté en raison de l'imperfection des machines qui parfois peuvent être vues d'endroits pareils pour ce que les personnes susdites n'y regardent point de si près; les personnes instruites et de marque doivent, au contraire, être placées dans le parterre et autant que possible au centre, dans les deuxième et troisième rangs car, outre qu'elles jouiront mieux du spectacle, en ces places-là toutes les parties de la scène et les machines se montrent dans leurs perfections; ces spectateurs de qualité n'en pourront donc discerner les défauts qui, parfois, ne sont que trop visibles pour les gens placés de côté ou sur les gradins, ainsi que nous l'avons marqué plus haut.[82]

What do we learn from this? The best view is in the pit, at the level of the house floor. The orchestra still has a function as a sort of extended pit for the ladies. Machinery and the single-line perspective set render the rising benches and the sides of the house very poor as a viewpoint. Why then do the sides of the hemicycle continue to be used when the side seats are bound to place the spectator in a position from which he looks more or less directly into the wings? Why did not a narrow, long, rectangular auditorium with a slight but adequate slope develop? Sabbattini

81. The importance of women as spectator-spectacle is already well established in the Italian theatergoing mentality, as a detail in the generally narcissistic nature of the public. Thus, Pigafetta, at the Olimpico *Oedipus*, was in the theater, along with others, for eleven hours without the slightest boredom: "stettero là dentro forse undici ore senza increscere punto . . . perciò che nel vedere tanti visi nuovi successivamente, e sempre, o nel'accomodarsi le Donne, o nel considerare quella ragunanza tutta, trapassò il tempo molto presto."
82. *Pratica*, Bk. I, ch. xl, p. 68.

has again given the answer. Socially, the auditorium had a measure of autonomy: the ladies in the orchestra were there to be looked at, and, if we are to lend credit to the writer, were insulated from the signors by a layer of older ladies lest mere contemplation should exceed itself. The hemicycle naturally surrounded this semi-circular orchestra. The long periods of social intercourse before the show began indicate that the audience came for the purpose of looking at itself.

In short, the evolution of the baroque perspective stage ideally demanded straight rows of seats stretching backwards. The social narcissism of the Italian courts acted however as a check upon the curve. Plebeian infiltrators at the peformances were relegated to the sides, there being no other social distinction apart from sex and nearness to the best viewpoint.

The growth of the lyrical drama, firstly in the private or quasi-private perfor-mances of the Roman and Florentine palace, and then in the public opera of Venice, is not entirely foreign to the disintegration of this form of auditorium. It is clear in any case that the eventual opening of the occasion to the whole range of a class society would affect such modifications of the theater buildings as were undertaken, and, where new ones were built, the form of the edifice itself. It seems that this is what happened in the passage from private to public of the Italian opera,[83] its trans-ference from Rome to the Republic of Venice, from aristocratic patronage to the merchant exploiter (for although the element of exploitation was by no means to the fore, the theater had to pay its way). In the first instance, the entire theatrical occasion would be privately financed, the audience being necessarily restricted, for it meant nothing commercially, everything socially. In the second instance, the ex-ploitation of the Venetian theater would be mixed. Such theaters were normally erected by patrician families or by the emission of shares, the proprietors securing their revenue by the letting of loggias, and the troupe by selling places on the ground floor.

In architectural terms this meant the maximum exploitation of space, and this again, since the floor of the house was already occupied by seats, could only mean further exploitation of wall space. Loggias are built all round the walls, and the "pigeon-cote" theater is born, turning the auditorium into a funnel with the pit at the bottom, atomizing the spectators and stratifying them vertically in a manner suitable for a class society.[84]

The opera did not change qualitatively the baroque perspective décor with all its conventions; but quantitatively it pushed it farther towards that intellectual and artistic atrophy which is generally admitted. The theater has never been farther along the road of "entertainment." It is true that it got off to a bad start: its early,

83. See Romain Rolland, *Histoire de l'opéra en Europe avant Lully et Scarlatti*, 1895, chs. 5 and 6, and Leclerc, *Origines*, chs. 8 and 9.
84. The point is nicely illustrated by a comparison of two theater plans by Carini Motta, one for a court, and the other for a public theater, reproduced by Leclerc, *Origines*, Pls. XLIII and XLIV. See also Peter Brieger, "The Baroque equation: illusion and reality," *Gazette des Beaux Arts*, March 1945, p. 145.

sincere efforts of humanist rebirth, the search for that San Graal of musicians, the melopoeia of the ancient Greeks, were soon engulfed by the fastuous appetites of the Princes of the Church.[85] Less trammelled by recitative, solo, and duet than was the legitimate stage by the presence of a literary text, the baroque of the lyrical drama surpassed itself and became virtually its own principle, independent of other artistic support.

85. Cf. Leclerc, *Origines*, pp. 128-29, and Rolland, op. cit., pp. 133 et seq.

CHAPTER TWO

MYSTERY STAGE AND STREET THEATER

'Soubz l'art theatrique sont comprins jeux publicques et prives ou il y a divers jeux et esbatemens.'

FERGET, *Mirouer de la vie humaine*, 1482

The Mystery Stage

NEVER AT ANY moment of the seventeenth century does the baroque completely monopolize the French stage. Nor, in France, is it ever purely Italian. Those native features which now resisted it, now were assimilated by it and thus modified it, are to be found not only in the Renaissance in France but as far back as the heyday of the mystery play, so that the history of the French theater leading up to the seventeenth century displays more continuity than has sometimes been supposed.

Decorations in the mystery staging tradition subsist in the seventeenth century, and are certainly used as late as the third decade. We may be sure of this from the manuscript left by Laurent Mahelot and Michel Laurent, *décorateurs* or *machinistes* of the Hôtel de Bourgogne.[1] It is the only iconographical document of any detail that we possess for that period, and as a result it has become in its isolation dangerously monolithic. Monopolized by the Confrères de la Passion in Paris, the mystery play, with its tradition of staging and decoration, is seen as entering the bottleneck of the Hôtel de Bourgogne, where it is slowly choked. The illustrations of the *Mémoire* are looked upon as its agony.

For the Hôtel de Bourgogne alone, to which we shall return, this is probably the case: the very sporadic exceptions later in the century, such as the *théâtre supérieur*, do not stem directly from that source, as we shall see; for in this and other instances we believe that the décors and machinery of the mystery play had a persisting effect, though in a modified form. The modifications they underwent are such that the mystery element in the French baroque theater has not been fully recognized, and what was partly indigenous has been written down as purely Italian.

Let us first summarize what is known of the mystery stage, setting aside for the moment its overall aspect, its existence as a stage-auditorium unit, for we shall return to that later.

It seems clear, as Professor Cohen has told us, that there was no fixed rule for the shape of the stage.[2] Elie Konigson has furnished us with an invaluable juxtaposition of the Rothschild and Bibliothèque Nationale manuscripts, both illuminated by Hubert Cailleau, the designer of the performance. (Fig. 17). As Nagler has reiterated after Stuart, not all the scenery is reproduced in the frontispiece,

---

1. MSS.BN Rés. 24330. Edns.: Dacier, *La mise en scène à Paris au XVIIe siècle.* Lancaster, *Le Mémoire de Mahelot, Laurent, et autres décorateurs de l'Hôtel de Bourgogne.*
2. *Théâtre religieux*, p. 85.

FIG. 17.—The Valenciennes mystery stage.

which is accompanied by miniatures figuring the mansions and *loca* for single days of the performance.[3] When space was available, the *mansions* (compartments or individual items of décor)[4] seem to have been placed in a straight line, reaching sometimes up to a hundred yards. But it was a most fluid form, and the well-known Fouquet miniature of the martyrdom of Saint Apollina tells a different story[5] (Fig. 18). Here the acting area of the stage is more distinct from the compartments than in the Valenciennes disposition. It is circular or semi-circular, and we are to assume that the public, or most of it, is gathered around in a semi-circle, though part of the public is to be seen massed below the stage at the far side of the picture, while in the background, on high, loggias for the more important spectators are interspersed with *mansions*.[6]

Apart from this, the main discussion as to the shape of the mystery stage centers upon the number of stories it comprised. The idea that the mystery stage had several

3. Elie Konigson, *La représentation d'un mystère de la Passion à Valenciennes en 1547*, Paris, 1969. A.M. Nagler, *The Medieval Religious Stage. Shapes and Phantoms*, New Haven and London, 1976, p. 51. Donald C. Stuart, *Stage Decoration in France*, New York, 1966, pp. 108–09. Rey-Flaud, *Le cercle magique*, pp. 218–22, sees the performance, most improbably, in the round.

4. On the meaning of the term *mansion*, see Cohen, ''Un terme de scénologie médiéviale: 'Lieu' ou 'Mansion'?'' in *Mélanges de Philologie et d'Histoire Littéraire offerts à Edmond Huguet.*

5. For a detailed interpretation of this, see Cohen, *Le livre de conduite du régisseur*, 1925, pp. xlvii–xlviii.

6. Although this again could be a trick of the miniaturist to introduce some audience into his picture. Southern, *The Mediaeval Theatre in the Round*, 3rd edn., London, 1975, pp. 91–107. The interpretations of Bapst, and Decugis and Reymond (*Le décor de théâtre en France du Moyen âge à 1925*, Paris, 1953, p. 18) are to be seen in the light of Southern's examination. See also Rey-Flaud, *Le cercle magique*, pp. 113–36.

étages, one above the other, a theory taken from the Frères Parfaict by Emile Morice,[7] was first attacked by Paulin Paris, who interprets *mansion* as a single item of décor.[8] This is further developed by Petit de Julleville and then recently by Cohen.[9] Thus, current opinion about the mystery stage has settled in the following way: Paradise normally occupied a second story, with seats for its various inhabitants and steps leading down to the main stage. However, when the mystery was played indoors, the serious restriction in stage width which ensued led to a bisection of the line of the compartments, half of them being placed on a higher stage, set slightly back, and presumably with steps leading down to the lower one. This would obtain for instance at the Hôpital de la Trinité. Lanson quotes Picot as claiming that the *mansions* were so disposed at the Trinité when the Confrères de Notre Dame de la Liesse played the mystery of Joseph there, in about 1538.[10] Cohen is quite firm about one thing: there were never five or six stories.

What of the actual elements of décor? In the Valenciennes mystery we can easily see the normal form of a house, palace, temple or other edifice; slightly raised on three or four steps, it was essentially a roof, open on three sides and supported at the front by two pillars. Occasionally it was labelled (''lieu pour jouer silete'' in the case of the Valenciennes picture), though the use of such *écriteaux*, says Petit de Julleville, was not universal nor in fact very general: it was often replaced by a prologue in which the scenes were described.[11] In the simple arched doorways we see an interesting fusion of the two possibilities of entrance: in the picture in question towers are to be seen behind the door marked ''Jerusalem'' and that marked ''Maison des Evêques,'' indicating place behind the stage. The stage itself is a sort of no man's land which can be localized as anything, according to the demands of the action and the place where the actors are standing. So we have the two phenomena of entrance in one: the place on the stage is indicated by the doorway, and the actor's positioning of himself in relation to this doorway; but it is also place ''whence,'' as was the case with the *frons scaenae* of the Roman theater. Paradise, highly stylized, is seen above one of the compartments, while the mouth of hell fulfils the function of a stage trap and leads below. All these are typical features.

7. Morice, ''La mise en scène depuis les mystères jusqu'au Cid,'' two articles in the *Revue de Paris*, 1835, vols. 22 and 23, pp. 5–40 and 73–107 respectively. According to Morice, not only were the stages placed on top of one another but occasionally one mystery was divided by different stages, each having a number of stories. See however Fischel, ''Art and the Theatre,'' *Burlington Magazine*, vol. LXVI, 1935, p. 13, who claims that the Frères Parfaict are merely speaking of ''the slight difference in level of three regions.'' Natalie Crohn Schmitt (''Was there a mediaeval theatre in the round?'' *Theatre Notebook*, vol. XXIV, no. 1, 1969) also uses the evidence of Paul on the road to Damascus, which we now adduce.
8. *La mise en scène des mystères*, 1855, p. 5.
9. Petit de Julleville, *Les mystères*, 1880, tome I, p. 288. Cohen, *Théâtre religieux*, pp. 78 et seq.
10. ''Etudes sur les origines de la tragédie classique en France,'' RHLF, tome X, 1903, p. 179 fn. 2.
11. Op. cit., tome I, p. 397.

FIG. 18.—*Le martyre de Sainte Apolline.*

The picture has been analyzed in great detail by Richard Southern. He seems effectively to destroy the theory that the stage was a raised one of heaped earth surrounded by *fascines* or branches bound together, and to establish that the level on the one side of the *fascines* is the same as on the other. But there is a habit common among theater historians when handling iconographical evidence, of isolating one picture which provides the evidence they want from the rest of a complete collection. We shall see this operating equally in the case of Terentian illustration. Here, the most cursory glance at the totality of the *Livre d'heures d'Etienne Chevalier*, of which the Martyrdom of Saint Apollina is but one item, reveals numerous examples of depicted events which have presumably nothing at all to do with theater, and are placed "upon" stage-like, apparently raised, decorative motifs of one sort or another, in similar positions to the so-called *fascines* of the Apollina miniature. One might mention the *Martyrdom of Saint Jacques the Elder*, or *Paul on the Road to Damascus* (Figs. 19 and 20). It is thus not unreasonable to conclude that whether the stage of

FIG. 19.—The martyrdom of Saint Jacques the Elder.

FIG. 20.—Paul on the road to Damascus.

the Apollina picture is raised or not, the ''fascines'' are just as likely to be a decorative motif as anything else. It is, in short, quite possible that they are without
descriptive value, and are not evidence of a raised, or indeed unraised, stage. Two
pieces of ''theatrical'' evidence adduced by Southern, the one of figures in front of
the barrier-motif, showing, for him, that there probably was not audience on that
side, and the other, the grey color of the trampled earth inside the fence and the

bright green grass in front of it, are to be equally seen in the Paul miniature, which has, for good measure, a perspective and a *gloire*!

In the determined search for theatrical evidence, Rey-Flaud disposes of these difficulties in an ingenious manner. While he certainly pays heed to the totality of the Fouquet pictures, he approaches the matter from a totally different angle. Firstly, Fouquet as an artist is known for his "réalisme fanatique." *Therefore* the "break" in so many of the pictures, represented by branches in *Sainte Apolline* and by other motifs in so many other miniatures, is *an integral part of the landscape or building depicted.* Yet this would clearly be ludicrous if one did not assume that the pictures are theatrically inspired—landscapes simply do not have ornamental barriers across them in reality. And so Rey-Flaud assumes a theatrical inspiration. It is interesting to note that among the many miniatures which he quotes neither the *Martyrdom of St. Jacques the Elder* nor *Paul on the Road to Damascus* figures. However this may be, the upshot of the author's deliberations is to see the barrier of Apollina as supporting, up to its foliage, a ditch which has been dug round the presumed circle, the spoil being used to create a slope around its outer circumference for a standing public. The author's reconstruction of the theater in detail is of the greatest interest.

With spectators surrounding the scene entirely, if they ever did, the compartment would naturally be modified so as to be visible all round: it would be supported by four pillars instead of having its back to a wall. The mystery theater in such a case would then vary between the convention of the arena and a form nearer to that single line of vision towards which the ancient Greek theater evolved. Evidence is unfortunately insufficient for us to state categorically that such a progression occurred in the case of the mystery; we cannot say definitely that in the earlier plays the audience surrounded the stage, and that this gradually ceded in popularity to the platform and back wall, in the way in which the ancient orchestra was gradually ousted by the *logeion* and *skené*. We may however note that the Fouquet miniature, which shows us a modified arena theater, is dated towards the middle of the fifteenth century, while the *Mystère de la Passion* at Valenciennes is dated 1547, the year before the famous edict of 1548, which tolls the death knell of the form itself. On the whole it seems not unreasonable to read into the Valenciennes picture one of the most advanced developments of the mystery stage. That this representation of the Passion was one of the most complicated and accomplished of its kind is suggested by the account of it:

> Aux fêtes de la Pentecôte de l'an 1547 les principaux bourgeois de la ville représentèrent sur le théâtre, en la maison du duc d'Arschot, la vie, mort et passion de Notre Seigneur, en vingt-cinq journées; en chacune desquelles on vit paraître des choses étranges et pleines d'admiration. Les secrets du Paradis et de l'Enfer étaient tout à fait prodigieux, et capables d'être pris par la populace pour enchantements . . .[12]

12. H. d'Outreman, *Histoire de la ville et comté de Valenciennes*, 1639, p. 396. Quoted by Morice, op. cit., p. 31, Petit de Julleville, op. cit., tome II, pp. 155-56, and Cohen, *Théâtre religieux*, p. 142.

Played in the courtyard of the Hôtel de Croy, its relative modernity is betrayed by the comparatively restricted number of compartments and the obviously "modern" looking stage front. It is just possible then that the French theater in its origin, after it left the Church, followed the same broad progression as the ancient theater: that of a circle breaking down.

Items other than the standard compartment were constructed as demanded by the dramatic work. In view of the very great distances covered by the action of the genre it is not surprising that the ship and the sea are recurrent motifs, reminding us of the orchestra at Athens which the Romans eventually made watertight for sea fights: in the *Mystère de Saint-Louis* a naval battle is staged.

Surely one of the most fascinating pieces of stage decoration ever to find its way onto a mystery stage is the Roman theater as such. There is one in the mystery of the *Trois Doms* (1509) and another in the *Mystère des Actes des Apôtres* (1536).[13] The ancient theater as something to be looked at, apart from its theatrical value, is something that we shall meet again.

As in the case of the Roman theater, awnings are occasionally used to protect actor and spectator from sun and rain. The Paradise also had awnings which were used to form clouds, occasionally decorated with a sun, moon, or stars, while beds were always hung with tapestries.[14]

Such is the splendour of the tradition of stage machinery which is brought over from Italy by its craftsmen[15] that the origins in the mystery of French machinery have been neglected. The details of the machinery itself have all been remarked upon, and it has become customary, in speaking of the genre, to refer to its intense naturalism, the tortured figure of Saint Apollina providing a stock illustration. But in so doing writers have tended to seal off the mystery, in this respect, from the subsequent history of the theater, from subsequent naturalisms, and indeed, following the development of the mystery play in its very restricted sense there is justification for such an attitude. Nevertheless we hope to demonstrate that in other theatrical forms mystery habits of machinery were handed down to the seventeenth century in France, though by that time inextricably assimilated by the superior lore of Italian stage management. This must be our excuse for dilating upon them.

A mystery machine was called a *secret*, and the person later referred to as a *machiniste* was a "facteur ou conducteur de secrets."[16] He was supplied before the play with a book in which were written down all the requirements of the show in terms of machinery: the "fainctes." An excellent account of the preliminary negotiation between "fainctier" and the municipality is to be found in Denys Godefroy's *Cérémonial françois* in his report of the Royal Entries of 1530.[17] His tasks were not a wit less varied than were to be those of his baroque counterpart: amongst

13. Cohen, *Théâtre religieux*, p. 100.
14. Ibid., p. 103.
15. Cf. Mignon, *Etudes sur le théâtre français et italien de la Renaissance*, 1923, pp. 63 et seq.
16. Cohen, *Théâtre religieux*, p. 143.
17. *Le cérémonial françois . . . recueilli par Théodore Godefroy . . . et mis en lumière par Denys Godefroy*, 2 vols., 1649.

them would be the fabrication of all sorts of animals, souls, or even plants.[18] Many of the animals had to be mechanically actuated. Flight, ascent and descent, appearance and disappearance, metamorphosis, all were present. The account of the Valenciennes play already quoted in part is rich in such detail:

> Car l'on voyait la Vérité, les Anges et divers personnages descendre de bien haut, tantôt visiblement, autrefois comme invisibles, puis paraître tout à coup; de l'Enfer Lucifer s'élevait, sans qu'on vît comment, porté sur un dragon. La verge de Moïse, de sèche et stérile, jetait à coup des fleurs et des fruits; les âmes d'Hérode et de Judas étaient emportées en l'air par les Diables; les Diables chassés des corps, les hydropiques et autres malades guéris, le tout d'une façon admirable. Ici Jésus Christ était élevé du diable qui rampait le long d'une muraille de quarante pieds de haut; là, il se rendait invisible; ailleurs, il se transfigurait sur la montagne de Thabor. On y vit l'eau changée en vin, si mystérieusement qu'on ne le pouvait croire; et plus de cent personnes voulurent goûter de ce vin; les cinq pains et les deux poissons y furent semblablement multipliés et distribués à plus de mille personnes; nonobstant quoi il y en eut plus de douze corbeilles de reste. Le figuier maudit par Notre-Seigneur parut séché et les feuilles flétries en un instant.
>
> L'éclipse, le terre tremble, le brisement des pierres et les autres miracles advenus à la mort de Notre-Sauveur furent représentés avec de nouveaux miracles.

The work of Konigson, confronting as it does the miniature of the *hourdement* and that of the different *journées*, and marginal notes and notices, has gone a long way towards elucidating the precise nature of these marvels. It is difficult to understand why this detailed exercise has not been carried out before. Biblical lore in action leaves little indeed for pagan myth to accomplish: its potential range is just as great. In the *Mystère du Vieil Testament* Lucifer sits proudly on the right hand of God the Father, and the fallen angels follow him, but a wheel "secrètement faite dessus un pivot à vis" lifts them up and drops them neatly into Hell. The clouds of glory which make up the *gloire* of the baroque stage, and which we have seen previously to be connected with medieval religious paintings,[19] are already there in the mystery, and practically indistinguishable from their better known successors: made of painted canvas they frequently concealed wooden platforms which could carry up to four persons, witness the scene from the *Actes des Apôtres:*[20] "Ici doit descendre une nuée ronde en forme de couronne où doivent être plusieurs anges feints, tenant épées nues et dards avec Gabriel et les trois autres . . ." and elsewhere, "Ici doit faire un tonnerre et une nue blanche qui doit couvrir les apôtres prêchant en diverses contrées et les apporter devant la porte de Notre-Dame . . ." The most frequent occasion for the mystery *gloire* was not unnaturally the Ascension: Jesus, "avec les trois anges, Gabriel, Raphaël et Uriel, sera tiré à part le premier, tout en paix, et les deux fils Syméon ressuscités (Carinus et Leontius) et les 49 qu'il mènera monteront secrètement en Paradis par une voie sans qu'on les voie, mais leurs statures de papier ou de parchemin bien contrefaites jusqu'audit nombre 51

18. Cohen, *Théâtre religieux*, pp. 146 et seq.
19. See p. 44.
20. Livre I, fol. 126 v°, quoted by Cohen, *Théâtre religieux*, pp. 153–4.

personnages seront attachés à la robe de Jésus et tirés amont, quand et quand Jésus et si seront les tables avironnées de nues blanches.''

In the *Mystère du Vieil Testament* it is made to hail, thunder, and rain. Moses strikes a rock with his rod, and water spouts forth, while the whole scene is on one occasion flooded.[21] Fire is also frequently used, and not merely in Hell, where sulfur is burnt. Traps in the floor are common, again in addition to the mouth of Hell. As examples of metamorphosis on the stage we may quote Moses throwing down a rod which changes into a serpent. The wife of Lot is changed into a pillar of salt, the Jews see their arms suddenly become withered and black, idols are reduced to powder.[22]

Flights up, down, and across the stage hold no terrors either for actor or ''conducteur de secrets.'' At Laval in 1493, during the performance of the *Vie de Sainte Barbe* characters flew across the stage, and at a peformance of the *Invention de la Sainte Croix* in 1511, at the same place, angels were to be seen in flight. For the *Actes des Apôtres* at Bourges in 1536 the magician Simon flew up in the air and was seen to fall suddenly and ''se rompre la tête et les jambes.'' ''Fainctes'' of this sort were commonly known as ''voleries'' or ''vouleries.''

All this, in content if not in perfection, equals the baroque and is almost purely native: it owes little to Italy, although we should not forget that very occasionally (and we may expect the habit to grow) an Italian *machiniste* might be summoned for the very important mysteries towards the middle of the sixteenth century, and Konigson has firmly attached the style of certain features of the Valenciennes *hourdement* to the Italian *quattrocento*.

To summarize, what were those native features which were to last into the seventeenth century? They were the habit of the *théâtre supérieur*, and the native tradition of stage marvel. We must not exaggerate this contribution: there were two things in this theater to be killed by the advent of the baroque, and which constitute analogies with the Greek and Roman theaters. Firstly, the conventional oneness of place between actor and spectator, and secondly the amphitheatrical form of the performance. The amphitheater disappears by submission to the rectangle; we are fortunate in possessing the Valenciennes picture, where we may see this process in its infancy. We must also note the relative absence of ''changements à vue.'' Cohen uses this term to indicate what would perhaps better be defined as stage metamorphosis. If, upon a stage, one object is made to change into another, that is, in a sense, an unconcealed change; but for us the expression must mean change of represented scenic place within full view of the spectator. Of this there is little, except the occasional use of a curtain drawn aside to reveal a compartment behind. Nor is there any proscenium arch to facilitate this changing of the whole scenic space for the purposes of the action.

Kernodle's work[23] has made an extremely important contribution to our knowledge of the proscenium arch. He has shown once and for all that it cannot have

21. Ibid., p. 155.
22. Ibid., p. 162.
23. *From Art to Theatre*, 1944.

developed in any regular way from the Royal Door of the Olympic Theatre. As a motif in the arts generally the arch obviously existed before the first proscenium arch theater, and possibly passed onto the stage in Italy from the street theater, though only because an increasing knowledge of the Roman theater had put archways on the stage in imitation of the *frons scaenae*. The surge of perspective places pictures or constructed scenes behind the arch, the prolongation of the Serlian tradition places houses, to become wings, down the sides of the stage, and the necessity for changing these eventually places the triumphal arch in front of the whole, responding to a need for concealment of change and framing what had become, to use Kernodle's phrase, a "theatre of pictorial illusion." We have seen such an order emerging in Sabbattini's work.[24] The process is of course gradual: the *scena ductilis* tradition prolongs the seeing of pictures through an arch well upstage, or halfway downstage, extending the inner stage well known to the seventeenth century. The problem of acting space, not difficult when the forestage is present in front of any décor, is solved with the advent of flat wings and the advance of the main archway to the front of the stage, framing a picture of which the actor is now a part. Before this, the decoration was framed and the actor was not, or at least he could step out of the frame. Now, both are part of a picture.

The importance for this process of the Triumphal Arch of the Royal Entry, erected in the street, must be considerable. It is along this channel more than any other that the motif becomes the great instrument of separation between stage and house which is the proscenium arch.

Yet sociologically the occasion of the prince's entry into a city is by no means unconnected with that of the mystery play. Both were municipal occasions, both were points of honor for various sections of the community, not the least amongst which were the fraternities and guilds of the towns concerned; and of the greatest importance for us, the mystery play not only figured in its own right in the general display of the Entry, but appeared suitably modified and shading off into other forms of show. The following quotation shows how near are mystery, Entry, and procession:

La relation de l'ordre de la triomphante et magnifique[25] *monstre des saints actes des Apôtres.*
Le premier jour de la représentation commença par une marche triomphale de tous les personnages, dans leurs costumes éblouissants de richesse; ces "acteurs" s'étaient réunis, à cet effet, hors de la ville, dans l'abbaye de Saint-Sulpice, la plupart à cheval ou montés sur des chars. Dès six heures du matin, le maire et les échevins, accompagnés de trente-six officiers de la ville . . . se rendirent à l'abbaye. Là, après avoir ouï la messe, chacun des acteurs se retira dans une chambre pour se vêtir . . . Sur les neuf heures, les magistrats de justice firent battre les tambours et sonner les trompettes et les fifres, pour donner le signal de se mettre en ordre, et faire faire l'appel. Sur les onze heures, le cortège se mit en marche vers les Arènes.[26]

24. See p. 39 n. 62.
25. Both these epithets are *de rigueur* in the accounts of the Royal Entries, but "triomphante" is particularly significant: it seems to be copied subconsciously from an Entry account.
26. Summarized by Girardot in his edition of the *Mystère des Actes des Apôtres*, 1854, from a contemporary account by Jacques Thiboust.

This tradition of the "monstre" preceding the mystery facilitates its assimilation into the shows of the Royal Entry. The example of Valenciennes alone, shows a rich clustering of paratheatricals around the date of the *Passion:* in 1540, entry of Charles Quint, with "les théâtres dressez à chaque rue, cinq arcs triomphaux . . ." etc.; in 1544 that of Maria of Hungary; in 1549 Philip II, son of Charles Quint. In 1548, the year after the *Passion,* the feast of the Principauté de Plaisance is reintroduced. That most popular of excuses for a triumphal demonstration, a victorious return from Italy, inevitably brought motifs from Italian entries and pageant. Thus, the history of Royal Entry and of street theaters in France is that of increasing Italian influences amalgamating with what the occasion had taken over from the mystery. This is the story that we must now follow, using some of its major landmarks.

Royal Entry and Street Theater

The resemblance between the *tableaux-vivants* of the street theaters of say 1500 and the mystery stage is strong. So is that between the French baroque stage of the 1660s and the street shows of that period, although the street theater, still popular, has changed comparatively little. There is a connection, in short, via the Royal Entry, between the mystery and the baroque. On the other hand we must also recognize the presence in the street theaters of the Renaissance of motifs and units of decoration from Italy, which appear, sometimes irrelevantly, upon the baroque stage.

Let us examine a series of typical Entries for the purpose of determining these features.[27] The Royal Entry is not, and cannot be, a normal theatrical manifestation. As we shall note continually, there is firstly a perfectly natural emphasis upon the thing to be seen. Anything offered in the way of laudatory couplets, song, or music, is again quite naturally, and strictly speaking, "occasional": there is no room, no time, no occasion for dramatic poetry of any length or any originality. Generally speaking, the royal procession considered as audience is the changing element. Contrary to the English mystery formula, the scene changed for the spectator when he moved to another, time being organized by a series of halts, as in the procession of actors in the French mystery play, or the stations of the cross in others. There is a further abnormality: the prince is not merely audience, he is actor as well, and knows it (Fig. 21). His dress and bearing indicate it sufficiently. To the onlooking population of a city the Royal Entry was a series of theatrical or pictorial objects before which, or through which, the hero appeared, halted, and passed on, action being supplied for the halt by the hearing of a song or recitation, by a ceremony of presentation or a machine descent, the procession being swelled by city notables

27. See Le Vayer, *Les entrées solennelles à Paris des Rois et Reines de France, des souverains et princes étrangers, ambassadeurs, etc.,* 1896. Kernodle (whose list of entries is very full for the period up to 1600) has this as Le Vager. See also *Entrées* in the Bibliography.

FIG. 21.—Entry of Henri II into Paris, 1549. The Prince: spectator and spectacle.

and musicians who had met the royal party, very much after the fashion of the "monstre."[28]

The overall scene is the street, the best prospect being the arrival of the monarch along a thoroughfare seen in perspective through a Triumphal Arch. All these general phenomena are of importance for the baroque stage, and in the accounts which follow they will be seen to be present in entries even before the Renaissance.

28. In Northern Europe, Kernodle tells us (op. cit., p. 62),"the one audience was the noble visitor—a moving audience that advanced from outer gate to city hall or palace." This is qualified by an earlier remark that "while the street theaters were designed for the royal audience, the procession, including the king, provided a show for the whole people." It was in other words a hierarchy of the spectacle.

The Prince was not the only one to realize that he was at once spectator and spectacle. Thus, Konigson (op. cit. pp. 12-13) offers the following analysis of the paratheatricals of Valenciennes:

> Les franchises exceptionnelles des bourgeois de Valenciennes signifient la possibilité concrète de jouer des rôles réservés habituellement aux nobles: porter les armes, jouter dans les tournois, imiter les entrées princières dans des spectacles à usage interne où les villes se donnent en spectacle l'une à l'autre ou se montrent à elles-mêmes comme dans un miroir. Jouer son rôle social dans une mise en scène où la ville entière est utilisée comme un théâtre, c'est pour le marchand, le maître de jurande, le magistrat communal, se confirmer dans la réalité de son être, apporter la confirmation d'une intronisation quasi-religieuse à l'exercice de ses fonctions dans la cité. Le mélange constant du sacré et du profane lors de ces fêtes—non pas dans la parodie—mais dans l'ordonnance même du spectacle qui superpose les offices religieux, les banquets et les représentations théâtrales, justifie le participant—nous pourrions dire l'acteur—dans son être social.

Most of them are to be found in one of the earliest entries described by Froissart and quoted by Godefroy, namely that of Isabeau of Bavaria, Queen of France, wife of Charles VI, in 1389.[29] Froissart mentions the waiting crowd in the streets of Paris, the noble ladies awaiting the Queen in the Church of Saint Denis, the nobles who are to accompany the litters. At the first gate of Saint Denis was a *ciel* bespangled with stars in which appeared children dressed as angels, singing, together with an image of Our Lady holding a child, "lequel enfant s'ébattait par soi à un petit moulin fait d'une grosse noix." The fountain of the Rue Saint Denis was covered with a cloth of azure, dotted with fleurs-de-lys of gold, its pillars adorned with the arms of the nobility of France. As was normal on such occasions, it was spouting wine in great rivulets, "clairet et piémont très-bon," and was surrounded by girls, singing, offering golden tankards and cups to those who wished to drink. Passing before them, the Queen stopped to gaze. Next, a long stage ("échaffaut") and upon it a Castle. Along the stage, Saladin, the Saracens, and Christians, and above them, the King of France and the twelve peers. When the Queen arrived in front of the showpiece the play commenced: King Richard, leaving his followers, went before the King of France and begged leave to go fight the Saracens. This the King accorded. King Richard then went back to his companions, and all, having drawn themselves up, assailed the enemy, a battle which lasted for some time. At the second gate of Saint Denis, another starry *ciel* with Father, Son, and Holy Ghost seated upon it, and within it, children dressed as angels, singing. Two angels came out of the gate of Paradise as the Queen passed under it, and crowned her with a rich crown, singing the while. Before the Chapelle Saint-Jacques, another stage, covered with *haute lice* tapestry, made in the shape of a chamber, and inside, organists playing. The entire street as far as the Châtelet was draped with the same material, "comme si on eût eu les draps pour néant." At the Châtelet itself was a castle made of wood, with watchtowers "faites aussi fortes que pour durer quarante ans," and showing, presumably through its entrance, a richly adorned "bed of Justice," with Saint Anne lying in it. Within the space of the castle, a preserve with copses full of hares, conies, and birds. A white stag appeared as the party approached, and a lion and eagle "faits très-proprement." Next, a dozen or so damsels, holding bare swords, which they stretched out between the eagle and the lion, on the one hand, and the stage and bed of justice on the other, protecting the latter from the former. At the Pont Notre Dame, yet another *ciel*, with the streets draped as far as Notre Dame. The final spectacle was that of a Genevan engineer who, summoned to Paris a month previously, had attached a cord to the highest tower of Notre Dame, with its other end made fast to the highest house on the Pont Saint Michel. As the party went through the Rue Notre Dame, he passed along the rope carrying two lighted candles, for it was by now dusk. And so the party entered the Church.

What do we deduce thus far? Firstly, that the *ciel*, well loved of the baroque *machiniste*, is perfectly popular in the street theaters at the end of the fourteenth

29. *Cérémonial françois*, pp. 637 et seq. Cf. Baskerville, *Pierre Gringore's Pageants for the Entry of Mary Tudor into Paris*, 1934, pp. xxv, xxvi.

century. Kernodle is right in saying that it can only come from medieval painting, though it may come to the street theater via the mystery. Secondly, there is no doubt as to the function of the crowd: that of audience. Next we note the existence of common objects as stopping points, as decorative foci in the procession: a fountain, for instance. The castle is a frequent showpiece. We see the *tableau-vivant* merging easily into a simple dramatic action, either wholly mimetic or having the simplest of texts, with the traditions of joust and tournament worked into the subject, reflecting the glorious past of the monarch or his ancestors in feats of arms, and his great qualities as an administrator: the latter theme expressing itself easily in personification and allegory. The stage, made in the shape of a chamber and covered with tapestry, is nothing more than a *mansion*, so that the influence of mystery staging is still apparent in the individual set as well as in certain incidents. The idea of a personage issuing forth to crown the entrant is most frequent, while the presence of a particularly audacious *machiniste* (for it is a long way from the top of Notre Dame to the Pont Saint Michel) is an interesting precursor of later machinery and flights, an attempt to show the prince marvel at the highest level. Lastly, though the gates of Paris are fairly and squarely entered, there is still no mention of a triumphal arch as such.

The normal progress of a Royal Entry into Paris from the North, by the Porte Saint Denis, ending at Notre Dame, permits us to compare in rough measure the setting of what may be called the same "theater" for different entries. A certain kinship between the stage of the mystery and that of the *tableau-vivant* comes to light. At the entry of Charles VII in 1437 we find that "Devant la Trinité était un grand théâtre, sur lequel étaient représentés les Mystères de la Passion, et Judas faisant sa trahison, ces personnages ne parlaient, ains représentaient ces Mystères par gestes seulement."[30] There is no reason to doubt that this performance was given by the Confrères de la Passion: the Passion was one of the most important plays in their repertoire. Since 1402 they had enjoyed the privilege of playing inside the enclosure of the Trinité, which was in any case hard by the Porte Saint Denis. It is interesting to see the way in which the normal mystery play is adapted to the needs of a processional audience: the text is simply suppressed. In the mind of the narrator,[31] mystery and *tableau-vivant* are lumped together: there is little difference between his brief account of the *Passion* and that of the other *échaffauts* and *théâtres:* "Devant le Sépulchre était un autre théâtre, où furent représentées la Résurrection du Sauveur du monde, et son apparition à la Magdeleine. A la porte de Sainte Catherine derrière Sainte Opportune, était un autre théâtre, où était le S. Esprit descendant sur les Apôtres et Disciples." This, appearing immediately after the mention of the *Passion*, might be confusing, but these two paragraphs almost certainly refer to *tableaux-vivants,* especially in view of the Confrère's privilege, and protection by Charles VII: it would have been difficult for anyone else to play anything approaching a normal

---

30. Godefroy, *Cérémonial françois,* p. 655.
31. Godefroy is reproducing an *extrait du recueil des offices de France par Jean Chenu, Advocat en Parlement.*

mystery in Paris at that time. Another account by Alain Chartier has this: "Tout au long de la grande rue S. Denis auprès d'un jet de pierre l'un de l'autre, étaient faits échafauds bien et richement tendus, où étaient faits par personnages l'Annonciation Notre-Dame, la Nativité notre Seigneur, sa Passion, sa Résurrection, la Pentecôte, et le Jugement . . . Et emmi la ville y avait plusieurs autres jeux de divers Mystères, qui seraient trop longs à raconter."[32]

Here, the *Passion* is thrown in with the rest: "par personnages" normally suggests a *tableau-vivant*. The multiplicity of the shows, a stone's throw from each other, is evident, and shows that they could not have been full mysteries, for it would have been impossible to watch a complete play with such frequency in the space of one day. Thus, we now have two "borrowings" from the mystery: the individiual *mansion*, and the actual performance of a play in mime. This latter compact form of representation is useful for insertion in any court occasion: we also find it in the very early court ballet, the "entremets" of the fourteenth century.[33]

At the entry of Charles VIII into Troyes in May 1486, we find the streets, as in Paris, decorated with cloth and tapestries depicting stories to the honor of the King, and, in view of his youth, a tableau of David felling Goliath with his sling and cutting off his head. This is still referred to as a *mystère*, as is yet another obvious tableau:

> Au dessus de la même porte était élevé un échafaud, sur lequel était représenté le Mystère de la trèssainte Trinité; il y avait auprès des orgues qui sonnaient, et un jeune enfant revêtu en forme d'Ange, qui descendit par subtile invention de cet échafaud devers le Roi auquel il présenta une croix d'argent, ainsi qu'on rapporte qu'un ange fit jadis à Constantin en lui annonçant qu'il vaincrait dorénavant en ce signe: de plus cet enfant bailla au Roi un écu, sur lequel était écrit le nom de JESUS en lettres d'or, et une couronne d'épines au-dessus, lui disant que cet écu représentait l'ancienne oriflamme pour l'empêcher d'être jamais vaincu.[34]

The absence of a text to this *mystère* is attested by the proximity of the sounding organs. We see once more the descent by mechanical means, the offering of a crown. We must also note that the allegorical flattery of the monarch remains biblical to the point of blasphemy, for it is not always to be so. The allegorical element certainly seems to represent an increase on that of the end of the previous century as does the number of *tableaux-vivants*, every incident in which has its allegorical significance: the Trinity "mystery" is a reference to the etymology of the word Troyes, developed from three castles, "totius Trinitatis nobile triclinium." The white cross, previously sent from Heaven by miraculous means to Charles VII for the greater terror of his foes, was to serve the same purpose for Charles VIII. The shield was to signify that Jesus having wished to enter the Kingdom of Heaven only by His own Passion, the King likewise would gain eternal repose after the tribulations of this life. From this account, as from many others, we likewise gain evidence of the wide spread of meaning of the word *ciel:* "Les quatre échevins de la ville revêtus de robes d'écarlate

32. Chartier was secretary of Charles VI and VII. Quoted by Godefroy, p. 658.
33. Prunières, *Le ballet de cour en France avant Benserade et Lully*, 1914, p.9. See also p. 12 for a mimed mystery in 1454.
34. Godefroy, op. cit., pp. 675 et seq.

et satin portaient sur le chef de sa Majesté un ciel ou dais de fin drap d'or luisant élevé sur quatre piliers,'' and ''Au dessus de la porte d'icelle Eglise était dressé un ciel ou pavillon fort riche, en forme de tente de guerre.''[35] Heaven is that beneath which the monarch walks.

By the middle of the sixteenth century the triumphal arch as a conscious motif in the Entry is well established. Mourey fixes its arrival with the entry of Henry II into Paris in 1549.[36] In the same year Jacques 1er Androuet Ducerceau publishes his *Quinque et viginti exempla arcuum* and two years later helps Louis Martin and Louis Fromont to construct triumphal arches for the entry of Henry II into Orleans. However, we shall call attention to its presence two decades earlier.[37] Certainly, the French monarchs had for fifty years past hardly spared themselves entries into the towns of Italy. Charles VIII into Naples, Rome, Siena and Pisa in 1495, Louis XII into Genoa in 1507 followed by Pavia and Milan. Francis I takes up the habit, with an entry into Milan in 1515. Godefroy's description of those entries occasioned by the early days of the campaigns are not interesting or informative: there is a certain reticence about the accounts suggesting that they are simply displays of armed might, with relatively little decorative effect. Gradually however we begin to hear of the citizens preparing the way for the conquering kings: the Pavia and Milan accounts are very full.[38] The ''tabernacle de verdure'' is most popular, decorated with Royal and other arms, and with welcoming scrolls attached. A triumphal chariot appears in the procession, suggestive of a preoccupation with the splendors of the Roman past. Although it still carries in it figures personifying the cardinal virtues (Justice and Prudence in the front seats, Fortitude and Temperance in the back), yet the Roman god Mars has now made his appearance.[39] The triumphal arch is widely used: ''toutes les rues étaient pleines d'arcs triomphants, et tabernacles de verdure.''[40] This is certainly one of the earliest references in French accounts to a Renaissance *arc de triomphe*, although the existence of such objects in Roman times was naturally known.[41]

35. Ibid., pp. 677–79.
36. *Le livre des fêtes françaises*, 1930, p. 36.
37. Morice, *La mise en scène depuis les mystères jusqu'au Cid*, p. 11, has something similar. He tells us summarily ''Henri II . . . abolit ces spectacles [échafauds] pour y substituer les arcs de triomphe.'' Bapst's statement that the mimed mystery is replaced by the *arc de triomphe* cannot be substantiated (*Essai sur l'histoire du théâtre*, p. 107).
38. Godefroy, p. 718.
39. Ibid., p. 721.
40. Ibid., p. 122.
41. La Curne de Saint-Palaye, *Dictionnaire historique de l'ancienne langue françoise*, quotes the following examples: ''Les Reis soleint anciennement faire lever e voldre ars ki fussent signe e à remembrance de lur victorie'' (Livre des Rois, MS des Cordel, fol. 64, r°, col. 2). His second instance takes us to the time of Henry II's entry into Paris:

> Face chasteaux qui voudra et théatres,
> Arcs triumphans, thermes, amphithéatres,
> Tours et dongeons, colosses monstrueux
> D'or bronze ou marbre, et palais sumptueux,
> Tout cela tombe et dechet en ruine.

(Les Marguerites de la Marguerite, fo. 3, v°. Liminary couplets by Jean de la Haye).

Meanwhile, the entries into Paris continue to display the familiar pattern; for that of the Queen in 1517 there is the usual descent from above at the Porte Saint Denis, the offering of a crown, feminine characters from the Old Testament, the personification of Justice, Magnanimity, Prudence, Temperance. Fountains are still used decoratively, allegory still thrives.[42] Although there is less evidence of the playing of full-length mysteries during the processions, on the occasion of the *Entrée des Enfants de France . . . en la ville de Bayonne* in 1530 we still read of "Comédies, facéties, et feintises si illustrement et ingénieusement comprises, que jamais fils d'homme ne vit ni ne oit parler de telles entreprises."[43] Of the value of the word "comédies" we may as usual entertain some doubt. At Bordeaux, for the same occasion "on jouait mystères à propos," but the decoration of the theater stages which follows indicates not a mystery proper, but yet another tableau. In fact, the word *mystère*, applied to the entry, is undergoing some interesting semantic changes. In the same year, for the entry of Queen Eleonor of Austria, a group of Italians is employed to furnish the decorations:

> Les Italiens, c'est à savoir Messire Mathée et ses compagnons, ont ce jourd'hui apporté au Bureau . . . des portraits en papier pour les inventions des mystères qu'ils seraient d'avis être faits à l'Entrée de la Reine Eléonor . . . et leur a été demandé quel prix ils voudraient avoir pour faire lesdits mystères esdits lieux: Lesquels ont fait réponse, qu'en les fournissant de bois ils voudraient avoir quatre mille livres tournois.[44]

Mignon also cites one Salvatori, a Florentine painter who spent twenty-one days working on the "échafauds."[45] Godefroy is not clear whether by *mystère* he means an individual item of décor, or the whole of the scene for a tableau, but he certainly does not use the term to indicate a dramatic genre.[46] The actor's rôle in the *tableau-vivant* is brought out by Lintilhac,[47] who shows how the amateur company of Basochiens graduated, as it were, from specific performances of their own to figuring in entries (rather like the Confrères) where their mute, motionless tableaux were a huge success. At the same time, there was a stage when regular mysteries and these dumb shows featured together in the entry. That of Eleonor, already quoted, is an example. Prior to her arrival, the Maîtres de la Passion are asked which mystery they intend to play.[48]

The Confrères were a body gathered together for the purpose of playing mysteries. Yet the same cannot be said of the Maître-Fripiers, who are asked exactly the same question in exactly the same terms, although it is clear that they were only to contribute a tableau: "et feront leurdit mystère selon le portrait qu'ils ont exhibé audit Bureau."[49] There is to be comedy, but it must be short: "Maître Jean de Pont-Alaix et Maître André Italien étant au service du Roi, auxquels mondit Sieur

---

42. Godefroy, pp. 753 et seq.
43. Ibid., p. 765 et seq.
44. Ibid., p. 783.
45. *Etudes sur le théâtre français et italien de la Renaissance*, 1923, p. 63.
46. See also ibid., loc. cit.
47. *Histoire générale du théâtre en France*, vol. II: *La comédie, moyen âge et Renaissance*, p. 47.
48. Godefroy, pp. 784-5.
49. Ibid., p. 787.

le Gouverneur a enjoint faire composer farces et moralités les plus exquises et le plus brief que faire se pourra.''[50] Finally (in 1530, let us recollect) there is to be the triumphal arch as a conscious motif, erected at either end of the Pont Notre Dame: ''et à chacun des bouts un arc triomphant, selon le devis et portrait que ledit sieur Gouverneur leur a baillé.''[51] Classical antiquity is slowly winning for itself a place beside biblical antiquity. Beneath a rainbow, there is the model of a ship, whose sailors speak of Mercury, Venus, Phoebus, Mars, Jupiter, and Saturn. Later, Bellona throws the apple of discord between Juno, Pallas, and Venus; the legend of the Gordian knot appears.

The entries of 1548 and 1549 are the apotheosis of this evolution. The central point of reference is by now undoubtedly the Roman triumph and Roman antiquity generally. The entry of Henry II into Lyons in 1548 is extremely well known, and its account was printed specially the year after.[52] Every one of the particular shows already mentioned is to be found in it, with several devices that had not previously been thought of, for Lyons is the great rival of Paris in this form of spectacle: *jeux, combats, naumachies,*[53] and so on: ''comédies, et maints autres passetemps, tant par eau que par terre.'' Everything is ''à l'antique'': the pageboys are dressed ''à la mode de l'antique chevalerie romaine'' and even have their hair cut that way: ''la tête à cheveux crêpés à la Césarienne.'' Gladiators appear and stage a combat. As for the soldiers in the procession, as might be expected, their accoutrement followed that of their Roman forebears. The monarch begins to hobnob with the ancient gods: with Diana and her companions, for instance.[54] On one of the gates is painted the story of Androcles and the Lion ''comme elle est taillée en marbre à Rome.'' The taste for antiquity goes so far that it falls into a premature pre-romanticism all of its own: ancient Roman ruins are faked for the occasion, with fragments of cornice, base, and half-column the better to represent their ''age.'' Perspective has appeared. In the famous *Perspective du Change* (Fig. 22) we see a representation of ancient Troy, with Neptune on one platform and Pallas on another. As the King passes, a horse comes halfway out of the earth on Neptune's side, and on Pallas' side an olive tree. At the Place du Grand Palais there is an elaborate showpiece the whole of which is backed by a low theater auditorium destined not to take spectators but, being ''Roman,'' to serve as a background and be itself looked at: ''Tout lequel simulacre était environné par le derrière d'un demi-rond de théâtre à quatre grands Thermes de Satyres mâles et femelles.''[55] The triumphal arch is multiplied, single,

---

50. Ibid., p. 789.
51. Ibid., p. 792. There is another example as early as 1514: *Le pas des armes de l'arc triumphal,* etc. Montjoye, Paris, 1514.
52. Ibid., p. 823. See also *La magnificence de la superbe entrée,* etc., *imprimée à Lyon avec privilège, l'an 1549.*
53. Yet again, the use of this word to designate a sea fight reminds us of Phaedrus and the orchestra of Dionysos at Athens made watertight by him in the third century B.C.
54. Godefroy, p. 837.
55. Ibid., p. ''851.'' Here, Godefroy's pagination is at fault, and reads 843, 850, 851 (to which we refer), 846, 847, etc.

FIG. 22.—The Lyons Entry of 1548. *La Perspective du Change*.

FIG. 23.—Le double Arc du Portsainct Pol.

Fig. 24.—Entry of Louis XIII into Lyons, 1622. Squared frontage of the Arc de Triomphe, resembling certain stages. General resemblance to the façade of the Olympic Theater.

double or treble, and always highly decorated (Fig. 23). Particularly interesting is the comparatively sudden preoccupation with the decorative detail of the Roman architecture. The narrators begin to cite religiously the orders of the columns, and the detached pieces are used for their virtue of symbolizing antiquity: obelisk, pyramid, and column, for instance. Nymphs and satyrs are worked into the pilasters, for the caryatid is becoming popular. All these things are "pièces détachées," of decorative virtue in themselves, to be moved here and there, juggled with and repatterned. The property-box of the baroque stage is filling at speed (Figs. 24 and 25).

Indeed, after the Lyons and Paris entries of 1548 and 1549 there is little left to invent. Only perspective is to become popular. The triumphal arch is taken for granted: no longer called *arc triumphant* as it was when it first appeared it is now *arc triomphal* or *arc de triomphe*, the *pièce de résistance* of the occasion. The individual showpiece is no longer referred to as a *mystère:* the word falls into disuse, and with it the word *échafaud.* In the entry into Lyons of 1564 there is more talk of perspective than before,[56] and we notice that the top story of a showpiece is being referred to as a *théâtre supérieur.*

The fourteenth and fifteenth centuries are the great age of urban expansion; the subject of the "city" becomes an obsession with the artist, one which he bequeaths to his descendants of the sixteenth century. Street and square become a universal setting, and in France it is the Italian mode of that setting that dominates, the street in perspective, bordered and dotted with archetype buildings.

56. Ibid., p. 898.

FIG. 25.—Paris Entry of 1628. The streets of Paris as the
nursery of baroque stage decoration: archway in perspective,
parallelism of side decorations, *ciel* and *gloire*. Floor in squared
perspective.

The perspective of a street and the concept of a décor or scene are merged in
the Royal Entry to the point where we cannot tell which is which. Contemporary
engravings bring this out well, and not the least of them an anonymous collection
from the house of the celebrated Lyons publisher, Jean Detournes (who, it will be
recalled, also published Philander's *Vitruvius* in 1552), and to which attention had
not yet been directed when the first edition of the present work was published[57]

57. Volume of vignettes without title or pagination. Est. BN. Ed. 5h Rés. and Est. AA1
     (under Jean de Tournes). In the *Inventaire du fonds français. Graveurs du XVIe siècle* (p.
     186) these are described as anonymous. One of the illustrations, undistinguished
     from the rest, bears the cross of Lorraine, mark of the engraver Geofroy Tory, as
     does the title page of the copy in the Réserve of the Cabinet des Estampes. There
     seems nothing to prevent us then from attributing the pictures formally to Tory,
     along with Bernard (*Geofroy Tory peintre et graveur*, Paris, 1857, pp. 192-95). Four of
     the engravings for the entry of Henry II into Paris in 1548 bear Tory's cross, and
     those for the Lyons entry of the same year seem to be either his or Bernard Salomon's
     (le petit Bernard). The background detail of the *Perspective du Change* (see Fig. 22) is
     strikingly similar to that of the collection in the Estampes. See also Lawrenson, "Ville
     imaginaire, fête, et décor de théâtre: autour d'un recueil de Geofroy Tory," in *Les
     Fêtes de la Renaissance*, Paris, 1956.

(Figs. 26 and 27). Steps of varying sorts lead up to the "stage" and to the houses which could easily be taken for angle-wings. There is in some of the engravings a forestage which leaves the back clear for the "décors." In general disposition, the urban motifs are not incomparable with the picture of the *Perspective du Change* (see Fig. 22), which is also a Lyons publication, and, more to our immediate purpose, they are those of the Royal Entry: obelisk, column, and arcade. Archways figure prominently in the collection. Street and stage are approaching synonymity: the ideal city was to find an inevitable medium in the theater.

Long before Torelli was summoned to France the baroque theater existed potentially in that country in the streets of its cities. In this particular canalization of the dramatic art, the mystery stage, via the Royal Entry, becomes the baroque stage, with perspective scenes, machinery, ascents, appearances, seen through a columned archway, a century before these adorn the court theater and *without reference to the development of the dramatic text*. These habits are to be found not only in the entry proper, but in all those festive activities centered upon the court, though the entry remains their chief breeding ground. In all those occasions familiar to the official chronicler, and to which we shall refer collectively under the title of "paratheatri-

FIG. 26.—The Detournes engravings.

FIG. 27.—The Detournes engravings.

cals,'' there is something of the baroque. We extract from the La Ferté collection in the Paris National Archives the following list of activities which our neologism is intended to cover: *fêtes, réjouissances, divertissements, cérémonies, réceptions, courses de bague, courses de chevaux, courses à pied, carnaval, carrousel, pompes funèbres, entrées, régales, galanteries, ballets, fêtes de l'arquebuse, sacres, couronnements, combats à la barrière, tournoi, joute,* and *mascarade*.[58] We could add with justification, since they were ultimately engulfed in this imperialism of the spectacle, *accouchements* and *consommations de mariage*.[59]

Contrary to some other aspects of theatrical history over the same period this paratheatrical activity develops fully, without let or hindrance, and at speed, as is natural since the history of France takes its monarchs to Italy. Triumphing over the Italian courts, it outdoes them in this form of expression. It out-italianizes the Italians. Within the century, it punctuates each phase in the story of a monarchy progressing towards centralized power. In its relations between "salle," if we may use the expression, and "scène," it displays a hierarchy of the spectacle, the central point of which is the prince. He is at once spectator and spectacle. When receiving homage after a ceremonial entry, the place where he sits for such a purpose is still called a *théâtre*.[60] In the gods who descend with gifts and crowns, he sees himself; and the crowd sees him. Remove the townsfolk, substitute scenic change *in situ* and under the discipline of a single stage, for the moving cortège of spectators, and one is not far from the aesthetic of the baroque period in France, for there is little room for dramatic poesy in either. Morice, in 1835, hit upon the same concept jokingly: "On obtenait enfin ainsi l'effet des décors mobiles de la *Belle au Bois Dormant*, à l'Opéra, et du *Sacre de Napoléon*, au Cirque-Olympique, avec cette différence qu'aujourd'hui c'est le spectacle qui se dérange, et qu'alors c'était le spectateur."[61]

In the middle of the sixteenth century there was still a mystery stage, there were still mystery performances in France. They had points in common with the Royal Entry, apart from lending it certain sets in earlier times: they were public and popular, and as often as not financed from public funds belonging to the municipality. Though the mayor, *échevins*, and even country gentry went gladly to these performances, they depended little on royal patronage. By sheer virtue of their traditional content they cared little for their contemporary knights and princes. The seam of "superlification" and "flagornerie" was lacking. They were the national theater of the time. The Royal Entry, on the other hand, was the nursery of a court theater, in spite of its crushing expense to the township. The figure of the prince dominated the day. He was the catalyst of that reaction in which mystery tradition was assimilated by the baroque. Small wonder that he adored this paratheatrical form, the effective sublimation of his narcissism, the perfect reflection of his megalomania.

58. Arch. Nat. 0^1 3259.
59. Pure, (*Idée des spectacles*, 1668, p. 162) has his own shorter list: "Comédies, Bals, Ballets, Mascarades ou Cavalcades, Feux de Joie, ou Joutes, Courses, Carrousels, Entrées, Revues ou Exercices."
60. E.g. Godefroy, op. cit., pp. 949 and 951.
61. *La mise en scène depuis les mystères jusqu'au Cid*, 1835, p. 13.

CHAPTER THREE

THE TERENTIAN STAGE AND RENAISSANCE
TRAGEDY AND COMEDY

The Arcade Screen

WHEREVER STUDYING THE origins of the shape of the Renaissance theater, we quit the direct line of Vitruvian tradition, we are compelled to come to terms with Kernodle's thesis.[1] The theory that all the arts, and in particular painting, have not only contributed to, but indeed conditioned form and convention in the theater requires serious consideration at any time, but particularly in the Renaissance where the "complete man," painter, architect, scenographer, humanist, whose archetype is Da Vinci, is common enough. The idea that art comes normally "before" theater and feeds it with its traditions is tempting in all conscience for the historian of the theater, working as he does in a field where iconography is sparse.[2]

The pitfalls are clear. If we exclude the use in art of motifs drawn directly from nature, surely a characteristic of Gothic rather than Renaissance art, we are left with only a limited gamut of largely geometrical forms, and these are bound to occur and recur wherever men invent or imitate. They will of course recur in painting, sculpture, engraving, architecture, and so on. So we must employ some circumspection in following "influences" along the gratuitous paths that these forms trace, of discerning parenthood amongst their often haphazard patterns. Kernodle tells us that "comparisons of two theatre forms have often been very useful and revealing; but, unless they go beyond the theatre and relate the stages to the whole tradition of Renaissance art they are inadequate. In the family tree we must not cry paternity where there is only cousinship."[3] Nor, one might add, must we cry relationship at all where there is merely coincidence. Where the later theater form resembles in any way the earlier, we are surely justified in seeking parenthood there rather than elsewhere. Thus, in the case of the mystery plays, the Hôtel de Bourgogne housed both these and later the plays of Hardy, Rotrou, and Corneille. Since both forms were confined within the same limited space we are naturally justified in seeking parenthood there before we seek it outside.

The second danger lies in the complete neglect of the dramatic text, for this leads inevitably to a one-way view of causality which cannot always be a good one, the implication being that it is always the shape of the theater which influences dramatic literature. This leads Kernodle into a somewhat mechanistic view of the "querelle des unités," which he sees as emanating from the internal dichotomy of

---

1. *From Art to Theatre*, 1944.
2. Kernodle makes an exception to his rule in the case of the Hellenistic theater, which, he claims, started a tradition of painting which finally influences the modern theater after some fifteen hundred years of painted conventions.
3. Op. cit., pp. 3–4.

a theater employing two conventions of staging at once; it becomes divorced from any basis in doctrinal discussion.[4]

This writer sees the flat, back-wall convention of the stage as "theatre of architectural symbol," and the perspective set as "theatre of pictorial illusion." This may well be, yet there is a dramatic text to be reckoned with, and the spectator does not merely view. What he hears changes his view. Racine was acted upon a stage that Kernodle would describe as theater of pictorial illusion, a concept which shocks, for Racine requires the support of pictorial illusion no more than does Aeschylus. Formally, by his own definition, Kernodle is right: the arrested baroque form of the "palais à volonté" was to some extent an illusory stage picture, as was *a fortiori* the courtly stage upon which Racine was played at Versailles and elsewhere. But Racine turned this theater into its own opposite because his convention of dramatic poesy was highly unnaturalistic and in addition he was capable of observing unity of place, taking the element of change out of what was only potentially a baroque set.[5]

However, when the weight of evidence for one particular motif in painting is great: the framing of a picture for instance as an integral part of the total picture, we may assume an interrelation. It was inevitable too that perspective should be worked out at first upon a flat surface, where experiment is far easier than with constructed forms in space, so that in a sense painting here fathers the perspective scene and there is some justification for seeking transfer of motifs from paintings in perspective, to the stage, provided always that first we look for, or give preference to, the working out of linear perspective upon the flat surface of stage decorations.

One of Kernodle's theories, that of the arcade façade theater, demands examination before we make any further attempt to study the antecedents of the seventeenth-century theater.

Briefly, it is as follows. The arcade screen is potentially present in the Greek *skené*, the Roman *frons scaenae*. It is a feature of medieval art, copied by painters from the Greek theater façade. In the *tableaux-vivants* of the sixteenth century it took on the meaning now of a throne of honor, now of a triumphal arch. It had small inner stages reminiscent of the mystery play sets. For Fischel the normal *mansions* of the mystery play could be combined into one large building. He instances as support a picture, the *Passion of Christ,* by Hans Memling. This produces something

---

4. Ibid., p. 6. It induces Fischel ("Art and the Theatre," *Burlington Magazine*, vol. LXVI, Jan.–Feb. 1935, p. 65), whom Kernodle acknowledges as a minor source of inspiration, into even worse error. "In France," he says, "at the time of Louis XIV [sic] Corneille introduced the well-known, tedious discussions on the Unity of Place. I think they arose from an inferiority complex of the dramatic poets in view of the splendid, movable opera stage which was capable of any adaptation." The writer is not deterred from this statement by the fact that neither Louis XIV nor the French opera set was born at the time of the *Cid.*
5. Cf. Rousset, *L'Intérieur et l'Extérieur*, 1968, p. 181: "Il [le dix-septième siècle] a créé son instrument pour un théâtre d'enchantement, qui convenait particulièrement au ballet de cour et à l'opéra, mais aussi à Corneille ou à Rotrou; *on peut se demander si Racine en avait un égal besoin.*" (Our italics.)

very like the Terence stage of the frontispieces to early editions of that author. Although functionally not illusionistic these arches could easily carry illusionistic details into and behind their façades. The arcades could be covered by curtains for the purpose of revelation. These habits, in their turn known to the illustrators of Terence, were reproduced by them and thus influenced later stages. Finally, the Olympic Theater at Vicenza is the crowning glory of this tradition.[6]

In a sense this pushes the European theater at many points nearer to the Graeco-Roman formula, for it assumes the arcade screen as an entity and a background; it is a line from the ancient to the Renaissance theater which tends to sidetrack Vitruvius. At the same time, placing as it does the *Olimpico* at the crown of this tradition, it is in contradiction to our own view of perspective on the stage breaking through the comparative solidity of what had been the *frons scaenae*, and belittles the rôle of archaeological reconstitution: the "solidity" of the *skené* to be broken through, would come not from any adherence to archaeological concepts but from the use of such a screen as a motif in the painting of the Middle Ages.

An examination of Kernodle's own examples, since they are likely to be most germane to his own thesis, will enable us to weigh the value of these ideas:

> The best description we have of the arcade in actual production tells us of a performance of the *Poenulus* in Rome in 1513 by the followers of Laetus. The stage was almost a hundred feet wide, twenty-four feet deep, and about eight feet high—much larger than most groups could afford. At the back of the stage was a highly decorated arcade screen divided into five sections by columns with gilded bases and capitals, each section framing a doorway covered with curtains of gold cloth. Above was a frieze of beautiful paintings and a gilded cornice. At the two ends of the screen were two great towers with doors, one marked "Via ad forum." These towers, relics of the castle towers so frequent in medieval art, soon disappeared from the Terence tradition but were important in the development of the proscenium. The screen with its upper story of paintings, shows a very close resemblance to the arcades built in street theatres throughout Europe.[7] (See also Fig. 28).[8]

Now, the rôle of Pomponius Laetus is in no doubt. He and his followers were out deliberately to reconstruct the ancient. Almost every stage unit in the description may be traced back to its Vitruvian source, and in no greatly mutilated manner. We need only note the depth, width and height of the stage, the so-called arcade-screen which is an attempt at a *frons scaenae* with the division into five columned entrances, a natural interpretation of the five Roman entrances. The same explanation is possible for the general run of Terentian or Plautian performance: it is true, as Kernodle says,[9] that the humanists, realizing that each of the principal

6. *From Art to Theatre*, pp. 154–73.
7. Ibid., p. 163.
8. This so-called setting for Parabosco's *Il Pellegrino* is a grim reminder of the snags awaiting those who accept iconographical evidence too readily: if it is the décor of *Il Pellegrino* it is that of every comedy of the Venice Terence of 1569! See Lawrenson and Purkis, "Les éditions illustrées de Térence dans l'histoire du Théâtre: Spectacles dans un fauteuil?" in *Le lieu théâtral à la Renaissance*, Paris, 1963, pp. 1–23.
9. Op. cit., p. 162.

FIG. 28.—Décor for *Il Pellegrino*, by Girolamo Parabosco. Serlian side-wings and reconstituted *frons scaenae*.

characters should have a house, would build about five of these together as an open street; but the façade of the Roman theater and the plays of Terence and Plautus match each other. Both authors, though Plautus in particular, wrote for a theater they knew, so that in realizing that there were five entrances the humanists were to some extent realizing the shape of the *frons scaenae.*

Again, for all we know, the Roman stage wall, like that of the 1513 *Poenulus,* had friezes and a gilded cornice above its doorways: it was certainly highly decorated. The "two great towers with doors" are a version of the Roman *versurae:* "versurae sunt procurrentes," as Vitruvius had remarked, and this is perfectly well shown by the fact that one of them is marked "Via ad forum," showing the designers to be aware of the localizing function of these entrances (at least on one side!). Cesariano's attempt at *itinera versurarum*, it will be remembered, has a similar indication.[10] The school of Pomponius Laetus might not have known what to make of Vitruvius' remarks about the various doors, but in placing them in a back wall (and fortuitously creating an arcade) these humanists were indulging in an intel-

10. See p. 24.

ligent piece of reconstitution, not introducing onto the stage of their time a motif from medieval art. Wherever two or three arched entrances are gathered together, there is an arcade. It occurs on and off the stage in the Middle Ages, in the Renaissance and baroque periods. It could hardly be otherwise where man-made forms are used.

Into a combination of Serlian side-houses and a manifest attempt at a *frons scaenae* Kernodle reads this theory. That the arcade screen exists in Terentian illustration is obvious: the Lyons (Trechsel) Terence of 1493 has pictures which cannot be held to depict a *frons scaenae* (Figs. 29 and 30), nor can the Roigny Terence picture (Fig. 31). Although there are five doors in the former, there is no solid space between them to make up the breadth of the wall. What we cannot say however is whether we must read this as absence of space between the doors, or presence of an arcade? One thing seems clear: there is a resemblance to the mystery *mansion*. Firstly, the period of Terentian illustration is that of the mystery play. Secondly, the concept

FIG. 29.—*The Adelphi*, Terence (Trechsel, Lyons, 1493).

FIG. 30.—*Hecyra*, Terence (Trechsel, Lyons, 1493).

of house in the comedies of Terence and the *mansion* would easily be allied in the mind of the illustrator. Thirdly, whenever the houses in the Terence illustrations jut forward they are virtually identical with the baldaquin type of mystery compartment.[11] Fourthly, the labelled houses in the illustrations resemble the *écriteaux* of the mystery; and fifthly, Fischel, whose work Kernodle found suggestive in formulating his theory, chooses to prove his point a picture in which mystery *mansions* are pushed together to form an "arcade."[12]

How far then is this type of illustration genuine? How far does it correspond to actual production? How far is it compressed into the narrow width of the page? Neither Kernodle's instancing of *Il Pellegrino*,[13] which is not, as he claims, a "formal arcade," nor his account of the 1513 *Poenulus*, eminently Vitruvian, is of much help.

11. See Fig. 17.
12. See p. 51.
13. See Fig. 28.

FIG. 31.—Illustration from the Roigny Terence. So-called "théâtre parisien au XVIe siècle."

Renaissance Performance

Do we find any traces of such décors in the College performances of the Renaissance? In spite of the many repressive actions by the authorities consequent upon the licence and ribaldry of College theatrical *ludi*, such performances were general, and a strong tradition was established by the sixteenth century.[14] When Plautus and Terence began to be acted in the Colleges, what was the nature of the stage decoration? We do not know and it is not easy even to hazard a guess as to how far it resembled the illustrations: from the examples of Terentian inspiration quoted by Kernodle, not at all. Neither Gofflot nor Boysse can help us.[15] If we are to believe Rigal, however, the students soon grew tired of the new genre and returned to their traditional forms: popular plays and satires against political and academic authorities.[16] He asserts that after 1567 there is no example of a Renaissance work being played in a College. Plays by College students, not necessarily in

14. Gofflot, *Le théâtre au collège du moyen âge à nos jours*, 1907, p. 13. Kernodle, in his bibliography, cites Claretie as the author of this work. It does in fact carry one of Claretie's innumerable prefaces.
15. Boysse, *Le théâtre des Jésuites*, 1800.
16. *Théâtre français*, pp. 113–15.

the Terence tradition, were popular and regularly financed by townships throughout the sixteenth century, and in or out of the College a stage was usually erected for the occasion. In the minutes of communal council meetings and in treasury accounts of provincial towns all over France these stages were variously referred to as "échafaud" or "théâtre." The use of "échafaud" would certainly seem to indicate a set after the mystery manner. Indeed at the time of these early Terence editions, the phrase "dresser un échafaud" normally means to put up a stage for a mystery play.[17] For the unpopularity of an attempt to produce original Latin comedy before a general public, we have the evidence noted by Professor Lawton, after Lintilhac: in 1502, a troupe tried to play a Latin comedy "nommé Térence" at Metz. The general public understood nothing, invaded the stage, and sent the players packing. The same play, given the next day before a closed audience of clergy, nobles, and scholars, was a success.[18] The literary influence of Terence in the second half of the fifteenth century may not be questioned.[19] Already in 1418 Alberti had written his Latin comedy *Philodoxius* in the Terentian style. But when such plays were performed in Italy at least they were performed before sets and upon stages which were also conscious revivals. In France we do not know how they were played. The illustration of the early editions of Terence occupies a mere moment, and cannot be erected into a theory of the arcade screen stage. It is not clear that the illustrations "illustrate" anything new in the way of staging, that they ever really appeared on a stage in France. It is possible that such a stage existed in Italy. Magagnato has recently collated the evidence in favor of this supposition and has added some of his own. The Trechsel Terence pictures which he produces are perhaps not particularly relevant, since they are French; more convincing is his reproduction of a *Coliseus sive Theatrum* from a Terence edition by Simon de Luere (Venice, 1497).[20] Here, spectators are to be seen in an amphitheater, facing the viewer, who may therefore imagine himself on the stage. On either side of the stage, half a small house is to be seen, suggesting that these, and perhaps three others, were arranged in a continuous curved line. Yet these remain book illustrations, and in the absence of evidence about Terentian production in France, we can only assume that the Trechsel Terence, and frontispieces like it, were imitated from the Italians, while the practice was not.

The arcade appears fairly frequently as a motif in seventeenth-century stage decoration, and we shall have occasion to refer to it later *en passant;* but it cannot be considered as ever forming the basis of a distinct and typical stage background for the French theater.

17. Thus, Poupé, *Documents relatifs à des représentations scéniques en Provence au XVIe siècle*, 1904, p. 14: "Séance du 13 octobre 1596. Item, ont conclu, arrêté et délibéré de donner à ceux qui ont joué l'histoire de Tobie par personnages quatre écus pour subvenir aux charges et artifices nécessaires du chafaud." See other monographs by the same author for the fifteenth and seventeenth centuries.
18. Lawton, *Térence en France au XVIe siècle*, 1926, p. 43.
19. Ibid., pp. 46–47.
20. Magagnato, *Teatri Italiani del Cinquecento*, Pl. 7.

We have already alluded to the resemblance of the Terentian illustrations to the contemporary mystery lay-out, and this has been recently further underlined by Raymond Lebègue who arrives at a similar conclusion along other paths. The pictures have, for him, the realism and the simplification of the mystery. The stages of the Trechsel, and their bases, resemble those of mystery and farce; the costumes are contemporary, the properties and stage play are both lifelike, the naming of characters so that they may be followed across the various scenes seems businesslike, as does the placing of the *mansions* in the *Adelphi*. Lebègue is convinced that the commentator counselled the artist. Again, like the mystery décors, the sets evince considerable simplification, notably with the houses reduced largely to a matter of lintel and curtains: a long tradition of the single curtain to the single house is to be discerned, for example, in the martyrdom of Saint Apollina, the Mons Passion of 1501, the Valenciennes Passion, Van der Goes' *Adoration of the Shepherds,* Royal Entries in the Low Countries, the Cambrai manuscript, and the miniature of Papon's *Pastorelle.*

The awkwardness, the narrowness of the street in the illustrations, is seen as a form of economy common also to the mystery illustrations, and Cherea's extreme difficulty, in the *Eunuch,* in entering at all via a nonexistent street, *could* have been alleviated by the use of a stool as in P. Balten's picture of a *kermesse.*

Now, the only consideration militating against the mystery décor inspiration is the nature of the art of xylography itself. The woodcuts are a form of currency circulating very freely across time and space, the same block often illustrating totally different things. It could be argued for example, that if the Trechsel version of say, Act III scene iv of the *Andria* is conceived after the pattern of a Lyons mystery compartment of the time, then the Venice Terence of 1497 is based upon a Venetian mystery of that date, and the same applies to the Venice Terence of 1545: apart from the detail of the stage sides, in Trechsel, all three are similar. Yet the probability is that Trechsel was copied for its obvious exceptional beauty, so that it could *still* be mystery based, since it is a prototype.

These problems were considered in some detail by Dr. Helen Purkis and the present author, during a 1963 colloquium on ''Le Lieu Scénique à la Renaissance.'' We concluded

1. That the probabilities of an allusion to a contemporary scenic reality were not well established.
2. That the relationship of the pictures with Pomponian or other Italian performances was not established at all.
3. The comedies of Terence are probably not stageable on the stages given to him by Trechsel.
4. The woodcuts belong to a tradition of scholarly exegesis: they are the visual extension of the literary exegesis which has accreted round the Terentian texts since Donatus.

The arguments of Raymond Lebègue do seem to weaken the first of these suppositions, though the high mobility of the woodcuts across Europe, and across time, must remain disconcerting if Trechsel is to illustrate a contemporary reality of 1493. The remaining three hypotheses seem to us still valid, and in particular when Lebègue affirms in conclusion that the comedies of Terence are actable on the stages depicted in the Terence of Trechsel we must continue to doubt whether any practical man of the theater would find them so.[21]

A study of the dramatic genres, of where and how they were played in the sixteenth and early seventeenth centuries, hardly reassures us as to the existence of a Terentian type of stage at all, much less an arcade screen type of Terentian staging convention after Kernodle's manner. We cannot even begin to consider the problem without adopting a position in the controversy involving the terms comedy, tragedy, pastoral, and tragicomedy—how far do these terms indicate Renaissance works (where the text is not known), and how far mystery plays or plays in the mystery manner? Here we are in among a veritable quarrel of Titans. Renaissance or mystery, Court or College, bourgeois amateurs or professional nomads? The great critics of the nineteenth and of the early twentieth centuries are by no means in agreement.

The theoretical substructure of the rebirth of the classical genres is too well known to bear repeating here. We must simply limit ourselves to remarking that whereas Horace, Aristotle, Terentian edition and the Renaissance grammarians are active influences and that actual literary creations stem from them, we must not accept too freely Lintilhac's juxtaposition of Vitruvius and Horace for France:[22] "Les indications de l'*Art Poétique* d'Horace pour l'histoire du genre [comédie] et celles de Vitruve pour la mise en scène, commentées par les Serlio et autres architectes de théâtres, achèvent de ressusciter la comédie antique dans l'imagination des lettrés."[23] What is interesting and important for the Renaissance and seventeenth century in France is rather the way in which Vitruvian interpretation was never put into practice. This we must develop at length in a later chapter: let us for the moment content ourselves with observing that Vitruvius can give no hint as to theater structure and none as to staging for the Renaissance period in France. All that we may assume is that if the text was genuinely in the humanist tradition, comedy or tragedy, it could not but be correspondingly simple. Yet this merely throws us back into the quarrel of the genres: for what, ideally, we ought to do is

21. Op. cit. Lebègue, "Le Térence de Trechsel" in *L'humanisme lyonnais au XVIe siècle*, Grenoble, 1974. Nagler abandons his customary astringent cynicism regarding iconographical evidence in this instance:

> This was Badius' idea of the Roman stage, and this idea is realized in the Lyon woodcuts which originated under Badius' supervision. To be sure, the woodcuts are meant to be book illustrations for the benefit of the readers but this does not exclude the possibility that they actually echoed theatre performances that had taken place prior to 1493. We are aware of the fact that the Pomponians had staged Roman plays and that Cardinal Riario had acted as their Maecenas. It is conceivable that Badius, during his stay in Italy, had gathered information about the physical aspects of these Roman revivals.

("The Campidoglio stage of 1513," *Maske und Kothurn*, Vol. 16, 1970, p. 234.)
22. There is some excuse for the tempting analogy in Italy, where Vitruvian interpretation did occasionally terminate in brick and mortar.
23. *Histoire générale du théâtre en France*, vol. II, p. 275.

to decide what is Renaissance tragedy and Renaissance comedy, and where these titles are used for other things. Unfortunately this is precisely where scholars cannot agree.[24] The incidence of acted Renaissance comedy, and particularly tragedy, is for some infinitely small. For others it is not so. The theory that these plays were hardly acted at all we may for convenience call, after Haraszti, the *Buchdramatik* theory.[25] For it we have Chasles, Brunetière, and Rigal. Against it, Faguet, Haraszti, Lanson, Carrington Lancaster, and Lebègue.[26]

Faguet, who is concerned with establishing some continuous line of development between the indigenous mystery and regular tragedy, sees *Josephus*, by Cornelius Crocus (1536), as the beginning of serious drama, no longer mystery, not yet tragedy; this he calls the "drame sacré,"[27] though in propounding this theory he does not deny the genuine humanistic urge of the regular literati such as Sibilet, Pasquier, Pelletier du Mans, Ronsard: "L'amour de l'antiquité et le désir de la faire revivre ont été les sentiments constants et universels des lettrés de ce temps."[28]

He points to the collaboration, as from 1548, of Basochiens, Enfants sans souci, and Confrères de la Passion, the first two companies retaining the right to play their own repertoire, "sur la table de marbre" in the case of the Basochiens, and in the Halles in the case of the Enfants sans souci. Garnier's *Antigone*, he claims, was played by the Confrères in 1579, and taken up by the Basochiens in 1580. He gives several examples of this shuttlecocking of plays: *Lucelle*, by Louis le Jars, a tragicomedy in prose, was played probably in 1576, at both the Hôtel de Bourgogne and the Hôtel de Reims, the courtly performance presumably by the Basochiens, the latter by the Confrères. Bouchetel's *Hécube* is played by the Basochiens in 1549 and the year after by the Confrères. On the whole, he discerns, the Basochiens give the most talked-of performances, the Enfants sans souci the most irregular, and the Hôtel de Bourgogne mixes its genres: classical tragedy (all Garnier, he affirms), what he calls "regular sacred tragedy" (e.g. Chantelouve's *Pharaon* in 1579), and all this with a continuing taste for the mystery: between Garnier's *Hippolyte* in 1572 and Jacques de la Taille's *Alexandre* in 1573, for instance, they put on the *Mystère du Vieil Testament*. Théodore de Bèze is given a place among the "tragiques réguliers," and this typifies Faguet's attitude towards regular tragedy: of Bèze he says "Il marque une autre méthode par où les poètes de ce temps arrivent à la tragédie classique. Ceux de la Pléiade, comme la Péruse, comme Jodelle, y viennent en partant de l'imitation du théâtre antique. D'autres y sont venus *en partant de l'ancien mystère*,[29] mais en l'allégeant, en l'émondant, de manière à le réduire aux lois de la poétique nouvelle, qu'ils connaissent et dont ils acceptent l'autorité."[30] Were this interpretation firmly

24. See, however, Lebègue, *La tragédie religieuse en France*, 1929, pp. 24 et seq., and p. 46.
25. RHLF, 1904, pp. 680–86.
26. See also Holsboer, *Mise en scène*, p. 98.
27. *La tragédie française au XVIe siècle*, 1883, p. 64.
28. Ibid., p. 24.
29. The italics are ours.
30. Op. cit., p. 93.

established we should be well placed to emit an opinion about the staging of such plays. Knowing, factually, from the *Mémoire de Mahelot* what the Confrères possessed at the Hôtel de Bourgogne in the way of scenery, knowing that it was admirably adapted to the playing of a reduced mystery, we could assume that these décors served for the plays mentioned by Faguet, the number of compartments being simply reduced or retained at their approximate five according to the nearness of Faguet's embryonic "regular tragedians"[31] to absolute unity of place. But in the years which followed its publication and in the first decade of our century Faguet's hypothesis was to receive a rough handling.

Its mainstay is immediately shorn away when we realize that Faguet, in his assertions concerning the playing of classical tragedy at the Hôtel de Bourgogne, is basing himself on the notoriously inaccurate Chevalier de Mouhy.[31] Rigal is quick to point to the fact.[32] Apart from this, Rigal's evidence is weighty: much of the Pléiade dramaturgy never saw the boards in any shape or form: Jean de la Péruse's *Médée*, Jacques de la Taille's *Daire* and *Alexandre*, Guillaume de la Grange's *Didon*, Rolland Brisset's *Thyeste* and *Baptiste*. Of "classical comedy" he says that it helps us little, since *Eugène* and *Les Ebahis*, for example, were indistinguishable from indigenous farce in the license of their content and in their form.[33] While admitting that in 1584 an ambulant troupe which had been playing the Pléiade repertoire in the provinces came to Paris and played at the Hôtel de Cluny, they cannot, he says, have played much since they were only there for a few days, whereas the first French troupe to install itself in Paris, that of Courtin and Poteau, in 1595, played "jeux et farces . . . mystères profanes licites et honnêtes." The Confrères, "gens ignares, artisans mécaniques ne sachant ni A ni B,"[34] were the last people to be entrusted with classical tragedy, and if all of Garnier had been played by such a troupe mention of it would certainly have come down to us.

For Rigal, the tragedies of the sixteenth century were never played upon a public stage. The earlier ones were doubtless written for acting, and were acted, before a specially benevolent restricted public predisposed in their favor. Losing their popularity, the authors gradually resigned themselves to mere publication. By consolidating mention of courtly and college representations scattered amongst such authorities as Rigal, Lintilhac and Lebègue, one arrives with difficulty at a sanguine total of half a dozen or so court performances and a score of college performances.[35] This is indeed a meager list to have commanded a staging tradition all of its own,

31. *Abrégé de l'histoire du théâtre français*, 1780, 4 vols.
32. *Alexandre Hardy et le théâtre français à la fin du XVIe et au commencement du XVIIe siècle*, pp. 88–89.
33. Ibid., p. 87.
34. Quoted by Rigal, pp. 91–92.
35. Rigal, op. cit., p. 85, Lintilhac op. cit., p. 295, Lebègue, op. cit., pp. 145 et seq. Cf. also Fransen, "Documents inédits de l'Hôtel de Bourgogne" (RHLF, 1927, p. 322), who quotes Valleran le Conte as stating that at Rouen, Strasbourg, and "Angres" (Angers or Langres) he not only played biblical plays, but plays by "Schodällen" (Jodelle).

and yet it would seem that none of these plays were staged by the Confrères in the mystery formula. We begin to see that militating against any sober "mise en scène à l'antique" is an attitude to the ancients in dramatic literature similar to one that we shall meet in theater decoration. Pierre Toldo is one of the first to draw attention to it.[36] He notes that du Bellay, in his *Deffense et Illustration*, places the Italians, Petrarch, Sannazaro, Pontano, Ariosto, on the same footing as the ancients. He notes the closeness of the Lyons *Calandria* in 1548,[37] a purely Italian venture in France, to Jodelle's *Cléopâtre captive* at the Hôtel de Reims in 1552. Mellin de Saint Gelais' *Sophonisbe* is a translation from the Italian. Charles IX, Henri III, and Henri IV were in close relationship with the Italian players, and directly interested in their success. Catherine de Medici, acquainted with all the magnificence of the Italian Renaissance theater, was only too happy to contribute to this taste in France.

Comedy, as a genre, was naturally more vulnerable than tragedy. In the comedy prefaces, alongside the appeal to the ancients, there is praise of their Italian imitators. Lintilhac indicates two translations of Ariosto's *Suppositi* even before the Pléiade, in 1545 and 1552, and at the same time as Toldo, remarks "Nos comiques de la Renaissance, devancés à l'école des anciens, depuis près de deux siècles, par les Italiens, furent séduits outremesure par ces derniers. Les imitations de ces devanciers parurent si brillantes qu'on en fut ébloui au point de ne plus voir les modèles anciens, qu'à travers elles, et même de ne plus regarder qu'elles."[38] The success of the Italians is unquestionable; as well as *commedia dell'arte*, they play *commedia sostenuta* with magnificent décors. In 1555 Alamanni's *Flora* is played before Henri II and Catherine de Medici, in 1584 *Fiammella* by the actor-author Rossi at the residence of the duc de Joyeuse in Paris, in 1585, before the Queen Mother and the court, Fabritio de Fornaris's *Angelica*, and in 1589 at the Hôtel de Reims, before Catherine de Medici, an Italian comedy by Cornelio Fiasco.[39] We may perhaps guess at the setting of this drama from a picture reproduced by Mourey[40] (Fig. 32). This set is not unlike the early seventeenth-century sets of the Hôtel de Bourgogne (see Figs. 40 and 41) with the addition of a perspective through the central arch. The characters of native farce merge naturally into their Italian counterparts; the ancient comedy and Italian comedy become genuinely mixed in the minds of dramatic writers towards the end of the sixteenth century. As Larivey says in the prologue to his *Laquais* "je sais que nos Français nous feront voir ci-après [des comédies], dressant un Théâtre autant magnifique, superbe et glorieux, que nation qui soit au monde, afin de n'aller chercher ailleurs, qu'en nos propres maisons ces honnêtes plaisirs, et utiles récréations,"[41] which shows the situation at the time of

36. "La comédie française de la Renaissance," RHLF, 1897, p. 382.
37. See Mignon, *Etudes sur le théâtre français et italien de la Renaissance*, pp. 72 et seq., and Prunières, *L'opéra italien en France*, 1913, pp. xx, xxi.
38. Op. cit., p. 285.
39. Ibid., p. 292.
40. *Le livre des fêtes françaises*, 1930, Fig. 35, and Jefferey, op. cit., p. 63. Also Lebègue, *Le théâtre comique en France*, 1972, p. 122. *The picture is in the Musée Municipal at Bayeux.*
41. Quoted by Toldo, RHLF, 1898, p. 602.

FIG. 32.—Courtly setting with Italian players and others.

his writing. Lintilhac concludes that Renaissance comedy was played only in the first flush of the Pléiade, at college and court, half a dozen times in fifteen years, and in Paris.

Lanson considers that Rigal has settled the matter of the Hôtel de Bourgogne once and for all: no classical tragedy was acted there.[42] But he widens the issue considerably by producing a long list of plays, at least thirty of which he claims to be "tragédies et tragi-comédies françaises." He makes it clear that the court is the big center of reception for sumptuous staging "à l'italienne" and that every genre reaching it would pass through this process. What we would call "regular" comedy, when played at the court, would be relegated to the mainstream of Italian influences: its staging would be influenced by that of the court ballet. The College theater, Lanson urges, is more prevalent than had been imagined: as the great mystery plays become more and more rare as a result of increasing scruples on the part of magistrates and clergy, coupled with the mistrust of nomadic troupes, the scholarly

42. "Etude sur les origines de la tragédie classique en France," RHLF, 1903, p. 191.

theater, no duller than any other at that time, must have attracted its public. Yet the author seems to go a long way on little evidence in assuming a very large public. He admits that the public was often restricted at the scholarly performance, though when the students played outside the audience was presumably general. Did the décor differ from that of the waning mystery? We cannot think so: everything that Lanson says suggests the contrary. The vocabulary of the accounts is the same: "échafaud," "dresser un théâtre": "Dans la série des représentations, jusqu'en plein XVIIe siècle, alternent, se succèdent, se croisent, mystéries moralités, farces, comédies, tragi-comédies, pastorales."[43] The only difference for Lanson between all these forms of performance is that the bourgeoisie of the towns probably regarded the new genres as a sort of *avant-garde* theater, *deformed* tragedy. We may, with the new material supplied to us by Holsboer, carry the speculation farther.[44] We know from her discoveries that the modified mystery set as depicted by Mahelot was a conscious creation and that it was renewed consciously when worn out. Also, it must have been used for some time before the period of the *Mémoire.*. It is natural to think that it would be imitated in the provinces by nomads in, say, the last two decades of the sixteenth century.

Haraszti sees no incompatibility between the Hôtel de Bourgogne mystery stage and the tragedies of Jodelle.[45] Montchrestien and all his predecessors were played there, he claims, and the chorus took the stage with the rest. (He is perhaps ignoring the size of the latter at the Hôtel de Bourgogne.) Two of Garnier's tragedies, he further affirms, were certainly played at Saint Maxent, one called *Hippolyte* and the other, incorrectly, *Marc Antoine et Cléopâtre*, witness Garnier's dedicatory remark: "Je vous consacre ce Marc Antoine chargé de son auteur . . . de vous dire que s'il a cet honneur de vous être agréable . . . les autres ouvrages de cette faveur se hâteront de voir le jour pour marcher en toute hardiesse sur le théâtre français que vous m'avez jadis fait animer au bord de la Garonne. . . ." Haraszti reasonably assumes that "animer un théâtre" is equivalent to "animare theatrum," that is, to produce.[46]

Thus, in our brief review, there is a gravitation towards a simple, and it must be admitted, uninspiring conclusion. Around the court, the staging of the play, whatever its nature, in general became Italianate with even less reference back to the ancients than with the Italians themselves.[47] The court is already the center of attraction for magnificence of staging, and we shall follow it later in this function. Elsewhere, the very limited staging demands of the new genres met and fused with a dying mystery convention.[48]

43. Ibid., p. 433.
44. Deierkauf-Holsboer, *Vie d'Alexandre Hardy*, 1947.
45. RHLF, 1904, pp. 681 et seq.
46. And see Jefferey, op. cit., pp. 68–69.
47. Cf. ibid., p. 63.
48. Ibid., p. 68. We are in agreement again with Jefferey who finds it "difficult to escape the conclusion that there is a continuity of stage design in France *without* a break at 1500 or 1550 . . ."

CHAPTER FOUR

VITRUVIUS FORMALIZED

Quant à la pourtraiture de Vitruve, elle s'est perdue par l'iniure du tems: au grand dommage et preiudice des ouvriers.' (Gardet's *Vitruve*, 1559).

Iconography

IN ITALY, THE Vitruvian impulse, although admittedly it ends in covered rectangular theaters and "infinite" stage space for decorations, does give rise to conscious reconstruction in terms of wood, stone, bricks, and mortar.[1] It is beyond doubt that such theaters as Serlio's and Palladio's are consciously inspired in this way. It is only subsequently that the demands of decoration in perspective, and stage marvel and change, impose with any finality the rectangle on the auditorium.

Yet in spite of the relative immediacy of the advent of Vitruvian study to France, there is no initial effort at a reconstructed building, even while the late Renaissance monarchs are building energetically in other ways. When Richelieu builds the Palais Cardinal and inaugurates it with *Mirame* in 1641 the theater in France is already potentially in the grip of the baroque, and the historical moment for reconstitution is past. The fact is occasionally glossed over with a regretful mention.[2]

We believe however that it is a negative fact of some significance. The long development of what we shall refer to as the "illegitimate" genres in the French theater: court ballet, machine play, and opera, together with "paratheatricals,"[3] takes place from the outset without the obstacle of a *frons scaenae*, however modified, without that hindrance to a one-way line of vision for the perspective set which is the auditorium *à l'antique*, without, in short, the restraining example of a French Olympic Theater. The result of this is that the Italian influences in stage decoration and magnificence do not, for France, have to overcome the barriers which confronted them in their own country: their flowering is immediate.

This canalization of Vitruvian study into academic channels in France further helps us to understand the way in which the Renaissance all over Europe, while paying lip service to the ancients, did exactly what it liked with them, often subconsciously, and in many spheres. It is the history of just such a process in the French theater, from its negative angle. It is the reverse side of a medal whose face is the rapid growth and ultimate hypertrophy of perspective decoration and stage marvel in the seventeenth century, and thus it illuminates the loss of the concept

1. We cannot accept Kernodle's thesis of the complete absence of connection between baroque perspective and the study of Vitruvius, any more than we were able to accept his claim that the *Olimpico* would have been the same had Vitruvius never been rediscovered. (Op.cit., p. 171, and see our p. 36, n.52.)
2. E.g. Leclerc, *Origines*, p. 13: "L'édifice théâtral, qui commence seulement au milieu du XVIIIe siècle, à faire figure de monument public 'autonome,' dans le paysage urbain."
3. See pp.71-2.

of that larger unity of place, of the sense of oneness between stage and auditorium which is the wider theme of our study. It helps us to see in a new light, for instance, exactly why Racinian tragedy was never performed in a theater edifice worthy of it, instead of leaving us to be satisfied with the trite generalization that the theater structure of one age is always that form most appropriate to the authors of the previous age.

This line of negative scholarship is then a detail in a general Renaissance phenomenon which has been admirably worked over by Michel and other historians of art.[4] The obsession with form, the desuetude of function, an artistic attitude applicable to theater decoration and architecture as well as to any other art, begins in Italy where, as Münz tells us, Roman ornamentation, in its richness and variety, is an active force while the laws of Vitruvius are still the property of a tiny number of initiates; "l'accessoire l'a emporté sur le principal," and this is to be renewed when the Renaissance makes its appearance in France, the Low Countries, and Germany.[5] The French Renaissance architects transmit to their successors their own pedagogical attitudes and an art which is essentially erudite.

Within the immediate sphere of architecture and the theater, there are many examples of the virtually instantaneous spread of Vitruvian study to France. One of the most impressive of these is the presence of Jocundus himself. He came to France some time before 1504, or possibly in that year, to construct an aqueduct at Blois, and was called to Paris on the occasion of the reconstruction of the Pont Notre-Dame, under the supervision of Colin de la Chesnaye and Jean de Boyac, "maître des oeuvres de maçonnerie de la ville de Paris," at first to examine the quality of the stones, later, in 1504, to help with the levelling.[6] A manuscript notice at the beginning of a collection in the Cabinet des Estampes of the Bibliothèque Nationale in Paris shows him working with the older Ducerceau on the rebuilding of the château of Gaillon for Georges d'Amboise.[7] His reputation as a scholar and as a practical architect is attested by no less authorities than Scaliger, Budé, and Sannazaro. Both Scaliger and Budé were his disciples, the latter thanking God for causing him to meet such a wise interpreter of Vitruvius.[8] The turn of the fifteenth and sixteenth centuries is in fact the moment of the brutal supplanting of the Gothic style in architecture by Italian novelty, and this revolution is the work of a small group of artists and artisans brought back by Charles VIII "pour oeuvrer de leur métier à l'usage et mode d'Italie," and installed by him at Amboise in 1497. Amongst the perfumers, the tailors and the gardeners was one Jérôme Pacherot, "tailleur de maçonnerie antique."[9] It was to such a small group that Jocundus belonged. The

4. Michel, *Histoire de l'art depuis les premiers temps chrétiens jusqu'à nos jours*, 1905–1929, Bk. III, pt. 2, ch. viii, pp. 468 et seq.
5. Münz, *La Renaissance en Italie et en France à l'époque de Charles VIII*, 1885, p. 170.
6. Michel, op. cit., Bk. IV, pt. 2, ch. i, pp. 500–01, 537–39.
7. Est. BN. 2i, *sur Jacques Androuet Ducerceau et sur son fils Jean-Baptiste . . .*, par Callen père (early nineteenth century).
8. Vasari, *Vite*, ed. Milanesi, 1878–85, Vol.V, pp. 265 et seq.
9. Michel, op. cit., Bk. IV, pt. 2, ch. 1, p. 499.

French were soon following the ancients via the Italians. There can be little doubt that Jocundus's Vitruvius was well read when it first appeared. Martin's preface shows us that a copy was in the hands of the King in 1521: "Dès l'année cinq cent vingt et un ayant ce livre été traduit et commenté en italien, il fut donné au Roi votre père par messire Augustin Gallo." In 1540 Serlio took up residence in the French court with the title (new at the time) of "architecte du roi," and dedicated to Francis I his *Livres d'Architecture*, so that his theater and his interpretation of Vitruvius' three scenes were known in France immediately.[10] Yet the career of Serlio in France is typical of the way things were going. He arrived in the full belief that he was to plan and construct buildings. He soon realized that he was to be entrusted with little actual building, and complained of the fact. According to Michel the only actual structures for which he seems to have been responsible at Fontainebleau were decorative pieces in its courts and gardens.[11] He is by no means the first of the stream of Italian architects who visit France. In 1528 the Florentines Rustici and Pellegrini, in 1529 Girolamo della Robbia, in 1531 Il Rosso, and in 1532 Primaticcio bring the Italian classical Renaissance to France. Meanwhile France's own first generation of classical architects is springing up, and these in their turn either study the Italians at home or go to Italy. Goujon, with Lescot and Philibert Delorme, is in the vanguard of the native classical revival. The first of these, illustrator of Martin's Vitruvius, may not have gone to Italy (we do not know), but he was certainly inspired by the Italian classical architects. Jean Bullant completed his studies before returning to France in 1537. Among the many writings of Jacques Androuet Ducerceau are *Monuments antiques d'Italie et de France* and *Livre des édifices antiques romains*. Philander, the humanist commentator of Vitruvius, imparted a Vitruvian flavor to a group of buildings in the Rouergue district, around Rodez, seat of the Bishop Georges d'Armagnac, whose friend and counsellor he was.[12]

With this school, developing after the death of Francis I, the Italian is somewhat abandoned for the more strictly ancient, but this movement again expresses itself in a rather distinctive manner: in the search for pure classic beauty, the emphasis is on columns, their order and measurement. This is an attitude which persists even throughout the seventeenth century, being sanctified by the Académie d'Architecture in its proceedings as from 1671. The significance of the structure as a whole is frequently missed, and this is particularly so with the theater, whose function is perhaps too specific, too restricted for it to be rebuilt "à l'antique": for more general edifices were certainly being rebuilt in France by devotees of Vitruvius. Perrault, in the preface to his own Vitruvius, gives us some examples: Louis de Foix is even called to Spain by Philip II for the Escurial; Philibert Delorme and Jean Bullant bring their Vitruvian lore to the Grand Palais des Tuileries.[13]

10. Complete details of the various editions are to be found in Charvet, *Sébastien Serlio*, 1869.
11. Op. cit., Bk. IV, pt. 2, ch. i, pp. 525–26.
12. Ibid., Bk. IV, pt, 2, ch. i, p. 532.
13. Perrault, *Les dix livres d'architecture*, 1673.

The seventeenth-century topographer Germain Brice would have us believe that at least one French theater built in his own time was in imitation of the ancients. This was the open-air theater in the Jardin des Tuileries. "Ce jardin," he tells us, "est à présent un des plus réguliers de l'Europe . . . il y a un Théâtre découvert qui a toutes les parties qui lui sont nécessaires, et déterminées par les Anciens, comme l'on voit dans ceux de Rome. On y a planté des arbres qui font le même effet que les décorations ordinaires. Il est fort grand, et peut contenir beaucoup de monde" (Fig. 33).[14] The plan tells a somewhat different story. The stage decorations (presumably the trees to which Brice refers) recede in a series of angle-wings, and the effect of hypertrophic development away from the *frons scaenae* is increased by a series of fleeing *allées* curiously reminiscent of the Olimpico. That part which might be construed as an orchestra seems to be the pit: it is labelled "salle de comédie," though this is taken to refer to the whole theater. There is a half-hearted attempt at an amphitheater: its curve is most tentative, and the *gradins* are on the whole pointed directly at the stage; there is no side seating. The auditorium, except for the fact that it is in the open, is hardly more advanced than are the timid attempts at indoor amphitheaters towards the end of the century. Strangely little is known of this theater.[15]

The priority of form over function is illustrated by the writing of Jean Bullant: "Reigle généralle d'architecture des cinq manières de colonnes, à sçavoir: tuscane, dorique, ionique, corinthe, et composite; et enrichi de plusieurs autres à l'exemple de l'antique; veu, recorrigé et augmenté par l'auteur de cinq autres ordres de colonnes suivant les reigles et doctrines de Vitruve."[16]

The Italian topographies of ancient Rome are not long in appearing in France. Marlianus's *Topographia antiquae Romae* is an early example in 1534, and his *De origine urbis Romae* is published in 1554.[17] Between 1533 and 1536 Philibert Delorme is in Italy, drawing ancient monuments. Particularly popular, presumably since it was the most prominent in Rome, was the theater of Marcellus. There are many attempts at a reconstitution. Among these we may mention Béatrizet's (Fig. 34).[18] The *frons scaenae*, completely reconstituted, would appear to be imaginative. There is no sign of the three face entrances, and Béatrizet has placed at the side important

---

14. *Description nouvelle de ce qu'il y a de plus remarquable dans la ville de Paris*, 1684, vol. I, p. 31, item "Jardin des Tuileries." The theater was demolished in the early eighteenth century and turned into the *bosquet du mail* set aside for the amusement of Louis XV in his minority. See also Babeau, *Le jardin des Tuileries au XVIIe et au XVIIIe siècle*, 1902, pp. 15–16, and Le Nôtre, *Plan du Jardin du Palais des Thuilleries de l'invention de M. Le Nôtre*, Musée de Carnavalet, Estampes, 20 A. Our own figure is taken from a larger plan in the same collection, abstracted in its turn from Blondel's *Architecture françoise*.
15. See ch. vii.
16. 1568. Re-editions, 1619 and 1647.
17. Copies of both works are to be found in the Christie Collection, University of Manchester.
18. *Theatrum Marcelli*, Est. BN Ed. 1a, n.d. (roughly midcentury).

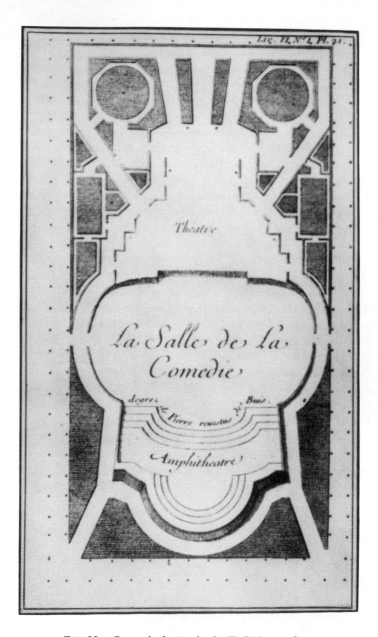

FIG. 33.—Open-air theater in the Tuileries gardens.

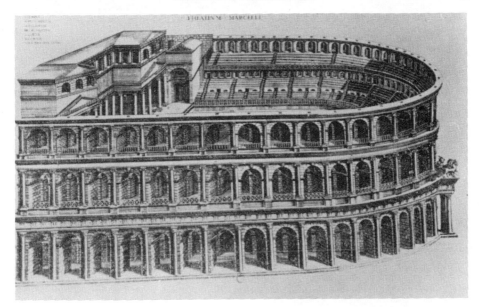

FIG. 34.—The theater of Marcellus according to Béatrizet.

entrances which, in the key, are described as *corus*, revealing the impression that a chorus was used in the Roman theater and that it entered directly onto the stage. The numbered key as a whole reveals considerable haziness as to the parts of the theater. The front of the building is described as *scaena*, but on the other hand the jutting *versurae* are called *proscaenium*. The engraving betrays a greater preoccupation with the detail of decoration (columns, pediments, capitals, cornices, entablatures) and with proportion (for example the increasing height, from top to bottom, of the three rows of columns around the periphery), than it does with the function of the theater. This is not an isolated case, and indeed this is not the only example of this engraving, which may or may not be an original work by Béatrizet. He worked for Lafréry, an editor from the Franche Comté who went to Italy in 1540 and played an important part in acquainting the French with the monuments of the city.[19] Béatrizet's Marcellus is typical of the idea of Rome propagated by Lafréry and others in France.

Surface features were also to attract the architect Jean Bullant, who tells us "Cet ordre Doiqure [sic] est au théâtre de Marcellus à Rome fort loué des bons Architectes."[20] In approximately 1560 Gérard de Jode publishes an engraving of the ruins of the Teatrum Bordeos[21] (Fig. 35). In 1575 Dupérac's *Vestigii dell'antichità di Roma*

19. See Est. BN Gc 6, also *Inventaire du fonds français*, Adhémar, *Graveurs du XVIe siècle*, vol. II, p. 350. Cf. Dupérac-Lafréry, *Nova Urbis Romae Descriptio*, in the exhibition hall of the Vatican Library.
20. Op. cit., p. 11.
21. From *Ruinarum variarum fabricarum delineationes*, Antwerp, 1560 (?). See *Inventaire du fonds français*, Linzeler, *Graveurs du XVIe siècle*, vol. I, p. 55.

TEATRVM BORDEOS

FIG. 35.—The Bordeos Theater according to Jode.

appear, including an engraving of the theater of Marcellus: *Vestigii del Theatro che fu edificato da Augusto in nome di Marcello suo nepote.* . . . In 1579 a plan of the city appears in Ducerceau's *Second volume des plus excellents bastiments de France.* It includes five theaters: the Marcellus, the Lapideum, the Balbus, together with the Palatinum and the Pompeii, all of which are repeated, enlarged and isolated from their urban context in his *Livre des édifices antiques romains* of 1584 (see Figs. 36, 37, and 38). They reveal clearly the same preoccupation with decoration and proportion, and the same indifference to function. The stage buildings are obviously conceived as a house, a fact which is particularly obvious in the case of the Balbus, where in any case the *frons scaenae* in the engraving of 1579 bears the legend "THEATRUM BALBI qui hoggi e la casa di S. Cesarini." In the case of the Marcellus, the Lapideum and the Balbus it is not clear whether or not Ducerceau has intended to depict more than one entrance through the face wall of the stage. There is a tendency for the *hospitalia* to be turned into windows. In the case of the Pompeii they are all represented as windows and no entrance is visible. There is no sign in any of the theaters of *versurae*, or jutting side-wings, and none of a stage. The seats of the auditorium abut directly onto the face wall of the scene building. A vague obeisance is made to archaeological restoration, but the architect, in a typically Renaissance manner, uses it to serve his own ends: those of the establishment of correct proportions and the establishment of the nature of outward decoration amongst the ancients. He has lost sight of the function of the theater, and to an even greater extent than Béatrizet. Philibert Delorme, on the site of the Marcellus, abandons all pretense at reconstruction, relying, like his successors of the Academy, on the theater merely as a source of information about columns:

FIG. 36.—The theater of Balbus according to Ducerceau.

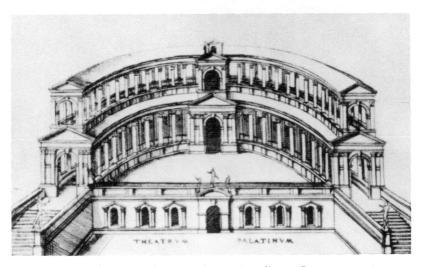

FIG. 37.—The Palatinum Theater according to Ducerceau.

Ch. XVII. Encore du chapiteau, épistyle, métope, triglyphe et couronne de l'ordre Dorique: le tout mesuré et décrit après les antiquités du théâtre de Marcel à Rome.

. . . étant le dit théâtre au côté de la place Montenaire, ainsi qu'il s'y voit au-jourd'hui presque tout en ruine, et n'en peut en avoir que bien peu de connaissance, si est que du temps que j'étais en ladite Rome (il y a environ trente ans) on y pouvait encore connaître et mesurer les deux ordres selon lesquels il avait été édifié savoir est l'ordre Dorique et Ionique, desquels il était orné par le devant et les faces des portiques.

FIG. 38.—The Lapideum and Pompeii Theaters according
to Ducerceau.

In his own time, he finds the building no more easy of access than it is now: "Avant
au dedans du théâtre je ne me voulus ingérer d'y entrer, pour autant que plusieurs
maisons y étaient bâties, et pour les accommoder on l'avait quasi tout abattu."[22]

These topographies remain popular throughout the sixteenth century, and the
admiration for Rome continues into the seventeenth in the same way. It is as though
the fixity of the illustrator's gaze precludes real investigation: the Roman theater
of Orange is described by Louis XIV as the "most beautiful wall in his kingdom."[23]
At about the same time, the French engraver Baugin produces a view of the *Face
méridionale du cirque d'Orange* (Fig. 39), and this again has some of Ducerceau's features: once more, the poles of the auditorium abut directly onto the *parascaenia* or
versurae and at their lower reaches onto the *frons scaenae* itself. There is again no

22. *Oeuvres*, 1626, Bk. V, ch. vii, p. 147b.
23. Sautel, *Le théâtre de Vaison et les théâtres romains de la vallée du Rhône*, 1946.

suggestion of a stage, and the *aula regia* is shown walled up. There could have been little idea in the mind of Baugin that entrance was made through the *frons scaenae*, nor has he any idea of the one-time function of the orchestra which he describes as ''Demy rond servant pour les combats y représentés.'' He has, in fact, turned it into a Roman circus.'

Edition

Alongside the activity of these engravers (some of whom, let us note, are practicing architects), Vitruvian exegesis and translation thrives. The immediacy of its presence is no more contestable than is that of the appearance of Vitruvian practice in all but the theater.

Alberti's *De re aedificatoria*, with a chapter on the ancient theater according to Vitruvius, in Latin, appears in France and elsewhere one year after the publication in Italy of the Jocundus Vitruvius, namely in 1512. Next, still in Latin, comes the Strasburg edition of 1541, and then Martin's translation, *L'Architecture et art de bien bastir du Seigneur Léon-Baptiste Albert . . .* (1553). By this time we are justified in saying that his work is well known in France. Martin's translations are popular in French humanist circles, and this one, published after his death, carries an epitaph by

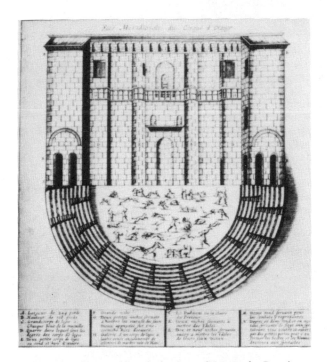

FIG. 39.—*Face méridionale du cirque d'Orange*, by Baugin.

Ronsard and homage by other notables.[24] Ever present to the scholastic architects of the seventeenth century, Alberti reappears in print along with many other colleagues in Fréard de Chambray's *Parallèle de l'architecture antique et de la moderne* of 1650.[25] By this time, we see that in the mind of the academician, the memory of the practical Alberti has gone the way of that of so many other practical men of the Renaissance: from Alberti and the others, Chambray merely requires the usual evidence about columns. He is quoted for the purposes of external, superficial decoration. He is formalized.

As might be expected, the spate of pure Vitruvian editions in France is even fuller. The Giunta edition of 1522 is reprinted in France the year after.[26] Philander, whose commentary is published in Rome in 1544, is reprinted in Paris in 1545, and again at Lyons in 1552 and 1586.[27]

A curiously early edition is a translation from the Spanish: *Raison d'architecture antique extraicte de Vitruve et aultres anciens Architecteurs, nouvellement traduite despaignol* [of D. Sagredo] *en Francoys . . .*[28] The translation of this translation, judging from the number of editions, is most popular of all. According to Colombier, there is an edition before 1539, and there are subsequent editions in 1542, 1555, 1604, and 1608.[29] Mid-century sees the several translations of Jean Martin, and corresponds roughly to the activity of Serlio in France. The latter's second book on perspective (containing his treatise on the theater), along with the first book of architecture, appears in one volume in 1545 in Italian,[30] and in the course of the same year in Martin's translation,[31] as does Van Aelst's translation from the Italian, *Reigles generales de l'architecture sur les cinq manieres d'edifices . . . selon la doctrine de Vitruve.*[32] In 1547 Martin publishes his translation of *de Architectura.*[33] There is a Paris re-edition in 1572. Gardet's translation, after many vagaries, appears in 1559,[34] and is re-edited in Paris in 1567 and 1568.

24. His translation of Sannazaro's *Arcadia* in 1544 is the only one of the century. Under the protection of Maximilian Sforza and later the Cardinal de Lenoncourt, Martin was well known to the men of letters of his time. See Marsan, *La pastorale dramatique*, 1905, p. 146, and Pierre Marcel, *Un vulgarisateur, Jean Martin*, n.d.
25. Alongside Palladio, Scamozzi, Serlio, Vignola, Barbaro, Cataneo, Bullant, and Delorme.
26. *M. Vitruvii de architectura libri decem.* Printed in Lyons, according to Brunet, and bearing a reprint of Jocundus's preface. See University of Manchester, Christie Collection.
27. *In decem libros M. Vitruvii Pollionis "de Architectura" annotationes*, Paris, 1545. *De architectura libri decem . . . accesserunt G. Philandri . . . annotationes*, Lugduni, 1552.
28. Paris, 1539.
29. "Jean Goujon et le Vitruve de 1547," *Gazette des Beaux Arts*, janvier–juin, 1931.
30. Paris, Barbé. Also Venice, 1560.
31. *Le premier livre d'architecture de Sebastien Serlio Bolognois mis en langue françoise par Jehan Martin, suivi du second livre de perspective.*
32. Antwerp, 1545.
33. *Architecture ou art de bien bastir de Marc Vitruve Pollion autheur Romain antique . . .* Barbé, who printed the Italian edition of Serlio's second book of perspective, apparently patrons this work. Also Cologne and Geneva, 1618, and Geneva, 1628.
34. *Epitome, ou extrait abrégé des dix livres d'architecture*, etc. Toulouse. According to the *adresse au lecteur* it was in the process of printing for four years, held up by the absence of the translator and by an outbreak of the plague.

The spate is well over by the seventeenth century, the only editions being Julien Mauclerc's *Traitte de l'architecture suivant Vitruve* (Paris, 1648), which is purely interested in columns, and the final "definitive" edition for this period, the fruit of the Academy of Architecture, Claude Perrault's new translation of 1673, with editions in 1674, 1681 (Amsterdam), and 1684. The ancient architect is however read and quoted through the century. His presence in the libraries of the colleges has been well attested.[35]

Transmission

In the blossoming of the Vitruvian tradition in France, what, in the details of the text (editions in the original apart), is transmitted? Firstly, the function of the Roman orchestra enjoys a prominence in the work of Alberti that it does not in Vitruvius. One wonders if any of the *seigneurs* who so persistently sat on the seventeenth-century stage had read this: "Et portait la coutume que les seigneurs ou magistrats avaient un certain lieu à part, convenable à leurs qualités, où ils étaient assis hors la presse du peuple. Icelle place était en l'aire même du milieu, et y avaient de beaux sièges bien parés de tapisserie pour ces personnages d'autorité."[36] Vitruvius' remark that the Greek *artifices* (whatever they were) played (or worked) in the orchestra[37] receives varied treatment, and Alberti in particular expands it largely, in just that direction that we have been noting in the case of the architects and engravers: to something approaching a translation of the passage he adds (in Martin's translation), "Et se parait celle partie des joueurs tant pour les Grecs que les Latins, de colonnes et travonaisons relevées les unes sur les autres, en semblance de maisonnages."[38] He is speaking of what Martin translates variously as *poulpite* or *poulpitre*, in other words the stage proper. So that not only has he added columns to look like houses, but it is not certain that he means the *pulpitum* to be clear of decorations and "maisonnages," not clear that he intends them to figure only at the back of the *frons scaenae*. If he means them to occupy parts of the *pulpitum* then we have something like Kernodle's Terentian stage, but springing directly from Vitruvius.

The mention of *scaena* tends to elicit the idea of decoration in other commentators too: it is again the mention of the orchestra and the stage that occasions Philander's definitions of the two scenes, *versatilis* and *ductilis*, the latter with such fruitful implications for the future of theater decoration.[39]

Perhaps the most obvious of the transmitted misinterpretations emanating from this servility to ideas of decoration is Martin's translation of the same passage. A

---

35. François de Dainville, "Décoration théâtrale dans les collèges de Jésuites au XVIIe siècle," RHT, tome IV, 1951.
36. Martin's *Alberti*, Bk. VIII, ch. vii, fos. 174,5.
37. "Ideo que apud eos tragici et comici in scena peragunt, reliqui autem artifices suas per orchestram praestant actiones," (Jocundus edn., Bk. V, ch. viii, fo. 87 v°).
38. Op. cit., fol. 175.
39. "Quod omnes artifices in scenam dant operam" (Philander, Bk. V, ch. vi, p. 155). See Allardyce Nicoll, *Development of the Theatre*, p. 91.

normal interpretation of this is Granger's: "because all the actors play their parts on the stage."[40] Yet "dant operam" is vague, and "artifices" debatable. The result, for Martin, is "Ce faisant, icelui Poulpitre sera beaucoup plus ample que ne sont ceux des Grecs: comme raison veut qu'il le soit, à cause que les Artisans y font leurs feintes et autres négoces pour la décoration du jeu."[41] The translator has eschewed the rendering of "artifices" as "actors." Our knowledge of the vocabulary of the mystery plays can leave us in no doubt as to what is meant by "fainctes." Martin means that the Roman stage must be bigger because workmen have to put up decorations on it. He sees what he was expecting to see: a stage with imper-manent, changeable decorations. This is surprisingly confirmed in his translation of Vitruvius' passage concerning the *periaktoi*, where there is a deliberate addition by Martin which does not appear in the Jocundus text: after the translation "pivots à trois faces" for "versatiles trigones habentes" he adds "mouvant à la volonté d'un conducteur qui fait les feintes."[42] "Conducteur" is as reminiscent of the mid-fifteenth-century performance as is "fainctes." This idea of contemporary deco-ration and scenic effect places him in difficulties when he comes to consider the question of the Greek chorus in the orchestra. Tied by his previous renderings of "artifices" he resorts to significant addition and dilation. His translation of the whole passage referred to[43] is this: "Le reste des Artisans est à faire ses negoces en l'Orchestre: et pourtant [i.e. pour ce] sont-ils appelés les uns Scéniques, et les autres Thyméliques, *c'est à dire partie attentifs aux décorations du jeu, et partie à la Musique de Harpes, Violons, Hautboys, Trompettes et telles sortes d'instruments.*"[44] "Négoces" sug-gests, if anything, unartistic industry, a type of occupation defined in the passage in italics which is pure addition.

To see what is happening we need only contrast this with Perrault's translation of the same sentence, in which "artifices" is read as though it were merely a syn-onym of "actores" used for the purpose of avoiding repetition: "De sorte que les Acteurs des Tragédies et des Comédies jouent en la Scène, les autres entrent dans l'Orchestre."[45] Martin reads as superficial decoration and accompaniment what is a primal division in the Greek theater. We cannot help wondering if it is not partly in this passage that Baïf drew his justification for expressing his search for the Greek *melopoeia* in the mixture of all things theatrical that was the early court ballet.

It may be further noted that Martin makes an addition to the text which intro-duces details of a social differentiation in the auditorium of which Vitruvius does not speak: "Les ouvertures des Escaliers par où le Peuple aura moyen d'aller aux places ordonnées selon les qualités des personnes."[46]

40. Loeb translation, based on the oldest manuscript of Vitruvius etc., 1931.
41. Bk. V, ch. vi, fo. 75.
42. Ibid., fo. 77.
43. "Reliqui autem artifices suas per orchestram praestant actiones. Itaque, ex eo scenici et thymelici graece separatim nominantur."
44. Op. cit., Bk. V, ch. viii, fo. 79 v°. The italics are ours.
45. Op. cit., Bk. V, ch. viii, p. 170.
46. Op.cit., loc. cit.

The one common factor that we may distinguish in the translations, is that for the most part the ancient theater is not living for them, and where it does live it is brought to life by the transference of detail from the contemporary theater.[47]

On the other hand, the entire fusion of ancient and modern inherent in the work of Serlio is immediately present in Martin's translation. Where the pure translation of Vitruvius remains without practical application except in terms of superficial decoration, the stage of Serlio corresponded to what the French designer knew and recognized as a modern trend in an already familiar phenomenon: it was the *avant-garde* of all the habits of decoration which had grown up in the mystery play and had been developed in the street theater. It seemed to give them sanctity. Even when translating Vitruvius the writer often has Serlio in mind. Goujon, in Martin's Vitruvius, for the three scenes, merely reproduces Serlio, and his stage and amphitheater are again Serlio's. Gardet does the same thing,[48] whereas the later and more scholarly Perrault is sceptical as to the existence in depth of the ancient Scene: "Il y a apparence que ces trois sortes de Scènes ne s'entendent que de celles qui étaient en peinture sur les machines tournantes qui servaient de Décorations, et non pas de l'Architecture de la Scène qui ne changeait point, mais qui faisait une partie de la Structure et de la Maçonnerie du Théâtre."[49] The great mass of Goujon's illustrations to Martin's Vitruvius are from the Jocundus edition, but otherwise he would appear to be inspired by the Como group of illustrators, of whom Cesariano and Caporali are the chief representatives.

Serlio, more than anyone, produces in the minds of these writers a contamination of Vitruvius, "scenography," and perspective. "Scénographie, qui comprend non seulement le front et les côtés d'un édifice, ains qui plus est toute forme soit ou superficie ou corps."[50] Gardet says much the same: "*Scénographie*. Cette diction signifiant le portrait ou montée en perspective, tant de la face ou rencontre, que des flancs, et côtés d'un bâtiment, ou de quelque autre chose que ce soit, dérive d'un terme grec [sken] par lequel ils entendent tout le toit de l'édifice."[51] The care

---

47. The false analogy survives in subsequent centuries. Cf. D'Aubignac, *Pratique*, Bk. III, ch. ix, p. 356:

> On y voyait des Cieux ouverts où paraissaient toutes leurs Divinités imaginaires, et d'où même ils les faisaient descendre pour converser avec les Hommes: l'Elément de l'air en peinture y souffrait des éclairs, et les véritables bruits du Tonnerre: la Mer y faisait paraître des Tempêtes, des Naufrages, des Rochers, des Vaisseaux, et des Batailles. C'était peu que la Terre y montrât des Jardins, des Déserts, des Forêts: qu'elle y portât des Temples et des Palais magnifiques, souvent même elle y paraissait entr'ouverte, et du sein de ses abîmes faisait sortir des flammes, des Monstres, des Furies, et tous les prodiges de l'Enfer des Fables.

> Also Brumoy, *Le théâtre des Grecs*, 1730 (in very much the same tone): "On y voyait des palais, des Temples, des places en perspective, et des villes dans l'enfoncement" (Preface, p. xcvi).

48. Op. cit, p. 141.
49. Op. cit., p. 170.
50. Martin's translation of the *Second livre de Perspective*, fo. 25 v°.
51. Op. cit., *Annotationes sur le Ier livre*, p. 11.

with which Serlio works out the vanishing points of his perspective has little to do
with Vitruvius and a great deal to do with perspective stage decoration to come. It
leads him naturally into a social hierarchy in his auditorium which is doubtless the
origin of Martin's addition noted earlier:

> La partie signée E représente l'orchestre, c'est à dire un petit lieu où sont les sièges
> des Sénateurs . . . Les sièges desdits Sénateurs, ou autres plus nobles spectateurs sont
> au lieu ou est mise l'F. Les premiers degrés signés par G sont pour les plus apparentes
> dames et demoiselles, celles de moyenne qualité se mettent en ceux de dessus. Le lieu
> spacieux marqué H est un passage pour les allants et venants, aussi est bien la partie
> I. Les marches mises entre ces deux sont destinées aux gentils hommes et autres per-
> sonnages de qualité. Depuis ledit I jusques au bout des degrés montant contremont,
> c'est la place des marchands et gens de métier. Le grand espace noté K est réservé au
> menu peuple.[52] (See Figs. 7 and 8.)

Serlio is already speaking of elaborate decorations, with machinery, and a full stage:

> On y voit en peu d'espace aucuns palais dressés par art de perspective, avec grands
> Temples et divers maisonnages proches et lointains de la vue, places belles et spacieuses
> décorées de plusieurs édifices, rues longues et droites, croisées de voies traversantes,
> arcs de triomphe, colonnes hautes et merveilles, Pyramides, obélisques, et mille autres
> singularités . . . D'avantage l'on y voit petit à petit lever la lune cornue.[53]

In fact, all the paraphernalia of the street theater prepared for the Royal Entry,
with the addition of superior machine effects: rising and setting suns, gods descend-
ing from the skies, a planet crossing, are to be found. It seems that his second book
of Perspective, appearing in Martin's translation in the midst of all the other Vitruvian work, is for France the chief medium whereby the negative aspects of Vitruvian study are transmuted into the baroque. For with Perrault's translation the
surge of fructifying error is well over, but by this time the fusion in the theater is
accomplished.

The Academy

The Académie Royale d'Architecture, founded in 1671 by Colbert, is the most
striking example of this negative line of scholarship. Last born of the Academies,
it is Colbert's last move in his attempt to bring the whole range of French culture
under some form of centralized discipline. Its proceedings bear every sign of this.[54]
Its purpose is the inculcation of rule: "Sur ce qui a été représenté par le Sr. Colbert,
surintendant et ordonnateur général de ses bâtiments, qu'il serait très utile pour
élever l'architecture à un plus haut degré de perfection que celui où elle est aujourd'hui de faire choix d'une personne très-savante en ce bel art pour en enseigner
les véritables règles aux jeunes gens qui se proposent d'embrasser la profession.
. . . ."[55] In such terms is Blondel summoned to its head.

52. Op. cit., fo. 63 v°.
53. Ibid., fos. 64–65.
54. See Yates, *The French Academies*, 1947, pp. 310–11.
55. Arch. Nat. 0¹ 15 (Maison du Roi), fo. 36 v°.

The *procès-verbaux* of this body, right from its inception, confirm the negative attitude of the architects to the problem of theater construction and their failure to see any other than a superficial guide to action in the work of the ancients. Once more, where the detail of decoration is followed slavishly, the function is ignored. The academicians reveal this the more in that one of their chief functions was the reading of the ancient writers and their Italian and French interpreters, at their weekly sessions.[56]

As we read through this document, its tone soon becomes apparent: it is dogmatic, authoritative. Blondel opens the proceedings at the first session by announcing that on the occasion of the next meeting "l'on dira ce que c'est que le bon goût." This theme lasts for five sessions. Thus based aesthetically, the members proceed to consider the position of Vitruvius. His authority is unanimously confirmed: "Il faut le considérer comme le premier et le plus savant de tous les architectes."[57] At the next meeting, Palladio is judged: "On peut lui donner la première autorité parmi les architectes modernes,"[58] a verdict which is arrived at without any reference to his theater. Scamozzi is graciously awarded second place,[59] and Vignola receives a mention.[60]

The treatment of Serlio is perhaps more illustrative of our point. Serlio's consideration of the theater, within the general bulk of his work, absolutely commands attention. Yet it receives none. His fidelity to the ancients is questioned, and this tends to dismiss his case. It is recognized that his drawings of ancient monuments are of value, "quoique non dans la dernière exactitude." Note is taken of his invention of temples, doors, public buildings (in which the theater is presumably engulfed), and of some rules of Geometry and Perspective: "Il doit être loué et estimé comme un auteur dans lequel les Architectes intelligents peuvent prendre plusieurs belles idées."[61] The severity of the academicians appears to increase, unless we assume that the works they consider are carefully prearranged in order of merit, for Alberti receives very short shrift from them: "Il doit être considéré comme un Auteur plutôt que comme un ouvrier de bon goût."[62]

The reports on the French architects show a touch of pride, echoed in Perrault's preface to his Vitruvius, in which he reviews the progress of French architecture. Bullant is acclaimed as the man "qui a suivi par une méthode facile, la doctrine de Vitruve, dans ses écrits,"[63] though Philibert Delorme is given the rank of first French architect.

56. Arch. Nat. 0¹ 1929 (1), 0¹ 1929 (2), (3) and (4) contain the detailed *procès verbaux*. 0¹ 1930 is a carton of statutes appertaining to the Academy. They are a copy of the original which is housed in the library of the Ecole des Beaux Arts. See also Lemonnier, *Procès-verbaux de l'Académie royale d'architecture*, 1911–24, 8 vols.
57. 0¹ 1929 (1), 6th session.
58. 7th session.
59. 8th session.
60. 9th session: "On a jugé qu'il devait être estimé."
61. 10th session.
62. 11th session.
63. 16th session.

The tendentious errors of Jean Martin in his translation of Vitruvius are rapidly realized: the Academy begins to read his work in detail on the 30th January 1673 (fifth meeting of that year), but soon decides to wait for the completion of Perrault's translation, because of the wide gaps between Martin's version and the meaning of the author.[64] The reading of Perrault's translation begins at the 22nd Assembly of the 11th June 1674. In sweeping away Martin's unwitting substitutions the Academy has swept away all sense of a possible connection between ancient and modern theater. It begins to read Book V on the 13th April 1676. Chapters 4, 5, 6, 7, and 8 of this book all concern the theater exclusively. This is all that appears in the *procès-verbal:*

> La compagnie faisant réflexion sur la règle que Vitruve donne pour la hauteur des colonnes mises les unes sur les autres,[65] par laquelle il ordonne que partout les supérieures soient un quart moindre que les inférieures, et à la note que Philandre a faite sur ce sujet, qui dit que cette proportion doit être entendue des diamètres des colonnes aussi bien que de leur hauteur; a jugé que cette règle ne peut aucunement être mise en oeuvre que lorsque l'on veut se servir de colonnes de même ordre.

The seventh chapter of the fifth book finds them interested again only in the proportions of the columns in the theater. Blondel, speaking of the theater of Marcellus, is simply concerned with its Doric capital as measured by Philibert Delorme and M. de Chambray, compared with capitals of the same order by Vitruvius, Vignola, Palladio, and Scamozzi. The two last-named writers are both read through without any question of the *Olimpico* appearing in the proceedings. Not only, as we have seen, does the Academy pass by Serlio's theater: it seems determined to chase the memory of it from his other works: "La 16e planche est remplie d'un dessin très capricieux. Cette figure d'un demi-rond qu'il donne à la salle étant plus propre pour un théâtre que pour l'usage auquel il l'emploie."[66]

On the 30th October 1690, the worthy members begin once more to read *De Architectura.* This time the theater does not entirely escape notice, and with their remarks upon it, summarizing their entire attitude, we may leave them: "On a lu les 4, 5, 6, 7, et 8e chapes. du Ve liv. de Vitruve et comme il n'y est parlé que des *Théâtres des Anciens qui sont présentement hors d'usage, on n'a trouvé aucune remarque à faire.*"[67]

The theater is not a distinct architectural form for these architects: even when they discuss the ancient theaters which come to their notice (Marcellus and Poli) they atomize the individual decorative elements and are merely concerned with passing value judgments on these. The ancients, the Italians and the French, are so many scholars presenting architectural theses to these self-appointed assessors.

We might perhaps epitomize the situation by saying that in the history of the French theater the five orders of columns have proved a more sterilizing factor than their sisters of dramatic literature: the three unities.

---

64. 9th session, 1673.
65. Ignoring the fact that he is speaking of columns in the *face wall of his theater.*
66. 20th session, 6th May 1680.
67. The italics are ours.

Material Obstacles

Yet it would clearly be a gross injustice to attribute the absence of an autonomous theater building in the seventeenth century entirely to the deadening influence of Vitruvian scholarship. The economic odds against such an establishment must have been considerable, as the briefest review of the circumstances will show.

These circumstances take the form of a series of developing restrictions upon building and the profession of builder. Much of this process is inherent in the semantics of the word "architect." In the modern sense he is at once a planner and a director of works. The first use of the word in France appears to be by Budé, who uses it of Jocundus in his *De Asse.* Under Francis I, when it is in regular use, it applies more to designers and decorators than to practical men. The man on the spot is the *maçon.*[68]

Gradually, the architect is endowed with practical responsibility and direct supervision over the work of the mason, but not without opposition from this latter, and his confraternity. The history of building itself in the seventeenth century is, like so many other histories of the time, one of increasing authority and discipline, mostly under the aegis of Colbert. The obvious magnificence of its achievements has possibly led to the exaggeration of its extent. In Paris, at least, building is centralized geographically as well as administratively: Pont Neuf, Place Dauphine, Louvre, Luxembourg, Tuileries, the Palais Cardinal are all in a restricted space, and the grandeur of these projects implies restrictions in other directions.

These take two forms: firstly, the internal struggle in the hierarchy of the building trade: the defense of privilege by *architecte, maitre maçon, compagnon maçon,* the last two struggling upwards; and secondly, the direct vetoes on building development emanating from the royal authority, and wielded in the later part of the century by Colbert himself.

A few examples will show us the extent of these. Direct restriction on building in Paris is not unknown in the sixteenth century, and is inspired by the depopulation of towns and villages, by the heavy migratory trends on the capital: in November 1584 there is an edict "par lequel est défendu de ne plus bâtir ès faubourgs de la Ville de Paris."[69] In 1576 the lower strata of the trade are cut down: a decree limits the number of *maçons* and *charpentiers jurés* to twenty-four.[70] The seventeenth-century projects make themselves felt particularly in the latter half of the century; the 12th October 1660 sees an *Ordonnance* "portant défense à toutes sortes de personnes d'entreprendre aucuns bâtiments tant dans Paris qu'à dix lieues à la ronde, sans la permission expresse de sa M. et ce pour achever les bâtiments du Louvre et Palais de Tuileries."[71] The immediate repercussion of this on the theatrical life of Paris is a classical example: the destruction of the Petit Bourbon by Ratabon, and the consequent eviction of Molière from that house:

68. Michel, *Histoire de l'art* etc., Bk. IV, pt. 2, ch. i, p. 503.
69. MSS. BN franc. 21677, fo. 63.
70. MSS. BN franc. 21678, fo. 178.
71. MSS. BN franc. 21675, fo. 95.

> Le roi ayant résolu par l'avis de M. le cardinal Mazarin son premier ministre de faire achever incessamment tant le bâtiment de son Château du Louvre que celui du Palais des Tuileries pour être joint ensemble suivant l'ancien et magnifique dessin qui en a été fait par les Rois ses prédecesseurs, et pour cet effet donne ses ordres au surintendant et ordonnateur général de ses bâtiments, et à l'intendant en exercice de faire abattre dès à présent tant l'Hôtel de Bourbon que les autres hôtels maisons et Bâtiments qui se trouveront dans l'enceinte dud. dessin.[72]

The entire area is placed under a building veto in 1667, pending the visit of the King.[73]

Only the architects, restricted in number, may build, and the architects are concentrated around the court. This is well demonstrated by the severity with which the lower orders are supervised.

> Sur ce qui a été représenté au Roi étant en son Conseil, que plusieurs Maîtres Maçons, Entrepreneurs et autres gens se mêlant des Bâtiments, osent sans aucun droit prendre la qualité d'Architectes du Roi pour se mettre plus en crédit; et sous ce titre donner des Dessins, bâtir toutes sortes d'Edifices, tant publics, que particuliers, lesquels pour la plupart se trouvent très-défectueux, par l'insuffisance desdits Maçons et Entrepreneurs. Et comme il est très-important d'empêcher le cours d'une licence si désavantageuse aux intérêts publics et si contraire aux intentions que Sa Majesté a de relever et faire fleurir les Arts, particulièrement celui de l'Architecture: SA MAJESTE ETANT EN SON CONSEIL, a fait très-expresses défenses a tous Entrepreneurs, Maîtres Maçons et autres gens se mêlant des Bâtiments, de prendre la qualité d'Architectes du Roi, sinon à ceux que Sa Majesté a choisis pour composer son Académie d'Architecture, auxquels Elle a donné des Lettres ou Brevets à cet effet; A peine de mille livres d'amende payable par corps . . .[74]

The same extracts from the *Registres du Parlement* contain a similar complaint at the level below: the Maître Maçons complain that their rights are being usurped, that the Compagnons Maçons are undertaking building, instead of remaining in their function of daily labor.

Carpenters were undergoing similar restrictions. A declaration of 1655 reduces the number of six "Jurés Maîtres Menuisiers de Paris" to four only.[75]

We may perhaps conclude this brief and random survey with the *ordonnance* of 1671, forbidding laymen to take the title of "architecte" or "maître maçon." It gives the following list of all previous rulings in this direction: December 1317, 3rd April 1574, 17th May 1595, 16th May 1598, 7th September 1616, June 1645, 4th September 1660, 29th July 1662, 26th February 1665, and 27th October 1667.[76]

It may well be that the Renaissance in Italy provided the ideal social structure for the birth of such edifices as the Olympic Theater at Vicenza. Its courts were small, many, and rich; the sources of patronage correspondingly numerous. Its Academies seem to have been free from the deadening hand of a centralist discipline.

---

72. Ibid.
73. MSS. BN franc. 7801, fo. 1.
74. MSS. BN franc. 21678, fo. 126.
75. MSS. BN franc. 21678, fo. 123.
76. Ibid., fo. 192.

None of these things obtained in France in the latter half of the sixteenth or in the seventeenth century. We have the example of Fouquet to remind us of the fate that lay in store for effective rivals of the monarchy, especially in the matter of theatrical activity. The theatrical troupes, in any case severely restricted in number, were helpless without a Maecenas, and the French Maecenas of the seventeenth century was hardly rich enough to build a theater outside the court, even if he was allowed to build.

CHAPTER FIVE

ATROPHY

WE MUST NOW turn our attention to the seventeenth-century theaters themselves. A basic bifurcation will form the framework of our study: on the one hand, those Italian influences whose nature we have described, battening upon the "illegitimate" genres, and thereby concentrated chiefly on certain theaters,[1] and on the other, at the Hôtel de Bourgogne, a vanishing mystery convention, already partly Italianized, whose further evolution towards the Italian Order is restrained throughout the century by the spread of classical doctrine in the drama. In this belief, we shall observe in our treatment of the Hôtel de Bourgogne the discipline of the theater, rather than of the author or genre.

The Early Hôtel de Bourgogne Style

It is in this playhouse that our examination must begin. For the period of the seventeenth century leading up to the first of the plays dealt with in Mahelot's *Mémoire* we must refer the reader to our previous treatment.[2] Whatever the staging of plays was, apart from the courtly Italianate performances, it was simple: probably a matter of curtains as much as anything. We may however add that for the Hôtel de Bourgogne, though not necessarily for any other theater, the form of the curved *décor simultané* (alternatively known as the *décoration multiple*), the curve of an average of five mystery *mansions* or compartments, round the sides of the stage, must have evolved gradually during the seventeenth century before the commencement of the *Mémoire* period. The simplicity of which we have spoken would seem to have been retained for the decoration of farces,[3] for such is the message of contemporary engravings (Figs. 40 and 41). In the first of our two figures, the famous players of the Hôtel de Bourgogne are depicted before a curtain flanked by two *guérites:* a favorite instrument of farce production. The whole is simple. But one of the curtains is drawn aside, revealing a more solid type of set behind. This suggests to us that for the farce at the end of the afternoon's entertainment, the entire face of the stage with its existing set might be concealed by curtains. The second and later engraving, by Bosse (1630), has no curtains, but yet retains the *guérites* and is otherwise of a

---

1. See p. 11. Cf. Martino's preface to d'Aubignac's *Pratique du théâtre*, p. xxv:

   > Il [l'opéra] tire à lui les intermèdes de musique de la tragi-comédie, les ballets de cour, toute la machinerie théâtrale; il vide à son profit le magasin d'accessoires et de décors de la tragédie et de la tragi-comédie. Et, dans le même temps, par l'effet de cette création d'un genre nouveau et de sa spécialisation le théâtre des poètes renonce de plus en plus à amuser les yeux ou à étourdir les imaginations par des spectacles surprenants.

   See also Vinaver, *Racine et la poésie tragique*, 1951, p. 79, and Schérer, *Dramaturgie classique*, p. 160.
2. See ch. 11.
3. See also Holsboer, *Mise en scène*, p. 103.

FIG. 40.—Farce décor at the Hôtel de Bourgogne.

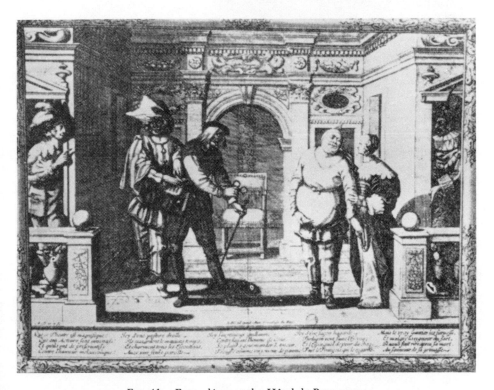

FIG. 41.—Farce décor at the Hôtel de Bourgogne.

simple enough nature in comparison with the sets for tragedy, comedy, tragicomedy, and pastoral of the Mahelot period.[4] Earlier pictures display greater simplicity (Fig. 42). The engravings of Pierre Perret are a matter of curtains only.[5] The other "scène de farce française" (Fig. 43) has a completely blank background with two *guérites*. Many of the engravings of the *Recueil Fossard*[6] use these tiny cabins, square or circular, by themselves or combined with curtains whether they depict French farces played by Agnan Sarat's troupe, or purely Italian Commedia dell'Arte (Figs. 43 and 44).

The *guérites* would be a natural item of decoration for the Confrères to possess, as they are in fact nothing but a simple and small compartment. Apart from them, we can only speculate as to the chronology of the development towards the curved *décor simultané* of the *Mémoire*. Perrault, in his *Parallèle des anciens et des modernes*, tells us:

> J'ai ouï dire à des gens âgés qu'ils avaient vu le théâtre de la Comédie de Paris de la même structure et avec les mêmes décorations que celui des danseurs de corde de la foire Saint-Germain et des charlatans du Pont Neuf; que la comédie se jouait en plein air et en plein jour . . . Les pièces qui nous restent de ce temps-là sont de la même beauté que le lieu où l'on en faisait la représentation. Ensuite on les joua à la chandelle, et le Théâtre fut orné de tapisseries qui donnaient des entrées et des issues aux Acteurs par l'endroit où elles se joignaient l'une à l'autre.[7]

Knowledge of the exact period to which Perrault's informants were alluding would no doubt have helped us, but we can safely place the reference within the first three decades of the century, in any case before the period of the *Mémoire*. There is no sign of the mystery compartment here. Perrault's "en plein jour" seems amplified by Holsboer's discovery that on the 17th May 1600, Valleran rented a large court-yard in the Rue du Cocq and built a stage there.[8] Haraszti affirms that Schelandre's *Tyr et Sidon* of 1608 demanded a *décor simultané*,[9] while Holsboer is sure that for the dramatist's rewriting of the tragedy as a tragicomedy in 1628, such a set is indispensable. It is quite certain that far more than curtains are in operation by this time. Fransen has produced an *acte notarié* of 1622 affecting the Comédiens du Prince

---

4. Cf. Fischel, "Art and the Theatre," *Burlington Magazine*, vol. LXVI, Jan.-Feb., 1935, p. 66:"When the author and stage-manager of the Théâtre de Bourgogne [sic] saw fit, the old mansions and sometimes the new style of Italian decoration were added to this standard framework [i.e., horseshoes with guérites] as shown in Bosse's engraving. In his *Mémoires* [sic], de Mahelot [sic] gives an exact account of all these possibilities." See also Kernodle, *From Art to Theatre*, footnote to p. 206, and p. 208, figs. 86 a and b.
5. Fig. 42, according to Adhémar, is not by Perret but by François Clouet. The signature Jenet equals Clouet.
6. *Recueil de plusieurs fragments des premières comédies italiennes qui ont estés représentées en France sous le règne de Henry III*, ed. Duchartre,1928.
7. 1692, vol. III, p. 191. Quoted by Despois, *Le théâtre français sous Louis XIV*, pp. 125–26, and Holsboer, *Mise en scène*, p. 105.
8. Deierkauf-Holsboer, *Vie d'Alexandre Hardy*, 1947, p. 346.
9. Quoted by Holsboer, *Mise en scène*, p. 123.

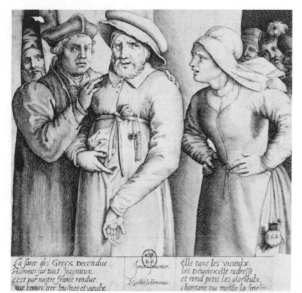

La farce des Grecz decendue.
Hommes fur tous ingenieux.
c'est par nostre france rendue.
qui ramoniirer toutnes et vueulx.

Elle taxe les vicieux.
les Devotex elle radreffe
et rend petis les glorieux.
chantant du monde la fineffe

FIG. 42.—French farce scene.

La bonne mere Guillemette.   Agnan Magifter.   Peronne.

Mon fils tu ès ja grãd, tu deurois te cognoiftre,
Et fage te monftrer pour vn iour te pouruoir,
Ne cours dõc point apres la fille de ton maiftre,
Il la faut courtifer autrement pour lauoir.

Ma mere laiffez moy, ie veux faire Peronne,
Car elle m'a donné vn fouftlet pour faueur,
Aproche mon foulas, ne t'enfuis ma mignône,
Par la mort d'vn etron tu as raui mon cœur.

Vous ne me tenez pas Magifter de village,
Puifque ie vous ay peu le dernier coup donner,
Ma foy vous eftes trop eucille pour voftre aage,
A dieu dõc Magifter, il m'en faut retourner.

FIG. 43.—French farce décor.

FIG. 44.—French-Italian farce décor.

d'Orange in which there is an obligation to "faire rétablir par lesdits comédiens ce qui serait par eux démoli audit lieu,"[10] and another, involving Valleran, of 1610, in the same tenor: "entretenir lesdits lieux de menues réparations," "rétablir" [le théâtre] "en la forme qu'il est à présent" if anything is demolished,[11] implying that alterations might be made to a theater, presumably for stage decoration, and a further deed of 1627 in which the *feinteur* of the Comédiens Royaux "sera tenu de retirer de derrière le théâtre les ramages, serges qui y auront servi."[12] Indeed Perrault himself launches a widely accepted supposition by dating the inception of tolerably painted scenery from Mairet's *Sylvie* (between 1621 and 1627),[13] although he asserts that Hardy and Garnier were played before the first type of setting he describes.

For the most conclusive proof of the weakness of Rigal's hypothesis that the troupes renting the Hôtel de Bourgogne at the beginning of the century were not preoccupied with decoration since all they had to do was to take over the décors of

10. RHLF, 1927, pp. 342–43.
11. Ibid., p. 334.
12. Ibid., p. 349. The passage is struck out in the original manuscript.
13. Bk. III, p. 194. Cf. Despois, *Le théâtre français sous Louis XIV*, p. 126. For the date, see Marsan, *La Sylvie,* édition critique, 1905.

the Confrères, we must turn to Holsboer's *Vie d'Alexandre Hardy*. A series of deeds discovered by this historian of the theater prove beyond reasonable doubt that while Valleran le Conte was playing at the Hôtel de Bourgogne in the early years of the century, fresh decorations were ordered frequently. As early as 1599 Nicolas Vattemen, Maître Peintre, undertakes to furnish to Valleran le Conte "toutes les feintes et peintures qu'il conviendra."[14] He makes the same promise later in the year, and in addition undertakes to "peindre trente aunes de toile de telle façon que bon semblera aud. Valleran qui fournira la toile."[15] In October of the same year the Maître Peintre Boniface Butays promises to furnish "toute peinture de ville, châteaux, rochers, feintes, bois, bocages, gazons, artifices et généralement toutes autres choses quelconques qui sera besoin et nécessaire faire et avoir."[16] The normal expression for décors is "feintes et décors," and it is quite obvious from the documents that the main constituent of these is canvas: there is constant reference to "toile." It is also clear that this painted canvas was regarded to some extent as stock, not *necessarily* to be renewed, which is not surprising in view of the recurrent elements of décor which characterize the plays of the time. These stocks sometimes changed hands as between actors even when ready painted. Thus Valleran, in 1606, cedes to Estienne de Rufin, amongst other things, "onze pièces de toile peintes servant à théâtre."[17] In the "acte d'association de la troupe de Mathieu de Lefebvre," made at a time when financial difficulties had caused Valleran to cease his productions at the Hôtel de Bourgogne,[18] we find the new troupe agreeing to share profits after the deduction of certain expenses amongst which are "peintures si aucunes en convient faire."

Now, Perrault's suggestion that the turn of the century settings were rudimentary may probably be dismissed, as we may dismiss any idea that they were summarily or rudimentarily painted. C. M. Fogarty, in an unpublished master's thesis, has demonstrated this convincingly, her conclusions being as follows:

> The period 1599–1612, in which Butay and Gouin were present both separately and together, at the Hôtel de Bourgogne is probably crucial to our understanding of the décor simultané convention as illustrated by Mahelot in his *Mémoire*. Both men fulfilled a number of rôles, those of actor, decorator, and Confrère de la Passion, at some time during this period, and it may be concluded, due to the varied perspectives which they acquired in these rôles, that they both became general men of the theatre. This experience in itself differentiates the period markedly from the brief duration of Vattemen's and du Val's work at the Hôtel de Bourgogne, since neither of these men, as far as we know, had any reserves on which to draw except their practice as painters. There was, however, a certain amount of overlapping in the periods of work of these painters and decorators . . . Certainly, any elements of the décor simultané convention which had been supported and reinforced as decorating techniques by Butay in 1599, could have been perpetuated beyond 1612 and Butay's last recorded presence at the Hôtel.

14. Appendix 10.
15. Appendix 11.
16. Appendix 12.
17. Appendix 19.
18. Appendix 22.

Boniface Butay belonged to a family of landscape painters, which becomes re-markable when we examine the wording of the agreement between him and Valleran le Conte of 5th October, 1599. He was evidently a man of some standing since in 1619 he was a member of the Academy of Saint Luke, the aims of which were to verse artists in the theoretical and historical background of art and affiliated subjects.

The high level of technical mastery of the consciously renewed convention, evident during the third and fourth decades of the seventeenth century can be partly explained by the nature of the association between Boniface Butay, Sébastien Gouin and the Hôtel de Bourgogne. They had leased the Hôtel, hired the Hôtel, acted in the Hôtel and painted décor for the Hôtel stage. There can be little doubt that their varied practical experience contributed to the sophisticated realisation of what has been viewed as the rudimentary convention. Their situation at the turn of the century made them ideally placed to perpetuate the convention; they were craftsmen and had the craftsman's conscience of the possibilities offered by their medium, modified by the practical considerations which their acting experience brought into focus.[19]

Over the last two decades, the dimensions of the theater have been the subject of renewed scrutiny. Roy, the late David Illingworth, Villiers, Wiley, and Barlow have applied themselves to the matter.[20] A new impetus to investigation had been provided by Mme. Deierkauf-Holsboer who, in 1960, drew renewed attention to the *Devis et marché de divers travaux à exécuter au théâtre de l'Hôtel de Bourgogne* (17th April, 1647).[21]

As we are immediately concerned with the stage itself, suffice it to say for the moment that Roy's findings for the shape and dimension of the stage prior to 1647 have not been seriously disputed, Deierkauf-Holsboer's width of 18 meters 20 (including walls) being invalidated. (Fig. 45). From an overall width of seven toises (i.e. 42 *pieds*, nearly 45 current English feet) Roy proceeds as follows:

Les dimensions du plateau utilisable pour le décorateur et les acteurs étaient né-cessairement plus restreintes [than the total width available]. Il faudrait déduire l'espace occupé des deux côtés par les coulisses, espace égal sans doute à la profondeur des loges de côté. Il resterait donc une ouverture de scène large de cinq toises (9.72 meters), moins peut-être, pour le décorateur, la largeur de deux petits chassis qu'il a dû placer oblique-

19. M.A. in French Theatre Studies, University of Lancaster, 1977: *Boniface Butays and the Hôtel de Bourgogne*. One must add that Védier, *Dramaturgie néo-classique*, pp. 72-73, takes Deierkauf-Holsboer's proof of the conscious renewal of the décor as de-noting the possibility that a *décor unique* as opposed to a *décor multiple* was in occasional use at the time.

20. D. H. Roy, "La scène de l'Hôtel de Bourgogne," RHT, 3, 1962, pp. 227-35. D. V. Illingworth, "Documents inédits et nouvelles précisions sur le Théâtre de l'Hôtel de Bourgogne," RHT, 2, 1970, pp. 125-32, and "L'Hôtel de Bourgogne: une salle de théâtre 'à l'italienne' à Paris en 1647 ?" RHT, 1, 1971, pp. 40-48. André Villiers, "L'ouverture de la scène à l'Hôtel de Bourgogne," RHT, 2, 1970, pp. 133-41, W. L. Wiley, *The Early Public Theatre in France*, 1960, and in particular *The Hôtel de Bourgogne: Another Look at France's First Public Theatre, Studies in Philology*, Vol. LXX, Dec. 1973, No. 5. Graham Barlow, "The Hôtel de Bourgogne according to Sir James Thornhill," TRI, I, 2, 1976.

21. *L'Histoire de la mise en scène dans le théâtre français à Paris de 1600 à 1673*, Paris, 1960, pp. 14-15. First published by Lemoine, *La première du Cid*, Paris, 1936.

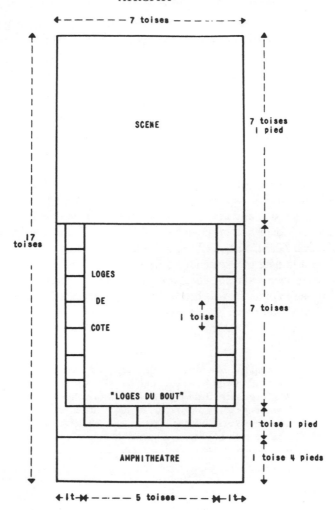

FIG. 45.—Roy's Hôtel de Bourgogne.

ment sur la scène, à l'avant des premiers compartiments latéraux, pour masquer les coulisses.[22]

The working depth of the stage would be 5 toises 3 pieds, less space behind the backdrop or upstage center compartment for a passageway and actors' *loges*. Consideration of the upper stage (*petit théâtre, théâtre supérieur, théâtre de Jupiter*), we will leave till later.

22. Lawrenson, Roy, and Southern, "Le *Mémoire* de Mahelot et l'*Agarite* de Durval," *Le lieu théâtral à la Renaissance*, Paris, 1964, p. 367.

The Hôtel de Bourgogne stage was, then, neither wide nor deep. The decoration at the back of the stage was usually (although not always) painted on a perspective backcloth.

With the aid of the backcloth, the different compartments could represent any of the motifs required for tragedy, comedy, tragicomedy, and pastoral: as we have noted, there seems to have been a certain use of "stock in hand": columned palaces, statues, temples, crossroads, arches, pyramids, inns, churchs, castles, drawbridges, fortresses, towers, prisons, and houses[23] are recurrent features in tragedy and comedy, while the pastoral shows us woods, forests, and copses, springs, fountains, rocks, sheepfolds, temples, and the mouths of caverns.[24]

It now seems sure that the simplicity of these décors has been exaggerated.[25] Mahelot's drawings are exact and detailed, nor do they show any sign of the deliberate exaggeration and search for magnificence which the professional engravers brought to their depiction of theater sets.[26] To instance the well-known passage from Rotrou's *Saint Genest,* as does Despois, who believes that "il ne s'agissait que de barbouiller à la hâte quelques aunes de toile"[27] is neither here nor there since in this the scene painter is not confessing to slapdash methods, but putting Genest right as to the manner in which to paint theater sets so that they look well from a distance; broad, generous lines are necessary:

Le décorateur

Le temps nous a manqué plus que l'industrie;
Joint qu'on voit mieux de loin ces raccourcissements,
Ces corps sortant du plan de ces renfondrements,
L'approche à ses dessins ôte leurs perspectives,
En confond les faux jours, rend leurs couleurs moins vives,
Et, comme à la nature, est nuisible à notre art,
A qui l'éloignement semble apporter du fard . . . [28]

We can however agree with Rigal that those palaces which only occupied one compartment must have seemed very small, though the ones which used up three would seem reasonable enough, the more difficult (and we might add, non-architectural) items being far less impressive: camps, seas, and mountains for example.[29] This is most evident from the sketches themselves. The *Mémoire,* whose illustrations

---

23. Lancaster, *History*, Pt. I, vol. ii, pp. 717 et seq. Holsboer, *Mise en scène*, p. 112.
24. Cf. Marsan, *La pastorale dramàtique*, p. 207.
25. E.g. Despois, *Le théâtre français sous Louis XIV*, p. 131.
26. For the difficulties inherent in the use of these iconographical sources, see Holsboer, *Mise en scène*, pp. 115–16.
27. Far more than "quelques aunes de toile" were involved in the average set. For this we have the evidence of Holsboer's *Vie d'Alexandre Hardy* and Scarron, *Le roman comique*, Pt. I, ch. 1: "La charrette était pleine de coffres, de malles et de gros paquets de toiles peintes, qui faisaient comme une pyramide."
28. Act II, scene i.

FIG. 46.—*L'Heureuse Constance*, Rotrou.

are very like the mystery set, abounds in details which might have been taken from a "livre de conduite."

Definition of Place

The most important characteristic of these decorations is that they symbolize rather than represent place, being in this not far removed from the Elizabethan placard announcement of place, or from our own view of the function of the *periaktoi* in the Greek theater. The actor, having positioned himself either in or in front of a given item of décor, moved downstage, when (we have assumed), by convention, the whole stage would become that place, as it did in the mystery.[30] The absent feature, as compared with the mystery, is the procession across the stage, although we suspect that this may not have vanished altogether. For instance, in Rotrou's *Heureuse constance* (Fig. 46) during the first scene, the King is passing from English stage right to English stage left, that is from the village to his capital, Buda. This goes on during the second scene, all halts indicating that he is a little farther on his journey. At some point in his progress, and still during the second scene, Rosélie comes out of the village "passant derrière": an expression that we take to mean following the King to some extent, that is coming after, rather than actually passing the King and his suite upstage and moving left. This latter movement would be

29. *Théâtre français*, p. 252.
30. Cf. Holsboer, *Mise en scène*, p. 109, and Rigal, *Théâtre français*, pp. 263–64.

meaningless, as Rosélie flees back to the village at the end of the scene. The particularly short scenes of Gombauld's *Amaranthe* (Fig. 47) also practically form a procession across the stage. Schérer has neatly categorized this type of movement, in its connection with change of place, by the use of the modern cinematographic concept, the *travelling*.[31] Attention is concentrated on the actor or actors while they are actually moving from one place to another, so that any disparity between the fictional and physical distance from one place to another is mitigated. In the words of Rigal "ce n'était pas le décor lui-même qui changeait, c'était l'action qui changeait de décor."[32]

In Auvray's *Madonte* (Fig. 48) the first two scenes of the play are clearly in the palace, described by Mahelot as "un palais bas, mais qui soit riche."[33] The known exiguity of such pieces of scenery together with the indication "bas" make it fairly sure that the palace was not meant to be entered. Thus Madonte, one supposes, stations herself for a moment in front of the palace before taking the stage to deliver her monologue.[34]

Apart from the convention already defined and taken over from the mystery (namely that the audience would accept the whole stage as being the place immediately defined), what was the nature of that place in relation to the audience? This is perhaps to be sought in comparison with the past and the future of stage decoration and convention at that time. The mystery play was not acted, at its greatest moments, in an enclosed building. There was, in fact, a living, socially significant place, as opposed to a mere closed hall, in which it took place: usually the market square. We surmise that when the initial definition of place had been carried out, by the positioning of the actors, the pictorial illustration of place was present to the mind of the public far less than it was later, and that some consciousness of "the play on the cathedral steps" or later "the play in the market place" remained with the spectator, just as we believe it to have done in the case of the theater of Dionysos. This we may contrast with the modern stage convention, where the function of the detailed stage setting throughout a scene is to reiterate continually the theme of "place."

In this, the "backward-looking" aspect of the representation of place in the *décor simultané*, it seems likely that some such psychological process subsisted, though to a far lesser extent, in view of the less significant actual physical place of the theater house. The spectator, aided by this stage movement of definition, and by the textual elaboration of place, would have either to cease worrying about this latter, or go home with his head full of considerations such as went into Scudéry's *Observations*,

---

31. *Dramaturgie classique*, pp. 179–80.
32. *Théâtre français*, p. 276. Konigson (q.v.) has cast serious doubts on any attempt to read the Valenciennes staging as a progression along the platform. But, for the plays of the *Mémoire*, see John Golder, "L'Hypocondriaque de Rotrou: un essai de reconstitution d'une des premières mises en scène à l'Hôtel de Bourgogne," RHT, 1979, 3, p. 269.
33. Lancaster, *Mémoire*, p. 70.
34. Act I, scene i.

FIG. 47.—*Amaranthe*, Gombauld.

FIG. 48.—*Madonte*, Auvray.

for he had no unified set throughout the scene to remind him constantly of place: he had in fact before him three or four contradictory compartments emphasizing its diversity.

This presumed attitude of the audience is matched by light-hearted notions concerning place on the part of the dramatic poet. Schérer's evidence that generally speaking the author of the time did not "see" his stage is very full.[35] Nevertheless, a few reservations must be made. Firstly, the incidence of stage direction is very varied amongst the preclassical authors: Scudéry, to quote at random, uses very few, Claveret and Auvray quite a lot; secondly, Hardy, being the paid dramatist of a single troupe, and possibly having even mounted the boards himself in the capacity of actor,[36] could legitimately be sparing of direction, since he could count on being present at rehearsal; and thirdly, we now know that the *décor simultané* was a consciously renewed convention, not a momentary utilization of old stock. However, without accompanying Schérer to the extent of saying that the preclassical drama was primarily narrative, we can perhaps agree that the evidence of the plays themselves suggests the extent to which the authors imagined that the convention for which they were writing could cover any sweep of space.

Our earlier experiments in practical theater scholarship applied to the problem of place and the Mahelot settings, not being particularly audience based, tended to confirm the hypothesis of audience puzzlement. The first of these experiments was an attempted reconstitution of Durval's *Agarite* (Fig. 49 and see n. 22). "Le système marche à un certain point," we averred, "mais il marche en grinçant, il marche à tâtons." And later: ". . . French staging at one of its most neuralgic moments; a convention built to work on a large outdoor platform (or amphitheater), was imprisoned and was about to explode, and that imprisonment formed one shockwave in the explosion which we call *la querelle du Cid*"[37] (Figs. 50a, 50b, 51a and 51b).

Author, and subsequently spectator, imagined the physical course of an action, and upon the stage the compartments were the sporadic (not always complete) milestones of the progress of that action.

Our present suspicion is however that the audience was not terribly preoccupied with the definition of place. We wonder if our concern with these matters was not a form of backward extrapolation from the *querelle du Cid* itself and Scudéry's remarks about place in the *Observations*. T. J. Reiss has more recently treated the author's imaginative sweep of vision and the apparently random nature of (for example) Hardy's plays[38], which he regards as not arising out of careless haste (in spite of

35. *Dramaturgie classique*, pp. 156 et seq.
36. Deierkauf-Holsboer, *La vie d'Alexandre Hardy*, p. 333.
37. Op. cit. p. 375, and "The Contemporary Staging of Théophile's *Pyrame et Thisbé*," in *Modern Miscellany Presented to Eugène Vinaver*, Manchester, 1969, p. 178. Jòhn Golder (see n. 32) returns usefully to this examination by reconstruction, in his monograph on Rotrou's *Hypocondriaque*.
38. T. J. Reiss, *Toward Dramatic Illusion: Theatrical Technique and Meaning from Hardy to Horace*, New Haven and London, 1971.

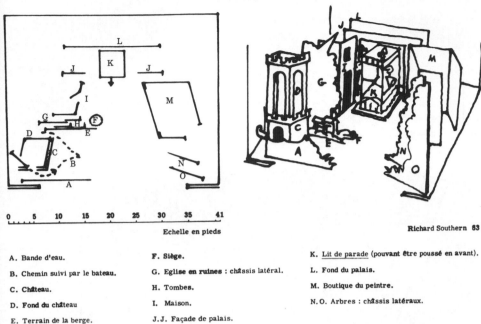

A. Bande d'eau.

B. Chemin suivi par le bateau.

C. Château.

D. Fond du château

E. Terrain de la berge.

F. Siège.

G. Eglise en ruines : châssis latéral.

H. Tombes.

I. Maison.

J.J. Façade de palais.

K. Lit de parade (pouvant être poussé en avant).

L. Fond du palais.

M. Boutique du peintre.

N.O. Arbres : châssis latéraux.

FIG. 49.—Reconstruction of Durval's *Agarite* by Richard Southern.

Hardy's enormous output), but rather out of an instinctive feeling for the needs of the spectator. For him, Hardy's texts are rhetoric before they are narrative. Multiple action, multiple movement, multiple setting correspond to the non-illusionistic expectations of the spectator. The stylized language is supported by the sets at the disposal of the authors. The compartments are luxurious, but *not* illusionistic. At times, we are told, the set appears to provoke the language—he instances Mairet's *Sylvie* and Auvray's *Madonte,* and he could equally well have instanced Théophile's *Pyrame.*[39]

As regards the "finish" of the compartments, we may now be satisfied indeed that this was of a highly competent nature, theatrically speaking. It is certainly not a question of "barbouiller à la hâte quelques aunes de toile."[40] Védier, in fact, goes further, and is one of the first theater historians, so far as we know, to point out the reconciliation, in painting, of the *tableau multiple* with the new practices of perspective:

39. We assume, naturally, that Reiss is referring to the set and poetic reference to it during actual performance—that Mahelot had in short, *set* the play to the best of his ability, otherwise we are in the absurd supposition that in the processes which bring the play into performance the designing of the set preceded the composition of the piece.

40. See p. 116.

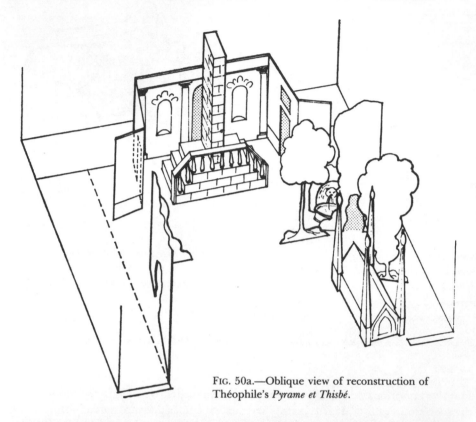

FIG. 50a.—Oblique view of reconstruction of Théophile's *Pyrame et Thisbé*.

FIG. 50b.—Théophile's *Pyrame et Thisbé*. Night scene.

FIG. 51a.—Mahelot's sketch for Théophile's *Pyrame et Thisbé*.

FIG. 51b.—Théophile's *Pyrame et Thisbé*.

Quant au décor de Mahelot, loin de pouvoir s'expliquer, comme on l'a cru, seulement par la persistance à l'Hôtel du décor simultané des mystères, tant bien que mal accommodé aux règles de la perspective, il faut bien plutôt y voir l'oeuvre originale de décorateurs qui trouvaient, dans les traditions de l'art plastique de leur temps, les éléments et le principe même de leurs compositions. La gravure et l'illustration, et la peinture de chevalet elle-même, avaient depuis longtemps accoutumé les yeux à se satisfaire d'un compromis entre l'ancienne et la nouvelle esthétique, par lequel la représentation multiple se conciliait avec le réalisme de la représentation de l'espace, et ne détruisait pas l'illusion.[41]

Miss Fogarty's findings complement such a view. This, and Reiss's analysis, constitute a refreshing development, for they drag the problems out of the mechanics of the conventional statement of place by exit and entrance into the realms of theatrical aesthetics. It is clear that all has not yet been said about the modified *décor simultané* at the Hôtel. In a reconstituted performance of Act IV of Théophile's *Pyrame*[42] (See Figs. 50b and 51b) the candle-lit stage conferred a marked blurring of outline upon individual items of the multiple set. The autonomy of the compartment was diminished. To the eye accustomed to modern stage lighting there was a pronounced effect of mystery and magic. Elements of the audience, faced with the question as to whether they had, at any point during the action, been puzzled as to the supposed locality of the actor, expressed uniform puzzlement at the question itself. If a modern audience, with more than two centuries of illusionistic décors behind it could react thus, how much less "puzzled" must have been the early seventeenth-century spectator?

A recent thesis by Lorelei F. Eckey[43] adds to the wave of rethinking. She has somewhat misinterpreted our statement that the author did not "see" his stage very well. By this, naturally, we did not intend the reader to infer that the writer had never heard of the Hôtel de Bourgogne or was ignorant of the shape, size, or convention of its stage, which would be absurd. Dr. Eckey does however seem to us to imply some form of close liaison between poet (who, it may be added, would be conscious of writing a subspecies of poetry: *le poème dramatique*) and the Hôtel designer, whereas in fact it is a fair assumption the writer would not know if his play was to be acted at all. In an heroic attempt to seek maximum corroboration of play texts by the Mahelot sets, Dr. Eckey alludes repeatedly to the use of the *tapisserie,* and the interesting possibility that one item could represent more than one place at different times in the play, without change, and, more startling, to heavy scene shifting without a front stage curtain. Not the least startling of her hypotheses is the suggestion that the compartments may not have been compartments at all, in the neo-medieval sense. This latter theory, and the idea of heavy scene shifting,

41. Op. cit., p. 189.
42. Crowther and Shaw, M.A. in French Theatre Studies, University of Lancaster, 1972.
43. Lorelei F. Guidry Eckey. *The Scenic Environment at the Hôtel de Bourgogne determined from analyses of twelve plays performed at the Hôtel between 1628 and 1634*, University Microfilms, Ann Arbor, Mich., 1972.

FIG. 52.—*Lisandre et Caliste*, Du Ryer.

seems to us to display a weakness of which she accuses others—the application of modern staging attitudes where they do not apply.

One feature of the *décor simultané* has received considerable attention; this is the use of a curtain placed in front of a compartment and representing some other scene, which could be drawn aside or dropped at an appropriate moment to reveal the set behind. In the words of d'Aubignac, the author "résout de cacher sous un rideau tout ce qui l'incommodera." That which hinders him is of course the excess of places in his play, over available compartments. Rigal has summarized previous false notions on the use of the *tapisserie* in the sixteenth century: those of Morice, who believes that three curtains sufficed for the whole play, of Sainte-Beuve who claims that no one cared at all about the representation or change of place, of Lemazurier who thinks that a curtain was raised to reveal change, and of Jarry who thought it was done by machines created for *changements à vue d'oeil.*[44] Bapst, Rigal, Cohen, Lancaster, and Prunières all agree that there must have been unconcealed change. The easiest way to operate this would be by curtain, and this is what we find later in Mahelot.[45]

One of the best known examples is the direction for *Lisandre et Caliste* (Fig. 52). Opposite a butcher's shop, there is a barred window, and according to Mahelot (and the text) "il faut que cela soit caché durant le premier Acte et l'on ne fait

44. Quoted by Rigal, *Théâtre français*, p. 243.
45. See Védier *passim* on the whole subject of curtains.

FIG. 53.—*Les Travaux d'Ulysse*, Durval.

paraître cela qu'au Second Acte et se referme au Même Acte. La fermeture sert de palais."[46] Not only is the *toile peinte* removed during the representation as Holsboer suggests, but it is replaced later.[47]

Similarly, in Durval's *Travaux d'Ulysse* (Fig. 53), Mahelot's comment runs thus: "Une mer; auprès, le fleuve du Styx où Caron paraît dans sa barque . . . le tout se cache et ouvre."[48] In this play, the Hell is hidden until required. Numerous

46. *Mémoire*, p. 68.

47. *Mise en scène*, p. 112. Schérer's interpretation of the Mahelot direction is at fault:

> Dans *Lisandre et Caliste* de du Ryer, le fond du décor représente une prison et l'étal d'un boucher. Mais "il faut que cela soit caché durant le premier acte, et l'on ne fait paraître cela qu'au second acte et se referme au même acte: la fermeture sert de palais." C'est donc qu'un palais est peint sur la tapisserie et constitue le décor de la plus grande partie de la pièce; mais quand l'action, à l'acte II, se transporte dans la prison et dans la boucherie, le palais fait place, pour un temps, à ces lieux nouveaux.

(*Dramaturgie classique*, p. 176).

Now, the *fond du décor* is neither the prison nor the butcher's shop, but the Petit Châtelet de la rue Saint Jacques. This is clear from Mahelot's commentary, which also tells us (and shows us) that the prison and shop window are opposite one another, an impossible disposition according to Schérer's interpretation. The palace does not replace for a while the two places, but only the prison. The text of the play corroborates this: Lisandre, in Act II, scene iii, uses the first-story window of the shop to talk to Caliste, who is opposite.

48. *Mémoire*, p. 83.

Fig. 54.—*Arétaphile*, Du Ryer.

examples have been listed by Schérer,[49] such as Du Ryer's *Arétaphile*, (Fig. 54) in which a tapestry representing one palace hides another, Mairet's *Sylvanire*, where the tomb is "caché de toile de pastorale," the same author's *Sylvie*, (Fig. 55) in which the enchanted palace and the altar only appear in Act V, as do the tomb and altar in his *Chriséide et Arimand*. The example of Corneille's *Galerie du Palais* is perhaps better known, where "on tire un rideau et l'on voit le libraire, la lingère, et le mercier chacun dans sa boutique."[50] The extreme example is the much quoted report on the *Prince déguisé* of Scudéry (1634-5): "Le superbe appareil de la scène, la face du théâtre qui change cinq ou six fois entièrement à la représentation de ce poème. . . ."

These methods of change are simple devices for extending the number of places. As Schérer points out, there is just as little real contiguity between the revealed place and the place that was hiding it, as there is between any other two items of décor. Simple extension is the object.

The change of place in this manner implies no extension backwards, although we shall meet with this later, to some extent, at the Hôtel de Bourgogne. The new place revealed is held to have the same frontage as the previous one, it occupies the stage space of the previous item. It is a change *in situ*.

49. *Dramaturgie classique*, p. 176.
50. Act I, scene iv.

FIG. 55.—*Sylvie*, Mairet.

In his search for a means of increasing the places, the stage decorator had taken over from the mystery what was in fact a form of *décor successif*. Imagining each item of decoration as a whole stage, the use of the curtain in this way would be tantamount to its use in the modern playhouse for the purpose of concealing change on the whole stage, but with this difference that the curtain itself represented a place, and had an acting area in front of it, unlike the modern proscenium arch curtain. This important difference has not been sufficiently stressed, for it places this device firmly amongst the old, dying features of the *décor simultané,* so that there seems little likelihood that it may be regarded as the father of the modern curtain scene-change. We should bear in mind how much the development of the proscenium arch curtain is conditioned by the existence of the proscenium arch which was lacking from the Hôtel de Bourgogne at this period. The position is once more analogous to that of the Greek *skené.* A passage from La Mesnardière's *Art poétique* falls into significant context here, for we see that he too was making the same comparison:

> Si l'aventure s'est passée moitié dans le palais d'un roi en plusieurs appartements, et moitié hors de la maison en beaucoup d'endroits différents il faut que le grand du théâtre, le *proskenion* des Grecs, je veux dire cette largeur qui limite le parterre serve pour tous les dehors où ces choses ont été faites et que les renfondrements soient divisés en plusieurs chambres par les divers frontispices, poteaux, colonnes, ou arcades.[51]

---

51. Quoted by Rigal, *Théâtre français*, p. 245. The writer also notes that the Middle Ages attributed to the Ancients the simultaneous system of staging. Also Holsboer, *Mise en scène*, p. 84.

The complete use of the full curtain to conceal scenic change implies total irruption through a more or less solid façade which, inherited from the mystery platform, was present in the sets of the *Mémoire*. And this was to be accomplished, not by any minor eccentricity of simultaneous staging but by the flood tide of baroque in the "illegitimate" genres, besides having been prepared, technically, in the use of the curtain in the French *ballet de cour,* and in *Mirame* in 1641. To express the concept in different terms, the compartment of the *décor simultané* could define the stage and in the body of the play could by defining, change it. It could also, in the odd instances where it was big enough, both be the place and define an extension of itself which was the stage. The actor in moving from a position in front of the compartment to "take the stage" was demonstrating the simultaneity of place "whence" and place "where" in this convention. The use of the proscenium arch and proscenium arch curtain will not only multiply indefinitely the possibilities of place "where" but will carry this through the solid back wall, gravely limiting the possibilities of place "whence," and thereby the intensity of the dramatic entrance.

THE ITALIAN ORDER AT THE HÔTEL DE BOURGOGNE

Such was the rôle of the French past in the Mahelot period of the preclassical theater at the Hôtel de Bourgogne. What was the importance of its more recent components? And what their future in this particular channel of the bifurcation we are considering? Vitruvius, perspective, Serlio and the three scenes, marvel and metamorphosis are all at hand and have not escaped the attention of previous writers on the subject. We shall see that some of these features at least, belonging to the native past of the French theater, pass over to the baroque tradition. The *théâtre de Jupiter,* or *théâtre supérieur,* will be one instance. For Rigal, the Mahelot set is little more than a direct inheritance from the Middle Ages, and indeed all that it owes to the mystery decoration has been fully brought out by him. Lanson has pointed out that the early decoration of this theater bears some trace of Vitruvian influence as interpreted by Serlio, an idea which is repeated by Lancaster and Holsboer.

Serlio's satyric scene is composed entirely of trees and cottages, quite undistinguished for anything that might be described as scenic purpose, as opposed to the comic and tragic scenes which are more clearly theatrical. The pastoral sets of the *Mémoire* are also, by comparison with the other sets, undifferentiated, although not to the same extent as Serlio's scene. The phrase "en pastorale" is meant to cover the whole stage.[52]

If however we examine those sets which most resemble Serlio, and are most purely pastoral, we find that the scene painter, as elsewhere in his document, is thinking in terms of separate items of decoration: rocks, caves, fountains, trees, woods, mountains, are separate things to be juggled with and re-arranged (Figs.

---

52. Du Ryer, *Amarillis*: "en pastorale"; Gombauld, *Amaranthe*: "il faut que le théâtre soit tout en pastorale . . ."; Hardy, *La folie de Turlupin*: "il faut que le théâtre soit en pastorale," and "en pastorale à la discrétion du feinteur" in the case of *Les trois semblables*.

Fig. 56.—*Amarillis*, Du Ryer.

56 to 60). There is not one set which could even remotely be conjectured to be a direct imitation of Serlio.

If in turn we examine those plays which are defined as comedies by their authors, and which bear some resemblance to Serlio's comic scene, we find quite noticeably that features from the pastoral and the tragi-comedy, as dictated by the exigencies of the dramatic text, are inextricably mixed in with details which might have belonged to the comic setting. In the case of Rotrou's *Ménechmes* (Fig. 61), the stage direction, unusually short and general, has a decided Serlian ring: "Il faut le théâtre en rues et maisons." But the sketch itself shows on the whole houses of a more ambitious, less homely type than those of the comic scene, and certainly of a type which is to be found in the tragi-comedies of the *Mémoire*.

Célimène, a comedy by Rotrou is closer to the pastoral than to the comic in its setting, demanding a fountain "en perspective" between two houses, balustrades, branches, and verdure.[53] Another Rotrou comedy, the *Heureuse constance* (see Fig. 46), has a similar set. The nearest approach in the *Mémoire* to the Serlian comic scene, Du Ryer's *Lisandre et Caliste* (see Fig. 52), is again a tragi-comedy. Claveret's *Angélie ou l'esprit fort* is pastoral in setting: "Au milieu du théâtre, il faut faire paraître forme de fontaine dans un palais. Le théâtre tout en bois et forêt de haute futaie, des routes et allées de verdure qu'on traverse et qui font presque le sujet de la pièce. . ."[54] So is Du Ryer's *Vendanges de Suresnes* (Fig. 62) and Rotrou's *Filandre,*

53. *Mémoire*, p. 92.
54. Ibid., p. 93.

FIG. 57.—*Clorise*, Baro.

FIG. 58.—*La folie de Turlupin*, Hardy.

Fig. 59.—*Astrée et Céladon*, Rayssiguier.

Fig. 60.—*Les Trois Semblables*.

FIG. 61.—*Les Ménechmes*, Rotrou.

although in the case of the last two the bucolic place is not vague but defined (Suresnes and the Seine). On the other hand practically all the stage motifs of Rotrou's *Bague de l'oubli* (Fig. 63) could belong to the Serlian tragic scene or to a pastoral setting: a palace in the form of a rotunda, with balustrades; a grotto, fountains, and garden.[55] His *Diane* is perhaps to the required formula: "Le théâtre doit être en perspective de frise, pilastre et balustres par haut et par bas, forme de portiques de l'invention du feinteur, rue et maisons fort libres d'où l'on puisse entrer et sortir aisément."[56]

Those plays which are called tragedies as opposed to tragicomedies support our conclusion. There is no evidence of any rigid adherence to the components of the tragic scene as set down by Vitruvius. The only illustrated tragedy of the *Mémoire* is Théophile de Viau's *Pirame et Thisbé,* (see Figs. 50b and 51b). It has nothing to distinguish it by genre: "Il faut, au milieu du théâtre, un mur de marbre et pierre fermé; des balustres; il faut aussi de chaque côté deux ou trois marches pour monter. A un des côtés du théâtre, un mûrier, un tombeau entouré de pyramides . . . Un antre d'où sort un lion du côté de la fontaine, et un autre antre à l'autre bout du théâtre où il rentre."[57] The wall is to be seen, endwise to the spectator, upstage center. This unusual arrangement occasioned d'Aubignac's outcry "combien fut ridicule dans la *Thisbé* de Théophile, un mur avancé sur le Théâtre, au travers duquel elle et Pyrame se parlaient et qui disparaissait quand ils se retiraient afin

55. Ibid., p. 69.
56. Ibid., p. 98.
57. Ibid., p. 71.

FIG. 62.—*Vendanges de Suresnes*, Du Ryer.

que les autres Acteurs se pussent voir . . ."[58] We can interpret this in at least four ways:

1. The wall was a permanent onstage feature, and by "disparaissait" d'Aubignac means "was held to be not there."
2. He means "disparaissait" literally, which would in turn mean that the upstage *ferme* or *toile* opened and the wall trundled downstage like the "lit de parade" in *Agarite* (see p. 120).
3. It was covered by a *tapisserie* when not in use, for that is one of the possible meanings of *fermé*. But the curtain would be a long way downstage.
4. Given the cramped space backstage, it was hoisted up and backward through the opening and closing curtain at the height of the *théâtre supérieur*.[59]

With Rotrou's tragedy *Hercule mourant,* however, which belongs to a somewhat later period (since it was staged at the beginning of 1634,[60] as against *Pirame et Thisbé* written between 1621 and 1624), a change has taken place: there is a determination to have the stage "superbe" (though this word is used throughout the *Mémoire*) and a conscious search for antiquity and dignity:

58. *Pratique*, Bk. II, p. 104.
59. Lawrenson, *The Contemporary Staging of Théophile's "Pyrame et Thisbé,"* in *Modern Miscellany*, 1969, pp. 170–71. An elaboration of the fourth possibility is to be found in Fogarty and Lawrenson, "The Lessons of the Reconstituted Performance," *Theatre Survey XXII*, 1981.

FIG. 63.—*La Bague de l'Oubli*, Rotrou.

Le théâtre doit être superbe. A un des côtés, il faut le temple de Jupiter, bâti à l'antique et enfermé d'arcades autour de l'autel; et que l'on puisse tourner autour de l'autel. Dessus l'autel, une cassolette et autres ornements. Il faut faire le piédestal rond comme l'antique, où est posé Jupiter. Sur l'autel carré, quatre petites pyramides garnies de leurs petits vases où sont des flammes de feu en peinture. Le temple doit être caché. De l'autre côté du théâtre doit avoir une montagne où l'on monte devant le peuple et descendre par derrière. Ladite montagne doit être en bois de haute futaie, et, dessous la montagne, doit avoir une chambre funèbre remplie de larmes, le tombeau d'Hercule superbe. Trois pyramides, deux vases où sortent deux flammes de feu en peinture, tous les travaux d'Hercule y doivent paraître, ledit tombeau doit être caché. Plus, au milieu du théâtre, doit avoir une salle à jour, bien parée de balustres et plaques d'argent et autres ornements de peinture. Au cinquième acte, un tonnerre, et après le ciel s'ouvre et Hercule descend du ciel en terrre, dans une nue . . . une prison proche du tombeau.[61]

Temple, altar, pedestal ''à l'antique,'' pyramids (like the other pyramids of the *Mémoire* where these are illustrated, they are doubtless in the form of the obelisk, as in Serlio and in the motifs of the Royal Entry), all these are the Vitruvian tragic scene as embellished by the Renaissance. But there is more in this set; there is the beginning of baroque machinery and the recurrence of pastoral items. Not even now are we in the presence of the pure tragic scene, and as we have noted, all these tragic ''items'' are to be found illustrating plays which are not tragedies. Lancaster observes that although tragedy was not in vogue at the Hôtel de Bourgogne at the

60. *Mémoire*, p. 102.
61. Ibid., pp. 102–03.

time Mahelot compiled this document, palaces with columns and conventionalized statues frequently appear in his drawings.[62]

This is most evident, but we are compelled to make the reservation that the incidence of motifs from the Renaissance in general and from Serlio in particular is hardly, if at all, influenced by considerations of genre. These interpenetrate in the stage set just as they do in the dramatic text. There is not the slightest sign of any slavish conformity to the teaching of Serlio: it is the play that is set, not some preconceived scene; the setting is only limited by the extent of the Hôtel de Bourgogne storeroom.

Védier adduces convincing arguments for the long coexistence, both in stage decoration and the pictorial arts, of the simultaneous setting or picture, and the unifying hand of perspective. He establishes that one cannot automatically concede that the ideal of the French stage designer moves toward a Serlian unity.[63]

Perspective

Holsboer notes that the perspective in the sets of Mahelot's period is best seen in the backcloth.[64] It should not however be concluded that the upstage decoration (normally called "le milieu du théâtre" in this document, where "milieu" does not usually mean anything in terms of stage depth) was always a backcloth. There are several notices which suggest the contrary, for example those of Rotrou's *Diane,* and Passar's *Célénie,* [65] which reads "Il faut au milieu du théâtre, un palais assez beau, forme de trois portiques . . . Derrière les trois portails, environ trois pieds faire paraître une frise où sont les armes du Roi." The only clear perspective backcloths in this portion of the *Mémoire* are Hardy's *Pandoste (deuxième journée)*[66] (where the street of houses depicted flees more sharply than the constructed compartments and is not mentioned as an item in the written directions), Hardy's *Cintie* (Fig. 64),[67] where the same conditions obtain, and his *Cornélie* (Fig. 65),[68] where the backcloth in perspective continues that of the compartments downstage, with the same vanishing point. Those *mansions* where the scene is not bosky and pastoral are constructed in perspective, which naturally demands the largest pair of items downstage.[69]

Mahelot is certainly not afraid of the word "perspective," but an examination of the context in which he uses it convinces us that he gives it a special, restricted

62. *History*, Pt. I, vol. ii, p. 718.
63. Védier, op. cit., pp. 78 et seq.
64. *Mise en scène*, p. 112.
65. *Mémoire*, pp. 98 and 103.
66. Ibid., p. 72.
67. Ibid., p. 72.
68. Ibid., p. 75.
69. This does not necessarily place the stage decorator any more directly under the influence of Serlio, who was not the only writer to realize this fact. Holsboer seems to suggest that it is specifically Serlian: "Le compartiment le plus proche des spectateurs présente le plus grand décor comme Serlio le préscrivait" (*Mise en scène*, p. 113).

FIG. 64.—*Cintie*, Hardy.

FIG. 65.—*Cornélie*, Hardy.

FIG. 66.—*Céliane*, Rotrou.

meaning. Two of the notices which carry sketches use it: Rotrou's *Céliane* (Fig. 66),[70] in which "au milieu du théâtre" there is to be "une grotte peinte en perspective," and Des Bruyères *Roman de Paris* (Fig. 67),[71] where, "au milieu du théâtre, il faut une perspective en fontaine, quatre rangs de balustres." The two sketches show us that, as compared with the perspective in the aforementioned Hardy sets, whose indications do *not* mention it as such, there seems little reason why the word should be specifically included here, for the perspective is hardly noticeable; and indeed when we examine the connotation of the word, in those notices which have no accompanying sketch, the specialized meaning becomes plain: it is the "milieu du théâtre" to which the term is applied,[72] suggesting not only that it is on the backcloth that the greatest perspective effects appear, but that the backcloth itself is called the "perspective": an idea which is made clearer in a later indication, that of Passar's *Heureuse inconstance*:[73] "Au milieu du théâtre un myrte planté proche de la perspective des trois portiques de pastorale,"[74] clinched by the indication for La Pinelière's *Foire de Saint Germain*,[75] "Au milieu du théâtre, dit la perspective," and Rayssiguier's *Calirie*,[76] where a ceiling is to be "refondré jusqu'à la perspective."

70. *Mémoire*, p. 87.
71. Ibid., p. 90.
72. Cf. Rotrou's *Célimène*, Hardy's *Frère indiscret*, and Passar's *Florice*.
73. *Mémoire*, p. 97.
74. Cf. Rotrou's *Diane*, ibid., p. 98.
75. Ibid., p. 100.
76. Ibid., p. 105.

FIG. 67.—*Roman de Paris*, Des Bruyères.

We conclude that although some attention is paid to perspective in this section of the *Mémoire* it is not very serious attention so far as it applies to the contructed scenery, which does not normally have the same vanishing point as the backcloth perspective; and further, that the term ''perspective'' can mean a mere backcloth not necessarily painted in pronounced perspective. This latter usage is doubtless borrowed from staging styles in which the backcloth or back shutters would nearly always be in perspective; the verbal usage is borrowed, in short, but the practice is not.

Parallelism

The parallelism of the sets in the *Mémoire,* that is, the matching of units down either side of the stage, has been adduced as evidence of Italian influence. It is true, for instance, that such a tendency is present in all the sets of the somewhat later scene designer Torelli, who occasionally observes an absolutely rigid uniformity of setting (see Figs. 96 and 97). Yet the Hôtel de Bourgogne was a small stage, and had to take at least two units on its either side, with occasionally a face item of décor occupying some space slightly downstage, which would again tend to restrict space available down the sides. Add to this that the stock of separate stage pieces available to the decorator of the Hôtel de Bourgogne was limited, and it is evident that some form of matching would have occurred anyway. The symmetry which Holsboer discerns in the sets is not very apparent.[77] The rigid parallelism used by Torelli and

77. *Mise en scène*, p. 108.

FIG. 68.—*La Folie d'Isabelle*, Hardy.

his like is so imperceptible here as to make one feel safe in concluding that such as
there is can hardly be deliberate, with the exception of those odd plays which, requiring three compartments, were given two more to make up the balance.[78] We
must recall once more that broadly speaking it was the play that set the stage for
ordinary purposes of tragicomedy, comedy, and pastoral in the time of Mahelot;
for two houses of like character to face each other across the stage a prime necessity
was that there should be two such houses in the play: a not unusual event. Not so
with Torelli and the machine play, in which the system of indicating change of place
was totally different, and the stage represented one place at a time, so that its detail,
if this was ornament of a general nature, could easily be placed in parallel down
the sides of the stage. In the perspective backcloths of Mahelot's sets, whenever the
defining function of the compartment in the simultaneous staging has ceased to
operate, when the painted picture is sufficiently vague, then only do we find in it
anything like Torellian parallelism. The nearest approaches are probably Hardy's
Folie d'Isabelle (Fig. 68), Baro's *Force du destin* (Fig. 69), and Rotrou's *Ménechmes* (see
Fig. 61).[79] In these we may say that there is an incipient parallel of *constructed* décor.
With the pastoral, the outlines of the set are so vague that the question does not
arise.

78. Ibid., p. 109.
79. *Mémoire*, pp. 74, 83, 89.

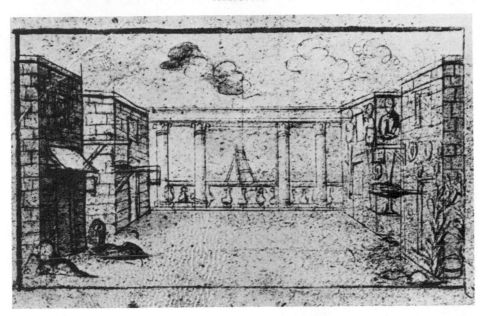

FIG. 69.—*La Force du Destin*, Baro.

Machinery

A small stage is particularly unsuited to elaborate machinery, and yet there is some evidence of the popularity of baroque mechanical tricks in the Mahelot drawings, as well as the retention of mystery effects of machinery. While with other features of the set it is always possible that Mahelot has omitted something in his notice,[80] we may be sure that major machine effects, because of their novelty on this stage and their complication, will be included. The simplest and most frequent device is the *nuit*, so frequent that in this case Mahelot does contrive to forget it sometimes.[81] In spite of the omissions however it is referred to many times,[82] and there can be no doubt at all of its being a stock-in-trade. It is to be distinguished from the personified figure of night, which also appears, sometimes in company wtih the stock *nuit*: "au dessus du temple, faire paraître la Nuit dans son char dessus

80. Lancaster is careful to list the omissions in each play.
81. *Mémoire*, p. 39; e.g. *Pyrame et Thisbé, La belle Egyptienne, Cornélie, Arétaphile* Act IV, *Célimène*.
82. *Les occasions perdues, Amaranthe, Le trompeur puni, Mélite* (actually Rampalle's *Bélinde;* its real identity is established by Lancaster), *Arétaphile* Act III, *L'infidèle confidente, Agarite, La Filis de Scire, L'heureuse tromperie, La Sylvie, La Place Royale, L'heureuse inconstance*, and *Cléonice*.

FIG. 70.—*La Filis de Scire*, Pichou.

un pivot tiré par deux chevaux, et faire paraître la nuit'' (Fig. 70).[83] A moon and stars are made to appear in Rotrou's *Occasions perdues*,[84] along with the night, while *Mélite* (i.e. Rampalle's *Bélinde*, see note 82) is provided with "une lune qui marche." These are among the simpler of the baroque tricks, and more complicated ones, although they do exist in the *Mémoire,* are not numerous. The cloud in which Hercules descends in *Hercule mourant*[85] is described thus: "Le globe doit être empli des douzes signes et nues et les douze vents, des étoiles ardentes, soleil en escarboucle transparente et autres ornements à la fantaisie du feinteur." Here is the full complication and lavishness of the baroque "descent."[86] It is the most complicated machinery of the *Mémoire,* though there are other examples of the same thing, somewhat terse by comparison: "Au quatrième acte, l'Amour paraît en l'air" (see Fig. 59) and "Au dessus du théâtre, une nue où est la déesse."[87] In Gombauld's *Amaranthe* (see Fig. 47) Dawn appears in a chariot drawn by two horses.[88] Flight is not necessarily implicit in these last two examples, and they may well have been contrived with a *théâtre supérieur,*[89] like the similar devices in the *Travaux d'Ulysse,* the notice of

83. *La Filis de Scire, Mémoire,* p. 84. See also D. H. Roy, ''Mahelot's Nights: a traditional stage effect,'' in *Gallica: Essays presented to J. Heywood Thomas,* Cardiff, University of Wales, 1969.
84. *Mémoire,* p. 66.
85. Ibid., p. 103.
86. Cf. Holsboer, *Mise en scène,* p. 146.
87. *Astrée et Céladon, Mémoire,* p. 76, and *Iphis et Ianté,* ibid., p. 106.
88. Ibid., p. 66. Holsboer, *Mise en scène,* p. 144, refers to the figure as ''vaguement indiquée''; it is however referred to in the notice and it is not difficult to make out in the sketch.
89. See pp. 143 et seq.

which reads: "Au-dessus de l'enfer, le ciel d'Apollon, et au-dessus d'Apollon, le ciel de Jupiter."[90] We must note in passing that only in one case, that of Rotrou's *Hercule,* is a flight obviously involved. The other examples seem to be mere apparitions.

As opposed to the use of machinery, in which one perhaps discerns some development towards the end of the Mahelot period, change upon the stage is confined to the use of a curtain in front of the compartment in the manner already noted. There is no drawing aside of shutters to reveal a further perspective scene within, no spectacular metamorphosis. The appearance of ships on seas, of running fountains, and all the naturalist repertoire of these notices, we relegate to their proper place, firstly the mystery tradition, and secondly, the growth of the dramatic pastoral, which is fairly short-lived. The rôle of the marvelous in this genre has been fully dealt with by Marsan:[91] fountains, magic, phantoms, apparitions, enchanted mirrors, philters, metamorphoses abound. It adopts the most familiar terms in its dealings with the ancient divinities.[92] Marsan is concerned with demonstrating the origins of the later lyrical drama in the pastoral. In this connection Etienne Gros utters a word of warning which may serve us in our attempt to follow the baroque and the native traditions of staging through the life of a separate theater: he remarks that the French pastoral disappears towards 1635 only to reappear in 1650 under the probable influence of the Italian opera.[93] The machines of the Hôtel were certainly not sumptuous. Whether or not the Marais theater used the simultaneous décor, that of the Hôtel would certainly be more developed and to this extent would preclude such sumptuosity, so that in a sense the end of this first period of the *Mémoire* marks the decline of one tradition of spectacle in that theater.

One feature of the Hôtel de Bourgogne stage in the early part of the century—a descendant of the mystery play via the street theater—has remained shrouded in obscurity. This is the *théâtre supérieur,* whose exact nature and function are not well understood.[94] It is generally admitted that when the Confrérie de la Passion took their plays out of the open air into the Hôpital de la Trinité at the beginning of the fifteenth century, in order to cope with a much narrower stage which could not hold

90. Lancaster (p. 40, fn. 1) comments on this "Une note dans les *Travaux d'Ulysse* indique *le soleil en son char de lumière, Jupiter en son trône de gloire,* mais puisque Mahelot ne parle d'aucune machine pour cette pièce, il semble qu'on ait négligé ces indications." However, the "trône de gloire" is present as the "ciel de Jupiter" in both notice and sketch, while the "soleil en son char de lumière" is present in the sketch as the "ciel d'Apollon." The text bears this out (Act V, scene v, 1st edn., 1631).
91. *La pastorale dramatique,* pp. 190 et seq.
92. Ibid., p. 198.
93. "Les origines de la tragédie lyrique et la place des tragédies en machines dans l'évolution du théâtre vers l'opéra," RHLF, April–June, 1928, p. 166.
94. Cf. Holsboer, *Mise en scène,* pp. 119 et seq.
95. Cohen, *Théâtre religieux,* p. 85; Jacob, *Recueil de farces, soties, et moralités,* 1859; prefatory notice on *L'Ancien théâtre en France,* p. xi. See also Cohen, *Théâtre religieux,* p. 77, on others who have held this theory.

the requisite number of compartments they were compelled to construct either one into the Hôtel de Bourgogne the Confrères imitated the disposition of the Trinité.[96] If so, they may well have reintroduced the *théâtre superposé*, a supposition strengthened by Fransen's publication of a lease made by the Confrères to the Comédiens Royaux in October, 1616: "En outre, ne pourront lesdits preneurs prétendre aucune chose au-dessous qui est sous la montée du petit théâtre de ladite grande salle."[97] He explains the phrase "petit théâtre" by analogy with two contracts discovered by Liebrecht, for alterations made to the Fossé-aux-Loups theater in Brussels in 1651 and 1652; Liebrecht tells us:

> Le 'théâtre' proprement dit,—ce que nous nommons aujourd'hui la scène—occupait le fond sur toute la largeur et sur une profondeur de trente-deux pieds . . . soit environ le tiers de la longueur totale. L'ouverture au rideau n'était que de dix-sept pieds . . . et le 'plateau' allait en se rétrécissant, de manière à ne laisser entre les portants du fond qu'un espace de sept pieds . . . Encore ce fond était-il occupé, entre les derniers portants et le mur, par un second petit théâtre nommé dans les contrats 'théâtre de Jupiter', dont le plancher était à trappes, pour permettre aux apparitions de surgir dans ce 'guignol'.
>
> Parfois le théâtre était à deux étages et constituait un reste curieux des mises en scène du moyen âge: 'Un téâtre avec un petit téaltre au dessus', dit le contrat de 1651; 'trois téâtres, un embas et deux aultres téâtres dessus' précise celui de 1662 . . .[98]

The little stages are to be found again in Belgium, in a description of the theater of the Troupe Royale by one of its actors, Du Cormier: "Il faudra un petit Théâtre qui tiendra depuis la 7e aile jusqu'au fond de la muraille, qui sera sur le devant, plus haut sur le derrière pour faire la pente" and "il faudra que le Théâtre ayt 42 ou 43 pieds de longueur pour la commodité du petit Théâtre de Jupiter, et du passage de derrière."[99]

In addition to this evidence, we have the familiar stage direction of Rotrou's *Saint Genest*: "Adrien, sur un théâtre élevé, représenté par Genest," while the present author has drawn attention to its existence in France in mid-century, attested by a passage from Dubreuil's *Perspective pratique*: "Quand on se servira de Théâtres supérieurs, c'est à dire d'un second, et même troisième étage. . . "[100] The spread of dates shows the device's wide use in the century, nor is there any doubt that the "petit théâtre" and the "théâtre de Jupiter" are the same thing.[101]

To this corpus of knowledge must be added Mme. Deierkauf-Holsboer's highly important discovery of the instructions for the rebuilding of the Marais after it burnt down in 1644. The relevant passage from the *Mémoire de ce qu'il fault faire au jeu de paulme des Marets* is as follows:

96. Cf. Rigal, *Alexandre Hardy*, p. 141.
97. "Documents inédits de l'Hôtel de Bourgogne," RHLF, vol. 34, 1927, p. 341.
98. *Histoire du théâtre français à Bruxelles au XVIIe et au XVIIIe siècle*, 1923, p. 38. Holsboer later agrees with Fransen in relating the two theaters (*Mise en scène*, p. 45).
99. Liebrecht, op. cit., p. 77.
100. "The 'théâtre étagé' in the seventeenth century," *French Studies*, Jan. 1950. *Perspective pratique*, Traité IV, Pratique xii, Pt. 3, 1649.
101. Liebrecht seems to have in mind two separate phenomena, although Fransen has not read Liebrecht this way.

Au dessus dudit théâtre il en faut faire un autre distant du premier de douze pieds de haut et de la même largeur du premier soutenu de huit piliers qui prendront depuis le dessous du premier théâtre jusqu'à la hauteur de dix-neuf pieds desquels piliers il faut que les quatre de devant soient de vingt-un à vingt-deux pieds de hauteur pour faire un appui fermé tant à l'entour du devant.

Le plafond doit être aussi de même bois sapin de même le premier et les bouffettes.

Ledit second théâtre ne doit avoir que deux toises de long au milieu et aux deux côtés de trois toises.

Il faut un escalier de dix-neuf pieds de haut et d'une toise de large en carré pour monter depuis le fond des deux théâtres jusqu'en haut.[102]

The *théâtre superposé* is not immediately apparent in the illustrations of the *Mémoire:* there is nowhere any sign of a structural framework. But when we reflect that in any of the functions of such a device in the body of the play the structure would be concealed by the decorator, and quite naturally, subsequently, by the illustrator, we can see what happened: the various "heavens" of those plays using such little stages, would be in the form of *tapisseries,* whether they were a "ciel d'Apollon" or a "ciel de Jupiter." At the moment of divine revelation, "le ciel s'ouvre" and the elevated thrones come into view.

We had hitherto supposed that the structure was only semipermanent, and that, if so, it might have been used down the sides of the stage. C. M. Fogarty[103] has argued plausibly that it was permanent, probably extended down the (English) stage left at least, and possibly the right, in the Mahelot period, for the following reasons:

1. Pillars would have been necessary at the side of the stage and across the back to support the roof beams, and would have provided a constructional basis for the *théâtre supérieur.*
2. It would have been a waste of space not to continue the facility down the sides, using pillars already provided.
3. Although Mahelot provides no direct pictorial evidence of a *théâtre supérieur,* a very significant number of the drawings show compartments with balustrades on top which could well have been destined to prevent actors from falling off the *théâtre supérieur* if they ventured too near the edge. These balustrades occur down the sides as well as across the back. This is supported by stage directions such as are found in *L'Heureuse Tromperie:* "a un coté du théâtre une chambre et une tour avec une fenestre pour descendre et monter il faut une eschelle." "If the actor is to climb," remarks Miss Fogarty, "then something must exist for him to climb onto." Roy has noticed that in the case of this play, the Mahelot sketch seems to show us, in the second compartment on the spectator's right, the wooden pillar supporting the lateral prolongation of the upper stage.[104]

102. Deierkauf-Holsboer, *Le théâtre du Marais,* tome 1, 1954, pp. 194–95, 108–110.
103. "A reconstruction of the interior of the Hôtel de Bourgogne." *Maske und Kothurn* XXVI, 1, 1980.
104. Op. cit., RHT, 1962, p. 235. Golder (q.v.) argues, on the evidence of his reconstruction of Rotrou's *Hypocondriaque* that there was no extension of the *théâtre supérieur* down the wings.

There are two obvious cases where its employment is demanded in the *Mémoire*. Firstly, the stage direction "Jupiter en son trône de gloire" from *Les travaux d'Ulysse*.[105] The notice tells us that above Hell there is Apollo's *ciel*, and above that, Jupiter's. Both appear in the sketch (see Fig. 53).[106] Apollo's sky, we are told, rests upon the roof of Hell. Access could then be from below, through traps, during the time that the Hell was hidden or from the back by a ladder.[107] This is surely a case of the "trois théâtres" of Liebrecht's document. The frequent appearance of Jupiter in the drama could give the little stage its name. We have already observed that no flight necessarily figures in these appearances.

The Hercules of Rotrou's play of that name would appear in like manner in his temple, while in *Iphis et Ianté*, we have the appearance of Isis in the air *near* the temple, according to the playwright's instructions,[108] but as we have seen, Mahelot has her *above* the temple on a cloud: a clear case for the *théâtre supérieur*.[109] Unfortunately no illustration accompanies either of these notices.

It is beyond reasonable doubt that the *théâtre supérieur*, having one, two, and even three stories, was used at the Hôtel de Bourgogne in Mahelot's time. Mme. Deierkauf-Holsboer's discoveries have proved that at the Marais the structure was solid enough, and in the light of the now proven high reputation of that theater in 1644 it is by no means impossible that it inspired the theater designers in Brussels.

The foregoing examination shows that the Mahelot sketches are a halfway house in which there is both Italian and indigenous tradition, now separate, as in the perspective backcloth which might be purely Italian, now fused, as in the case of the *théâtre supérieur* which, following the general processus of the Royal Entry motifs, finishes by supporting a pagan god, having commenced in the Christian mystery. It is possible, as Lancaster suggests, that some of the *merveilles* were borrowed from the court ballet where they had been in vogue for some time.[110]

If too much of Serlio has been read into the document, the influence of the Renaissance generally has not been exaggerated and what we have called the "curved" *décor simultané* is nearer to Italian sets of the time than it is to the mystery stage, at least in disposition. This prompts the remark that the sets are more Sabbattinian than they are Serlian, although Sabbattini did not publish until 1637 and although there is no direct evidence that his work was well known in France in the seventeenth century.[111] With Serlio, the houses of the set are joined together and do not create "streets" except in the case of the first, downstage, pair of houses;[112] so

105. See *Mémoire*, p. 92.
106. Etienne Gros, *Les origines de la tragédie lyrique*, p. 147, fn. 2, has noticed the same thing.
107. *La bague de l'oubli* (Rotrou): "A côté du jardin et du palais, il faut un échafaud tendu de noir qui soit caché; il s'ouvre au cinquième acte, à la première scène."
108. Act V, scene v: "La déesse Isis paraît en l'air près de son temple."
109. See p. 142.
110. *Mémoire*, p. 40.
111. Leclerc, *Origines*, feels however that Sabbattini is merely publishing methods that had been in vogue for some time.
112. See p. 42.

that even if acting took place on the inclined portion of his stage, which is unlikely, entrance could not be made in such a manner (see Fig.7). With Sabbattini, this is no longer so: the houses have spaces between them like the various décors of the Mahelot sketches; the actors can, and do, make entrance between them or occasionally through them. They are literally narrow side streets used for entry:

> Il sera bon de les tenir aussi étroites que possible afin que les façades des maisons puissent être plus longues et, par conséquent, comprendre plus grand nombre de portes, fenêtres, arcades et boutiques—toutes choses qui les feront paraître plus grandes et donneront plus de profondeur aux perspectives ainsi que plus de plaisir aux spectateurs; leur étroitesse, toutefois, ne devra point aller jusques à incommoder les comédiens, ni les danseurs et mauresques, principalement lorsqu'il leur faudra y entrer ou en sortir avec célérité.[113]

So we must not say outright, as does Lancaster, that the lay-out of the set belongs to the Middle Ages, but rather that it is perhaps medieval in function and already partly Italianate in disposition, since, in being forced into a curve by the constraint of a closed theater, it is naturally tending towards a perspective set.

Its nearness to contemporary Italian dispositions may be understood by a comparison of the sketches themselves with Sabbattini's arrangement of angle-wings, which again we can compare with the frontispiece of Scudéry's *Comédie des comédiens*, printed in 1635 and played at the Marais (Fig. 71). A drawing reproduced by Bapst (Fig. 72) of an Italian theater shows a set similar to those of Mahelot except that the palace "au milieu du théâtre," as Mahelot would have put it, has, in comparison with its French counterpart, taken unto itself two side portions, the mystery tradition being presumably less prominent; the number of compartments is less, and the stage is nearer to the "palais à volonté" of the later *Mémoire*.

It would be natural to expect such a set to develop toward a proscenium arch type of stage, with a full curtain,[114] and with flat wings assuring the scene changing, as opposed to the angle-wings of the Sabbattinian type. We believe that such a development was largely arrested, for the Hôtel de Bourgogne, by the subsequent history of dramatic literature as it affected that theater, and that the Italianizing traditions inherent in the first part of the *Mémoire* were swallowed up by other theaters and other genres. Let us then see what the Hôtel subsequently made of these teeming elements.

Second Period of the "Mémoire"

The second part of the *Mémoire* is a mere index, without notices, so that we have only the plays themselves to go by. They represent a stage in between Mahelot's work and the later work of Michel Laurent. Some of them were produced during the time covered by the first period of the *Mémoire*. *La Veuve*, *La Suivante*, and *Médée*, all by Corneille, are certain examples. Their appearance at this time in the Hôtel

---

113. Sabbattini, *Pratique pour fabriquer scènes et machines de théâtre*, trans. M. and R. Carnavaggia, Bk. I, ch. 10, p. 12.
114. Cf. Rigal, *Théâtre français*, p. 254.

FIG. 71.—Frontispiece of the *Comédie des Comédiens*, Scudéry.

de Bourgogne repertory suggests, together with other evidence, that they had first been played by the Marais Troupe and had been taken over by the Hôtel when they passed into the immediate *domaine public* on printing. Of the first, Corneille himself says: "Cette comédie n'est pas plus régulière que *Mélite* en ce qui regarde l'unité de lieu."[115] In fact, it covers several places in one city. *La Suivante* on the other hand observes the unity of place fairly well, the scene being in front of a house

115. *Œuvres*, ed. Marty-Laveaux, tome I, p. 394.

FIG. 72.—Early seventeenth-century Italian Theater.

and garden. Mairet's *Sophonisbe*, played probably within a year of *La Suivante*,[116] requires several rooms in a palace, and some other place.[117]

These plays are in fact employing the system of staging of their time, possibly with a little more sobriety, a little more progress toward unity than the other plays outlined in Mahelot's section of the *Mémoire*. We are not therefore able to say exactly how they were produced in the period leading up to 1646–7, that is to say the time at which this second list was compiled. La Mesnardière, in his *Poétique*, published in 1639, seems to be complaining of any simplification such as Corneille desires:[118]

> La Scène, autrement le Lieu où l'Action a été faite, désignant pour l'ordinarie une Ville tout entière, souvent un petit Pays, et quelquefois une Maison; il faut de nécessité qu'elle change d'autant de faces qu'elle marque d'endroits divers. Qu'elle ne découvre pas un Jardin, ni une Forêt, pour la Scène d'une Action qui s'est passée dans le Palais;

116. *La Suivante*, according to Lancaster, *History*, Pt. I, vol. ii, p. 605, was played in 1632 or 1633.

117. Cf. Rigal, *Théâtre français*, p. 286.

118. *Poétique*, pp. 412–13.

et que même en ce Palais elle ne fasse pas voir dans l'Appartement du Roi ce qui doit avoir été fait dans le Cabinet de la Reine.

Scudéry (*Didon,* 1637) says: "Cette pièce est un peu hors de la sévérité des règles, bien que je ne les ignore pas; mais souvenez-vous (je vous prie), qu'ayant satisfait les savants par elles, il faut parfois contenter le peuple par la diversité des spectacles et par les différentes faces du théâtre."[119] The struggle towards simplification is especially apparent here. It is in any case an uneasy second stage in the atrophy of the multiple staging system.

The effect of Mairet's *Sophonsibe* was in fact a rapid outcrop of tragedy at the Marais, in competition with the still popular tragicomedy at the Hôtel de Bourgogne,[120] so that we must be chary of attributing the initial simplification of staging to the Hôtel: we might, on the contrary, take it as evidence that the Marais welcomed a genre which did not demand complicated *décors simultanés.*[121] The palace and Médée's dwelling both provided entry, in Corneille's *Médée,* on to a public place, and this will become an increasingly popular instrument for preserving unity, and increasing exploitation of place "whence."[122] But this is still in its infancy and Corneille readily admits that he prefers Médée to weave her charm in her room rather than have her do so on the "place publique:" "je ne puis comprendre comme, dans son quatrième acte, il [Sénèque] lui fait achever ses enchantements en place publique; et j'ai mieux aimé rompre l'unité exacte du lieu, pour faire voir Médée dans le même cabinet où elle a fait ses charmes, que de l'imiter en ce point."[123] Much the same may be said of the *Cid* at the Marais, while the *Illusion Comique,* also played in 1636 or 1637, would use every liberty then existing on the stage.

Yet we can only proceed by analogy in speculating how these plays were staged when they ultimately entered the repertory of the Hôtel de Bourgogne, in 1646 or 1647, or some time before those dates.

In 1638 d'Ouville's *Arbiran,* a tragicomedy, is played. The author has unity of place in mind, but is not prepared to sacrifice too much to it: "Cette scène ici est la ville de Salerne, qui se changera pourtant tantôt en celle de Naples." He would have preferred to have the play in one particular place, but is not prepared to mutilate the action for that purpose. Rotrou's *Les captifs,* first played probably in the same year,[124] limits place to the vicinity of Haegée's house. Corneille's *Horace,*

119. Quoted by Rigal, *Théâtre français*, p. 288.
120. Lancaster, *History*, Pt. II, vol. i, p. 29.
121. Cf. ibid., Pt. I, vol. ii, p. 711, and Rigal, *Théâtre français*, p. 284: "L'intérêt de Mondory était de favoriser les idées nouvelles; mais parce qu'elles devaient lui faire perdre tout un magasin de décors les règles aristotéliques ne pouvaient que déplaire à l'Hôtel de Bourgogne."
122. Act II, scene i: *Nérine*: Contentez-vous, Madame, il sort de son palais.
     Act I, scene iii: *Cléone*:

     > Vous pourrez au palais suivre cet entretien
     > On ouvre chez Médée, ôtez-vous de sa vue . . .

123. *Examen, OEuvres*, ed. Marty-Laveaux tome II, p. 334.
124. Lancaster, *History*, Pt. II, vol. i, p. 264.

first played (probably at the Marais) in 1640,[125] and naturally adopted by the Hôtel on publication, takes place in a single room. *Cinna,* probably played in the same year, would appear also to have moved from the Marais to the Hôtel.[126] We may take it to represent the *décor simultané* almost at its point of disappearance. Corneille himself admits a duplicity of place: "Il est vrai qu'il s'y rencontre une duplicité de lieu particulière. La moitié de la pièce se passe chez Emilie, et l'autre dans le cabinet d'Auguste."

There has been some discussion as to what this actually means on the stage. D'Aubignac is cited by Lancaster to show that only a single room was to be seen on the stage, Corneille, as he says in his *Examen,* breaking the *liaison de scènes* in Act IV, Scenes iii–iv, so that the stage could represent two apartments in the imperial palace;[127] but we can go farther than this. Corneille broke the *liaison de scènes* because he could not reconcile himself "à faire que Maxime vînt donner l'alarme à Emilie de la conjuration découverte, au lieu même où Auguste en venait de recevoir l'avis par son ordre, et dont il ne faisait que de sortir avec tant d'inquiétude et d'irré-solution."[128] Accordingly (and this is the essential of place in the *Examen*), "Emilie ne parle . . . pas où parle Auguste." In other words, one room in a palace was used, and this defined the stage as either "chez Emilie" or the "cabinet d'Auguste" as the story required. The necessity for two compartments subsisted to a minor degree, and the compartments were not there. Lancaster sees, in the notice on *Cinna* of the later (Laurent) section of the *Mémoire,* evidence of the use of a curtain to conceal the "cabinet d'Auguste" upstage, while the downstage region would be Emilie's apartment, but this does not necessarily follow.[129]

Tragicomedy still lingers on with its greater extension of place. Place in this genre is however limited geographically, though not numerically. This is the case with Scudéry's *Andromire* (printed in 1641 and therefore played either in that year or some time before), which is comparatively rich in place, though his *Arminius* requires only space before a Roman camp. Du Ryer's *Esther,* styled "tragedy" though it has a happy ending, requires one or two rooms in the palace, and possibly a space before it. Puget de la Serre's *Thomas Morus* demands several places in the vicinity of London. It is significant that none of these, with the possible exception of *Andromire,* is an importation from the Marais, so far as we can discover.

Corneille's *Polyeucte,* played in 1641 or 1642,[130] and *Pompée,* played not later than 1643 at the Marais,[131] exploit, in the interests of unity, the weapon of place "whence" in what is by now a familiar manner since in the latter "le lieu particulier est, comme

---

125. Ibid., Pt. II, vol. i, p. 311. Marty-Laveaux (tome III, p. 251) claims it for the Hôtel de Bourgogne. See also Holsboer, *Mise en scène,* p. 132.
126. Lancaster, *History,* Pt. II, vol. i, p. 312.
127. Ibid., Pt. II, vol. i, p. 317.
128. *Examen,* Marty-Laveaux, tome III, p. 380.
129. *History,* Pt. II, vol. i, p. 317.
130. Ibid., Pt. II, vol. i, p. 320.
131. Ibid., Pt. II, vol. ii, p. 499.

dans *Polyeucte,* un grand vestibule commun à tous les appartements du palais royal.''[132]

The comedies of these years which figure in our list (d'Ouville's *Fausses vérités* and Corneille's *Menteur*) display a limited *décor simultané* convention. The former requires the street, and rooms in two houses, the latter shifts from the Tuileries to the Place Royale. *Le Menteur* is probably an importation from the Marais.[133]

The incidence of tragedy at the Hôtel de Bourgogne now increases perceptibly. Of the drama either probably or certainly played at the Hôtel between 1644 and 1646, and figuring on the list of the decorator, if we discount those of uncertain genre, nine plays are tragedies, six are comedies, and five are tragicomedies.[134] Of the tragicomedies, Gillet de la Tessonerie's *Sigismond* observes the unities, as does Magnon's *Josaphat;* Rotrou's *Dom Bernard* takes place vaguely in a palace, while Le Vert's *Aricidie* exhibits a limited number of places in Rome. Only Gillet de la Tessonerie's *Art de régner* displays something like the exuberance of the past, and here there is a special motive for the multiplicity of place, as its purpose is to act as instruction for the young Louis XIV with a lesson on one of the virtues in each act. Of the tragedies, *Hippolyte, La mort de Crispé, La mort de Valentinien,* and *La Porcie romaine* may be described as regular so far as place is concerned. *Genest* requires a prison for Act V, *Scévole* two different places, *Alcidiane* a palace, a park, and some third place nearby.

Rodogune and *Héraclius,* in their treatment of place, for which Corneille craves a specific type of indulgence, strike us as so typical of this intermediate period that we shall deal with them in a little more detail. Of the comedies, *La dame suivante* is

132. *Examen,* Marty-Laveaux, tome IV, p. 20.
133. Marty-Laveaux, tome IV, Notice, p. 278 and fn. 4.
134. Tragedies: *Hippolyte ou le garçon sensible,* Gilbert, printed 1646; *Saint Genest,* Rotrou, played about 1645; *La mort de Crispé,* Tristan l'Hermite, played about 1644; *Rodogune,* Corneille, played between 1644 and 1646 (or the same title by Gabriel Gilbert); *Scévole,* Du Ryer, played about 1644; *La Porcie romaine,* Boyer, printed in 1646; *Théodore vierge et martyre,* Corneille, played in 1645 or 1646; *La mort de Valentinien et d'Isidore,* Gillet de la Tessonerie, played in 1646; and *Héraclius,* Corneille, played in 1646 or 1647.
   Comedies: *La dame suivante,* d'Ouville, printed in 1645; *Jodelet ou le maître valet,* Scarron, printed in 1645; *Jodelet astrologue,* d'Ouville, printed in 1646; *Les trois Dorothées,* Scarron, privilege of 1646; *La soeur,* Rotrou, played about 1645; and *Le songe des hommes éveillés,* Brosse, printed in 1646.
   Tragicomedies: *Sigismond,* Gillet de la Tessonerie, printed in 1646; *Dom Bernard de Cabrère,* Rotrou, played about 1646; *Josaphat, fils d'Abenner,* Magnon, privilege of the 31st Aug. 1646; *Aricidie,* Le Vert, printed in 1646; and *L'Art de régner* de Gillet de la Tessonerie, printed in 1645. (All datings and attributions are Lancaster's.) We have assumed that plays printed in 1645 and 1646 were produced within the period, though not those printed in 1644. If however we include those printed in 1647, this adds:
   Tragedies: *La soeur généreuse,* Boyer; *Sémiramis,* Gilbert; *La véritable Sémiramis;* Desfontaines; *La mort d'Asdrubal,* Montfleury père; *Séjanus,* Magnon.
   Comedies: *La coiffeuse à la mode,* d'Ouville.
   This makes a total of fourteen tragedies, seven comedies, and five tragicomedies.

limited to Paris, *Jodelet ou le maître valet* needs two rooms in a house, and the street, *Jodelet astrologue* is more diffuse, demanding several houses and a garden. *Les trois Dorothées,* like *La dame suivante,* is limited to a town, Toledo. *La soeur* requires the space before three houses, while *Le songe des hommes éveillés* is limited to a castle. Tragedy is clearly leading the movement towards a single set. Out of the remaining plays on the list, not one is a tragicomedy. The only tragedy which is not set in a single room, palace, or hall, is Magnon's *Séjanus* (printed in 1647), requiring two rooms in a palace. Comedy continues to be the most lax of the genres, Scarron's *Dom Japhet d'Arménie* romping with the picaresque verve of its author over two towns, and d'Ouville's *Coiffeuse à la mode* presenting the familiar street scene with three houses leading onto it.

We conclude that the mass importation of tragedy from the Marais, together with the growing popularity of the genre, had largely simplified the set at the Hôtel de Bourgogne. What is normally made as a general statement about the theater of the time would more wisely be limited to this one, for what we assume to be the early simplicity of the tragic sets at the Marais gives place to an intensive development of the machine play.

The defining function of the compartment has disappeared from the Hôtel to a great extent, and possibly completely. Where there are two or more houses in a play, they tend to indicate place "whence," and lead out on to a street, where the greater part of the action takes place; a return to the "suddenness" of entry of the ancients is taking place, matching the return to ancient precept in dramatic literature. The frequent use by the dramatic author of the expression "il rentre," meaning "exit," even when there is no specific place to enter, is indicative of this. A theoretical reflection of this physical fact is to be found in Corneille's heart-searching about multiplicity of place, in particular in the *Examens* of *Cinna, Héraclius,* and *Rodogune,* and the *Discours des trois unités.* He refers to place in the *Examen de Rodogune:* "l'unité de lieu s'y rencontre en la manière que je l'explique dans le troisième de ces discours, et avec l'indulgence que j'ai demandée pour le théâtre."[135] He says of *Héraclius:* "il lui faut la même indulgence pour l'unité de lieu qu'à *Rodogune*."[136] What is this indulgence? He explains in the *Discours des trois unités:* "Nos anciens, qui faisaient parler leurs rois en place publique, donnaient assez aisément l'unité rigoureuse de lieu à leurs tragédies . . . Nous ne prenons pas la même liberté de tirer les rois et les princesses de leurs appartements."[137] What then is his solution? Firstly, the limits of a town if absolutely necessary, or better, only one or two specific places in the town (*Cinna, Le Menteur, La Suite du Menteur, Le Cid*). Next, to mitigate this license, he would wish

> . . . *que ces deux lieux n'eussent point besoin de diverses décorations* . . . Cela aiderait à tromper l'auditeur, qui ne voyant rien qui lui marquât la diversité des lieux, ne s'en apercevrait pas, à moins d'une réflexion malicieuse et critique, dont il y en a peu qui

135. Marty-Laveaux, Tome IV, p. 421.
136. Ibid., tome V, p. 153.
137. Ibid., tome I, p. 119.

soient capables, la plupart s'attachant avec chaleur à l'action qu'ils voient représenter. Le plaisir qu'ils y prennent est cause qu'ils n'en veulent pas chercher le peu de justesse pour s'en dégoûter; et ils ne le reconnaissent que par force, quand il est trop visible, comme dans le *Menteur* et la *Suite, où les différentes décorations font reconnaître cette duplicité de lieu,* malgré qu'on en ait.[138]

This passage teaches us much: Corneille would appear to be wishing, retrospectively, that the plays referred to had not been staged with a simplified *décor simultané,* for it is difficult to read the passage any other way. He wishes to discard the *mansions* as defining elements: "Les jurisconsultes admettent des fictions de droit; et je voudrais, à leur exemple, introduire des fictions de théâtre, pour établir un lieu théâtral qui ne serait ni l'appartement de Cléopâtre, ni celui de Rodogune dans la pièce qui porte ce titre, ni celui de Phocas, de Léontine, ou de Pulchérie, dans *Héraclius;* mais une salle sur laquelle ouvre ces divers appartements."[139] By this, we should note, Corneille is reclaiming that very liberty of the ancients which he has just said the moderns cannot enjoy; he too is restoring the drama of entry, place "whence," onto a vague terrain which the spectator has no reason to suppose (since any decorative reminder of the fact is to be removed) different from the place in which he finds himself. He has in any case already contradicted his statement in his treatment of the unity of action:[140]

L'auditeur attend l'acteur; et bien que le théâtre représente la chambre ou le cabinet de celui qui parle, il ne peut toutefois s'y montrer qu'il ne vienne de derrière la tapisserie . . . Je n'ai vu personne se scandaliser de voir Emilie commencer *Cinna* sans dire pourquoi elle vient dans sa chambre: elle est présumée y être avant que la pièce commence, et ce n'est que la nécessité de la représentation qui la fait sortir de derrière le théâtre pour y venir.[141]

This new exploitation of place "whence" is what Rigal has in mind when he speaks of the "dernière façon d'être" of the *scène simultanée,* using the *chambre à quatre portes* of the later *Cid* as his example. It is, he says, a sort of *décor multiple,* but there is complete unity of place for the spectators.[142] Place "whence" defines place "where." The convention is not far from the "a foro" and "a peregre" of the Vitruvian side entrances, nor from the localizing rôle of the main doors in the *frons scaenae.*

When the three *discours* appeared at the head of the 1660 edition, Corneille could see the way in which his theater had tended. Lingering habits of staging between 1640 and 1647 (the last probable date of the performance of *Héraclius*) had not provided him with the convention he would have wished.

138. Ibid., tome I, p. 120. The italics are ours.
139. Ibid., p. 121. Also quoted by Schérer, who defines the convention as the "lieu composite" (*Dramaturgie classique,* p. 191).
140. Marty-Laveaux, tome I, pp. 108–09.
141. This "nécessité de la représentation" could also be used to argue the non-utilisation of a proscenium arch curtain, which, if present, would have removed the "nécessité," and if we accept this we must accept it for the year 1660, date of the publication of the *Discours,* as well as for the date of *Cinna.*
142. *Théâtre français,* pp. 290–91.

We find in this list of plays very little trace indeed of those incipient baroque devices which we have noted in Mahelot's part of the *Mémoire*. The stage of the Hôtel is being swept clear of machine and marvel and is developing into the *palais à volonté* of its final period. Etienne Gros gives the following list of plays showing the invasion by the machine of early regular tragedy:[143] Corneille, *Médée*, Rotrou, *Iphigénie en Aulide*, Desfontaines, *Martyre de Saint Eustache*, Puget de la Serre, *Thésée*, D'Aubignac, *La Pucelle d'Orléans*, Rotrou, *Les Sosies*. It is significant that only one of these, so far as we can ascertain (Corneille's *Médée*), ever reached the Hôtel de Bourgogne. *Médée* is then an exception for this theater. Act V, Scene vi has "Médée, en l'air dans un char tiré par deux dragons." But this machine effect was first implemented at the Marais. Was it retained at the Hôtel? The text seems to demand it:

> Epargne, cher époux, des efforts que tu perds;
> Vois les chemins de l'air qui me sont tous ouverts;
> C'est par là que je fuis, et que je t'abandonne
> Pour courir à l'exil que ton change m'ordonne.

In any case the machinery of D'Aubignac's *Pucelle d'Orléans,* a play probably acted about 1640, must give us pause and prompt the reflection that the arrival of the unities did not immediately and automatically preclude machine effects. For D'Aubignac, the chosen terrain of the play must not shift (since the stage cannot shift physically), but he rules that if this simple precept is observed the back and sides of the stage may be made to change freely.[144]

Generally speaking, however, in shunning the *Deus ex machina,* classical doctrine precludes from the Hôtel de Bourgogne stage one of the great standbys of the baroque theater. As Corneille says, "Dans le dénouement je trouve deux choses à éviter, le simple changement de volonté, et la machine."[145] The flight, descent, and ascent by machine tend to be banished. Sudden appearance, where it takes place, is reminiscent of the earlier period and is effected in the same way, by the use of the *tapisserie:* in Tristan l'Hermite's *Folie du sage* a curtain is drawn aside to show the heroine dead on a couch. The same thing occurs in Mairet's *Sophonisbe* although this, probably produced first in 1634, is an importation from an earlier period. The device is frequently used in Corneille's *Illusion comique.*[146] Perspective, undoubtedly

143. *Les origines de la tragédie lyrique*, p. 173.
144. *Pratique*, Bk. II, ch. 6, p. 102. Holsboer, *Mise en scène*, p. 75. The machinery required for this play and the fact that it has a front stage curtain after the final act ("le théâtre se ferme avec la toile de devant") suggest that it was played at the Palais Cardinal. (Lancaster, *History*, Pt. II, vol. i, p. 359. But see Védier, op. cit., p. 20 and fn. 1, and especially pp. 113–20. This author raises serious doubts as to its peformance at the Palais Cardinal.
145. *Discours des trois unités*, Marty-Laveaux, tome I, p. 105.
146. See also p. 158 and Fig. 74, where Mount Sinai appears by the same method in Puget de la Serre's *Martyre de Sainte Catherine*.

used increasingly, must still have employed a single vanishing point in the single-room sets.

Only one notable exception is to be found: that of Desmaret's *Mirame*, and this has a peculiar destiny since it is brought in not from the Marais but from the Grande Salle du Palais Cardinal, which it opened in 1641.[147]

This, if it was a total one, must have been a curious invasion. The details of the staging of *Mirame* are well known to us (Fig. 73a). In spite of the comparative simplicity of its decoration, the play belongs to the baroque tradition: it is the Cardinal's first effort at theatrical splendor. We know that the Palais Cardinal had a proscenium arch and a proscenium arch curtain (Fig. 73b). (The curtain did *not*, as we stated in the first edition, open in the middle and run laterally.)[148] By baroque standards the single décor was simple enough: colonnades decorated with statues which functioned as fountains down either side of the stage, in parallel. On top of the colonnades, vases which also served as miniature fountains. Upstage, a balustrade, with trees right and left, and beyond, a backcloth perspective of the sea.[149] There was a sun and a moon, both made to rise by machinery.

> La France, ni possible, les pays étrangers n'ont jamais vu un si magnifique théâtre, et dont la perspective apportât plus de ravissement aux yeux des spectateurs . . . de fort délicieux jardins, ornés de grottes, de statues, de fontaines et de grands parterres en terrasse sur la mer, avec des agitations, qui semblaient naturelles, aux vagues de ce vaste élément, et deux grandes flottes, dont l'une paraissait éloignée de deux lieues, qui passèrent toutes deux à la vue des spectateurs. La nuit sembla arriver ensuite par l'obscurcissement imperceptible tant du jardin que de la mer et du ciel qui se trouva éclairé de la lune. A cette nuit succéda le jour, qui vint aussi insensiblement avec l'aurore et le soleil qui fit son tour.[150]

So runs the *Gazette*. Arnauld had declared previously that the machines would cost more than 100,000 livres.[151] The entire venture involved Richelieu in an expenditure of between 20,000 and 30,000 écus.[152]

How was all this adapted to the Hôtel de Bourgogne of the time? The initial failure of *Mirame*, according to the (admittedly prejudiced) Abbé de Marolles, was due to the machines.[153] Could the Hôtel hope to do better than the Palais Cardinal? We cannot think so. The play could only be transferred to that stage because of its basic simplicity of setting, for it still preserves unity of place. It must have been played before a much simpler décor, with the possible inclusion of the sun and moon effects, which could still have been possible achievements at the Hôtel de Bourgogne: we have seen that they were present in the earlier part of the *Mémoire*.

147. Another example of this exchange is Gilbert's *Téléphonte*, which, according to Lancaster (*History*, Pt. II, vol. ii, p. 390), was probably also performed at the Palais Cardinal by the combined actors of the Marais and Hôtel in 1641.
148. See for example Wiley, *Hôtel de Bourgogne*, p. 94.
149. Celler, *Décors*, p. 26.
150. Quoted by Lancaster, *History*, Pt. II, vol. ii, p. 376.
151. Ibid., loc. cit.
152. Celler, *Décors*, p. 18.
153. Ibid., p. 28.

FIG. 73a.—Décor for *Mirame*, Desmaretz.

FIG. 73b.—Proscenium arch and curtain, Palais Royal.

We cannot do better, in leaving this moment in the fortunes of our theater, than draw attention to the illustrations contained in Puget de la Serre's *Martyre de Sainte Catherine*. Their significance for this period makes it difficult to understand why they have not been used more frequently (Figs. 74–78).[154] The play probably figures in the second list of the *Mémoire* though unfortunately we cannot be quite sure that the play of the *Mémoire* is Puget de la Serre's *Martyre* and not that of d'Aubignac or Saint Germain.[155] The first edition has an engraving to each act. The trestles of the stage are fully visible; there are two side "compartments," a semicircular recess midstage, and a central door with an extension scene. Act I depicts the Empress, and messengers bearing the royal regalia who come to tell her that the Emperor is on his way to the temple for the sacrifice in celebration of victory. A charioteer is to be seen though the door, probably, says Lancaster, as a symbol of the Emperor's victory.[156] In Act II, a chandelier has appeared in the doorway, the Emperor and Empress are on stage. Act III shows us the Empress visiting Saint Catherine in prison. In spite of this, Catherine is out on the stage, and the extension scene is in darkness, the back lighting having been extinguished. This may have been done to indicate the conventional shift of place from the central part of the palace to the gaol.[157] In Act IV, the recess and central door are blocked by twin thrones, while in Act V, Mount Sinai has appeared in the manner already shown.[158]

These illustrations may, as Lancaster states, be "intermediary" between Mahelot and the settings of Racine and his contemporaries, but they are certainly more than midway. We distinguish in them few remnants of the *décor simultané*. It is not at all clear that the side-pieces are really compartments, for the balustrade, cornice and entablature above them are continuous, and further, we cannot be sure that these so-called "compartments"[159] are not solid: there is no visible access to them, although their pillars are disengaged from the motifs in between. Lancaster sees

154. Paris, 1643. The setting for Act III is reproduced by Laumann, *La machinerie au théâtre depuis les Grecs jusqu'à nos jours*, p. 55, Fig. 14, without explanation or attribution. Mme. Deierkauf-Holsboer has used Act IV to decorate the front cover of Vol. II of her *Marais*. The plates have been briefly studied since by Jacques Heuzey: "Le Martyre de Sainte Catherine tragédie en prose de M. de la Serre—étude de cinq gravures de l'édition de 1643," RHT, 4, 1967, pp. 383–86.

155. Lancaster makes this reservation in his *Mémoire*, but in his *History* assumes that it is in fact the play of the second list (Pt. II, vol. i, p. 363, fn. 14).

156. Lancaster (ibid., p. 364) devotes some space to a description of the pictures.

157. This is an interesting possibility, for it means scene-changing by blackout, which is unusual. The following example has come to our attention (from *Atalante et Hippomène, Ballet héroïque en trois actes*, MSS. BN franc. 24352, fo. 261):

I, iii: Le théâtre s'obscurcit.

II, vi: Le théâtre s'éclaircit et la forêt se change en un jardin agréable ornée de jets d'eau et de statues.

See also Prunières, *Ballet de cour*, p. 156.

158. See p. 155.

159. Lancaster, *History*, loc. cit.

FIG. 75.—*Le martyre de Sainte Catherine*, Act II.

FIG. 74.—*Le martyre de Sainte Catherine*, Puget de la Serre. Act I.

FIG. 76.—*Le martyre de Sainte Catherine*, Act III.

FIG. 77.—*Le martyre de Sainte Catherine*, Act IV.

FIG. 78.—*Le martyre de Sainte Catherine*, Act V.

them as representing an antechamber in which Catherine first appears, and a prison. Catherine's first appearance is with her cousin Emilie at the beginning of Act II, but this does not prove the necessity for an antechamber, especially as there is no sign of any special compartment for the Empress, who at the beginning of the tragedy is in her own apartment, specifically described as "chez l'impératrice." This leaves us with that ubiquitous stage nuisance, the prison, to dispose of. Would not the blacked-out recess of the stage, unnoticed by Lancaster, have served this purpose? Neither of the "compartments" defines any place, they are gratuitous and nondescript parts of what, as a whole, is a "palais à volonté." Let us risk the obvious by saying that the "palais à volonté" is so called precisely because it is gratuitous.

A form *of théâtre supérieur*, which Lancaster omits to mention, is present in Act I, where heralds are seen, no doubt trumpeting the Emperor's proclamations after his triumph over the Scythians.

With stage settings such as these, the Hôtel de Bourgogne is well on the way to the "palais à volonté," which with the "chambre à quatre portes" is to constitute the seventeenth-century equivalent of the *frons scaenae*.

Third Period of the "Mémoire"

The third part of the *Mémoire*, that specifically attributed to Michel Laurent, consolidates these processes. It is the last part to apply to the Hôtel de Bourgogne, since the fourth part dates from 1680, when the troupes which had amalgamated on the death of Molière in 1673, that is, Molière's company and that of the Marais, went to play at the Guénégaud. During the period under consideration, the Hôtel de Bourgogne was in a position to maintain what was by now a leadership in tragedy, making little effort to rival the Marais, or what was after 1673 the "troupe du Roi" at the Guénégaud, in the matter of machine plays.[160] The list comprising the third part of the document was composed, according to Lancaster, between January and November, 1678.[161] There are fifty-three plays listed. The scenes of twenty-three of these are described as "palais à volonté" or "théâtre à volonté" or, more rarely, some equivalent phrase.[162] The prominence of indoor plays helps the evolution of the box set, forestalling the use of wings "à l'italienne." The setting would undoubtedly be simple though perhaps not bare, as Despois would have us believe: "L'unité de lieu impliquait nécessairement l'unité du décor. Aussi faut-il bien se dire que, pour toutes les pièces qui n'étaient pas ce qu'on appelait des *pièces à machines,* et dont le théâtre du Marais eut longtemps la spécialité, la mise en scène était à peu près nulle."[163] The remaining plays fall into several categories: Firstly, remnants of the old repertoire, comprising chiefly those plays for which Corneille had craved indulgence. His "fiction théâtrale" without the use of compartments appears to be operating in the case of the following directions:

Le menteur. "Le théâtre est un jardin pour le premier acte, et pour le second acte il faut des maisons et des bâtiments et deux fenêtres."

Cinna. "Théâtre est un palais. Au second acte il faut un fauteuil et un tabouret à la gauche du roi."

Rodogune. "Théâtre est une salle de palais. Au second acte il faut un fauteuil et deux tabourets. Au cinquième, trois fauteuils et un tabouret."

In the *Cid,* the decorator has devised a simple room corresponding to Corneille's "fiction," which has to serve all four places, in the way in which Corneille would have wished, and in addition, "quatre portes," each one obviously meant to come from one of the four places in the play: place "whence" and place "where" are synonymous. The result is the box set. Quinault's *Mère coquette* is also a "chambre à quatre portes" but one in which the fusion is not present to the same extent: the room represented is one room: "la scène est à Paris dans une salle du logis d'Ismène."

Next, we note the open-air sets which yet preserve unity. The military camp is the usual locality, as in Racine's *Alexandre,* "tentes de guerre et pavillons," and Du Ryer's *Scévole,* "tentes et pavillons de guerre."

Next, indoor or outdoor sets having unity of place, but in which some specific reference is made to the backcloth or the "fond de théâtre":

Andromaque (Racine). "Théâtre est un palais à colonnes, et, dans le fond, une mer avec des vaisseaux."

160. Cf. Lancaster, *History*, Pt. III, vol. i, p. 17, and Pt. IV, vol. i, p. 15.
161. *Mémoire*, p. 28.
162. E.g. *Bérénice*: "Le théâtre est un petit cabinet royal"; *Tartuffe* and *Le misanthrope*: "Le théâtre est une chambre."
163. *Le théâtre français sous Louis XIV*, p. 130. See also Holsboer, *Mise en scène*, pp. 130 et seq.

Iphigénie (Racine). "Théâtre est des tentes, et dans le fond, une mer et des vaisseaux."

La Troade (Pradon). "Théâtre est un camp, des tentes. L'optique[164] est une ville ruinée, un fleuve devant."

Two of the sets are described as "une salle," that of *L'Avare,* which adds "et sur le derrière un jardin": the garden in the play being strictly place "whence," and Poisson's *Les femmes coquettes,* which also has the indication, exceptional in this part of the *Mémoire,* "le rideau abattu et se lève pour commencer," proof that an opening curtain was only rarely employed at the Hôtel in about 1670.[165] We may also add Thomas Corneille's *Dom Bertrand de Cigarall:* "théâtre est un cabaret, deux portes fermantes dans le fond."

Apart from the completely diffuse stage decorations, there is one most interesting category; this is the set which has a pair of houses downstage (it is difficult to imagine more), and a further scene upstage:

L'Ecole des femmes (Molière). "Théâtre est deux maisons sur le devant et le reste est une place de ville."

La fille capitaine (Montfleury). "Théâtre est deux maisons sur le devant, et le reste est une grande salle—quatre colonnes au milieu."

Jodelet ou le maître valet (Scarron). "Théâtre est des maisons sur le devant, et sur le derrière une chambre, une alcôve. Il faut un balcon sur le devant."

La femme juge et partie (Montfleury). "Théâtre est deux maisons sur le devant et le reste est une chambre."

Crispin gentilhomme (Montfleury). "Théâtre est des maisons mêlées d'arbres, et sur le derrière un cabaret."

We conclude from this that where duplicity of place was required, a further modification in the old simultaneous décor had taken place, not merely this time in the number of *mansions*, if it is still legitimate to call them so at this period, but in their orientation. The stage as a whole could be treated as providing one possibility of place at a time, and the forestage would be flanked by two houses. Change of place, instead of sweeping round a curved lay-out and thereby, in the early days of the Mahelot settings, partaking of the processional character of the mystery play, was being effected by a retreat in depth and in so doing was moving with the times. It is not easy to say whether some form of midstage curtain or shutter was used to conceal the upstage place until required. This would imply that the action of the plays must move from downstage houses to the upstage place with the progress of the intrigue, which is not necessarily the case, though it does occur very often.

The simplest, and what we might call the classical form of such a disposition appears to be the use of the houses purely as place "whence," leading onto a public square or street, which is the main part of the stage. Molière's *Ecole des femmes* provides us with such an instance. The house of Arnolphe is used only as place

---

164. That is, "la perspective."
165. Date of the performance according to the Frères Parfaict, tome XI, p. 49.

"whence" in the play, leading out onto the square.[166] This is not accomplished without some constraint. There are several scenes which would obviously have been better indoors, notably that of the "maximes" (Act III, Scene ii) which is however skilfully guided to the outside of the house; in Act III, Scene i, Arnolphe calls for "un siège au frais ici . . ." The play resolves itself into a series of open-air encounters.

Montfleury's *Femme juge et partie* is another example of this downstage symmetry. There is use for only one house in the play, and that again for purposes of place "whence." Act I, Scene i, involving Béatrix, Constance's *suivante* and Gusman, Bernadille's valet, is clearly outside the house of Bernadille:

Gusman, *apercevant Bernadille,* "Mais je le vois qui sort . . ."

The second house, however, could be anybody's. We can imagine that it belongs to Constance, but there is nothing to tell us so in the text. Here we surmise that the gradation of place upstage as the play advances took place upon near-baroque lines: there is in fact what we take to be a *scena ductilis* in rudimentary form, for Laurent's indication adds: "La coulisse s'ouvre à la fin du troisième et l'on passe un fauteuil sur le théâtre. Une porte au milieu du théâtre." The first three acts, which take place in the street, are played on the forestage. For the beginning of Act IV a shutter which had hidden the upstage half is drawn aside revealing the court-room. The use of the "porte au milieu du théâtre" becomes obvious:

Act IV, Scene i.

Julie

Eh bien! à le chercher as-tu perdu ton temps?
Et Bernadille enfin . . .

Octave

Madame, il est céans;
Et nous l'avons conduit avec assez de peine.
Je viens de le laisser dans la chambre prochaine.
Il est dans un transport qu'on ne peut exprimer:
Il tempête, il menace, il veut tout assommer.
Pour vous en divertir, voulez-vous qu'il avance?

Julie

Oui, qu'il vienne . . .

and Act IV, Scene iv:

Bernadille

Que l'on prenne le soin de chercher Béatrix,
Et qu'on l'amène ici.

166. There is no major reason for the appearance of a second house in the Laurent notice: it must be there for simple purposes of "parallelism."

Octave

Dans peu je vous l'amène . . .
(aux deux valets)
Cependant, remenez-le en la chambre prochaine.

Meanwhile, in Act V, the forestage can still be used as the street: Don Lope and Constance meet Julie on the street, and she ultimately takes them across the courtroom and through the door upstage center:

Julie

Entrez, pour le savoir, dans mon appartement.
Ce que je vous veux dire a de quoi vous surprendre.
Bernadille s'y plaint, que vous pourrez entendre;
. . . .
. . . . Il paraît, suivez-moi.
(Elle se retire avec Constance et Don Lope.)

Finally, Act V, Scene vi:

Octave

Frédéric vous veut voir; entrez dans cette salle.
(Béatrix passe dans la salle voisine.)

The same formula is observed in the same author's *Fille capitaine*, with the exception that the room is a room in one of the houses. *Crispin gentilhomme* is a variation on the same theme.

The disposition could be adapted to the plays of earlier times. Scarron's popular *Jodelet maître*, first played at the Marais,[167] then at the Hôtel during the second period of the *Mémoire*, is evidence of this. Two rooms, as well as the street, are required for this play. The play opens with the street scene, in which the balcony of Dom Fernand's house is used. In Act II the scene moves to the interior of that house, and remains there for the rest of the play, the only visible variation in the text being Act V, in which "Béatris enters by a little door with a candle in her hand": an obvious reference to Laurent's alcove. It looks decidedly as though the façade of Dom Fernand's house, with its balcony, is a *ferme* halfway upstage, opening to display the interior for Acts II, III, and IV, while the alcove at the back is revealed, presumably by a curtain, for Act V.

We are left with a small group of plays which are diffuse in their staging:

Marianne (Tristan l'Hermite). "Théâtre est un palais au premier acte . . . au second acte c'est une chambre . . . au quatrième, il faut la prison. Au cinq, le palais et un fauteuil et abaisser le rideau pour la fin."

Crispin musicien (Hauteroche). "Théâtre est deux chambres différentes qui se changent à tous les actes."

167. Lancaster, *History*, Pt. II, vol. ii, p. 457. But see his fn. 7.

Dom Japhet d'Arménie (Scarron). ''Théâtre est village jusqu'au troisième acte, qui laisse voir des bâtiments, un balcon du côté du roi, une fenêtre au-dessus qui s'ouvre et ferme.''

Tristan's *Marianne* as staged by Laurent is a puzzle. There is no evidence of an act curtain, and the assumption that there was none is reinforced by the remark ''abaisser le rideau pour la fin.'' In this section of the *Mémoire* we now have a curtain for the beginning of the play, and one for the end, but none to mark a scene change as between acts. The peculiar problems raised by a play requiring several compartments in 1636 and staged again at some much later date prior to 1678 are considerable. There are three possible rooms in the palace, a prison, and a street. Bernardin, staging the play at the Odéon in 1897, gave it a complete simultaneous set, with all the required compartments. Madeleine cannot see how such a set could still be in use in 1636. Lancaster sides on the whole with Bernardin.[168] It is certain that the staging at the Hôtel de Bourgogne was very different. Such general details as have emerged of the categories of play in this third period requiring two or more places (for example *Cinna, Rodogune,* and *Jodelet maître*), preclude any assumption that the full number of compartments was used, yet the extreme complexity of place in the play silences all conjecture as to what was substituted. We assume a *tapisserie* for the prison in Thomas Corneille's *Comte d'Essex:* ''Théâtre est un palais et une prison qui paraît au quatrième acte,''[169] for ''paraît'' might well mean this.

In the case of Scarron's *Dom Japhet d'Arménie,* as in that of the *Menteur,* it is infinitely to be regretted that no notice of their staging appears in the second part of the *Mémoire* in which they both figure, for it would have provided us with invaluable evidence of the development from one to the other. The notice of the third part reads decidedly as though a *ferme* or a midstage curtain is used: ''Théâtre est village jusqu'au troisième acte, qui *laisse voir* des bâtiments.'' Let us now place this against the evidence of Scarron's own stage directions:

Act I: Théâtre représente une place du village d'Orgas.

Act III: Le théâtre représente un salon de la maison du Commandeur.

Act V: Le théâtre représente une place où donne la maison du Commandeur, décorée de balcons.

It is immediately clear that in the performance at the Hôtel de Bourgogne the Act V elements are already there when Act III opens. Act III, according to Laurent, only reveals ''des bâtiments'': there is no mention of an interior, ''chambre'' or ''salon.'' Downstage, we conclude, is the village square, and when the full remaining set is revealed upstage in Act III, the actual house of the Commandeur, for the duration of Act III, ''defines'' a room within it which is the stage itself, unless the ''salon'' is ignored completely. The defining function ceases with Act V.

---

168. Madeleine, *Tristan, La Mariane*, édn. critique, 1917, p. xxii; Lancaster, *History*, Pt. II, vol. i, p. 52.

169. On the question of prisons and their disappearance under the classical impact, see Holsboer, *Mise en scène*, pp. 134 et seq.

Hauteroches' *Crispin musicien* contains valuable information. The direction "deux chambres différentes qui se changent à tous les actes" refers not to a complete change, but to a change from one house to another, Acts I, III, and V being set in Phélonte's house, Acts II and IV in that of Dorame. The writer is an actor of the Troupe Royale, and his anxiety to make matters of staging clear in his text, his fascination with the *ferme,* stand us in good stead. At the end of Act I:

> Phélonte se retirant, ses six Laquais entrent par les deux côtés du Théâtre, et s'y étant rangés sur une même ligne, jouent un air pour discerner l'Acte. Ensuite on pousse deux châssis qui les couvrent, ces châssis, qu'on nomme *Ferme,* doivent représenter la salle de Dorame, de même que le reste du Théâtre, dans laquelle se passe tout le Second Acte. Il faut qu'à cette Ferme il y ait deux Portes qui marquent deux Cabinets.

Exit and entrance, we note, can be made through the *ferme.* The end scene of the act rules out any possibility of an act curtain.[170] At the end of Act II, the *ferme* opens, revealing the six musical lackeys, and we are back in Phélonte's house. The process is repeated for Acts III and IV.

Only one play remains, and that another example, as with Desmaret's *Mirame* in the second list, of the exceptional importation from another theater and another convention. It is Molière's *Princesse d'Elide.* Divorced however from its context in the *Plaisirs de l'Ile enchantée* at Versailles in 1664, the play is simple enough and in no way fraught with technical difficulty. It requires no scene change, although one may well wonder how the stage of the Hôtel de Bourgogne would support a balletic *intermède* of any size, and how the limited number of musicians would fare in 1676.[171] It does not seem that Dawn, opening the play, was even in a chariot as was customary; there is no mention of it in the account of the *Plaisirs:* "Aussitôt qu'on eût tiré la toile un grand concert de plusieurs instruments se fit entendre, et l'Aurore, représentée par mademoiselle Hilaire, ouvrit la scène et chanta ce récit . . ." The scene itself, as depicted by Laurent, is quite simple: "Théâtre est une forêt. Il faut un grand arbre au milieu." Lancaster expresses interest in the tree but fails to stipulate whether it is the tree of the first *intermède* or that which appears after the end of the play, a machine mentioned in the récit: "Pendant que ces aimables personnes dansaient, il sortit de dessous le théâtre la machine d'un grand arbre chargé de seize Faunes dont huit jouèrent de la flûte, et les autres du violon avec un concert le plus agréable du monde." We may be quite certain that the Hôtel was not capable of managing the appearance through a trap of a machine carrying sixteen persons. The tree referred to by Laurent is almost certainly that climbed by Moron in his terror on the appearance of the bear at the end of the third scene of the first *intermède.*

To summarize, in the Mahelot sketches, native and Italian, old and new, are mingled. But the Italian influences apparent in them do not distinguish genre as

---

170. The play is published in 1674.
171. A Royal edict (12th Aug. 1672) limits the number of violins and other instruments to twelve (Arch. Nat. 0¹ 16, fo. 142 v°). See also Mélèse, *Le théâtre et le public à Paris sous Louis XIV*, 1934, p. 417.

does Serlio, and the illustrations are Sabbattinian as much as Serlian, although a few years earlier than the publication of *Practica di fabricar scene e machine ne'teatri*. There is little real evidence, except in the perspective backcloth, of baroque parallelism in the decorations, there are one or two examples of the use of machinery: the medieval *volerie* with a pagan twist and the *théâtre supérieur* appear, in baroque clothing, from the mystery and the street theater. The word "perspective" is borrowed from the baroque theater to indicate the backcloth. This theater is Italian in disposition, the curve of its separate items tending naturally towards a perspective scene. But it is largely medieval in function, and this function will be hard-lived.

The *décor simultané*, in one of its further modes, lingers on into the next period of the *Mémoire*, and in fact has a longer life than is usually admitted. Paradoxically, a purifying breath comes from the Marais. Tragedy is beginning to sweep away stage effect, and it reduces the number of compartments. But in the years leading up to the compilation of the second list, a form of *scène simultanée* is very much alive: it has a new orientation, developing up or downstage instead of across the stage. It has been called by Schérer the *décor composite*; we refer to its growth in terms of the concept of place "whence," which, with the increasing observance of the unities, increases in importance and is itself an unconscious return to the ancients, gradually ousting diversity of place on the stage.

The composite décor was potentially developing towards the baroque stage. In its revelation of new place, upstage or downstage, but mostly, one assumes, the former, it was in constant danger of giving itself over to effects with the "coulisse qui s'ouvre," which is the English Restoration shutter or the Renaissance *scena ductilis*. These possibilities are arrested by the mass of regular tragedy, which takes the existing elements of staging at the Hôtel de Bourgogne and disciplines them into the "palais à volonté." The "palais à volonté" says "thus far and no farther" to the onslaught of perspective at that theater; it endows it with a perspective scene which does no more than continue the lines of the auditorium.

We have little pictorial evidence of the "palais à volonté." There cannot be much doubt that, following the line of the Hardy illustrations in Mahelot's sketches, and the engravings of the *Martyre de Sainte Catherine* (see Figs. 74–78), but particularly if an outside scene, it would exploit perspective to some extent, on and off the backcloth. The frontispieces of editions of Racine and Corneille teach us nothing. The engraver is here concerned with removing the picture from any scenic connotation and making it as impressive as possible. He is in fact illustrating the published work of literature and not the performance. This is however far from the case with comedy, and in particular that of Molière. A monograph by Herzel has demonstrated that the early editions of Molière, and especially the first collected works of 1682, do, in their illustrations, present viable theatrical evidence, that in his earliest plays (to 1663) "he accepted without question the unified exterior setting that he inherited from traditional French and Italian farce; in *Tartuffe* and *Le Misanthrope* (1664, 1666) he experimented successfully with the intense concentration that could be achieved by confining the action of a full-length play to one room; in *Dom Juan* and in several cheerful farces (1665–7) he allowed the action to float freely from one location to another, even changing the setting in the midst of continuous action . . .''[172] Of those comedies by Molière staged at the Hôtel de Bourgogne during the period of Michel Laurent, namely *Le Misanthrope, Tartuffe,* and *L'Avare, L'Avare,* as Herzel points out, definitely requires two places: ''Théâtre est une salle, et sur le derrière, un jardin.'' This is clearly to be seen in Brissart's frontispiece for the 1682 edition.

The period witnesses the atrophy of machine effects at this theater; they are most frequent in the first section of the *Mémoire,* and diminish progressively thereafter. The situation is doubtless imposed to some extent by the physical surroundings, by the exiguity of the stage. The rôle in this disappearance of the seigneurs who sat on the stage is extremely obscure. We cannot believe, as Rigal does, that the ''scène simultanée'' was condemned in 1636 by the first appearance of the seigneurs on either side of the forestage, much less that after that date ''la décoration ne disposa guère plus que de la toile de fond qui pouvait changer au cours de la représentation ou rester la même . . .''[173] for all the evidence of the *Mémoire* is against this. Despois quotes a letter from Montdory to Balzac concerning this first known appearance of the phenomenon, which applies to the Marais, and not the Hôtel de Bourgogne. Tallemant, as this author says, speaks of it as a recently established usage, and d'Aubignac does not even mention it when writing of the inconveniences of theater buildings, while the seigneurs certainly seem to be claiming no rights on the stage in 1648 at the Hôtel, when Scarron shows it to us as occupied by the poor authors, who, entering free of charge, would consequently tend to come in greater number and overspill onto the stage.[174]

The purity of the Hôtel de Bourgogne stage is chiefly a matter of choice: the choice of the dramatic author, who does not want machinery in his plays. The physical difficulties are contributory factors. Laurent himself, one suspects, was quite capable of staging a machine tragedy or even an opera, if required to do so. But these genres simply did not enter the repertoire of the Hôtel to any significant degree.[175] Once the pastoral has been left behind in the Mahelot period, its exper-

172. Eugène Vinaver has pointed out how frequently these illustrators depict precisely that which could not appear on the stage. See Picard, ''Racine and Chauveau,'' *Journal of the Warburg and Courtauld Institutes,* vol. XIV, Nos. 3–4, 1951. Roger Herzel, ''The décor of Molière's stage: The testimony of Brissart and Chauveau,'' *PMLA,* vol. 93, Oct. 1978, no. 5, pp. 925 et seq.

173. *Théâtre français,* pp. 292–93. Cf. Holsboer, *Mise en scène,* p. 125.

174. Despois, *Le théâtre français sous Louis XIV,* pp. 116–18. We cannot however accept his suggestion that this kept the machine out of Racinian tragedy. Celler, *Décors,* p. 142, voices the same curious hypothesis: ''peut-être que Racine eût beaucoup plus osé dans sa mise en scène, s'il n'avait pas eu, comme encadrement à son drame, deux perspectives de costumes à la mode,'' as does Fritsche, ''La scène de Molière et son organisation,'' *Le Moliériste,* vol. IX, June–July–Aug., 1887, pp. 76–77.

175. Laurent, if it is he, was familiar enough with the court theaters and all their concomitant splendor; this is suggested by two entries from the ''comptes de la maison du roi'' (Arch. Nat. O[1] 2984 (7) dated 1685) in which we find:

iments with the machine genre are few. The tradition of pastoral machine effect lingers on in a revival of Sallebray's *Jugement de Pâris,* of which Loret says:

> Plusieurs Perspectives changeantes,
> Plus de Vingt Machines volantes,
> D'admirables éloignements,
> Des Feux et des Embrasements,
> Enfin, cette pompeuse Scène,
> Où l'on ravit la belle Hélène.[176]

In the case of Rotrou's *Deux Sosies,* of which the *Mémoire* tells us nothing, it is the Marais which makes of it a "pièce à spectacle," the *Naissance d'Hercule,*[177] while after the *Jugement de Pâris* Lancaster finds only Boursault's *Yeux de Philis* which could be described as a machine play,[178] although machines, he points out, were used in Villier's *Festin de Pierre* and Gilbert's *Amours d'Ovide.*[179] The troupe rapidly understood that their best competitive weapon was the regular tragedy.

The Italians

After the last general amalgamation of troupes which creates the Comédie Française, the Italians move into the Hôtel late in 1680. They flood the stage with machinery—of a kind. It seems fitting that this old house, when, at the last, it had to submit to the indignity of spectacle, should commit widespread slaughter in its

> A ~~Saint~~ Laurent la somme de £54 pour ouvrages faits au théâtre de Chambord en ladite année 1685.
>
>   and
>
> A ~~Saint~~ Laurent la somme de £390 10s. pour raccommodage et augmentations faits dans la salle des Comédies de Fontainebleau.

There is no reason to suppose that this is not the Laurent of the *Mémoire.*

176. Cf. Lancaster, *History,* Pt. II, vol. i, p. 240. The *Muse historique* is describing a performance at the Hôtel on 27th December 1657. For this rather simple play (published in 1639) to have acquired such an incrustation of splendor, a great deal of imagination must have been required of the stage manager; but the major effort of imagination is probably Loret's. Raymond Picard, in his review of our first edn., (*Revue des Sciences Humaines,* Apr.–June, 1958) quotes precisely the *Jugement de Paris* to cast doubt on our suggestion of a growing specialization in the seventeenth-century theater houses. The argument appears to be based upon the supposition that one swallow makes a summer.

177. Cf. RHT, 3, 1950, p. 272.

178. *La métamorphose des yeux de Philis changez en astres, Pastoralle, Représentée par la Troupe Royale,* Paris, 1665. Act II, scene vii, "L'Amour en l'air." Act III, scene v (last scene of the act), "Jupiter assis dans un Trône de gloire."

179. E.g. *Les amours d'Ovide, Pastorale héroique,* Paris, 1663, Act V, scene ii:

> *Céphise*: Dis, les Grâces du Ciel sont-elles revenues?
> *Aminthe*: Oui, leur superbe char a traversé les nues.

agony. We may entertain the most severe doubts as to the lavishness and efficacy of the machines which were produced, but this could only enchance their effect, for the Italians treat us to the most rollicking and persistent guying of the Opera known to the century. In *Arlequin Mercure galant* Mercury appears flying on Jupiter's eagle, which he has has "borrowed." His winged feet are wet and will carry him through the air no longer, *"perche passando per una strada, una servanta* m'a vidé un pot de chambre dessus."[180] In the *Toison d'Or comique*, Jason makes a speech to the Queen from his Car, and then falls out.[181] Jupiter descends, in the prologue to the *Divorce*, mounted on a turkey, which Arlequin offers to cook for him: "aussi bien les Dieux de l'Opéra qui sont bien montés quand ils viennent s'en retournent toujours à pied"[182] the scurrilous attacks gather momentum: Momus, seeing Jupiter leave his heaven on foot, asks him why, as a *pis aller*, he does not use one of the Opera machines:

> A la charge d'en faire les réparations auparavant; car, comme vous savez, on ne s'expose guère dans ces sortes de Voitures qu'après une visite d'Experts; encore aurait-il fallu faire passer la Machine par le feu, pour en étranger tout le mauvais air, et comme vous pourriez dire, une certaine teinture de Taverne et de Cuisine qui sont les parfums ordinaires des Dieux habitués à l'Opéra.[183]

The *théâtre supérieur* does not of course escape. Arlequin, as Apollo, sits ludicrously on a raised throne.[184] The "changement à vue" thrives, in the same intention of satire: caverns change into mountains, palaces into gardens, butterflies into nymphs, lanterns into shepherds, and so on. The use of the *ferme* to reveal new scenes is very frequent indeed; but the prime function of the spectacle is the pastiche of spectacle itself. The Italians leave the Opera machine hanging ridiculously aloft, like the falsely clever Socrates in the *Clouds* of Aristophanes.

Let us conclude that for this theater there is no regular evidence, throughout the period treated, of either a proscenium arch or a permanent proscenium arch curtain. A front curtain seems to have been used sporadically, to begin and end plays. It had, in any case, been catered for in the 1647 contract, and we cannot expect to find regular evidence for it in stage directions.[185] A simplified scene continues the lines of the auditorium; in their tussle with the problems of unity of place, the authors have resorted to the drama of entry, the exploitation of place "whence." What more striking witness of this necessity, inherent in the establishment of the unities, could we quote than that of Voltaire, who in his *Commentaires sur Corneille* supports the three unities, and as a solution to their problems, proposes that Parisian theaters should have "une scène semblable à celle de Vicence," the only one worthy

---

180. Gherardi, *Le théâtre italien*, Paris, 1700, vol. I, p.2.
181. Ibid., vol. I, pp. 213 et seq.
182. Ibid., vol. II, p. 109.
183. Ibid., vol. V, pp. 3-4.
184. Ibid., vol. V, p. 176.
185. See Védier, op. cit., pp. 118-19.

of Corneille?[186] This instinctive solution is also arrived at in a more practical sphere by the theater projects of Cochin and La Guêpière in the eighteenth century.

The complete *décor successif* never storms the citadel of the Hôtel de Bourgogne, and until the Italian occupation that theater is farther away from habitual scene changing with a proscenium arch curtain than it was at the beginning, since the *tapisserie* is used less and less. The successive scene is revealed as a specific child of the Opera tradition, of the Italian Order, necessitated by the fact that that convention closed in the scenic space. The "palais à volonté" and the "chambre à quatre portes," operating with unity of place, are the modest seventeenth-century *frons scaenae*. In this desert of baroque distances they make of the shoddy little stage an oasis of the dramatic entrance. Racine and the regulars save one of the Parisian theaters in a way in which the Italian or the English theater is never saved: they save it from the wand of Circe.

186. *OEuvres*, ed. Moland, vol. XXXI, p. 328, *Remarques sur Cinna Acte II, scène 1ère.* Also vol. XXXI, p. 212, *Remarques sur le Cid.* For further criticism of the French stage lay-out, see vol. XXXII, p. 366, *Remarques sur le troisième discours.*

CHAPTER SIX

HYPERTROPHY

HAVING SEEN HOW, in one theater in Paris, the forces of baroque decoration were ultimately halted, we must now follow them as they batten upon the rest of the French stage, growing in frequency and splendor, to the detriment of dramatic action and poesy, until little or no semblance of the legitimate stage is to be seen in those representations which fall under their spell.

The Theorists of Perspective

Our examination of the advent of the Italian Order has tended to stress the manner in which decorative convention has contributed to an irruption into the flat face wall of the stage, towards a prolongation, figured or factual, of the scenic space beyond. The theoretical bases for this are worked out by the writers on perspective in the sixteenth and seventeenth centuries. They, as well as the Italian practitioners who arrived in France, have their share in its advancement.

They are not immediately aware of what they are doing in this direction. Their earlier efforts are disinterested, theoretical in the extreme, and do not apply in any obvious way to the theater, so that their history for us will be in some degree that of a growing theatrical consciousness.

The first Italian painter to reduce the principles of perspective to some sort of order is Paolo Uccello.[1] An early English writer is John Peckham, Archbishop of Canterbury. The first French theorist of any note is Jean Pélerin, alias Viator.[2] He acknowledges his predecessors: Vitellio or Vitello,[3] and John Peckham, as will the majority of his successors, for the *perspecteurs* are a tight little family group, developing all the dissensions of such a social unit. Where his predecessors however had applied themselves to geometry and optics, Pélerin is concerned with the direct application of perspective to painting, so that in this sense at least he is the father of French scene decoration.[4] He is also near to the court: his epitaph describes him as "secretarius regius," and it seems that he was secretary to Louis XI.[5] There are several triumphal arches in his work. Pélerin died in 1532, but his work reappears unexpectedly in 1626 and 1635.[6] People certainly continued to read him: one of the

1. 1389–1472.
2. *De artificiali perspectiva*, 1505, 2nd edn., 1509, 3rd edn., 1521, facsimile 2nd edn., 1860.
3. A Polish author of the twelfth century.
4. See Kernodle, *From Art to Theatre*, p. 196, who reproduces from *De artificiali perspectiva* a view seen through a city gate, which he describes as "City gate as proscenium frame."
5. Tross edn., 1860, *Notice*, p. i.
6. At La Flèche, ed. by Mathurin Jousse. The text of the 1526 translation from the Latin of the 3rd edn. was presumably never printed. Jousse prints a new text with

three copies of the third edition in the Bibliothèque de l'Arsenal has the following longhand inscription: "De Bibliotheca parisiensi pp. Minimorum ad plateam regiam. 1638. Dono. D. Niceron," and this is interesting, for Niceron himself is a well-known writer on perspective.[7]

The year 1532 sees a Paris edition of Dürer's perspective, translated from German into Latin, which again seeks to apply perspective to painting, and this brings us to what we might call the Vitruvian "injection" in France. It takes place through Serlio. We have already noted the appearance of Martin's translation of Serlio's second book of perspective in 1545,[8] containing a treatise on the theater, and a Paris edition in Italian in the same year. These represent, once more, a form of "consecration" for future writers. The overall Vitruvian message is that of the importance of perspective in architecture, and in Vitruvius, scenery is allied to architecture. Goujon, the illustrator, emphasizes perspective in word and in drawing. The practice of perspective is henceforth an observance of ancient canons, and a form of perfectionism in painting and architecture. Its future is assured. The lateness of theatrical application from Italy has been noted by Günter Schöne, who observes that the formation of the Italian renaissance perspective set, beginning only at the outset of the sixteenth century, thus occurs towards the end of the development of linear perspective in pictorial art. There is a natural further time-lag as between Italy and France.[9]

In French writings there is however no specific mention of the theater, and this continues to be the case with Jean Cousin in 1560.[10] Nevertheless, he is a practical man, describing himself as "maistre painctre," and all his examples are clearly intended for practical use. Perspective is growing in popularity. Yet even when Cousin speaks of its application to "aires, planchers, et côtés d'une salle ou chambre" there is no mention of the theater, though like most of his colleagues he is very much aware of the universal applications of his method; this is so with Jacques Androuet Ducerceau as well—his Leçons de Perspective positive (1576) are equally negative from this point of view.

Yet the typical perspecteur is a man of many parts, and these parts are often admirably suited to the man of the theater: geometrician, architect, and engineer, sometimes engraver or painter, he represents a combination of accomplishments

a reprint of the plates in 1635 (Tross edn., Notice, p. iii). Lavedan, Histoire de l'urbanisme, p. 22, alludes to a seventeenth-century translation by Martellange. Cf. Brion-Guerry, pp. 159–162.

7. Notice of the Tross edn., p. 111.
8. See p. 98.
9. Premier livre d'architecture, trans. Martin, Jean Goujon, Aux Lecteurs: ". . . pour induir tous ouvriers à se munir d'icelles Géométrie et Perspective, sans lesquelles ils ne vont jamais qu'à tâtons." Schöne, Günter, "Les traités de perspective, sources historiques du théâtre," TR/RT, vol. III, no. 3, 1961, pp. 176–90. Unlike Védier, Schöne appears to assume that scene changing by proscenium arch curtain is an automatic end-product of the perspective set.
10. Livre de Perspective de Jean Cousin.

which are prerequisites for the construction of baroque décors and machinery; Salomon de Caus,[11] after purveying his talents as architect and engineer to the Count of Flanders, the Prince of Wales, and the Elector Palatine of Bavaria, ultimately settles down as architect and engineer to Louis XIII. He seems conscious of no theatrical applications for his art, and yet some of his contrivances are theatrical and undoubtedly intended for use in fête or court ballet: "Machine par laquelle l'on représentera une Galatée qui sera traînée sur l'eau par deux dauphins, allant en ligne droite, et se retournant d'elle-même, cependant qu'un cyclope joue dessus un flageolet . . ."[12] "Machine par laquelle sera représenté un Neptune, lequel tournera circulairement, à l'entour d'une Roche, avec quelques autres figures lesquelles jetteront de l'eau en tournant."[13] The second book of his *Raison des forces mouvantes* is devoted entirely to "grottes et fontaines." Some of his figures, although he may not have the theater in mind, show how the "extensionist" powers of the art were being applied to interiors: "Pour peindre contre la muraille d'une chambre une continuation de ladite chambre avec aucunes figures, et aussi poser les ombres à tout ce qui est peint dans ladite chambre."[14] Perspective made everything look bigger, longer, more magnificent, hence its attraction. Its exponents were already taking on those "magical" properties later to be attributed to Torelli, who is called "the wizard." Another potential complete man of the theater is Desargues, who, according to Poudra, was so appreciated by Richelieu that he was summoned to be the Cardinal's engineer and architect.[15]

During this period of staging simplicity in France it is not surprising to find the writers failing to realize the possibilities of the instrument they are handling. Marolois' *Opera mathematica* (1614), containing also his edition of the architectural and perspective writings of Vredeman Vries, is such a work. But the influence of Serlio is making itself felt: we cannot say definitely to what the authors are applying their perspective, whether to mere illustration, to constructed pieces of architecture, or simply *in vacuo*. One of Marolois' plates (after Vries) is most theatrical, and reminiscent of Serlio's comic scene.[16]

One process is working itself out that is to be of great utility to the baroque theater. The divers applications of perspective to different objects and natural phenomena are creating a stockpile of possible "pieces." Vaulezard speaks of individual units: galleries, gardens, floor-boards, rooms, as coming within the practice of perspective,[17] yet never mentions theater decoration, although his general intention is merely decorative: we are never clear as to how perspective is to be applied to these objects, whether they are to be painted or constructed, or what their purpose is to

---

11. *La perspective, avec la raison des ombres et miroirs . . .*, London, 1612. *Les raisons des forces mouvantes*, Frankfort, 1615, and Paris, 1624.
12. Bk. I, Pl. 32, Problem XXIV (*Raison des forces mouvantes*).
13. Ibid., Bk. II, Problem XXVII.
14. *La perspective*, 1612, ch. 8.
15. *Oeuvres de Desargues*, ed. Poudra, Paris, 1864.
16. Pt. V, Pl. 42: "Un marché, avec une maison de ville, et des rues."
17. *Abrégé ou raccourci de la perspective par l'imitation . . .*, 1633, p. 77.

be. It is apparent that a stage decorator could take the whole of Vaulezard's *Abrégé*, as he could many of the other works, and simply apply it wholesale to the theater. The theatrical effect of perspective is implicit in the title of Niceron's work although it again does not touch the stage explicitly: *La perspective curieuse ou magie artificielle des effets merveilleux.*[18] With Abraham Bosse we reach a point where decorative perspective is naturally applied to illustration. Bosse's work as an engraver is well enough known, but his prowess as an exponent of perspective suggests some reserve as to the faithfulness of his engravings, which would undoubtedly employ perspective to the utmost, possibly in falsification of the theatrical scene represented.[19]

Practical application is not the strong point of these writers. They are concerned firstly with the theory of perspective, and then vaguely with its decorative possibilities for which they fail on the whole to point out any practical use; nor is this surprising, for we are hardly out of the first period of Mahelot's *Mémoire*, when perspective on the theater backcloth was limited, and an entire set in continued perspective an unusual thing. Yet 1641 is the year of *Mirame*: a revolutionary event in the progress of the French theater towards the baroque, and 1642 marks a revolutionary access of theatrical consciousness in perspective writing with the publication of the first volume of Dubreuil's *Perspective pratique.*[20] By the time Dubreuil has reached his third volume in 1649 the theater set is perhaps the main object of his figures.

The stockpiling of items now becomes specifically theatrical; the items themselves are "pièces détachées" in the manner of theater flats, and can be shaken up to form any ensemble, like a kaleidoscope. The spread of perspective, as we can see from Dubreuil, is helping towards the stylization of the baroque decorative piece just as it helped to stylize the whole of architecture. Constant references remind us that Dubreuil is handling a repertoire of objects which can be used for ornamentation, theatrical or paratheatrical:

> Des pièces détachées qui ne sont autres que Perspectives ordinaires: mais coupéés, divisées, et séparées, mouvantes, tournantes et coulantes. Qui peuvent serviraux Autels, et Oratoires des Eglises; aux Jardins, et Maisons de Plaisance, aux Alcôves, Théâtres, Ballets, etc.[21]
>
> Ce que je dis . . . se doit entendre des pièces qui sont en un jardin, au bout d'une Allée, d'une Galerie, sur un Théâtre, aux Ballets aux Alcôves etc.[22]

---

18. 1638.
19. *Moyen universel de pratiquer la perspective sur les tableaux ou surfaces irrégulières.* Paris, privilege of 1643, etc. It was Bosse who undertook to popularize and complete the works of the mathematician Desargues in this field and instituted a course in perspective at the Académie de Peinture (MSS. BN franc. 12345, 1663, p. 86).
20. It is just possible that the illustrations of the second and third volumes are by Bosse. The frontispiece of the work is by him, and Duplessis (quoted by Weigert, *Inventaire du fonds français: graveurs du XVIIe siècle*, tome I, 1939, p. 498) sees Bosse's manner in the explanatory figures to the text though he makes no formal attribution.
21. Title page of traité IV.
22. Bk. III, *Instruction sur le Traité IV.*

Dubreuil, we may see, begins by including all decorative possibilities in his figures. Imperceptibly however we realize that he is speaking mainly, if not exclusively, of the theater. His descriptions of the *scena ductilis* and *versatilis* do not for instance inform us that they are for stage use, yet it is difficult to imagine many other applications:

> Ensuite de celles-là suivent d'autres [pièces] qui outre qu'elles sont détachées, elles sont encore changeantes, soit par le mouvement des Triangles, qui peuvent en un moment donner trois faces différentes à ses Perspectives, soit par le coulement de deux châssis, qui étant unis l'un à l'autre font voir une belle Perspective, de Bâtiments, de Jardins, de Bois de Rochers etc. Mais si on tire ces châssis de part et d'autre, ils se séparent par le milieu, et se glissant dans des coulis qui sont dessus et dessous, font voir une autre pièce de Perspective, cachée derrière toute autre que la premère.[23]

The remainder of this instruction rings the changes upon these possibilities, and still Dubreuil does not give the theater pride of place: we do not hear of it until later, and by that time it is patent that he cannot be talking about anything else: "Et si l'on veut que les Perspectives des côtés se changent comme celles de fonds, on pourra se servir de triangles, selon la largeur et la place qu'on aura sur le Théâtre."[24] All this permits us to surmise that previous writers, in particular Vaulezard and Marolois, have the theater in mind to a greater extent than is immediately apparent.

The whole range of mechanical "changements à vue" is to be found in Dubreuil, including the type of *versatilis* which was installed in the Gracht theater in Brussels at about the same time (see Fig. 112): "L'on peut encore faire changer de Scène par de simples châssis, au milieu desquels il y aura un essieu, ou seulement deux pointes de fer qui poseront sur des pivots, pour peu qu'on remue ces châssis ainsi montrés, ils donneront tantôt une face et puis une autre."[25]

No method of change is left unexamined: *ductilis, versatilis,* the relieve and shutter, the grouping of several flats one behind the other down either side of the stage. Like his Italian predecessors he can see that the triangle gives rise to problems of space (Fig. 79): "Sans cette invention de triangles, on serait plus longtemps à changer une Scène: mais aussi faut-il bien plus de place pour eux (à raison qu'ils doivent se tourner) que pour de simples châssis."[26] Sometimes he uses a combination of triangle and *coulisse*,[27] while to save space he does not hesitate to use revolving parallelograms (Fig. 80), machines which, he implies, are in current use: "Pour les corps de devant, que je fais d'un angle obtus, pour donner plus de creux aux Perspectives; l'on peut faire deux petites machines en forme de Rhombe, *comme ils sont*

---

23. Ibid., loc. cit.
24. Ibid., loc. cit.
25. Ibid., loc. cit.
26. Bk. III, traité IV, pratique x.
27. Bk. III, traité IV, pratique xi. This too, he admits, needs more space, and, he seems to imply, both methods are infrequently used: "Les deux pratiques, x et xi . . . supposent un espace plus que l'ordinaire des théâtres."

FIG. 79.—Dubreuil, tri-
angles.

ordinairement aux Théâtres."[28] The proscenium arch curtain is not present to the mind
of Dubreuil: all changes are unconcealed. In some instances one feels that, change
apart, here is the typical set of the second part of the *Mémoire:* Traité IV, pratique
i shows us a set with two houses represented by flat wings, in front, with a garden
on a large single flat behind (Fig. 81). There is to be a space between the two for
the actors to pass. Every type of scene involving every possible architectural and
topographical feature is constrained into a perspective set. Whenever possible the
architectural sets comprise an arch or arcade through which a second element is
discerned. The good "religieux de la Compagnie de Jésus" is concerned with the
application of perspective decoration to his own domain as well as to the theater,
and says in his pratique vi: "Cette pièce et les précédentes de ce Traité peuvent
aussi bien servir, pour des Oratoires, où on met le Saint Sacrement le grand Ven-

28. Ibid., pratique xii. The italics are ours.

FIG. 80.—Dubreuil, *Scena versatilis*.

dredi, en y ajoutant quelque pièce de dévotion, qu'au bout d'une Allée et d'une Galerie, qu'en une Alcôve et sur un Théâtre.''

Pursuing this line, he restores the *gloire* to an ecclesiastical function (Fig. 82): ''Si c'est pour mettre le S. Sacrement: il faut le poser entre le premier et le second châssis, . . . Je dis si c'est pour y mettre le S. Sacrement: car on peut se servir de ces nuées en des Théâtres et des Ballets, où on veut représenter le Paradis, même on peut y faire monter, et descendre des personnes . . .''[29] With Dubreuil then, every natural and architectural phenomenon that can be reduced to perspective is so reduced, and every form of unconcealed change is submitted to the general discipline of perspective, including those forms of *scena versatilis* which were to disappear in the search for space. A glance at his book convinces us that he was not a very competent ''expert'': he has used his predecessors to good effect (Niceron accuses him of copying Desargues)[30] and he is vastly concerned with selling his wares. His interest for us is the way in which he realized the theatrical possibilities of his work, where his contemporaries, whether they realized this or not, preferred to remain ''universal.''

29. Traité IV, pratique ix.
30. Poudra, *Desargues*, Pt. II, p. 202.

FIG. 81.—Décor by
Dubreuil. Compare
decorations of Mahelot's
Mémoire.

Apart from the *scena versatilis* which makes him a fellow of Sabbattini and Danti, there is one constant factor in the work of Dubreuil which the "illegitimate" stage was to discard as a principle at the turn of the century. This is the optimum viewpoint in the center of the house, from which every perspective is calculated. From this Dubreuil professes not only to calculate (he never enters into details as to his calculations) the general perspective picture, but also the rake of the stage and of the skycloth, which must also observe the same vanishing point (Fig. 83).[31]

The implications of such a restriction for the shape of the theater house have already been treated for the Italian theater.[32] In France the same conditions favor the retention of the rectangular house, not with equal, but with greater force, for the possibilities of building are less than they were in Italy.

31. Traité IV, pratique x. A later work is examined by Meaume, *Traité de la perspective, manuscrit inédit de Sébastien Le Clerc (vers 1680)*, Nouvelles Archives de l'Art Français, 1876, p. 308.

32. See pp. 45 et seq.

FIG. 82.—The *gloire* returned to its ecclesiastical function.

Possibly the greatest, certainly the most elaborate of the writers and practitioners is Andrea Pozzo.[33] He properly concludes our brief study of the theorists. Publishing in French as well as Italian, he too uses a line of perspective continuing that of the auditorium, presupposing one single line along which the view is perfect. He uses the oblique wings which are to become a subject of discussion in the eighteenth century.[34] Having determined his vanishing point O on the horizontal plane (Fig. 83) he determines it on the vertical plane in very much the same manner as Sabbattini was doing earlier in the century (Fig. 84). The equivalent amongst the theorists of Servandoni, no geometrical form is too complicated for the prowess of Pozzo, including curved colonnades, the most detailed interiors, and indeed a com-

33. *Perspectiva pictorum et architectorum* . . . 1st part, Rome, 1693. *La perspective propre des peintres et des architectes*, Rome, 1700.
34. Though he is preceded in this by the lesser known Troili, *Paradossi per praticare la prospettiva senza saperla*, Bologna, 1683.

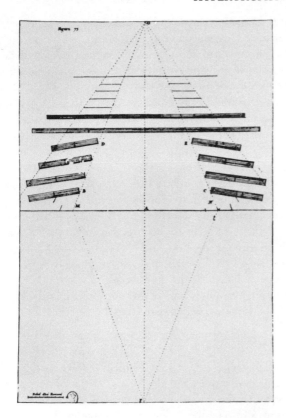

FIG. 83.—Pozzo, oblique flat wings in perspective.

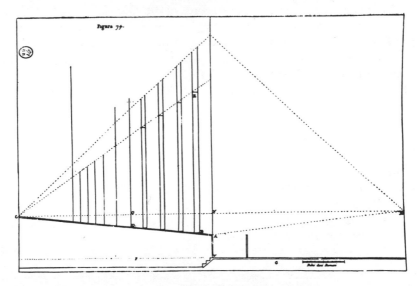

FIG. 84.—Pozzo, oblique flat wings in perspective.

pletely curved building with a domed ceiling, with only a small section removed from the front so that the spectator may look within (Fig. 85). There is by now not the slightest sign of the use of the angle-wing. Everything is worked out on flats which are divided according to the rules of perspective into the tiniest possible manageable units from which they may be formed into the shapes required (Fig. 86).

If we make one exception, the use of oblique perspective, of a vanishing point assuming a viewpoint elsewhere than in the auditorium, Pozzo represents the apotheosis of theory, as Servandoni a few years later is to represent the apotheosis of practice.[35]

The growth of a native school of perspectivists, of whom Bosse represents the militant, anti-Italian faction, nevertheless owes much to the Italians, as is apparent from the writers' own acknowledgements. The name of Ducerceau is linked with that of the Italian Ligorio. Hondius cites Guidus Ubaldus and Vignola. The latter writer's *Due regole* in the edition of 1611 is to be found together with Serlio and Niceron in one volume, in the Bibliothèque de l'Arsenal.[36] Marolois in his turn mentions and comments on Serlio. Dubreuil acknowledges, amongst a host of others, Barbaro, Vignola, Serlio, Sirigatti, Guidobaldo, and Accolti.

All the time the ancient reference continues, mainly through the Italians. The favorite subjects are the orders of columns in their perspective.[37]

The Practice of Perspective

The progress of practice follows to some extent that of theory, for here again perspective does not reach the legitimate stage until the 1630s, any more than it was a conscious theatrical proposition to the writers before the 1640s.

Its first appearance on anything approaching a legitimate stage in France is undoubtedly with the Lyons performance of the *Calandria* in 1548: "Une nouvelle mode et non encore usitée aux récitements de comédies qui fut qu'elle commença par l'avènement de l'Aube qui vint traversant la place de la perspective."[38] The Italian Nannoccio constructed the set which was a normal Serlian scene of houses terminating in a backcloth of the city of Florence. Yet this was but a fleeting visit. We may regard the use of perspective in the *Calandria* as pertaining to the street theater rather than to the legitimate stage.

The court ballet, in spite of its pretentious staging, uses perspective only in a very limited way before it merges with the opera and machine play and monopolizes baroque production. An examination of a contemporary engraving of the *Ballet comique de la reine* (1581) will tell us why (Fig. 87). The polarization of stage and auditorium is not complete; at the end of the Salle du Petit Bourbon farthest from

---

35. It should not be forgotten, however, that Pozzo is also a very practical scene designer.
36. Arsenal, fol. Sc. A. 1352,3,4.
37. E.g. Bosse, *Traité des manières de dessiner les ordres de l'architecture en toutes leurs parties* . . ., 1664.
38. *La magnificence de la triomphale entrée* . . ., quoted by Prunières, *L'Opéra italien en France avant Lulli*, 1913, p. xxi.

FIG. 85.—Pozzo, circular perspective.

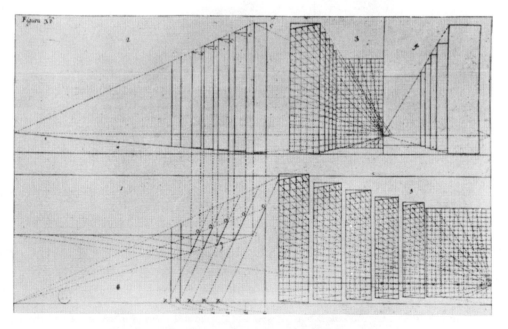

FIG. 86.—Pozzo, flat wings reduced to units for perspective purposes.

FIG. 87.—The Petit Bourbon, *Ballet comique de la reine*, 1581.

their Majesties there is a slightly raised stage filling the apse of the Hôtel. One archway is to be seen through another, but that is as far as the perspective goes. A stage is not yet a *sine qua non* of the ballet, the audience is not organized facing the stage, but almost surrounds the area of the dance. There is little point in perspective. The *Ballet des Polonais,* given at the Tuileries in 1573, illustrates this point even more clearly (Fig. 88).

    With the *Ballet comique de la reine*, however, the seeds are sown for such a movement, since it was Beaujoyeulx, the author, who dramatized the ballet, and its dramatization which eventually moved it onto the stage. But even later there is only limited perspective, the stage being used for the actual *entrée* and the dancers then moving down to the central area, often by means of ramps leading down from the

FIG. 88.—The Tuileries, *Ballet des Polonais*, 1573.

stage. It is true, as Kernodle says, that with the early ballets of the seventeenth century, *Alcine* in 1610, for instance, and the *Triomphe de Minerve* in 1615, the scene is presented as "a unit at one end of the stage,"[39] but this does not mean that the stage was the main dancing area, for it was, as Kernodle admits, shallow, with such perspective as there was worked into cut-out painted curtains,[40] nor does it mean that the gaze of the onlooker throughout the ballet was on the scene. Kernodle instances *Renaud* as the first appearance in elementary form of the Italian type of perspective scenery with angle-wings. It should be added that two ramps led down from the stage to the body of the hall in the Louvre.[41] Perspective was there in

39. The *Triomphe de Minerve* is the work of an Italian, Francini, as is *Renaud* in 1617.
40. *From Art to Theatre*, p. 203.
41. Prunières, *Ballet de cour*, p. 116.

embryo, but depth, and the retreat of the actor from a surrounding audience, were not; this is further demonstrated by the fact that it was quite easy for the large, unorganized public to prevent a ballet from being danced by sheer weight of numbers.[42] The conditions of its composition correspond to this undifferentiated *mise en scène*, for differentiation arrives with the individual composer. "Le ballet de Lully et de Benserade avec ses épisodes et ses intermèdes en style récitatif, avec ses décors et ses machines, est un spectacle nouveau, plus proche de l'opéra que du ballet de cour classique. Il porte l'empreinte du génie du Florentin et n'est plus, comme au temps de Louis XIII, une oeuvre anonyme et collective."[43]

Gros gives 1647 as the date after which the ballet becomes a regular public spectacle.[44]

We have seen how sporadic was the use of perspective in the *Mémoire*. Its employment in France at the beginning of the century is kept alive not by the legitimate stage, not by the court ballet, but by the Royal Entry and the street theater erected for that occasion. These nurse the traditions brought from Italy at the time of the *Calandria* until such time as the stage is sufficiently Italianate to use them. For the entry of the Queen into Lyons in 1600: "Il y avait en perspective plusieurs figures représentant les principales provinces et gouvernements de France, avec les armes et écussons des Royaumes, Duchés et Comtés"[45] (Fig. 89). The perspective mentioned is not one in the normal sense of the word; it is rather an amphitheater. The idea of perspective is maintained in the Entry by the recurrent vista which it offers through the triumphal arch. The perspective-through-the-arch is just as popular in 1660 as it is in 1600; in the fêtes of this year for the royal marriage the Place Dauphine was used as a natural perspective: at the apex of its triangle, on top of a building pierced by an arch, there was a huge pyramid by Le Brun. The statue of Henri IV on the Pont Neuf and the distant outline of the Louvre were to be seen through the arch[46] (Fig. 90). By this time, as our figures very well show, there is a conflict between the concept "amphitheater" and the concept "perspective" which finds an echo in the problem of form attaching to the theater auditorium.

Mirame, in 1641, is the first example of the normal baroque use of stage perspective (see Fig. 73a). It is an obvious first step towards the full baroque set. Only two wings are required, so that the perspective must have been a sharply fleeing one to give the necessary effect of distance, and this would carry with it the customary evils of disproportion between actor and scenery. It is, however, a completely framed perspective, upon which the entire action unfolds itself and upon which the view is concentrated. The play, as we have already seen, observed the unity of place. The apparent extending effect of perspective on place, as Kernodle has shrewdly remarked, did not escape the notice of the classical theorists, and classical doctrine

---

42. This was the case with the *Triomphe de Minerve* (MSS. BN franc. 24357, fo. 183).
43. Prunières, *Ballet de cour*, pp. iv–v.
44. *Philippe Quinault, sa vie et son oeuvre*, 1926, p. 97.
45. *L'Entrée de la reine à Lyon* . . . , Pierre Mathieu, 1600, p. 27a. Engraving by Perrissin.
46. Magne, *Les plaisirs et les fêtes en France au XVIIe siècle*, 1944, pp. 76–77.

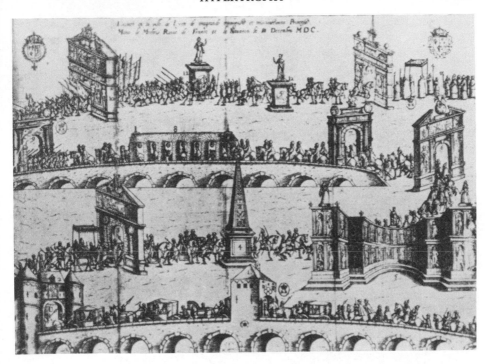

FIG. 89.—The Lyons Entry of 1600.

FIG. 90.—The Place Dauphine during the fêtes for the marriage of Louis XIV in 1660. Struggle between the amphitheatre and the perspective "stage."

accommodates itself comfortably to the single perspective set, always provided that we take the "view of one person" to imply the view extended to the vanishing point by the optical illusion. His quotation of Castelvetro is plausible: "The place for tragedy is restricted not only to one city or town or landscape [*campagna*] or similar place, but also to that view which can be seen by the eyes of one person."[47]

However, our attempt to follow the traditions of *mise en scène* down the line of one particular theater convinces us that these considerations did not count for very much with the French theorists. There was one main theater for the regular drama, if we discount the courtly performances and the comedy of Molière's troupe, and that was the Hôtel. There, the stage was shallower than at the Palais Royal, and the irruption of perspective was halted; there was little there for the eye to embrace, at least in the matter of space extending backwards.

The full onslaught of the Italian Order is felt in Paris with the arrival of Giacomo Torelli and the *Finta Pazza* at the Petit Bourbon in 1645.[48] By the time of the *Finta Pazza* a proscenium arch is added and all is ready for the exploitation of the space to be seen through it (Figs. 91 and 92).[49] The illusion of depth, by comparison with *Mirame*, is most evident. The appearance of the *Perspective du Pont Neuf*, with the statue of Henri IV, is symptomatic,[50] for now it is not the play that is being set.

47. *From Art to Theatre*, p. 201. Castelvetro, *Poetica d'Aristotle vulgarizzata et sposta*, 1570.
48. On the work of Torelli see also a review of the exhibition of seventeenth-century scenography and costumes in Venice, 1st September–14th October 1951, by Hélène Leclerc, in RHT, 1951, pp. 397–98. Also, by the same author, a review of another exhibition: *La scénographie italienne de la Renaissance à nos jours*, RHT, 1, pp. 19 et seq. Also Bjurström, *Giacomo Torelli and Baroque Stage Design*, 1961.
49. D'Ormesson (*Journal*, Wednesday, 27th December, 1645) is doubtless exaggerating when he tells us "En toutes ces faces différentes, la perspective était si bien observée, que toutes ces allées paraissaient à perte de vue, quoique le théâtre n'eût que quatre ou cinq pieds de profondeur." The *Mercure* of the 7th March, 1645 (Also Arch. Nat. 0¹ 3264, pp. 1–2) gives the true dimensions. The apse was 7 *toises* in depth, and 8½ in width. For the *Finta Pazza*, Bjurström places the king and his courtiers firmly in the apse, which is where they are for the Estates General of 1614. This is where, in our first edition, we had placed the stage. We remain puzzled. The engravings certainly do *not* prove that it was at the non-apse end: and yet one cannot assume that Bjurström has taken the Estates General to be a dramatic performance. The Estates family of engravings proves nothing in this respect. Such stage as there is for the *Ballet comique de la reine* (1581) is unquestionably in the apse. The *Mercure* of 1645 gives a stage height of six feet, a width of eight, and a depth of eight. The extra half-a-toise of depth could easily be accounted for by a forestage; the "forestage" of the Estates General is after all enormous. Holsboer (1960, p. 28) quotes the *Mercure* of 1605 (we take her to mean 1645): ". . . En l'un des bouts de la salle, directement opposé au dais de leurs majestés était élevé un théâtre . . ." Sauval (*Antiquités*, tome II, p. 209, gives ". . . assez élevé pour qu'au-dessus de l'ouverture de la scène il y ait une loggia à balcons." This might just be the continuing lower balcony going round the back of the apse in the Estates family of engravings. If that is what it means then for Sauval the stage was the apse. The *Mercure* calls the apse a "demy-rond." Beaujoyeulx calls it "demy-theatre." Bjurström (p. 122) shares our puzzlement as to d'Ormesson's dimensions.
50. Cf. p. 136.

FIG. 91.—The Petit Bourbon. The *Finta Pazza*, 1645. Décors by Torelli.

FIG. 92.—The *Finta Pazza*.

The spectator is being presented with natural perspectives that he knows, by type at least, but sometimes in detail as here, figured upon the stage. The irrelevance of the Pont Neuf to the action is shown by the fact that in the Italian performance another place, of equal local interest, was substituted.[51] The second of the engravings is a most general scene, repetitive, vaguely tragic. The ubiquitous obelisk of the street entry has again found its way onto the stage. It will be noted that far more flat wings are employed, though it is not always easy to tell their number. Again reminiscent of the *Olimpico* is the fact that Torelli uses three vanishing points to his back perspective, not unlike the three streets at Vicenza. This becomes a popular habit. It would have the attractive advantage of offering a correct perspective to more than one small section of the public, and could vary the final archway with an arcade.[52]

Now that change and stage depth have been added to perspective of the type seen in *Mirame*, little remains to develop except infinite elaboration and variation upon the theme. There is a stock-in-trade of objects and forms which can be re-patterned *ad infinitum*. The comparatively shallow stage of the Palais Royal does not survive the attack—for the Italian opera of *Orfeo* in 1647 Torelli modifies it considerably.[53] The machines and decorations of *Orfeo* pass without visible let or hindrance into Corneille's *Andromède* (1650). Act III of *Orfeo*, for instance, was "Un désert affreux, des cavernes, des rochers avec un antre en forme d'allée au bout de laquelle à travers l'obscurité se découvrait un peu de jour."[54] This becomes the prologue of *Andromède* (Fig. 93).

There are variations of the three streets on the perspective backcloth: the cut-out upstage in the first act of *Andromède*, creating three vistas along the same sight-line, is obviously the same as that for Act II (Figs. 94 and 95). In fact, Torelli, in *Andromède*, seems to have abandoned the three vanishing points for this motif, and to have gone back to a single point throughout, for it is also the case with Act IV (a double-storied arcade) and Act V (Fig. 96). The most irregular possible of motifs: jagged rocks rising from a stormy sea, are forced into a perspective in parallel (Act III), while Acts IV and V, again, may be said to represent peaks of parallelism in this type of set.[55]

51. Saint Mark's Square.
52. See also Holsboer, *Mise en scène*, pp. 50 et seq.
53. Prunières, *L'Opéra italien*, p. 104, Celler, *Décors*, p. 75, and Holsboer, *Mise en scène*, p. 52. Nor is this the end of its transformation: on the 22nd February, 1674, the Vigaranis modify it further to take the new opera house of Lully (Rouchès, *Inventaire des lettres et papiers manuscrits de Gaspare, Carlo et Lodovico Vigarani*, 1913, p. 194.
54. *Gazette* of the 8th March.
55. The gratuity of the settings in Acts I and IV evokes the criticism of d'Aubignac (*Pratique*, Bk. III, ch. ix, p. 357). The decoration must be *necessary*: "C'est en quoi je trouve un assez notable défaut dans l'*Andromède*, où l'on avait mis dans le premier et quatrième Actes deux grands et superbes Edifices de différente Architecture, sans qu'il en soit dit une seule parole dans les vers; car ces deux Actes pourraient être joués avec les Décorations de tel des trois autres qu'on voudrait choisir." In other words, he is complaining that the setting does not set the play.

FIG. 93.—Corneille, *Andromède*, Prologue.

FIG. 94.—Corneille, *Andromède*, Act I.

FIG. 95.—Corneille, *Andromède*, Act II.

FIG. 96.—Corneille, *Andromède*, Act. V.

FIG. 97.—The Petit Bourbon. *Noces de Thétis.*

In the *Noces de Thétis*, in 1654 (Fig. 97), also at the Petit Bourbon, Torelli goes no farther in his practice of perspective, although Celler has described it as the summit of decoration and machinery in the years preceding the King's marriage, which no doubt it was.[56] Torelli returns in it to the three vanishing points for his vista seen through a magnificent arcade, but otherwise it has little to distinguish it for our purpose from *Andromède.* The grotto of the prologue is again identical with the similar scene in *Andromède,* so that it has now made its way through three spectacles.

From now on the growth of the perspective on the French stage accompanies that of the opera.[57] The scene leaves the Petit Bourbon for the Salle des Machines in the Tuileries. It was the intention of Mazarin to give Paris a huge theater for the growth of the opera which he had made his special care, in the hope of causing a spectacular diversion from the growing anti-Italian tensions. Its rows of wings retreating in perspective must have gone more deeply than those of any other theater in the century.[58]

56. *Décors*, p. 88.
57. Cf. Holsboer, *Mise en scène*, p. 154.
58. Rouchès, *Inventaire*, p. xix, gives the following proportions: length 140 feet, width 62½ feet, height 54 feet from stage floor to rafters.

Perspective was taking the scene as far away from the audience as it possibly could, although the retreat was taking place along or near to the sight-line of large sections of the audience, particularly in a narrow auditorium.[59] Within these limits it was playing its part in the devaluation of the dramatic entrance. It helped to achieve this at a time (we may say between 1640 and 1670) when the classical drama was consolidating its position on another stage.

Perspective on the stage is a piece of publicity: publicity (and therefore exaggerated) for the new, splendid, disciplined architecture, which, strictly within the immediate sphere of the court, and under its aegis, was springing up in Paris, and which the Parisian public could see for itself, with its perspectives decked out and underlined on the occasion of the Royal Entry. It rejoins in this that flattery of the centralized monarchy with which the baroque theater is permeated.[60]

At Versailles, where nature had been bullied into geometrical forms at the instigation of the monarch, the open-air fêtes and performances continued the tradition by exploiting the natural perspective of the numerous avenues. Here, depth is unrestricted, space unlimited. The open-air plays of Versailles may be described as the wishful thinking of the theater technician in terms of stage depth.

The exteriors of buildings were also used and in one instance, at least, the length of two jutting *corps de bâtiment* limits the perspective, so that the outcome is not altogether unlike a Roman theater with over-developed *versurae*, the whole in the hands of a somewhat timid baroque artist. This was the playing of *Alceste* in the Cour de Marbre during the first day of the fêtes of 1674 (Fig. 98). The perspective cannot crush the solidity of the back wall although it is underlined by the decorator himself, further underlined in the illustration by the engraver Lepautre, and by the offical narrator of this fête, whose comments are relevant: ''Le Théâtre qui se trouva préparé pour la Tragédie contenait toute la petite cour pavée de marbre. Les deux côtés étaient ornés de Douze Caisses de grands orangers, qui se terminant dans le fond de la Cour, laissaient voir en face dans le point de la perspective les huit Colonnes de marbre qui portent le Balcon doré et qui font l'Entrée du Vestibule du Corps de Logis du milieu.''[61] The writer, we notice, calls even the solid façade

---

59. We ignore the growth of *loges* round the sides of the house.
60. And not only the baroque theater, cf. the passage from Corneille's *Menteur*:

Géronte

Paris voit tous les jours de ces métamorphoses:
Dans tout le Pré-aux-Clercs tu verras memes choses;
Et l'univers entier ne peut rien voir d'égal
Aux superbes dehors du palais Cardinal.
Toute une ville entière, avec pompe bâtie,
Semble d'un vieux fossé par miracle sortie,
Et nous fait présumer, à ses superbes toits,
Que tous ses habitants sont des dieux ou des rois.
(Act II, Scene v).

61. Arch. Nat. 0¹ 3263. This document is a manuscript *recueil* of official accounts of the *Fêtes de Versailles* from various sources. The present account is from the Impri-

Fig. 98.—*Alceste* in the Cour de Marbre.

of a building "une perspective," using the term normally applied to a painted back-cloth.[62] The depth of the acting area created by the two wings of the building is considerable but cannot of course be intensified by false perspective. The narration goes on to reveal what the engraving does but vaguely: the highly developed parallelism down the sides. In fact, everything that the baroque genius can do to a solid building, it has done. Between each pair of orange trees on either side is an equal number of marble pedestals carrying porcelain vases which in their turn carry smaller orange trees. Before each pedestal is a table of gold and azure, laden with girandoles of crystal and silver, each carrying ten candles. Behind the boxes carrying the larger orange trees, are twenty-four more large pedestal tables, and each carrying a lighted girandole of crystal. On either side, twelve orange trees, twelve pedestals, twelve vases, twelve smaller orange trees, twelve pedestal tables and one hundred and twenty candles, twenty-four more tables, and twenty-four more girandoles.

Any feature, architectural or natural, which corresponded to the Italianate staging vogue was pressed into service. The King himself was well versed in spotting such possibilities; for the fêtes of 1668 "il jeta les yeux sur les personnes qu'il jugea

merie Royale, 1676. Along with the fêtes of 1668 it is signed Félibien. See also Félibien, *Les divertissements de Versailles, donnez par le Roy au retour de la conqueste de la Franche-Comté*, 1674, and Celler, *Décors*, p. 152.

62. Whereas he might more properly have referred to it as a *frons scaenae*! The eight coupled columns at the back of the stage separate the three doors of the vestibule, comparable to the three doors of the Roman building.

Fig. 99.—Façade of the Grotte de Versailles.

les plus capables pour disposer toutes les choses propres à cela. Il leur marque lui-même les endroits où la disposition du lieu pouvait par sa Beauté naturelle contribuer davantage à leur Décoration.''[63] It would indeed have been surprising had the ''style Louis XIV'' at Versailles not provided ample opportunity for perspectives through an arcade. The best instance is that of the *Malade imaginaire* played before the grotto in the *divertissements* of 1674. The façade of this, when closed, resembles a *frons scaenae* (Fig. 99). The arrangements remind one once more of the Olympic theater and the piercing in depth of its three doors:

> Le devant du Théâtre . . . était avancé au devant des trois portes de la grotte, les Côtés étaient ornés d'une agréable feuillée; mais au travers des portes où le Théâtre continuait de s'étendre l'on voyait que la grotte même lui servait de principale décoration . . .

63. Arch. Nat. 0¹ 3263, p. 2 (Félibien). See also Félibien, *Relation de la feste de Versailles du 18e juillet 1668.*

Fig. 100.—Interior of the Grotte de Versailles.

Au fond des trois ouvertures l'on voyait les trois grandes Niches ou tout ce
Groupe de figures de marbre blanc dont la Beauté du sujet et l'Excellence du travail
font une des grandes richesses de ce lieu (Fig. 100).[64]

Thus, the gates are opened, and the façade, instead of forming a back wall, is made
to form an arcade screen in midstage, through which a highly lit continuation scene
is visible (cf. Fig. 97). The solid building, already predisposed in its "style Louis
XIV," has been made to conform to the insubstantial discipline of the stage designer.

Three engravings of the *Plaisirs de l'Ile Enchantée* of 1664 illustrate the employment
of open-air perspective. The first (Fig. 101), the *Théâtre d'Eau,* is the purest spectacle:
it exploits decoratively three avenues retreating in natural perspective, as a background for a display of fountains. The second (Fig. 102) shows neatly the way in
which the baroque vision made spectacle of everything. To the narrator, the illustrator, the stage manager of the period, not only was all the world a stage, but if
it was not a stage conforming to baroque canons, then it must be compelled to do
so. The feast of the first day of the *Plaisirs* is depicted by Silvestre. Although it is
not strictly speaking a theatrical show, his engraving cannot be distinguished in
general presentation from that of an actual performance. The diners, grouped in a
great amphitheater are for all the world like a human perspective setting, and Silvestre has depicted them from precisely the angle which would achieve this impression. The servants bringing the victuals are indistinguishable from a *corps de ballet.*[65]

64. Arch. Nat. 0¹ 3263, *Divertissements de Versailles,* 1674, pp. 19–20 (Félibien). See also
    Celler, *Décors,* p. 154.
65. Védier, op. cit, pp. 48–49, says much the same thing.

FIG. 101.—The *théâtre d'eau* in the fêtes of 1664. Open-air perspective.

Our third engraving (Fig. 103) repeats the general lines of the preceding one. The most striking feature of both is the forcing of a round figure, amphitheater or lake, into the framework of two retreating straight lines. The enchanted palace on the *Ile d'Alcine* has two jutting wings, so that the perspective may be the more impressive, and terminates obediently in an archway. The significance of this development has been sensitively expressed by Jean Rousset:

> La dissociation de la scène et du parterre se parachève, jusque dans un spectacle de cour, où elle est moins habituelle.
> Ce qui symbolise ici cette disjonction de l'auditoire et du spectacle, c'est la surface d'eau séparant l'actrice (Alcine), sur son île ou sa baleine, des spectateurs massés au bord du bassin. Cette surface d'eau remplit la fonction du cadre de scène coupant le plateau de la salle dans un théâtre régulier.[66]

During the time of the fêtes it is however chiefly the avenues of Versailles which predestine the site of the theatricals and discipline their perspectives: "C'est dans cet endroit de l'Allée du Roi que le Sr. Vigarani avait disposé le lieu de la Comédie. Le théâtre, qui avançait un peu dans le carré de la Place s'enfonçait de dix toises dans l'allée qui monte vers le Château, et laisait pour la salle un Espace de treize toises de face sur neuf de large."[67] The use of the phrase "s'enfoncer," in view of our study of the irruptive forces of perspective, takes on a wider meaning. At this period the noun "enfoncement" is used quite unconsciously to mean a perspective

66. Rousset, *L'Extérieur et l'Intérieur*, p. 66.
67. Arch. Nat. 0[1] 3263, *Fêtes à Versailles, le 18 juillet 1668,* pp. 13–14 (Félibien).

FIG. 102.—Banquet of the first day in the fêtes of 1664. Open-air perspective.

FIG. 103.—Third day, fêtes of 1664. Amphitheater with perspective.

scene.[68] Allowing for the absence of change, regular tragedy, whenever it goes to Versailles, is subjected to the same treatment; Racine's *Iphigénie,* played on the fifth day of the fêtes of 1674, is an example:

> La décoration . . . représentait une longue allée de Verdure, où de part et d'autre il y avait des bassins de fontaine et d'espace en espace des Grottes d'ouvrage rustique, mais travaillé très délicatement. Sur leur entablement régnait une Balustrade, où étaient arrangés des vases de porcelaine pleins de fleurs . . . Cette allée se terminait dans le fond du théâtre par des tentes qui avaient rapport à celles qui couvraient l'orchestre et au-delà paraissait une longue allée qui était l'allée même de l'orangerie bordée des deux côtés de grands orangers et de grenadiers entremêlés de plusieurs vases de porcelaine remplis de diverses fleurs. Entre chaque arbre il y avait de grands Candélabres et des Guéridons d'or et d'azur, qui portaient des Girandoles de cristal allumées de plusieurs Bougies. Cette allée finissait par un portique de Marbre.

The classical tragedy is gobbled up by the prototype spectacle: one recognizes all the set pieces which served for *Alceste* in the same year.[69] The narrator has an unimportant addendum which, one feels, he had almost forgotten: "Sur ce théâtre orné de la manière que je viens de dire la troupe des Comédiens du Roi représenta la Tragédie d'Iphigénie, dernier ouvrage du S. Racine."[70]

The passage of the court ballet, the machine play and their accompanying variations into the opera, a concentration which is accelerated after the performance of *Andromède* in 1650, affects the history of perspective in the seventeenth century but little. Stage and auditorium remain polarized, fixated along a single line of vision. The main supporting instruments of cleavage between the two are already there: proscenium arch and proscenium arch curtain, but these we shall discuss later. Until the end of the century then, the spectator looks through an archway at a stage picture which, provided he can swallow the convention of frequent change with or without curtain, he may suppose to be an infinite prolongation of his own position in the house.

It is in the first half of the next century that we see the final barriers to complete cleavage fall. Servandoni, greater than Torelli, Gaspare Vigarani, or his successor Bérain, is to destroy the last citadel. In 1724 he comes to Paris, in 1726 he is employed by the Académie Royale de Musique to design the sets for a new opera, *Pyrame et Thisbé,* which earns him praise from the *Mercure.*[71] In 1727, a new success with the revival of Lully's *Proserpine.* In 1728 he is appointed "premier-peintre-décorateur" to the Académie, and his first décors in that capacity, those of *Orion,* are a great triumph.

His vital contribution to perspective on the stage is oblique perspective.[72] With

---

68. E.g. for the performance of *Phèdre* during the fête given by Colbert at Sceaux in 1677: "Un théâtre magnifique, avec des enfoncements admirables." Arch. Nat. 0¹ 3263, 5e vol. *bis* of the *Mercure* of June.
69. See pp. 194.
70. Arch. Nat. 0¹ 3263 (1674), pp. 40 et seq., Imprimerie Royale 1676.
71. Bouché, "Servandoni," *Gazette des Beaux Arts,* tome IV, August 1910, pp. 123–24.
72. Barsacq, "Lois scéniques," *Revue Théâtrale,* No. 5, April–May, 1947. Such, at least is the traditional view. Per Bjurström, however, pointing out that the décors of *Orion*

his superior knowledge of this, Servandoni was able to vary the forestage, to choose
a point of departure for his oblique perspectives which ignored the discipline of the
proscenium arch. This naturally entailed a certain amount of contempt for what
was traditionally regarded as legitimate acting area, and here again we discern the
baroque militating against dramatic action, or at least against the actor, for such a
disposition would seldom leave a clear area downstage. With the introduction of
oblique perspective came the disintegration of symmetrical perspective: Servandoni's oblique sets did not proceed symmetrically down an oblique line: objects
were disposed in their proper places, in their natural (naturalistic) places, according
to a preconceived picture. To express the matter within our own terms of reference,
the stage had become an autonomous picture, existing in its own right with no
reference to the spectator, who is now supposed, conventionally, not to be there.[73]

Celler claims that the disproportion between the sharp perspective of the decoration and the human figures on the stage was little corrected in the eigtheenth
century, so that Noverre, in his letters on the dance, protests against the bad visual
effect created.[74] This is to ignore the work of Servandoni. He paid special attention
to this very problem, and (further evidence of his contempt for dramatic action)
went so far as to create obstacles on the stage to prevent the actor from approaching
the more sharply fleeing pieces of decoration and thus dwarfing them.

Finally, his application of the real elevation of objects to the stage completes the
movement in the vertical plane. The extension backwards of the spectator's view
is at an end; the oblique perspective, apparently quitting the stage in its lines, seals
off this retreat in depth. The autonomy of the stage as a box is completed by the
greatly enhanced height of Servandoni's sets.

We have reached that moment in the hypertrophy of the Italian Order when,
with Louis Jouvet, we can really define the stage as a "boîte à illusions."

Proscenium Arch

The proscenium arch defining the stage picture and separating it from the auditorium, is a picture frame. When it is finally established on the stage the public
can be in no doubt that it is looking at anything but a picture. The spectator has,
in his mind, one more obstacle to cross before total acceptance of the drama. This
does not mean to say, as Kernodle's work, taken as a whole, would seem to suggest,
that every framed picture from the Hellenic era onwards is some sort of ancestor
to the proscenium arch. It does not even seem certain that there is always any
connection between the long series of paired-off objects farthest down-stage in those
theaters where the proscenium arch was not yet in use, and the arch itself. Referring
to the early Italian perspective scene, Kernodle notes how, already, "formalistic"
objects appear, lumped together (on the Serlian stage for example), with naturalistic

and *Phaéton* had their oblique perspective on the backcloth alone, tends to minimize
the "innovation" ("Servandoni, décorateur de théâtre," RHT, 3, 1954, pp. 150-
59).
73. See Leclerc, *Origines*, Pl. XI.
74. *Décors*, p. 161.

side-houses in perspective: arcade screens, triumphal arches, center pavilions, obe-
lisks and castle towers, formal architectural façades and cloth curtains. But he sees
the development of the perspective stage from that moment as a reshuffle in which
"gradually the illusionistic structures were separated from the formal architectural
pieces by conceding two conventional places for the non-illusionistic: the one, the
decorative framing elements at the very front of the stage, and the other, the arcade
façade at the back."[75]

This strikes us as dubious, at least for the French stage. Our Torellian sets and
the open-air decorations of Vigarani reveal that all the things mentioned by Kernodle could and did appear, regimented in flat wings down the sides of the stage,
as much as they appeared in front framing arches or back pieces. We are left with
the simple conclusion that the origin of the proscenium arch is the arch—chiefly
triumphal. It is just possible that the back archway or arcade, since it is present
before the front framing arch, suggested this latter, but this is susceptible of no
direct proof. The only thing that does seem probable is that they both found their
way onto the stage via the Royal Entry and the street theater and arches.

We have briefly noted the way in which the triumphal arch persisted throughout
the century. It is there well before the formal proscenium arch, and with Vigarani
achieves virtual identity with it. For the entry of the Queen Mother into Angers in
1619, there are four, each with its allegorical motif: Felicity, Concord, Abundance,
Piety.[76] For the reception of Barberini, nephew of the Pope and papal legate, in
1625, it is a portico through which he passes.[77] In 1628 Louis XIII contemplates at
length and with satisfaction the Arch that greets him: "Cet édifice d'ordre dorique
était dédié à sa clémence, dont on apercevait, sur le faîte, la figure allégorique
soutenant un arc-en-ciel. Il portait toutes sortes de cartouches, rappelant par des
symboles, les effets de cette clémence, et, dans un cadre central, montrait Sa Ma
jesté, assise dans un char, traînant derrière elle les Vices enchaînés et recevant la
couronne des mains de la Victoire."[78] His route from that point was studded with
arcs de triomphe. There is no doubt here of the isolated and autonomous function of
the arch; it stands in its own right as an instrument of the monarch's narcissism.
Mention has already been made of the arch of the 1660 entry.[79] The construction
of these monuments was automatically a part of the duties of Vigarani, going hand
in hand with his other tasks as a landscape artist, machiniste, decorator and builder
of temporary theaters. The normal arc de triomphe naturally resembled the proscenium frame that he constructed for the Salles des Machines (Fig.104). Others resembled the leafy arcades which led to the scenes of the performance in the Versailles
fêtes: for the same entry we have at the Carrefour de la Fontaine Saint-Gervais an
arch made of palm fronds supporting an image of Mount Parnassus. The summit

75. From Art to Theatre, p. 189.
76. Arch. Nat. 0¹ 3259, from the Mercure of 1619.
77. Ibid., Mercure of 1625.
78. Magne, Les plaisirs et les fêtes en France au XVIIe siècle, pp. 52–53.
79. See p. 186.

FIG. 104.—Proscenium arch by Gaspare Vigarani for the Salle des Machines.

carries the sovereign's medallion, just as the more formal proscenium frame would carry the arms of the prince in the same place.

The use of these motifs carries steadily on through the century and beyond. In 1686, at Bourges, for the birth of the duc de Berry, "il y eut partout des arcs de triomphe,"[80] and in 1704 a firework display for the birth of the duc de Bretagne still represents the same motif.[81]

These things have hardly altered from the time when the 1548 Lyons entry sets their tone. In the latter half of the seventeenth century, nevertheless, the baroque theater has stepped into line, quite naturally, with them. They are not, in origin, utterly Italianate; the indigenous mystery contributes its lore of devices to them. But by this time these are quite indistinguishable from their Italian counterparts, and, as we have seen, are managed, in France, more by Italians than by anyone else.

In the open-air theaters of Versailles, Vigarani would not question the fact that as the stage picture, being unconfined in a rectangular room, had to be defined somehow, it could only be defined by an arch. So the autonomous arch is to be

80. Arch. Nat. 0¹ 3260, *Mercure* of October.
81. MSS. BN franc. 7801 (De Cotte), fo. 310.

found in these theaters, which are in any case far nearer to the street shows than are indoor performances. It is the commencement of the *allée* which forms the natural theater perspective. Thus, for the fêtes of 1668, the proscenium arch is at once a stage framing device and a tribute to the monarch: on either side of it, two statues, of Victory and Peace, render homage to the King for his victory over the Spanish.[82] For *George Dandin,* on the same occasion, "Deux colonnes torses éclatantes d'or et d'azur, entre lesquelles on avait posé des statues de marbre blanc, soutenaient de chaque côté un très-riche plafond extrêmement exhaussé."[83] The width of the proscenium opening was 36 feet.[84]

Along with the apparent splendor of these arches goes that transience which characterizes the Versailles occasions as a whole: the proscenium arch is after all only made of wood, as against the solidity of its indoor sister.[85] For the *Malade imaginaire* before the grotto, a free-standing arch was imperative:

> Le frontispice était une grande corniche architravée, soutenue aux deux extrémités par deux massifs avec des ornements rustiques et semblables à ceux qui paraissent au dehors de la Grotte. Dans chaque massif il y avait deux niches, où sur des piédestaux on voyait deux figures représentant d'un côté Hercule, tenant sa massue et terrassant L'Hydre et de l'autre côté Apollon appuyé sur son arc, et foulant aux pieds le serpent Python.
>
> Au-dessus de la Corniche s'élevait un fronton dont le Tympan était rempli des armes du Roi.[86]

Without redoubling the examples, which abound, we can see the immediate source of the proscenium arch of the Salle des Machines. And we have a good idea of the type of scenic frame with which Vigarani would endow any indoor theater with whose modification he might be entrusted. Such a case would be the Palais Royal, which he was charged to alter when it was allocated to Lully on the death of Molière, for the Opera; even when first built this theater had a proscenium arch *à l'italienne,* which was no more than natural, as it was an Italianizing venture on the part of Richelieu. We must conclude then that the proscenium arch, when it arrived in France, did so upon the full wave of the Italian advent, and was not slowly abstracted from amongst the various symbolic pieces of baroque scenography.

It must obviously have been adopted sooner or later at the Hôtel de Bourgogne, although we do not know when. Proceeding along the same lines as Kernodle, it would be easy for us to note the presence of integrated framing pieces in the sets of the *Mémoire*: they are all there: the two side-houses in Rotrou's *Ménechmes* or Hardy's *Cynthie* for example[87] (see Fig. 64), the early "castle frame" in Hardy's

82. Nolhac, *La création de Versailles*, 1901, p. 62.

83. Celler, *Décors*, p. 138.

84. Arch. Nat. O¹ 3263, p. 15.

85. Arch. Nat. O¹ 2984, p. 10 (*Comptes de la maison du roi*): "A Barrois, peintre, la somme de . . . 340 livres pour avoir peint six grands châssis qui ont servi au frontispice du théâtre de l'Amour et de Bacchus y compris deux statues de pareille peinture, et une fontaine en manière de profil."

86. See p. 196.

87. *Mémoire*, p. 72.

Parthénie (*première journée*);[88] but we would also have to note the exceptions to this framing "rule": those in which the largest compartment does not appear downstage: Durval's *Agarite*,[89] Théophile's *Pyrame et Thisbé* (see Fig. 51a) and others. It seems much more likely that the actual elements of the set in the *Mémoire* pictures had very little to do with the ultimate framing of the Hôtel stage, and that this frame, whenever it came, was imposed by the force of the Italian example. Of the Marais, we know strictly nothing in this respect. The first proscenium arch of which we know is that of the Palais Cardinal in 1641, after which time it is rapidly developed in the Petit Bourbon, the Salle des Machines, the Guénégaud, and the first Opera in the jeu de paume de la Bouteille.[90]

Paradoxically, the proscenium arch, coming into the theater from a completely undifferentiated paratheatrical form, a form in which spectator and spectacle are integrated, the street entry, takes on the function, along with its curtain, of saying "thus far and no farther" to the spectator.[91]

The Proscenium Arch Curtain

The proscenium arch frames the picture. The curtain, attached and inseparably allied to it, serves, so far as we can make out, one main purpose during the century, that is, the sudden revelation of that picture. At the same time as we were working on the first edition of the present volume, Georges Védier was undertaking a profound study of the seventeenth-century French front stage curtain which reached precisely this conclusion, although he otherwise tends to revolutionize our ideas.

He begins with the postulate that a front stage curtain and multiple staging are not absolutely, nor immediately, mutually exclusive. When a curtain is used, it is not used in the modern sense of *décor successif*, not used for the purpose of concealing the changing of the entire stage décor between acts. The set suddenly revealed, he claims, was the new, Italianate, illusionistic set. The curtain once down, the unity of the illusion is ensured. Thus

1. The front stage curtain, as employed in the sixteenth and seventeenth centuries, has nothing to do with the separation of acts and is not used to conceal total change in the modern manner—and will not be until the nineteenth century.
2. On the Italian stage of the sixteenth century, it reveals the décor to the spectator and is the instrument of that illusionism current in the pictorial arts.
3. It tends to keep this role in France.
4. It symbolizes and consecrates, in Italy and France, the unity of illusion.
5. The unity of illusion, become a veritable aesthetic canon, excludes systematic

88. Ibid., p. 75.
89. Ibid., pp. 80–81.
90. See Nuitter et Thoinan, *Les origines de l'opéra français*, 1886, p. 148. The width of it was thirty feet.
91. It is true that the spectator in France, as in England, had a great tendency to ignore this injunction. The *seigneurs* on the stage resist the division.

curtain closing between acts and this condemns change in time and place as *invraisemblable*, ensuring the triumph of *les règles*. (An interesting inversion of causality relatively to the normal view.)

Védier, then, links the sixteenth-century Italian perspective set with the curtain.[92] So that, whereas throughout the present work we envisage the Italian order as moving in the direction of the modern proscenium arch and proscenium arch curtain concealing total change of space behind, here we have an early Italian order which, combining illusionistic set and front stage curtain actually retards that development, although in making that statement we must reserve judgment on the role of the *changement à vue*.

Now, it has been known, since the publication of the *devis* of 1647, that provision for a curtain was to be made at the Hôtel de Bourgogne in 1647 in the form of two lateral beams, eighteen inches apart, the one to carry the *frise*, the other the curtain itself.[93] As this provision results from an advancing of the stage, it is possible that the curtain was there before 1647. Such is the clear opinion of Védier, who avers that it was in constant use in the second half of the century—except as an act curtain. The first famous instance of a front stage curtain, as we know, is at the Palais Cardinal in 1641.[94] But Védier is strongly inclined to think that there was one at the Hôtel de Bourgogne at the very least from 1630 onward. He disposes of objections which are now familiar: that Mahelot would either have shown or mentioned it had it been there, for example. He might not have done, replies Védier, quite simply because he took it for granted. Corneille, in his *Discours des trois unités*, declares that the public, so far as he can judge, had never found itself inconvenienced at the beginning of a play, by seeing a character walk onto the stage to that place where he or she might be presumed to be before the play began.[95] Writing in about 1660, Corneille is speaking of the Emilie of *Horace* (1640). This had seemed to us ample reason for assuming no curtain, and Lancaster had assumed that possibly it was not used for all types of play.[96] But Védier, having pointed out that Corneille is speaking for 1660 as well as 1640, and that in 1660 there can be no doubt as to the existence of the curtain, finds a solution:

> Le rideau s'ouvre quelques minutes avant l'entrée en scène des personnages; il reste ouvert pendant tout le cours de la pièce; il ne se ferme que quelques instants après que le dernier personnage a quitté la scène.[97]

It must be conceded that Védier has severely rocked our previous notions, though he makes out his strongest case for the curtain in the *pièces à grand spectacle*.

92. Op. cit, ch. III.
93. See p. 114.
94. We repeat that this did *not* open in the middle and run laterally. See Védier, p. 97, and Vanuxem, *Revue du XVIIe siècle*, 2e trimestre 1958, No. 39, fn. 9, p. 213.
95. See p. 154.
96. *Sunset*, p. 339.
97. Op. cit., p. 140.

In the specific case of the Hôtel de Bourgogne, to the best of our knowledge, he does not mention the Gherardi collection of *canevas à l'italienne* and illustrations (of 1700), when the house is given over to the Italian players. Here, although a curtain at the top of the proscenium arch, often with an inscription, is frequent in the drawings, it is by no means *de rigueur*. It is, for instance, replaced by foliage in the engraving for *Mezzetin, Grand Sophie de Perse*,[98] and elsewhere, while it is absent from the engraving for *La fille de bon sens*.[99] It seems clear, however, that an opening and no doubt closing curtain must have been in use by then. Thus, Arlequin, in the *Banqueroutier* (19th April 1687), says: "Je me suis placé au milieu du premier banc de l'Amphithéâtre. D'abord qu'on a levé la toile, je me suis écrié—Fi, quelle vilaine décoration."[100]

The curtain seems to appear first in the early court ballets: *Alcine* in 1610, *Renaud* in 1617, and the *Aventure de Tancrède* in 1619.[101] But once the curtain is down, for it "falls" at the beginning of the ballet, we assume that it stays down, especially as the dancers mingle with the public. It is the curtain of initial revelation, operating in the Roman manner; for the *Délivrance de Renaud*, "Lorsque tout fut prêt pour la représentation, la toile, qui représentait un palais en perspective, s'abaissa, laissant voir la montagne des Génies. . . . "[102] The "palais en perspective" tells us that this is the curtain in a rudimentary form serving as an initial decoration: not a purely masking instrument. The purpose of revelation, at the same period, is not necessarily served by a curtain, for at the *Triomphe de Minerve* of 1615, danced at the Petit Bourbon,

En bas, était une grande Nuée qui cachait toute la scène, afin que les Spectateurs ne vissent rien jusqu'au temps nécessaire.[103]

Au même instant que le roi fut assis et eut commandé de commencer le ballet, cette nuée s'entrouvrit par le milieu et de l'ouverture sortit une autre nuée assez petite en sortant de ladite ouverture, mais à mesure qu'elle avançait elle s'agrandissait en largeur et hauteur.[104]

As with *Mirame* we find the first proscenium arch, copied from the existing wealth of Italian precedent and requiring no immediate French ancestor, so do we find for that play, the first proscenium arch curtain.[105]

In the regular classical drama, the entr'acte was a compulsory feature, but it seems almost certain that there was no act curtain, and there was not the slightest

98. Vol. II, p. 407.
99. Vol. IV, p. 99.
100. Vol. I, p. 425. See also Duchartre, *La comédie italienne*, 1925, and Lancaster, *History*, Pt. IV, vol. ii, pp. 602 et seq.
101. Holsboer, *Mise en scène* p. 140, Prunières, *Ballet de cour*, pp. 111, 154, 156.
102. Celler, *Décors*, p. 7.
103. This naïve explanation of function would of itself tend to suggest the novelty of the idea of any initial masking device.
104. Arch. Nat. 0¹ 3264, pp. 3–4 (from the *Mercure* of 1615); Prunières, *Ballet de cour*, pp. 149 et seq.
105. Schérer, *Dramaturgie classique*, pp. 208 et seq.

need for one. Lancaster unaccountably endows Corneille's *Andromède* with a curtain concealing the change between the prologue and Act I. Having described the prologue setting he adds: "As a general curtain was used in this courtly theater to conceal the stage, this setting could easily make way for that of the first act, representing a public square surrounded by palaces."[106] Now, it will be observed that Lancaster passes imperceptibly from the assumption of a general (that is proscenium arch) curtain, which is correct, to that of a general curtain as an act drop, which is in doubt. In fact he himself paraphrases the very passage from the *Gazette* of 18th February 1650, which so justifiably causes Schérer to hesitate in his treatment of the question. The curtain "se lève pour faire l'ouverture du théâtre, mais avec une telle vitesse que l'oeil le plus subtil . . . ne peut suivre la promptitude avec laquelle il disparaît, tant les contrepoids qui l'élèvent sont industrieusement proportionnés à sa grande étendue."[107] Later, "la toile qui s'était levée avec tant de promptitude à l'ouverture du théâtre, descendant avec la même vitesse, le ferme." As Schérer properly remarks, there seems to be no room for an act curtain here. At the beginning of Act I of *Andromède*, the mountains of the prologue are still there: "Cette grande masse de montagnes et ces rochers élevés les uns sur les autres qui la composaient, ayant disparu en un moment par un merveilleux artifice, laissent voir en leur place la ville capitale du royaume de Céphée." The change was at the beginning of each act, and after a moment during which the spectator would admire (or if he was La Fontaine, ridicule) the scene, the play would continue. However, for the later Parisian work of Torelli (*Les Noces de Pélée et de Thétis*, 1654, *Psyché*, 1656, *Rosaure*, 1658), Bjurström, if we read him aright, assumes that a growing demand for *vraisemblance* imposes the act curtain: "Scene changes were now made between acts so that, even if the curtain had not fallen, no heed was paid to this event as part of the spectacle."[108]

The treatment of the curtain question seems to us to have been partly vitiated by a failure to distinguish between the "legitimate" and the baroque. Schérer observes with surprise that "even" the Hôtel de Bourgogne, home of the Troupe

---

106. *History*, Pt. II, vol. ii, p. 680.
107. See Schérer, *Dramaturgie classique*, pp. 172 et seq.
108. Cf. the oft-quoted lines from La Fontaine's *Epître à Monsieur de Niert sur l'opéra* (*OEuvres*, ed. Régnier, tome II, pp. 155–56):

> Quand j'entends le sifflet, je ne trouve jamais
> Le changement si prompt que je me le promets,
> Souvent au plus beau char le contrepoids résiste,
> Un Dieu pend à la corde et crie au machiniste,
> Un reste de forêt demeure dans la mer,
> Ou la moitié du ciel au milieu de l'enfer.

The play would run on from the prologue to Act I, as is clear from the stage directions, in particular those of Corneille's *Toison d'or*: "l'Hyménée, présentant le portrait de la Reine aux deux côtés du théâtre, en fait changer les débris en un jardin aussi magnifique que surprênant, qui sert de décoration au premier acte" (*OEuvres*, ed. Marty-Laveaux, tome VI, p. 233). Bjurström, "Notes on Giacomo Torelli," *TR/RT*, vol. III, no. 1, 1961, p. 22.

Royale, did not always use a curtain, and calls attention once more to its exceptional employment in the revival of Tristan's *Marianne* in 1678. Yet the fact that this troupe was called "royale" does not impel it to employ a curtain. If it did not, it was because in its career up to 1680 it consciously attempted to monopolize the works of those authors whose plays required none. It did not specialize in the baroque genre, for which a curtain was an inescapable appendage; it does not seem to have had a proscenium arch—indispensable for the smooth functioning of a forward curtain. Védier himself fails to draw conclusions from this bifurcation, although he is able to produce much more evidence for a curtain for the "illegitimate" genres and consequently in theaters other than the Hôtel de Bourgogne. His theory is of course the opposite of our own, stated immediately above: *because* there was an "initial revelation" curtain at the Hôtel, with only that function, Védier suggests that the demands of continuity of illusion ultimately made *changement à vue* give way to the unities. We are still inclined to take the more orthodox view, and to think that their origin in practice is of an aesthetic and doctrinal nature. It is surely in the *pièce à machines* and the *grand spectacle* that the initial fillip is administered to that weakening of "belief" in the illusion, which ultimately (much later) demands the act curtain for scenic change.

The value of the dichotomy that we are attempting to follow becomes clearer. If we assume, unlike Védier, that there was no curtain for *Cinna*, we may reason thus: it is ten years after *Andromède* the Corneille makes his pronouncement that although the theater represents the room of the person speaking, he cannot enter it save from behind the *tapisserie*.[109] What could indicate more clearly that Corneille was thinking in terms of two different genres as between *Andromède* and *Cinna*? We believe this dichotomy to hold good for Corneille and the other important dramatist to whom it could apply: Molière. Physically, as we have been at pains to show, it tends to choose different theaters for its manifestations.

Conversely, when evidence shrewdly brought forth and undoubtedly valid for the "legitimate" stage is applied to the baroque, it can again be misleading. The difficulties catalogued by Sabbattini in the operation of curtains are quoted by Schérer immediately after his statement that there was no act curtain for *Andromède*, and in apparent justification of this. The troubles in question saw the light of print in 1637, and at least cannot refer to any later period. Now Torelli, the decorator of *Andromède*, as Schérer himself observes, had personally perfected a system of counterweights for machinery.[110] Further, he had done this before he came to France. If we are asked to believe that Torelli, the "wizard," would encounter difficulty in the frequent and smooth operation of a proscenium arch curtain in 1650, we must be permitted to express our scepticism. But we would admit that it might have given Michel Laurent trouble, though only at the Hôtel de Bourgogne, in 1678, since it is assumed, except by Védier, that the notice "abaisser le rideau pour la fin," being the only example, indicates rarity of usage.

109. Cited by Schérer, *Dramaturgie classique*, and see our p. 154.
110. *Dramaturgie classique*, p. 173, quoting Leclerc, *Origines*, pp. 174–75.

There is one piece of undeniable and perplexing evidence for the act curtain. D'Aubignac, in his *Térence justifié*, correcting the errors of Ménage concerning the curtains of the ancient theater, refers to Donatus, and the use of the *siparia*: "Siparium . . . ne fut autre chose, dit-il, qu'une toile légère, qui empêchait que le peuple ne vît les changements qui se faisaient dans les intervalles des Actes, et laquelle servait peut-être, comme ce qu'ils nomment aujourd'hui la toile de devant, qui ne fait point partie de la décoration, et qu'on tire seulement quand on y veut changer quelque chose, afin que le peuple ne s'aperçoive point du désorde qui se fait en ces ajustements et qu'il soit plus agréablement surpris en voyant soudainement une nouvelle face du Théâtre."[111] The date of the publication of *Térence justifié* is 1656, but its editor remarks "il y a plus de quinze ans que cette réponse est achevée." If this is true, there was an act curtain for the explicit purpose of concealing change in about 1640! Dare we surmise that it had a brief life until the arrival of Torelli made the unconcealed change on a large scale, from act to act, a practical and dazzling proposition?[112]

From 1640, on, the Italians are virtually in complete charge of baroque theater staging and paratheatrical festivities, and naturally use a full curtain, though it is a difficult matter (and not very important to us) to decide how it opened. For the fêtes of 1668, "quand elles [leurs Majestés] eurent pris leurs places sur le haut Dais qui était au milieu du parterre, on *leva* la toile qui cachait la décoration du théâtre."[113] This, as opposed to "tirer la toile," could be taken to mean a curtain rising vertically, but the most interesting thing about the passage is that the narrator still, in 1668, sees fit not only to use "toile," the earlier usage for "rideau," and which in any case lingers through the whole period, but also to observe (superfluously, one would have thought, by this time) that it is this "toile" which is hiding the stage. This function still appears novel to him, and he is still penetrated by the sense of revelation: "Et alors les yeux se trouvant tout à fait trompés, l'on crut voir effectivement un jardin d'une beauté extraordinaire." For the Carrousel at the marriage of Louis XIV, the laterally opening curtain is used, "la toile qui cache le grand théâtre se tire,"[114] and "tirer la toile" is again used for the *Plaisirs de l'Ile Enchantée* in 1664.[115] As late as 1688, during the spectacle which celebrates the marriage of M. le Prince de Conti, the lateral curtains can still seem to be a novelty:

111. *Térence justifié, ou deux dissertations concernant l'art du Théâtre* . . ., 1656, p. 232. Védier has noticed the same passage (op. cit. pp. 108–10.)

112. D'Aubignac, in the *Pratique* (Bk. III, ch. vi, p. 238), seems to contradict this previous statement:"Il [le poète] doit bien prendre garde . . . de supposer dans l'intervalle d'un Acte, une chose qui ne peut vraisemblablement avoir été faite sans être vue; ce qui arrive quand on suppose qu'elle a été faite dans le lieu de la Scène: car étant ouvert et exposé aux yeux des Spectateurs, ils doivent vraisemblablement avoir vu tout ce qui s'y passe." It is not, unfortunately, conclusive evidence that the stage was not hidden by a curtain during the act interval.

113. Arch. Nat. 0^1 3263, p. 16. The italics are ours.

114. MSS. BN franc. 17460, fo. 311.

115. Arch. Nat. 0^1 3263, pp. 39–40.

"Quand Monseigneur le Dauphin fut placé on tira deux rideaux qui étaient au devant du théâtre *au lieu de toile*."[116]

The foregoing examples strongly suggest that the use of an act curtain was, to say the least, seriously limited.

Machines and Scene Change

The word *machine*, as is apparent from the court ballet of the second half of the sixteenth century and of the street theater of that time, is one of considerable extension. It is applied to rocks, triumphal cars, chariots, ships, stars, and all the array of constructed animals which figured in pantomime or procession. This extension is retained in our period, and it is only the machine play which brings to the word a passing restriction to machines for ascent, descent or flight. It is in fact applied to any item of stage decoration which is not actually a stationary flat wing. It assumes the meaning at one time fulfilled in the Royal Entry by the word *mystère*.

Lancaster sees the origins of the machine play in the medieval theater, the court ballet, and the Italian drama. It should by now require no further emphasis that a most important addition to this list is the street theater of the Royal Entry, and indeed the whole gamut of paratheatricals in the sixteenth century. In that century, they keep alive in France incipient tricks of baroque staging, interfused with the native tradition of mystery marvels, until such time as the seventeenth-century stage can feed upon them and upon the court ballet to produce the *pièce en machines*; by which time, between 1640 and 1650, history has prepared a fresh injection of more recent Italian accomplishments.

The collective, unpolarized nature of the early court ballet has been dealt with. The earlier *entremets*, while already using machines in the wider sense of the term, is even more collective, and the machines indeed serve to underline the undifferentiated nature of the gathering: as early as the fifteenth century mummers would enter the royal dining hall, upon a car figuring a bark, castle, or some monster. This would discharge its mummers on the same level as the diners.[117] The machine is part of the concept of a cortège, close to the mystery play in this.

Salle and *scène*, we have observed, are not particularly meaningful terms in the ballet of the first two decades of the seventeenth century, so that in the *Ballet comique de la reine* of 1581 (see Fig. 87) we need not be surprised to find them even less so. During the first *intermède* of this ballet the Tritons and Sirens execute a typical manoeuvre: they make a complete tour of the room before their final couplet announces the *fontaine de Glauque*, a machine which arrives at that moment. The machine is still a machine in the earlier sense of the term; it is a vehicle for entry. Composed of two parts, the lower represents a sea, protruding beyond the upper portion, which is the fountain proper.[118] Alongside this simple conception of the machine, descent and the *gloire* are to be found; indeed, they had been present in the street theater

116. Arch. Nat. 0¹ 3261, p. 8 (*Mercure* of July). The italics are ours.
117. Prunières, *Ballet de cour*, pp. 7–8.
118. Celler, *Décors*, p. 161.

for some time: for the *entrée de Mercure* a cloud which had been suspended from the roof descended to the accompaniment of thunder (much as the gods appear in Vitruvius), and Mercury was revealed. The cloud stopped half-way to the ground, Mercury delivered himself of a *récit*, Circe touched him with her wand, and the cloud completed its earthward journey. Jupiter later descended in the same manner. Thus, the machines of the *ballet comique* divide into two categories: the newer, early baroque form of the *gloire*, and the older and more indigenous rolling machine on wheels. Most of the remaining machines of the ballet are of this nature: that for a later entry of the Dryads, and the chariot of Pallas are examples. Ascent from below is apparently new (since the floor of the Petit Bourbon had been modified for this effect) but practiced.

The *Triomphe de Minerve* in 1615 has an Italian, Francini, in charge of the machines; he even makes a scale model of them (in the ratio of six to one) to show the Queen how they worked.[119] At this time, all the machine effects may be said to be present in the ballet, far closer to the court (which could afford them) and to its lavish paratheatrical spectacles and fêtes than was the drama. In the ballet of the *Délivrance de Renaud* in 1617, rocks vanish, a mountain turns upon itself. In the *Ballet des Néréides* in 1619: "La mer avait un mouvement artificiel et représentait si bien les flots eux-mêmes, et des ondes bleues qui haussaient et baissaient qu'on n'eût pas cru que cela se pût représenter sans eau."[120] The gods come down, but still mingle with the crowd in a familiarity which belongs to the sixteenth-century illusion of antique grandeur rather than to that of the seventeenth: "Voici descendre les Déesses, premièrement sur le Théâtre, et puis du théâtre en la salle. . . ."[121] The same truth emerges from a scrutiny of these early machines as did from our examination of perspective: the early court ballet does not easily abandon its quality of undifferentiated spectacle.

The play *Arimène*, by Nicolas de Montreux, at the château de Nantes in 1596, although, as we have mentioned, somewhat of an anachronism for France at that time, must certainly take pride of place in our account of the fortunes of the *scena versatilis* in one of the normal dramatic genres: the pastoral. Four pentagonal cylinders, with decoration painted in perspective, provided five possible scene changes. Lawton is of the opinion that these were placed across the back of the stage; as a space between the pentagons provided exits for the actors, he has shown that it would be a geometrical impossibililty for more than a small number of spectators to see only one face at once: the rest must have seen either two or three. Lancaster has the machines down the sides of the stage.[122] The relevant passage from the *Recueil*

119. MSS. BN franc. 24357, fo. 182 v°.
120. MSS. BN franc. 24353, fo. 42 v°.
121. Ibid., fo. 43.
122. See Celler, *Décors*, pp. 4–5, Marsan, *La pastorale dramatique*, pp. 214 et seq., Prunières, *Ballet de cour*, p. 146, Lawton, "Notes sur le décor scénique au XVIe siècle," *Revue du XVIe siècle*, 1929, tome XVI, p. 335, Holsboer, *Mise en scène*, pp. 137–38, Lacour, *Mise en scène et représentation d'un opéra en province vers la fin du XVIe siècle*, pp. 93 et seq., Destranges, *Le théâtre à Nantes*, 1893, Lawrenson, "La mise en scène

factice des oeuvres d'Ollenix du Montsacré (anagram of Nicolas de Montreux), could be read either way:

> Entre les Pentagones étaient les sorties des acteurs et toutes différentes. Le fond s'ouvrait, pour rendre à la vue des spectateurs les choses qu'on avait besoin de tirer de dessous la terre. A l'un des bouts était la grotte du Magicien, faite à la souvagine, et convenable à l'horreur des esprits, de laquelle il sortait quand il était appelé sur le théâtre: à l'autre bout était planté un antique rocher. . . Derrière les Pentagones était la musique, composée diversement de toutes sortes de voix, et d'instruments. . . Aux deux bouts du Théâtre, on voyait plusieurs rangs de lampes ardentes, pleine d'huile de senteurs, et qui jetaient des lumières de diverses couleurs.

"Le fond s'ouvrait": this seems to mean a clear space upstage center, though there would be room for two *telari* on either side of this without moving any one of them downstage. Alternatively it could be read as a stage trap. The use of the word "bouts" seems to indicate that the magician's cave and the rock were on either flank of the row of pentagons, possibly downstage, creating a curved décor. It was not in fact generally realized that there were two editions of this play in 1597, Nantes and Paris, and by juxtaposing the slightly varying scene descriptions in the two we have been able to demonstrate that *le fond* was almost certainly a trap, and that the pentagons were along the back, the outside two possibly reaching a little way up the (narrow) stage. (See n. 122.)

Let us now attempt to place the pentagons of *Arimène* more fully in their immediate context of scenography. Prunières sees in the play the general influence of the *Ballet comique de la reine* of 1581, and this is very likely.[123] Lancaster, properly drawing attention to the appropriate passage from Vitruvius on the *periaktoi*, suggests the same ballet as an intermediary to this source, and here we must cry halt.[124] For there may be revolving machines in this ballet, but they are neither pentagonal nor even triangular like the *periaktoi*. They are a sophisticated form, ahead, though not chronologically, of the machines of *Arimène*. We must seek elsewhere for our context, and firstly in the *épître au lecteur* in Charles Estienne's translation of Terence's *Andria*, quoted by Lawton.[125] In a letter to the duc de Mercoeur, Montreux says that he has "imitated the ancients in his play." He may, as Lawton suggests, have read this letter, which is in the form of a treatise on the theater of the ancients: "Aux coins [de la scène] vers les lieux de la Scène qui demeuraient pour ornement, étaient deux machines comme tours triangulaires dans lesquelles se faisaient les feintes: comme quand il faisait quelque pluie, ou tonnerre, ou avènement des dieux, et telles choses. Ces dites tours changeaient, mutaient, et tournaient de face, à même

dans l'*Arimène* de Nicolas de Montreux, *Bibliothèque d'Humanisme et Renaissance, Travaux et documents*, tome XVIII, 1956, pp. 286 et seq.

123. Prunières, *Ballet de cour*, p. 146.
124. *History*, Pt. I, vol.i, p. 31, fn. 3. See also Celler, *Décors*, pp. 4–5.
125. Lawton, "Notes sur le décor scénique au XVIe siècle," *Revue du XVIe siècle*, 1928, tome XV, 1, 161.

que les Scènes se changeaient et variaient.'' Now this is a near-translation of Vitruvius on the same subject. Not only this, but the wealth of Vitruvian translation and edition which, along with Terentian and Plautian edition, characterizes the first half of the sixteenth century, was there for him also, the more so in that he is professedly imitating the ancients. He could have read Alberti's eighth book, or Martin's translation of him; he could have read the Giunta edition of Vitruvius of 1523 or Philander's Paris edition of 1545, or any of the translations of Serlio or Vitruvius. He might conceivably have read Vignola on *Le due regole della prospettiva pratica*, in which Danti describes the functioning of the turning machines and which was published in 1583, fourteen years before *Arimène*.[126] This, and works like it, are the real intermediary between the Vitruvian *periaktoi* and Montreux, not the *Ballet comique de la reine*.

It is most difficult to trace the fortunes of this machine in the seventeenth century. By the time of Torelli and *Andromède* we can be sure that it would not be employed exclusively to create a complete stage picture: it would no doubt cease to be regimented down the sides or across the back of a stage, but would be mingled in with the other methods of *ferme* and *coulisse*, as Dubreuil occasionally has it in 1649.[127] Alternatively, flat turning wings might be employed as in the Gracht theater of Liebrecht's reconstruction (see Fig. 112).

Scene changing by this time would seem to be mainly assured by the lateral *coulisse* and the central shutter or *ferme*. The latter is a compromise development in depth of the *scène simultanée* and borrowed by the Hôtel de Bourgogne no doubt from baroque staging tradition at a time when unity of place was causing a certain amount of trouble. Kernodle has developed the same idea at length, but appears to err in not realizing the extent to which the *ferme*, covering the whole stage, representing very often a house, and parting in the middle to reveal the interior of the house, must have been restricted to the Hôtel de Bourgogne and, to a lesser degree, Molière's theaters.

The Italian tradition used the shutter well upstage, to reveal an inner scene. Our iconography should be sufficient to show that this practice was transferred bodily to the French stages, and would undoubtedly be used for machine plays at the Marais, since those plays had little use for the single change of place by a *ferme* placed somewhere downstage. Such a set would render flight, almost a law of the genre, most difficult.

We must therefore disagree with Kernodle when he says that in France, in a peculiarly French way, the baroque scene emphasized flat, two-dimensional forms, as opposed to the Italian long rows of wings, and that the French scene emphasized the *ferme* as opposed to these.[128] This was not all the work of the French baroque scene, which, since it was largely built by Italians, had little to distinguish it from

126. Lacour, *Mise en scène et représentation d'un opéra*, pp. 97–98, divines that the producer was an Italian, Cosmo Ruggieri.
127. See pp. 176–8.
128. From *Art to Theatre*, pp. 210–11.

its Italian counterpart. The movement the author describes does occur, but it is not typically baroque, not typically French. It is typically Hôtel de Bourgogne, and an expression of the power of resistance, against the baroque, of French classical dramatic practice in its early stages. The Hôtel steals a weapon from the baroque stage with which to defend itself.

The growth of three devices which intermingle increasingly and grow in magnificence, remains to be followed through the "illegitimate" genres. They are the *théâtre supérieur*, its mobile cousin, the *gloire*, and of course the flight. All three were present in the French mystery play,[129] and it is in the sixteenth century that these native forms become intermingled with their Italian kinsmen; it is in this form that they come down to the seventeenth century. In such a state is the *théâtre supérieur* to be found in the first part of the *Mémoire*. From the mystery play it has passed into the street theater, and is handed back to the public stage, after the death of the mystery, and indeed, aside from its development, in new Italian clothing. The latter would not be very noticeable, perhaps, in the earlier contracts of the Hôtel de Bourgogne, where these small stages are mentioned, but it is very much so with Dubreuil, who works them into his perspective and *scena ductilis* set, and completely so with the final machine stage of the Marais theater. Here we find the *théâtre supérieur* in perfectly current use in 1671: De Visé, writing of his own play in the *Mercure*, describes it thus: "Je crois que l'on ne doutera point de la grandeur du spectacle du celle [la pièce] des *Amours du Soleil*, puisqu'il y a huit changements magnifiques sur le théâtre d'en bas, et cinq sur celui d'en haut.[130]

The concept of Heaven, Earth, and Hell, sky, sea, or the underworld, Christian or pagan, is not far distant from many of the examples of the *théâtre supérieur*. By now it is naturally the pagan cosmos which it used. We found in the *Mémoire* a triple *théâtre supérieur*, with Hell, a "ciel d'Apollon," and above it a "ciel de Jupiter."[131] The meaning of the expression *théâtre de Jupiter* is made abundantly clear; there are many instances in which Jupiter appears, sitting aloft and delivering orders. In Act V of Corneille's *Toison d'Or* (at the Petit Bourbon in 1660) the heavens open, and theaters of Apollo and Jupiter appear, reproducing, no doubt more magnificently, the effect of the *Travaux d'Ulysse* (see Fig. 53).[132] Lancaster fails to notice this resemblance, though he does point out that this helps to explain Fransen's "petit théâtre" and Liebrecht's "deux théâtres,"[133] the more so in that Liebrecht's contract of 1662 was precisely for a stage on which to play the *Toison d'Or*, so that in the

129. See pp. 57–8.
130. Quoted by Fournel, *Contemporains de Molière*, vol. III, p. xxiv. Lancaster, *History*, Pt. III, vol. ii, p. 527, gives the probable date of performance as the winter of 1671. Thanks to Mme. Deierkauf-Holsboer (*Le théâtre du Marais*, tome I, pp. 108–10, and see our pp. 143–6) we can now understand why de Visé talks in such good round terms of "*le* théâtre d'en bas," and of "*celui* d'en haut."
131. See pp. 142–6.
132. *OEuvres,* ed. Marty-Laveaux, tome VI, p. 244. Such a scene is often the final one of an act, an apotheosis.
133. *History*, Pt. III, vol. ii, p. 506 and fn. 4. See our pp. 144 et seq.

expression "trois théâtres, un en bas et deux autres dessus" we can now understand that the lower *théâtre* is the stage proper. In fact the whole history of scholarly bewilderment over the 'théâtre de Jupiter' of the early Hôtel de Bourgogne contracts[134] stems firstly from a failure to study and connect with the theater proper, paratheatricals in the sixteenth century, and the baroque spectacles of the seventeenth as a separate genre, having partly indigenous roots in the street theater as well as in more immediate Italian examples.

The *gloire*, the *vol*, and the *ciel* reach the seventeenth century in France in the same way: through the street theater.[135] The individual flight, or at least vertical ascent and descent of one person, had been known to the mystery.[136] The *ciel* was well known to the street theater: it could be a mere canopy, covering the prince, or a simple sky effect; and then, like the other devices, it took on movement. Clouds surround the *gloire* and constitute its "glory." They are used in every possible way not only for aerial movement but for this combined with revelation: they are an upstage moving aerial curtain. In the prologue of the *Toison d'Or*, the heavens open— a thing that they frequently do in these plays, and Mars appears "un pied en l'air et l'autre porté sur son étoile." In the first act "un nuage descend jusqu'à terre, et s'y séparant en deux moitiés . . . laisse sur le théâtre le prince Absyrte." Sometimes it is more obviously the "théâtre de Jupiter" which has taken wings: at the end of Boyer's *Jupiter et Sémélé* we see Jupiter in his palace "qui s'avance insensiblement vers le milieu du théâtre. . . ." Sémélé is to be found "au fond du Théâtre d'en haut dans un ciel lumineux." Flights straight across the stage are improved on by oblique flights. Where a mystery play descent carried, to the general amazement, four people,[137] the public now requires a hundred to amaze it. Carlo Vigarani, for Cavalli's *Ercole Amante*, constructed a machine 60 feet deep by 45 feet wide, and carried in it the royal family together with sixty other people in the final apotheosis.[138] Molière's *Psyché* probably contains the largest *gloire* of the century, three hundred divinities appearing on the clouds in the last *intermède*.

It would be at once fruitless and tedious to reduplicate the examples of machinery to which attention has been so fully and frequently drawn by historians of the theater. Never were contemporary official chroniclers more punctilious and repetitive than those who guide or drag us through the accounts of machine play, opera, ballet, and court occasion.[139] The examples quoted are sufficient to make clear the effect

134. Including our own: "The 'théâtre étagé' in the seventeenth-century French theatre," *French Studies*, Jan. 1950, p. 55.
135. See pp. 60 et seq.
136. See pp. 57–8.
137. See loc. cit.
138. To the feigned alarm of the enemies of the Vigarani family, "fearing" the annihilation of the royal line in an aerial disaster. Cf. the abbé de Pure, *Idée des spectacles*, 1668, p. 314: "Nos princes nous doivent être plus chers que nos plaisirs; et ce ne sera jamais de mon conseil qu'ils s'exposeront à de pareils dangers, quoique sur la foi de toute la Philosophie."
139. We can certainly attribute to fatigue that slip of the hack who wrote of some carnival in Italy in 1678, "On avait cependant vu descendre par le Po des girandoles et des

of the baroque *essor* on the shape of the stage in relation to the auditorium. The masking provided by the proscenium arch opening is greatly enhanced in importance. Machines, operated by a cumbersome system of counterweights, require increasing height behind the top edge of the proscenium arch as they increase in size and splendor. In the fêtes of 1668 the proscenium arch pillars to which reference has been made "soutenaient de chaque côté un très-riche plafond extrêmement exhaussé pour faciliter le jeu des machines."[140] Depth below the stage, as well as height above it, is required. When the jeu de paume de la Bouteille is altered to create the home of the Comédie Française, it is found necessary to dig more than twenty feet below the level of the stage for the movement of the machines.[141] At the same time the sides of the rectangular edifice prove themselves insufficient for the extensive demands of scene changing with the flat wing and for the flight across the stage. The Palais Royal undergoes structural alterations in this sense. After the performance of Molière's *Psyché* in the Salle des Machines on 17th January 1671, the Palais Royal is further altered for the purpose of staging the same play there.

The entire space behind the proscenium arch has become a vast independent funnel bustling with activity, and the proscenium opening by comparison is a tiny hole through which the public is allowed to see the illusory result.

The Baroque Aesthetic

The aesthetic of the baroque centers in the first instance around the presence and function of the prince, and hence around the social necessity for "flagornerie" and "superlification." The seam of flattery is continuous through the Royal Entry of the sixteenth and seventeenth centuries. By the same token, it is present in all functions concentrated upon the court. Of the early court ballet, the *Ballet de la reine* of 1581, thanks to the efforts of Baltazarini, is an excellent example. Monarchs change, but the theme goes on. In the entry of 1614 there is the tableau of the antique bark of Lutèce, sailing on a stormy sea with Regent and King, experienced pilots, at prow and poop "se rendant maîtres des vents contraires."[142] At the end of the century, the mood is the same: the *Mercure* of February and March 1683[143] describes thus the carnival of that year: "Figurez-vous la Grandeur et la Richesse de la première Ville du monde, mettez-vous devant les yeux l'heureuse tranquillité dont sa Majesté fait jouir les peuples, et vous vous représenterez aisément tout ce qui s'est pu passer pendant ce temps de réjouissance dans un lieu ou rien ne manque et d'où toutes les cours de l'Europe tirent tout ce qu'elles ont de brillant." The ethos of

Dauphins sur de petites machines flottantes" (Arch. Nat. 0¹ 3260). As the attentive La Ferté points out in a marginal note, "c'est vraisemblablement gondoles qu'on a voulu dire."

140. See p. 204.
141. Nuitter et Thoinan, *Les origines de l'opéra français*, p. 144.
142. Magne, *Les plaisirs et les fêtes en France au XVIIe siècle*, p. 44.
143. From Arch. Nat. 0¹ 3264, p. 1.

the paratheatrical occasion, based on some historical event, is perfectly reflected by d'Aubignac.[144] In the event, he is speaking of Richelieu:

> . . . ces grands Politiques ont de coutume de couronner leurs ministères par les plaisirs publics, et de faire que leurs plus glorieux travaux ne soient que des moyens, ou des prétextes pour donner aux Peuples qu'ils gouvernent, tous les divertissements imaginables. Leurs victoires ne se marquent que par des jours de Fêtes, et par des Jeux. Toutes les dépouilles et les richesses des Etrangers ne s'apportent des extrémités de la terre, que pour composer la pompe et les décorations des Spectacles, et les Sciences les plus curieuses ne sont cultivées que pour produire des Hommes capables d'en inventer, et de les entretenir.

It is the rôle of the early machine play and the later opera, to adapt this theme to the stage as such. All the allegorical possibilities of ancient myth were ready developed and awaiting the attention of the producer. By the time of the opera, the immediate political justification for the occasion is no longer systematically exploited, but it is curious to note how the authors of the French machine play cling to historical occasion outside its normal context.[145] In 1647, Mazarin had launched the "Italian" campaign with *Orfeo* at the Palais Royal. Corneille's *Andromède* was thus originally mooted because it was thought desirable to have for the next carnival a similar sort of play, but in French.[146] In the same spirit, soon after *Orfeo*, Denis Buffequin at the Marais stages again the *Descente d'Orphée aux Enfers*, now called *Le mariage d'Orphée et d'Euridice . . . la grande journée des machines*, just as, in 1662, the Comédiens du Marais turn back to Chapoton's *Orpheé* in riposte to *Ercole Amante* at the Salle des Machines. The *Toison d' Or* is commanded by Sourdéac to celebrate peace with Spain and the Spanish marriage in 1660.[147] Lancaster suggests that Corneille saw in the story of the Golden Fleece a means of indicating that peace could be brought about by love and marriage.[148] The historical purpose of the play is explained in its prologue, in which France makes an impassioned plea for peace. We see in this the forerunner of the "flattering" prologue which first appears with Boyer's *Amours de Jupiter et Sémélé* in 1666 at the Marais.[149] The King, with Monsieur, Madame, and a goodly court gathering were present on the 11th January,[150] so that the prologue would not fall upon deaf ears. These prologues, particularly in plays conditioned by the political event, remind us of the verses addressed to the monarch as he halted before some *tableau-vivant* to receive a crown or similar gift, though they do not exhibit the same *mièvrerie*; Boyer neatly introduces his flattery into a dialogue between the tragic and comic muses:

144. *Pratique*, pp. 5–6, and see the entire chapter.
145. Cf. Lancaster, *History*, Pt. III, vol. ii, p. 497.
146. Lancaster, *History*, Pt. II, vol. ii, pp. 677–78.
147. Cf. Racine's *Nymphe de la Seine à la reine*, which we might, in this sense, describe as a "poème en machines."
148. *History*, Pt. III, vol. ii, pp. 503–05.
149. According to Gros, *Les origines de la tragédie lyrique*, p. 190.
150. MSS. BN franc. 24357, fo. 231 vº, from the *Gazette* of 1666, p. 72.

Thalis

Votre règne est passé, le mien vient à son tour;
Vous êtes du vieux temps et de la vieille Cour;
Tout le monde aime à rire, et j'en sais la méthode:
Vos tristes entretiens ne sont plus à la mode;
Louis m'aime en un mot, j'ai pour lui des appas.

Melpomène

Il vous aime il est vrai, mais il ne me hait pas,
Et pour dire tout haut ce que j'en ose croire,
Louis me doit aimer puisqu'il aime la gloire.[151]

Jupiter is not unnaturally represented as the great lover—an obvious reference. Boyer's next play, *La fête de Vénus*, celebrates the victorious peace of 1668, following the War of Devolution. As in the *Toison d'Or*, Victory and Peace appear in the prologue, following exactly in this the pattern of the Royal Entry. This *rapprochement* throws a new light upon the identification of Louis and Jupiter in these plays. Lancaster maintains that there is no reason to believe that the Molière of *Amphitryon*, any more than Boyer, was intentionally drawing a parallel between Jupiter and the King.[152] In the Royal Entries, which these plays (excluding perhaps *Amphitryon*) resemble in their social and political motivation, in their prologues, machines, and production, the identification is clear and intended.

The indigenous machine play is a stepping-stone to the opera in the matter of royal flattery as well as in other things. The opera sheds to a large extent the last social links with the Royal Entry. It consolidates the domestic, as opposed to the political, flattery of the prince. This is inevitable, for it is a confined genre, at least encouraged, when not actually financed, by the monarchy. The enclosed theater naturally reflects the life of the King in his more domestic surroundings. This constitutes its great advantage for the worthy Chappuzeau, by contrast with the uncomfortable republican neighbors of France: "Dans un Royaume les Comédiens ont à qui faire agréablement la Cour; le Roi, la Reine, les Princes, les Princesses, et les Grands Seigneurs."[153] The wider issues of historical flattery on the state occasion do not disturb Bossuet and the "opposition dévote." Yet the opera does disturb them. During the period of cultural screening after 1672, when the opéra finally replaces the ballet in the affections of Louis, when it is dangerous to speak against it, they are on the whole silent. They tacitly condone the cultural superstructure of the prince's private life. This function of the opera is not in doubt. As Gros says: "L'opéra ne glorifiait pas seulement le Jupiter mortel dans ses victoires; il le glorifiait dans les secrets sentiments de son coeur. La morale de l'opéra était pour lui un continuel encouragement; l'oeuvre entière était faite pour lui plaire,

---

151. Quoted by Lancaster, *History*, Pt. III, vol. ii, p. 509.
152. Ibid., p. 513.
153. *Le théâtre françois*, 1673, edn. of 1876, Pt. III, ch. xvi, p. 101.

pour célébrer ses victoires sentimentales autant que ses exploits guerriers."[154] When, many years later, the monarch tends to renounce the pleasures of this world, and it is safe to speak up, the retrospective opposition provides good evidence of the real function of the opera.

The machine and the flight find their proper context in this climate of "flagornerie" and "superlification": they are the symbols of the monarch's identification with the gods (pagan for the avoidance of blasphemy) and thence of his absolute power over the material world. It is this that makes them, immediately, the essential of the court function, and it is this message that they pass on to the general public through the machine play at the Marais in particular and at public performances elsewhere. Thus it is that they become the central vehicle of expression in what is ostensibly a form of the drama. They tend to become an autonomous means of theatrical expression, crushing text and dramatic action beneath them. They are bandied about, irrespective of any relevancy to text or action, not only from theater to theater, from play to play, but from court, whence came their central inspiration and finance, to the town, whenever the *échevinage* feel anxious to repay the endless compliment which they constitute. The early court ballet provides instances of the King lending machines to the Hôtel de Ville for the purpose of entertaining—the King! Thus, at the *ballet du roi* in the Hôtel de Ville on the 16th February 1627, Louis, remarking that there were many machines in his ballet at the Louvre, offered to have them transported to the Hôtel.[155] The initiative of the *échevinage* in furnishing such spectacles is perhaps not as spontaneous as has sometimes been made out. There is only one *fons et origo* of the baroque spectacle. As Chappuzeau remarked, still in defense of the monarchy, "Les Comédiens tirent de chez les Rois des douceurs qu'ils ne trouveraient pas chez les Bourguemestres, qui ne leur pourraient donner ces riches et pompeux ornements faits pour des Entrées, des Carrousels, et d'autres actions solennelles, de quoi les Princes leur sont libéraux.[156] The baroque machine forms itself into a stock of dramatic possibilities which becomes in the end a repertoire in its own right. The décors of *Mirame*, for all that they "set" a play which, in all but spectacle, was regular, serve with no difficulty for a ballet: that of the *Prospérité des armes de la France*, on the 7th February 1641.[157] The machines of *Orfeo* go into *Andromède*, and no doubt the same ones are used for the ball given in the Salle du Palais Royal for Lundi Gras in 1647, when, amongst other machines and marvels, the chairs, instead of being brought by lackeys, came up by machinery through the floor.[158] The last scene of *Psyché* uses the décors of the apotheosis of *Ercole Amante*.[159] At the closing of the Marais in 1673, and the fusion of that troupe

---

154. *Philippe Quinault*, p. 720.
155. MSS. BN nouvelles acquisitions franc. 9745, p.247.
156. *Théâtre françois*, Pt. III, ch. xv, p. 100.
157. MSS. BN franc. 24375, fo. 209.
158. Celler, *Décors*, p. 67.
159. Although the story, retailed amongst others by Celler, *Décors*, p. 76, that *Psyché* was ordered for the purpose of employing a well-known Hell machine already in the stock of the King's *machiniste*, is discredited by Lancaster, *History*, Pt. III, vol. ii, pp. 520–21.

with the players of the Palais Royal, the actors are ordered to take to their new house "les loges, les *théâtres*, et les décorations qui étaient dans la salle du Palais Royal."[160] In the building of the Salle des Machines, this independence of the machines from the theater is very evident; their construction leaps ahead of that of the house, with no evidence of any attempt at co-ordination.[161] Gaspare Vigarani, writing to the Cardinal d'Este in 1660,[162] says that they are little worried about the machines, for as much as possible has been made ready for them outside the theater. In 1669, for the winter ballet at Saint Germain, some of the machines are built in Paris and transported to Saint Germain.[163] In 1675, for *Circé*, by de Visé and Thomas Corneille, at the Guénégaud, the machines used have been bought previously from the marquis de Sourdéac after the failure of his own opera project.[164]

It is quite frequent for the privileged spectators to watch the machines on their own, presaging Servandoni's *féeries*, without the accompaniment of text or action: this happens in the case of *Orfeo*: "Enfin, le trente 8bre (1647) Leurs Majestés donnèrent le bal dans la grande salle des comédiens au Landgrave de Hesse, où l'on fit aussi jouer les machines de cette fameuse comédie."[165] Like the static motifs of the Royal Entry, the machines have their own conventions, one might almost say *grammar*, apart from the text.

However, the economic demands of the growth of machinery effect certain concentrations, around the court, culminating eventually in one genre, the opera, from which the Street Entry, tourney, carrousel and early ballet, are far distant. Machines require money, and only courtly patronage can provide this. The accounts of the *Menus plaisirs du Roi* for 1679 are revealing on this score. For four opera performances charged to this head of account in 1679, and played in the winter of 1678, we read under "dispositions" 18,082 livres 14 sols, and under "machines" 18,787 livres 7 sols.[166] In short, the machines cost more than the rest of the staging and general organization. At the same time the machine play tends to remove the spectators from their position on the forestage, although they were apparently to be seen there even at the opera.[167] With the final establishment of Lully's opera in 1674 the process of concentration is complete: from that time onward all the baroque elements which had been scattered across the dramatic pastoral, the ballet, the machine play, surge into that genre, where the public may see them all at once. In this way the opera becomes a sort of boil which draws away the impurities from the regular drama. The looser type of spectacle at Versailles and elsewhere also begins to decline,[168] for

160. The italics are ours. Beauchamps, *Recherches sur les théâtres de France*, 1735, ch. 1, p. 207.
161. Rouchès, *Inventaire*, No. 55, Letter from Lodovico Vigarani to the cardinal Rinaldo d'Este.
162. Ibid., No. 77.
163. Ibid., No. 306.
164. Despois, *Le théâtre français sous Louis XIV*, pp. 121 et seq.
165. MSS. BN franc. 24357, fo. 217.
166. Arch. Nat. O¹ 2984.
167. Despois, *Le théâtre français sous Louis XIV*, pp. 121 et seq.
168. Cf. Celler, *Décors*, p. 157.

the King has made it quite clear that the opera is his new love. As a result, the whole range of the baroque tends now to be confined to one public theater of royal patronage, the opera at the Palais Royal, with the Guénégaud limping weakly after it. The very process by which Lully oppresses the legitimate genres helps the process of purification: the final reduction of the number of singing voices to two and of violins to six, [169] discouraging any attempt at imitation, throws back the emphasis on the dramatic text.

Next, we note that however the Royal Entry and festival could endow the individual theater with its motifs and machines, one feature could not survive this transplantation; this was the collective nature of the occasion, the hierarchy of the spectacle. The prince, we have stated, was on these occasions at once spectator and spectacle: he viewed the showpieces, he viewed the crowd; and the crowd viewed the monarch and the showpieces. [170] This form survives, as might be expected, in the processions and ceremonies of the seventeenth century, in which it is an inescapable duty for the prince to show himself. Louis XIII, at the declaration of his majority, mounts, like his forebears, onto a *théâtre*. [171] When Louis XIV entered Paris in 1660, there had been prepared for him a rich canopy of gold brocade; but he did not use it, fearing that it might stop the people from seeing him. Nor is the bourgeoisie unwilling to maintain its rôle of third element in the spectacle: artisans, architects, engineers are paid by the Hôtel de Ville, and in fact maintained for such occasions: the *échevinage* accepts this responsibility. [172] At the same time, the early court ballet, not in any case completely "polarized," is open to the bourgeoisie— that they may see the monarch dance, for in this genre he is still spectacle himself. D'Aubignac once more goes to the heart of the matter: "Enfin la gloire et la grandeur des Spectacles ne pouvaient mieux venir que de celui qui s'était rendu lui-même le plus glorieux et le plus grand Spectacle du Monde. [173]

Gradually, after the first Italian performances, from 1645 onwards, the monarch and the court go off the stage. They cease to be direct spectacle. Jupiter, upon whom the King had so often gazed while being gazed on himself, is left to deputize. The King becomes, at best, a central point in the auditorium. From now on we detect in the organization of court spectacle a nostalgia for the missing layer in the hierarchy of the show. Repulsed from the rigidly exclusive Italianate opera-ballet, the public flows back to the Marais, which is beginning to imitate its wealthier rival. [174] *Orfeo* and the *Grande journée des machines* provide the first instance. On the

---

169. *Ordonnance* of 30th April 1673, confirmed in 1675, 1682, 1684, and 1716. Arch. Nat. 0¹ 618, No. 1. See also Mélèse, *Le théâtre et le public sous Louis XIV*, pp. 417–18.

170. See pp. 60 et seq.

171. Magne, *Les plaisirs et les fêtes en France au XVIIe siècle*, p. 46.

172. Cf. ibid., pp. 19–20.

173. *Pratique*, pp. 16–17.

174. The popularity of the machine play is such that, if we are to believe Bontems, *Nouveau recueil de pièces comiques et facétieuses*, it was even attempted by young amateurs:

> Plusieurs jeunes hommes et jeunes Demoiselles du Marais, ayant ces jours passés voulu jouer la Comédie d'Andromède, pièce célèbre à cause des Machines extraordinaires qui

court stage itself the more collective paratheatrical forms occasionally figure, reduced to mere spectacle: Loret notes with enthusiasm the "combat à la barrière"
contained in the *Nozze di Peleo e di Teti,* (1654),[175] but this hierarchy is a barrier to
the view through the proscenium arch, the growth of which, with its curtain, and
with the complete perspective set, constrains the "thing seen" irresistibly into one
small area.

In the closed fêtes at Versailles, on the other hand, the nostalgia for the crowd
as spectacle is appeased in a particularly nauseating manner. At the end of the feast
in the fêtes of 1668, the King gave the order to throw open the gates to the hungry
crowd massed around them, so that they might fight over the remains of the meal:
"La destruction d'un arrangement si beau servit encore d'un divertissement, par
l'empressement et la confusion de ceux qui démolissaient ces châteaux de masse-
pains et ces montagnes de confitures."[176] This became a regular practice: "Après
que leurs Majestés eurent fait collation au son des violons et hautbois, toutes les
tables furent abandonnées au pillage ainsi qu'elles ont accoutumé de l'être en ces
sortes de rencontres."[177] Sometimes the crowd was allowed in merely to augment
the audience; this was the case with the ballet of the 1668 fêtes.[178]

In the early *brevets d'opéra* the atrophy of this nuclear form of the spectacle is
realized, and a fruitless attempt made to prevent it. The court is given every in-
ducement to join in the singing: "Voulons et nous plaît que tous gentilshommes
Demoiselles et autres personnes puissent chanter . . . sans que pour ce ils dérogent
au titre de noblesse ni à leurs privilèges charges droits et immunités . . . "[179] Lully's
privilege of 1672 contains the same remarks. The ineffectiveness of this royal fiat
is sufficient proof that the hierarchy of the spectacle is disintegrating, under the
pressure once more of the polarization of stage and auditorium.[180]

servent à sa représentation: lorsqu'ils auraient voulu distribuer les Personnages entr'eux,
la plus jeune des filles qu'ils avaient choisies pour être leurs actrices, âgée d'environ de
dix-sept ans, aurait dit franchement aux autres, qu'elle voulait être Persée ou qu'autrement elle n'en serait point. Eh bien, dirent les autres, vous serez Persée, puisque vous
le désirez, et ainsi jouèrent gaillardement leur comédie.

However, *recueils* of this type are unreliable, and we reproduce the anecdote in the
pious hope that it is apocryphal.

175. *Muse historique*, p. 486, quoted by Prunières, *Opéra italien*, p. 161.
176. Quoted by Celler, *Décors*, p. 137.
177. Arch. Nat. 0¹ 3263, from the Imprimerie Royale, 1676. *Fêtes de 1674*, 5e journée,
     p. 42.
178. Cf. Celler, *Décors*, p. 136.
179. Arch. Nat. 0¹ 13, fo. 137 v°.
180. We do not regard the machine flight out from the stage towards the spectators,
     which Corneille claims to have introduced into France with the *Toison d'Or* in 1660,
     as a form of resistance to this movement. It is merely an exploitation of the estab-
     lished proscenium arch picture, deriving its shock value from the very fact that the
     public regards itself as sealed off from that picture. It is the aesthetic of the three-
     dimensional cinema.

The baroque carries with it, as part and parcel of its purpose of flattery, an illusion of antique grandeur. The seventeenth-century writer or producer had not the advantage of the modern historian in knowing that what we call the Renaissance was in his time a *fait accompli*: thus, the illusion is continuous from the sixteenth to the seventeenth centuries. It is the French Renaissance scholars, at their work of reconstitution, who pave the way for the Italian Order. The major Italian importation into the royal occasion occurs when Jodelle, Mellin de Saint-Gelais, Daurat, Ronsard, and Baïf become involved in the court festivities and collaborate with the Italians to that end.[181] The court ballet is for them a sincere attempt at an approximation to the combination of Muses in the ancient theater. Baïf's Academy, working on the union of poetry and music, opens the gates, through the ballet, for the opera to enter France:

> Car leurs vers avaient la mesure
> Qui d'une plaisante batture
> Frappait l'oreille des oyants
> Et des choeurs la belle dance,
> En chantant, gardait la cadence,
> Au son des hautbois s'égayant.[182]

Some little time later, the same idea, though under less scholarly control, inspires Baltazarini in the *Ballet comique de la reine*: "L'antiquité ne récitait point ses vers sans musique, et Orphée ne sonnait jamais sans vers."

Now, in these examples, there is much talk of music, but little of machines. These are the contribution of the seventeenth century to the illusion. It is already there with d'Aubignac: "Ces Ballets, dis-je, où l'on a représenté par deux fois la machine du monde, les Cieux, la Mer, la Terre et les Enfers, *surpassent* sans mesure tout ce que nous pouvons rencontrer de ces illustres Divertissements dans les Mémoires de l'Antiquité."[183] It is well to remember that the theorists use the ancients as authority for this type of spectacle. In particular, d'Aubignac's reservations about machine effects are based on his conviction that the Greek Maecenate was extensive enough to permit them, while the French patronage, at his time of writing, is not. Nevertheless, the "relèvement du théâtre" to which he looks forward is to be achieved by the rich, well-done machine play of the future: "Nous ne sommes pourtant pas dans un siècle, où nous ne puissions espérer que les libéralités des Princes, l'étude des Poètes, le travail des Ingénieurs, et les soucis de nos Comédiens ne relèvent la magnificence du Théâtre ancien."[184] Not reconstitution, but eclipse, is now the object. The *Gazette* is launching a slogan when it cries of *Andromède* that the Greeks and the Romans are surpassed. With the *machiniste*, the illusion is cer-

181. Prunières, *Ballet de cour*, p. 41.
182. Quoted by Prunières, p. 66.
183. *Pratique*, p. 15. The italics are ours.
184. *Pratique*, Bk. III, ch. ix, p. 357.

tainly genuine, witness Torelli in his dedication to Mazarin of the *Noces de Thétis*:
"L'emploi qui m'occupe depuis si longtemps à la cour . . . je m'y consacre avec
tout le respect que je lui dois, tous les soins et toute l'industrie dont je suis capable
de relever le Théâtre Français." For the King, the opera is the summit of the century's culture; the "privilège d'opéra" which passes, on Lully's death, to his son-
in-law Francini, speaks of "la Beauté et la Magnificence de ces Spectacles qui ne
plaisent pas moins à l'esprit qu'à l'oreille et aux yeux et qui par cette raison sont
les plus nobles Divertissements des personnes qui aiment les Beaux Arts."[185] The
work of scholarly palingenesis is left completely behind; the attempt to equal ancient
glory is forgotten, since it has already been "surpassed." If the Renaissance itself
is an illusion of antique grandeur, the baroque theater is the illusion of an illusion.

By comparison with the legitimate theater, the baroque is without intellectual
content, or even genuine emotion. It is transient, and this quality expresses itself
marvellously in the open-air theaters, particularly of Versailles. There is implicit
in this transience a contempt for the theater edifice as a totality which is almost a
mal du siècle. The Vigarani family are the great constructors of temporary (but sumptuous) stages in the park of Versailles. Already, to allay the impatience of the court
occasioned by the unfinished Salle des Machines, they construct a "théâtre volant"
made of tapestries, for Cicognini's *Serse*.[186] Of that constructed in 1677 at Sceaux,
we are told "il paraissait avoir été mis là par enchantement à cause du peu de temps
qu'on avait eu pour le dresser."[187] In 1665 we find that Carlo Vigarani has been
to Versailles where he has built a theater in six days.[188] But the best effort must be
accounted that of 1682, for a performance of Quinault's opera *Persée* in the park.
The King had said that he would give several days' warning when he was pleased
to have the opera, so that there would be time to build the theater. However, the
arrival of fine weather and his desire to let Mme. la Dauphine see the opera before
her confinement changed his mind so that he gave only twenty-four hours' notice.
At midday, the structure was well under way, when the arrival of rain decided His
Majesty to postpone the entertainment. He was nevertheless promised a theater for
the evening, in the *manège*. At eight-thirty in the evening the theater was ready, in
a building where horses had been undergoing dressage at midday![189]

The decline of the text inherent in the growth of the opera needs no further
development. Let us simply note in Servandoni, yet again, the logical culmination
of that autonomy of the machine which was beginning, as we have noticed, almost
to evolve a "grammar," an articulation of its own. There is some reason for be-
lieving that Servandoni actually achieved this. His career at the Académie Royale
finishes, at his own instigation, in 1737, and in 1738 he is given the decrepit Salle
des Machines in which to try out his first diorama project.[190] Left to himself, every-

185. Arch. Nat. 0¹ 613 (1).
186. Rouchès, *Inventaire*, No.107, pp. 38–39.
187. Arch. Nat. 0¹ 3263, p. 4 (5e vol. bis of the *Mercure* for June).
188. Rouchès, *Inventaire*, No. 217, p. 99.
189. MSS. BN franc. 24357, fo. 243 v°.
190. Bouché, "Servandoni," *Gazette des Beaux Arts*, tome IV, August 1910, p. 124.

thing impelled him towards the "spectacle muet": the opera had the monopoly of song, orchestral accompaniment and ballet. He had neither the means nor the desire to indulge in the legitimate drama. He was left with two weapons: painting and light. His first spectacle, then, has no text, no music, no movement, and, final *carence,* no men! It is the Church of Saint Peter in Rome. Accused of monotony, he evolves slowly towards an action of pure visual imagery; accepting the criticism, he says in the preamble to the program of his next show: "C'est aussi ce qui l'a porté à choisir un Sujet qui pût occuper agréablement pendant un temps assez considérable, et avec une variété capable d'ôter à une longue attention ce qu'elle peut avoir de fatigant et même d'ennuyeux."[191] He has in short introduced change and movement:

> L'ouverture de ce spectacle se fera par la Représentation du Chaos, et dès que les yeux des Spectateurs y auront été amusés quelques temps, cette masse informe s'agitera dans toutes ses parties et se développera au bruit du Tonnerre et au feu des Eclairs.
> Chaque Elément prendra la place que la Nature lui a destinée; le Feu, représenté par des transparents, s'élèvera dans la plus haute Région; l'Air se séparera des Eaux qui formeront les Mers, les Fleuves, les Torrents, pour entourer et arroser la Terre; et celle-ci, parée d'Arbres, de Fleurs et de Fruits, fera voir une riante image de la Nature naissante, telle que les Poètes nous la représentent sous le premier Age du Monde.[192]

Slowly, he traverses problems similar to those of the early silent cinema. Still conscious of a lack of variety, he adds machines, and silent characters and even music now to "donner une espèce de vie à ce Spectacle."[193] He reveals himself as genuinely preoccupied with the organization of successive visual images into an articulated, poetic whole. He defines the diorama as "une Poésie qui parle aux yeux,"[194] and asks: "Pourquoi la Peinture ne s'efforcerait-elle pas d'avoir l'avantage d'occuper seule toute l'attention des Spectateurs? Pourquoi n'aspirerait-elle pas à la gloire de faire oublier quelques instants ses Soeurs?"[195] The machine play and the opera in the seventeenth century, in their ostentatious triumph over matter in general and gravity in particular, in their naturalism of the supernatural, are the artistic superstructure of the monarch's illusion of omnipotence, of his subjective identification with a deity. This is no longer true of Servandoni's diorama. The seam of *flagornerie* has given out. Yet in his greater perfection of naturalist spectacle he surpasses them and attains something of the epic sweep of possibility of the cinema.[196]

The Italian Order, progressively excluding dramatic poetry and action from its theaters, could not yet invent a poetry to replace them. It bequeathed these problems in France to an eighteenth-century Italian, who, hampered by the very privileges which the darling child of that order, the opera, had gathered about it, went far to solving them.

191. *Description du spectacle de Pandore,* p. 4.
192. Ibid., pp. 4–5.
193. Program of the *Descente d'Enée aux enfers,* 1740, pp. 6–7.
194. Bouché, "Servandoni," *Gazette des Beaux Arts,* p. 136.
195. Preamble to the program of the *Forêt enchantée,* 1754, p. 6.
196. His *Spectacle de la chute des anges rebelles* (1758) sweeps from Book 1 to Book 6 of Milton's *Paradise Lost.*

CHAPTER SEVEN

THE RECTANGLE AND THE AUDITORIUM

THE ANCIENT THEATER, in its progress towards sophistication, tended to evolve towards a single line of vision. There is some evidence to suggest the point that we have already touched upon,[1] namely that theater form in France, from the outdoor period of the mystery onwards, followed a similar line. Cohen claims that the amphitheater was a much more frequent disposition than has been supposed.[2] Fouquet's miniature of the *Martyre de Sainte Apolline* (see Fig. 18) is the most notable example.[3] At Metz in 1437, we are told in a contemporary account, all around the stage were seats and *loges* for the lords and ladies.[4] Cohen further quotes an anonymous description of a performance of the *Acts of the Apostles* by the Confrères themselves, where the theater was built in the round, "after the ancient manner of the Romans," with the audience sitting around in twenty rising ranks, topped by three rows of *loges* and galleries. At Bourges there is the same form in 1536: here, the Roman theater of Avaricum is used.[5] At Saumur again they use "quelques restes de théâtre ancien."[6] Near the village of Doué (Maine et Loire) an old quarry was transformed into an amphitheater in the fifteenth or early sixteenth century, and it seems probable that performances were held in it, notably that of the *Actes des apôtres* in 1539 (Fig. 105).[7]

The indoor mystery play, on the contrary, would of necessity be confined to a rectangle: the Confrères, from the Hôtel de Flandres to the Trinité and thence to the Hôtel de Bourgogne, would be subject to this impediment. By the commencement of the seventeenth century, all trace of the popular collective amphitheatrical form of the theater proper is lost. For the early part of the century, not only was the theater subject to the rectangle, but by virtue of the Confrères' monopoly, it was subject to *one* rectangle, that of the Hôtel de Bourgogne.[8]

The most readily available accommodation was the *jeu de paume* or *tripot*. The nature of this indoor tennis game made the building long, narrow, and high, although the roof stood upon supports well above the top edge of the wall, for the

1. See p. 55.
2. *Théâtre religieux*, avant-propos, p. xiv.
3. But see pp. 53–5. We must beware of deducing from this miniature any details of stage frontage. The parapet of the raised stage is no more than a conventional motif of the miniaturist, as a glance at any other Fouquet miniatures in which there can be no question of a mystery (or other theatrical) performance will show.
4. Cohen, *Théâtre religieux*, p. 80.
5. Girardot (ed.), *Mystère des actes des apôtres*, p. i.
6. Cohen, *Théâtre religieux*, avant-propos, pp. xv–xvi.
7. Lebègue (ed.), *Le mystère des actes des apôtres*, 1929, p.27.
8. See also Dubech, *Histoire générale illustrée du théâtre*, 1931–4, vol. III, p. 128 (fig.): "Une salle de spectacle rectangulaire au début du XVIIe siècle."

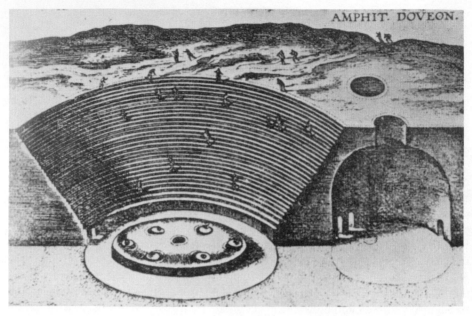

FIG. 105.—The amphitheater, Doué.

purpose of letting in light. It would normally have a gallery for spectators.[9] The matter has been treated in some detail by Holsboer, who remarks that such buildings were already numerous in 1579.[10] A loss in popularity in the game may have made more courts available during the seventeenth century.

Mme. Deierkauf-Holsboer has happily completed our knowledge of the movements of the Montdory-Lenoir troupe which was to found the Marais theater. They establish themselves in 1629 at the jeu de paume de Berthault, where they played Corneille's *Mélite*, while a lease of the 12th December 1631 shows them as playing in the jeu de paume de la Sphère in the rue Vieille du Temple, not far from their final home. In 1632 they rent the tripot de la Fontaine, in the rue Michel le Comte, and on the 8th March 1634 they sign a contract by which they take over the jeu de paume du Marais.[11] This very understandable and automatic choice of the

9. In the richer and private tennis court this open wall space was probably filled in by windows. That still existing at Chantilly (the present museum) is an example.

10. *Mise en scène*, pp. 38 et seq. See also our article "Les lieux du spectacle (XVIIe siècle)" in *L'Architecture d'Aujourd'hui*, No. 152, 1970. This demonstrates a tendency towards a centrifugal effect in siting, nearer to and indeed beyond, the old fortifications of Philippe-Auguste, away from the city center, presumably because land would be cheaper on the outskirts.

11. *Le théâtre du Marais*, tome I, pp. 16–17. See also Dulaure, *Histoire physique, civile, et morale de Paris, depuis les premiers temps historiques jusqu'à nos jours*, 5th edn., 1834, tome VI, p. 81.

tennis court goes on through the century, Molière being one of the chief victims. From the jeu de paume des Métayers he moves in 1645 to the jeu de paume de la Croix Noire. In 1650, according to Beauchamps and Dulaure, he installs a theater in the jeu de paume de la Croix Blanche, rue de Bucy, Faubourg Saint Germain.[12]

The modifications carried out to the Croix Noire in turning it into a theater, completed 8th January 1645, are revealing, for they show us what is to be a repeating pattern and, it will be observed, are already copied from the Marais:

> Dresser portes et barrières . . . fermer le jour du dit jeu, de maçonnerie ou charpenterie, en sorte que les dites fermetures puissent subsister, faire deux rangs de loges . . . de la façon de celles du Marais, les ais du plafond et devant lesquelles loges établis à doubles joints; remonter le théâtre audit jeu de la Croix Noire et faire la quantité des loges telles et semblables qu'elles étaient au jeu des Métayers; les dites loges garnies de sièges et barres . . .[13]

The *jeu de paume* was not to be Molière's only acquaintance with the constraining rectangle. On his return to Paris in 1658 he plays *Nicomède* in the Salle des Gardes du Vieux Louvre. The report of an inspection by the Académie d'Architecture on the 27th May 1707 gives us a professional view of its shape: "La Compagnie a seulement observé qu'il n'est pas ordinaire que des salles aient trois fois autant de longueur que de largeur, comme celle-ci qui, selon toute apparence, a été faite de cette proportion par rapport à son usage particulier, de servir à de grandes assemblées."[14]

After the example of the Illustre Théâtre, we must note the tribulations of the Comédie Française when, in 1687, the opening of the Collège des Quatre Nations causes it to be ejected from the Guénégaud. The players seek accommodation now in a series of private residences, since they presumably have more funds than their illustrious predecessors. They attempt in vain to secure the Hôtel de Sourdis, in the rue Neuve des Fossés-Saint-Germain-l'Auxerrois, the Hôtel de Nemours on the quai des Augustins, a house in the rue de l'Arbre Sec,[15] the Hôtel de Lussan in the rue Croix-des-Petits-Champs,[16] the Hôtel de Sens in the rue Saint-André, and a house opposite the Hôtel de Lussan. Finally they come to rest—in another *tripot*, that of the Etoile—in the rue Neuve des Fossés-Saint-Germain-des-Prés![17] The Ital-

12. Beauchamps, *Recherches sur les théâtres de France*, 1735, p. 209. Dulaure, op. cit., tome VII, p. 90.
13. Holsboer, *Mise en scène*, p. 4. The same author's *Théâtre du Marais* reveals that this installation is copied from the new Marais as rebuilt after its total destruction in the fire of 15th January 1644 (p. 121 and see our pp. 236–7).
14. Arch. Nat. 0¹ 1929 (3).
15. This must have been the most hopeless of their efforts, since the vicar of Saint-Germain-l'Auxerrois had already succeeded in having the King withdraw his consent for the Hôtel Sourdis.
16. The building had actually been bought when permission was again revoked as a result of ecclesiastical opposition.
17. For a full account of these peregrinations, see Bourdel, "L'Hôtel des Comédiens Français," RHT, tome II, 1955, pp. 145 et seq.

ian players meet with similar trouble when they try to build a theater in the Faubourg Saint Germain in 1680, before occupying the Hôtel de Bourgogne.[18]

The Amphitheater

Meanwhile, in paratheatricals generally, and particularly in outdoor rejoicings, free of the material and economic pressures which bear upon the public theater, the amphitheater persists, as do many of the other features of these occasions. Wherever the hierarchy of the spectacle persists, so does the amphitheater. At the carrousel of 1612 for the marriage of Louis XIII, the camp of the Place Royale is described thus by Châtillon, "topographe du Roi": "Les Echafauds joignant les Pavillons qui environnaient la Place . . . étaient construits en degrés rampants en forme de ceux des théâtres et amphithéâtres des anciens Romains."[19] The crowd, according to the *Mercure*, is equally "antique" in proportion, amounting to fifty thousand souls. Where the court is playing at its own game of surpassing the ancients, for which a massive public is required, the amphitheater is inescapable. It is the very impermanence of the occasion, its freedom from major architectural restraints (for, unlike the public theater it ignores those of a rectangular periphery when it is indoors), which permits and encourages the more narcissistic, collective arrangement. Across the century, in these accounts, the word amphitheater recurs: for the *ballet du roi* at the Hôtel de Ville in 1626,[20] for that of the 18th February 1635,[21] ("Galeries et degrés allant en forme d'amphithéâtre jusqu'au faîte de son plancher"), for the Ball and firework display of 1649 at the Hôtel de Ville, and so on.[22] Where the indoor accommodation already has galleries, their angles are hidden by the rising amphitheater of seats that reaches up to them: the *ordonnateur* does not accept the discipline of the periphery: "Cette salle était accrue d'une Galerie tout autour, au-dessus et au-dessous de laquelle étaient des sièges en forme d'amphithéâtre qui doublaient son espace et le rendaient capable de deux fois autant de personnes."

Until the very end of the century, the public auditorium, on the other hand, remains cabined within the existing walls of a building made for other destinies, and even the courtly theater house can only reach out timidly towards the complete ellipse or amphitheater which it had left behind it in the Italian sixteenth century.

The Hôtel de Bourgogne

The foregoing facts make the history of the auditorium form in the century a comparatively simple one. It is not until the eighteenth century, generally speaking, that those problems of line, visual and auditory, and of the general aesthetics of form which the Italian Order brings with it, are tackled and a compromise sought— charily in architecture, lavishly on paper.

18. Mélèse, *Le théâtre et le public sous Louis XIV*, p. 44.
19. Arch. Nat. 0¹ 3264, p. 5 (*Mercure* of 1612).
20. MSS. BN nouvelles acquisitions franc. 9745 (114), fos. 237 v° et seq.
21. MSS. BN franc. 2453, fos. 65 v° and 66.
22. Arch. Nat. 0¹ 3260 (*Gazette* of 7th September).

The general disposition of the Hôtel de Bourgogne is known to us. A narrow, shallow stage, a long narrow house, with two rows of *loges* round the three house walls, and the floor entirely occupied by the *parterre* or pit.[23] Copied possibly from a *jeu de paume* or the Hôpital de la Trinité,[24] the Hôtel must have had a *parterre* matching relatively that of the Marais in its first and second forms. It was certainly the main element of accommodation, given the fact that the spectators stood in it and the very considerable compressibility of the human person. It would constitute the normal, steady source of revenue for that theater certainly, and possibly for the Marais, for Molière's theaters, and towards the end of the century for the Guénégaud.

At the beginning of our period then, the greater part of the public is disposed in a completely anarchical manner,[25] while Despois surmises that even under Louis XIV the *parterre* of the Hôtel would constitute one half of the total house.[26] The license and unruliness of the pit have been very thoroughly chronicled.[27] They continue, like the pit itself, through the century. The simple fact that a standing audience can turn in any direction has been too much neglected in the consideration of this phenomenon. Despois has asked whether the disorders were not part of a repressed desire on the part of the masses to take a more organic part in the spectacle. With the proviso, as regards the masses, that it is the officers of the royal household who cause as much trouble as anyone else, we may develop the statement. The stage of the Hôtel, would-be focus of attention, is a narrow platform at one end of a crowded rectangle. The standing public is discouraged from approaching it by an iron grille which is still there in 1726.[28] The public arrived up to two hours beforehand, brawled, tippled, diced, and wenched because the spectacle, shorn for the moment of any collective social purpose such as the mystery play possessed, could not by its very nature and surround be any sort of focus: it was not the sole purpose of the gathering. The form itself of the Hôtel de Bourgogne buildings, from what we can gather, reduces the relative importance of the theater proper. We have seen what were its probable approximate dimensions,[29] but the site itself is much

23. See Rigal, *Alexandre Hardy*, p. 141, and our pp. 114-6.

24. Rigal, *Théâtre français*, p. 201.

25. Stools could be bought haphazard or placed by the troupe (Fransen, *Documents inédits de l'Hôtel de Bourgogne*, p. 327). For the court performances, seats would be brought and placed in the pit (Dulaure, *Histoire physique etc.*, tome VI, p. 76). This no doubt happened when Valleran played a farce before the King in 1607 (Rigal, *Théâtre français*, p. 51), and when the Dauphin Louis was taken to the Hôtel de Bourgogne for the first time on 7th February 1609 (ibid., p. 54, fn).

26. *Le théâtre français sous Louis XIV*, p. 370. This would however depend on where we place the *parterre* after the 1647 reconstruction.

27. Ibid., pp. 154 et seq., p. 161 and passim; Rigal, *Théâtre français*, pp. 203, 204, 213, 214; d'Ormesson, *Journal*, Monday, 2nd October 1645, etc., etc.

28. Op. cit., p. 129.

29. See pp. 114-5. The *plan Gomboust* shows only the exterior of the building and is otherwise uninformative.

larger: "une masure contenant dix-sept toises de long sur seize de large."[30] The theater was surrounded by dimly lit corridors which undoubtedly served many of the aforesaid purposes. The stage no longer forms an effective crystallization for the assembled crowd, which makes of the performance its own collective occasion, at the lowest level.[31] As late as 1694, de Visé in the *Mercure galant* remarks that the pit whistles for the fun of whistling, and because it finds this pastime more diverting than the play.[32]

The sources of patronage in Italy in the Renaissance and early seventeenth century were more numerous, richer, and more cultured than those of France.[33] There, the divers small courtly audiences tended to form into some version of the ellipse. This type of auditorium, transmuted in the growth of the public opera theater, remains curved in spite of the fact that for obvious economic reasons stemming from the numerical growth of its public, it uses the loggia for the purpose of exploiting its wall space.[34] Because this does not happen in France, even to the baroque auditorium, the *loges* remain a besetting nuisance. The rows of them at the Hôtel de Bourgogne follow the line of the rectangular walls. Lancaster, summarizing the various evidence of individual ownership, notes *loges* for the King, the Lieutenant Civil, Angoulevant, "prince des sots," the "anciens maîtres" (the Confrères), the "maîtres et gouverneurs," the Sieur de Fonteny, and others called "de court bouyon" and "des Thonneaux."[35] The writer is however unjustified in claiming that the entire upper gallery was called the *Paradis*. The statement would appear to be based on the terms of the lease of 24th October 1607,[36] in which occurs the phrase "la moitié du lieu dit le Paradis." The word "lieu" is not only too indefinite to connote the whole gallery, but further, later leases give a contrary view, that of 1635 saying "à la réserve . . . du lieu étant au-dessus de la loge appelée le Paradis" and that of 1639, once more "ladite loge appelée le Paradis." Thus it seems to have been a single *loge,* most probably facing the stage.

We can now form a picture of two galleries round the three sides of the hall, divided sporadically, and not completely, into *loges.* A minority of spectators, partially differentiated by privilege, looked down on the homogeneous throng. The "loges de face" were the only ones which provided a suitable view of the stage, and would be farthest from it. The others would face into the house throughout

30. Lease published by the Frères Parfaict, *Histoire du théâtre français*, tome II, p. 224, quoted by Holsboer, *Mise en scène*, p. 43. See also Rigal, *Théâtre français*, pp. 36–37, and Lancaster, *History*, Pt. I, vol. ii, p. 712.

31. Cf. the English theater of the time, where the public also arrived very early, also diced and drank, and also scared away the respectable bourgeoisie.

32. Quoted by Despois, op. cit., p. 161.

33. Cf. pp. 106–7.

34. Cf. p. 47.

35. *History*, Pt. I, vol. ii, p. 712. See also Fransen, *Documents inédits de l'Hôtel de Bourgogne,* pp. 325 et seq., 349, 350 and 351, Holsboer, *Mise en scène,* p. 61, Léris, *Dictionnaire portatif historique et littéraire des théâtres,* 2nd edn., 1763, p. xiii, and Beauchamps, *Recherches sur les théâtres de France,* p. 200.

36. Fransen, op. cit., p. 330.

their length. There is here neither the autonomy of the Italian court auditorium, nor the disciplined single line of vision demanded by the perspective set which is beginning to take the stage at this time. In a hopeless attempt to remedy this the Comédiens Royaux, most significantly, can think of only one thing. In their *Remontrances au Roi en faveur de la troupe royale des comédiens* they undertake, if freed from the yoke of the Confrérie, to rebuild their house after the fashion of those in Italy.[37] We must regret the absence of further evidence of what the Comédiens envisaged in this phrase. Of which Italian house were they dreaming? Vicenza, Sabbioneta, Parma? The only justified supposition is that their project involved the suppression or serious diminution of the pit, the installation of an amphitheater. As it was, this, and to a greater or lesser extent all the other theaters of the seventeenth century in France were to allow the rectangular periphery to dominate the interior arrangement of the auditorium to a far greater extent than in Italy.

Yet it is precisely around the chronology of the rectangle's modification that recent controversy has been at its most intense, and the interesting possibility emerges that the modifications to the Hôtel of 1647 may be of greater significance in the movement towards the Italian Order than we had imagined. The sovereignty of the *jeu de paume* shape may possibly have been shorter-lived than we had thought.[38]

Roy's article of 1962 had left us with a rectangular auditorium prior to 1647 measuring 9 toises 5 pieds by 7 toises[39] (see Fig. 45). It seems certain that the entire floor, excepting naturally the stage, was occupied by an unraked stand-up pit. *Loges* there certainly were, at least down either side, though how many we cannot be sure; on top of them an upper gallery, or *paradis*, and there was an amphitheater: "the floored gallery of the first banks of loges on the two sides of the Bourgogne extended around the rue Mauconseil end, jutting out there some fifteen to twenty feet into the *parterre*, and around six feet above the ground level. In this space was constructed the *amphithéâtre*, a sort of steep bleacher section rising precipitously up to the eaves of the building."[40] C. M. Fogarty has argued that the auditorium loges probably met the stage as this would save space at the back (assuming no doubt a limited number of loges on either side) for the base of the *amphithéâtre*: a possible explanation of the 1647 contract's expression "plus l'amphithéâtre sera fait . . . le plus commodément que faire se pourra" since at that time the number of loges was probably increased.[41]

37. Rigal, *Théâtre français*, p. 214 fn; Holsboer, *Mise en scène*, p. 45. Lancaster, *History*, Pt. I, vol. ii, p. 712, reverses the causality of this interesting fact. He says "even the actors themselves, in 1631, admitted the desirability of rearranging their house so that it might resemble Italian theatres."

38. See Wiley, *The Hôtel de Bourgogne. Another Look at France's First Public Theatre*, in *Studies in Philology*, vol. LXX, December, 1973, no. 5, pp. 28 et seq.

39. Mme. Deierkauf-Holsboer now having recanted on her previous width of 9 toises 2 pieds. (*Le théâtre de l'Hôtel de Bourgogne*, vol. II, Paris, 1970, p. 58.)

40. Wiley, op. cit. This is probably the most lucid account that we have.

41. C. M. Fogarty, "A Reconstruction of the Interior of the Hôtel de Bourgogne." *Maske und Kothurn* XXVI, 1, 1980.

It is with the contract of 1647 that scholars (and at least one man of the theater) have wrestled over the last two decades in particular. The late David Illingworth returns to the charge in 1970, supporting Roy's dimensions from other sources, mainly eighteenth century, and voicing (for the first time since Niemeyer in 1947) the possibility that the end may have been rounded à l'italienne in 1647. His article is printed side by side with that of an eminently practical man of the theater, André Villiers, who attacks Deierkauf-Holsboer's stage width of 9 toises 2 pieds by demonstrating that cross-timbers of such length were not available, and that 1647 is but a few years after the advent of Torelli and the *Finta Pazza*, not to mention *Mirame*, both heavily financed. Illingworth further develops his theory in 1971 in another monograph, basing himself on Niemeyer's publication of Dumont's half-plan of the theater in *Parallèle de plans des plus belles spectacles d'Italie et de France*, Paris 1777, and assurances from Charny (1716) and Des Boulmiers (1769) that the theater still had its "construction primitive."[42] With the assistance of John Golder he establishes the successive plans of the house (Fig. 106).

Neither Deierkauf-Holsboer (who simply denies the possibility) nor Wiley are able to accept this convention. For Wiley, the 1647 contract establishes two new ranks of end loges, with a dividing wall three feet distant, separating them from the *amphithéâtre*. There is a consequent reduction of space in the parterre. He disposes of Niemeyer's theory of a horseshoe-end auditorium by disposing of one of that author's main arguments—that the last Mahelot drawing of the *Mémoire*, described tentatively by Lancaster as "l'intérieur d'un théâtre" is most probably an unfinished sketch for the décor of Benserade's *Iphis et Ianté*. To Illingworth, Wiley objects that there is not the slightest indication of curvature in the 1647 *devis*, which is otherwise highly detailed, and that it would have required a new series of pillars. The amphitheater would have had to be curved too, for symmetry, and there would be a waste of space behind the two tiers of loges. There is no evidence that the Marais, which the Comédiens du Roy were purporting to copy, had a rounded end à l'italienne.[43]

Wiley argues that the theater would have been modernized in 1716, when the Italians resumed possession after their exile. Barlow, however, contests this in 1976 and adduces new evidence from the sketchbook diary of Sir James Thornhill in 1717, apparently vindicating Niemeyer, and he even raises the possibility of raked floors in the lateral lines of loges in 1647.[44] He places the amphitheater *in front* of the curved rear loges, which is unquestionably the message of Thornhill's sketch, and raises it somewhat above floor level so that its occupants may see over the heads of those in the *parterre*, without interfering with the view of those in the boxes. All this hinges upon the veracity of Thornhill, who is clearly no theatrical incompetent, and above all upon the extent of the 1716 alterations, about which there is doubt (Figs. 107, 108).

42. Illingworth, RHT, no. 2, 1970, and no. 1, 1971.
43. Deierkauf-Holsboer, op. cit., vol. II, loc. cit. Wiley, op. cit., ch. IV.
44. Barlow, "The Hôtel de Bourgogne according to Sir James Thornhill," TRI, vol. 1, no. 2, Feb. 1976, pp. 86 et seq.

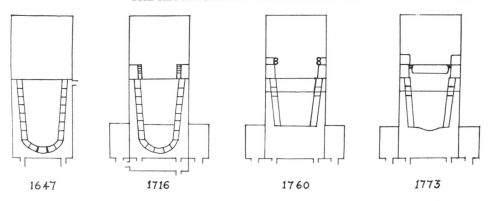

1647   1716   1760   1773

FIG. 106.—The successive states of the Hôtel de Bourgogne according to Illingworth and Golder.

All that we can be sure of then, regarding the Hôtel de Bourgogne auditorium in the second half of the century, is that it had two rows of loges, each of nineteen, a gallery above the second row, an *amphithéâtre* at the back, with a somewhat exiguous base, and a shortened *parterre*; and there, no doubt momentarily, the matter rests. What forces itself on the attention, within the terms of our overall thesis, is that it is the moment of incidence of the arrival of the Italian Order that is in question, and that there is more than half a century's difference between the opposing views.

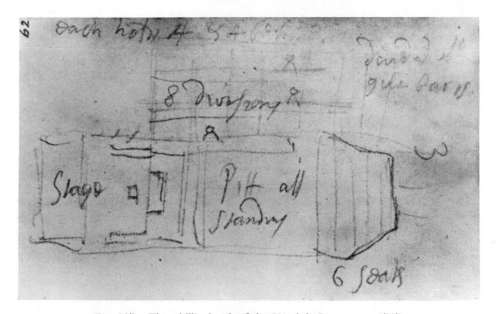

FIG. 107.—Thornhill's sketch of the Hôtel de Bourgogne, 1717.

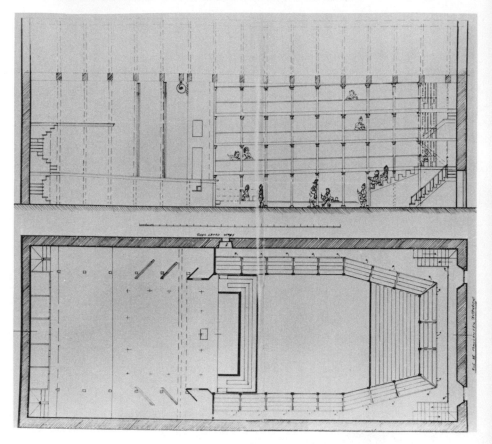

FIG. 108.—Barlow's reconstruction of the Hôtel de Bourgogne.

The Marais

The indefatigable researches of Mme. Deierkauf-Holsboer have finally dragged this house, after centuries of neglect, into the light of day. We have now a very good idea of the aspect it must have presented after its rebuilding and reopening in October 1644. We can do no better than to give the main details of her interpretation of her discovery, *Mémoire de ce qu'il fault faire au jeu de paulme des Marets*. Two rows of eighteen *loges*, one above the other, ran down either side of the house, the lower row sloping upwards slightly from the stage to the back of the house. Each *loge* was 6 feet wide, 6 feet high, and 4 feet deep, access to it being made from a gallery behind occupying another 2 feet of depth; each was furnished with two 10-inch benches and a folding seat resembling the modern French *strapontin*. Facing the stage were four more *loges*, also 6 feet wide, but furnished with chairs instead of benches, and therefore probably meant for more important members of the audience. Behind them was a gallery 3 feet wide, separated from the back of the house by a 6-foot-high partition with two doors. In between this partition and the back of the house two stairways led to the second *loges* and the *paradis*.

The pit, separated from the house entrance by two partitions, occupied the entire width of the *jeu de paume*, i.e. 36 feet, reaching in length from the partitions to the stage edge, that is, adding the 3-foot gallery behind the face *loges*, these *loges* themselves (4 feet) and nine side *loges* each of 6 feet, a total of 61 feet. Down the sides of the pit ran a narrow bench capable of resting some eighty spectators tired of standing.

Above the second *loges*, down both sides, ran the *paradis*, furnished with a long bench at the back.

On the ceiling of the face *loges*, but lying back from them, was constructed the *amphithéâtre*. Eighteen feet high at its highest point, measuring from the ceiling of the *loges*, it was 24 feet wide and, by the author's calculations, 4.75 meters deep.[45]

As the writer herself remarks, the troupe has not simply installed a timid theatrical layout inside a *jeu de paume*: it has seized and modified the tennis court with little or no thought of any eventual return to the original function of the building, though this continues to condition completely the overall design of the house. Nevertheless, it is a small move towards autonomy. It should be noted, however, that the lengthening of the auditorium is not accompanied by broadening, and the stage is in this respect farther removed from the most important part of the audience.

The Petit Bourbon

The evidence for the Petit Bourbon is naturally copious. Sauval's measurements are as follows: "Sa largeur est de dix-huit pas communs sur trent-cinq toises de longueur, et la couverture si rehaussée que le comble paraît aussi élevé que ceux des édifices de Saint Germain et de Saint Eustache."[46] This length of 70 yards by a width of about 18 would make it an extraordinarily long building, but the iconography of the subject bears this out on the whole; bigger than the Grande Salle du Louvre, it housed those paratheatrical ceremonies whose public could not be contained in this latter.[47] An engraving of the prologue to the *Ballet comique de la reine* (see Fig. 87) gives us an idea of the long rectangle, with two rows of galleries, the higher one set back, and the décor occupying the apse. The holding of the Estates General of 1614 gives rise to a whole family of engravings. Piganiol publishes a picture of the assembly, bearing the *sculpsit* of Hérisset and the *delineavit* of Dela-

45. *Le théâtre du Marais*, tome 1, pp. 110–13. See in particular the reconstructions of the theater, Pls. VII–X. But see the article by John Golder, "The Théâtre du Marais in 1644: a new look at the old evidence concerning France's second public theatre." *Theatre Survey*, XXV (2) 1984, 127–52.
46. Quoted by Despois, op. cit., p. 24.
47. Cf. Madeleine Horn-Monval ("Le théâtre du Petit-Bourbon," RHT, tomes I-II, 1948,pp. 46 et seq.) who, in a footnote, gives Sauval's 35 toises as 70 meters, presumably on the assumption that the toise is two meters and not two yards.

Fɪɢ. 109.—The Petit Bourbon, 1614. "Tenüe des Etats Généraux du Royaume sous LE ROY LOUIS XIII."

monce (Fig. 109), the original of which is to be found in the Cabinet des Estampes of the Bibliothèque Nationale,[48] as is a similar engraving by Métezeau,[49] and another by the Polish engraver Ziarnko.[50] The three pictures have minor points of resemblance and difference which are of no interest for the history of the theater. They confirm, as distinct from the sixteenth-century engraving, the capacity of the hall, the galleries following the lines of the rectangle, with a row of ground-floor *loges* rising backwards.[51]

The Palais Royal

The tensions as between function and form apparent in the Petit Bourbon are those of the general purpose hall connected with the court, serving for balls, ballets, and other "unpolarized" spectacles, and yet in increasing demand as theaters in which the stage decoration continued in depth and by *trompe-l'oeil* the lines of the

48. *Nouvelle description de la France*, 1718, tome I, p. 204. Est. BN Qb[1].
49. Est. BN AA[5], dated 1617. Mme. Horn-Monval (RHT, 1948) produces as original another copy of this from the Bibliothèque de l'Arsenal. It has in fact been reproduced by Lavisse, *Histoire de France depuis les origines jusqu'à la Révolution*, tome VI, pt. ii, p. 160.
50. Reproduced by Holsboer, who gives no source. Est. BN Qb[1]. See ch. VI, fn. 49.
51. Cf. Holsboer, *Mise en scène*, p. 50.

FIG. 110.—*Le Soir*.

auditorium. The Palais Royal is an excellent expression of this struggle. The chief sources of our knowledge are Sauval, an engraving, *Le Soir* (Fig. 110), Blondel's plan (Fig. 111), and the set for *Mirame* (see Fig. 73a).[52] We cannot lend credit to the arguments put forward by Fritsche.[53] In an attempt to bring the facts somewhere near to Sauval's two claims that the house contained up to three thousand spectators, or four thousand, which are today in general disrepute,[54] he finally reaches a figure of about one thousand four hundred; he does this by casting doubts on the accuracy of Blondel's plan, in which appears a second, inside wall to the auditorium, which would have reduced the capacity. The argument is not relevant, since as Fritsche is aware, Sauval died in 1670, while Vigarani's modification of the house for Lully's opera, in 1674, is almost certainly that which appears in Blondel.[55] We may recall

52. Sauval, *Antiquités de la ville de Paris*, 1724, tome II, pp. 161 et seq., and tome III, p. 47. The *Le Soir* engraving was falsely identified by Bapst as the "haute salle du Petit Bourbon." See Holsboer, *Mise en scène*, p. 52; Blondel, *Architecture françoise*, tome III, liv. v, no. ix, planche III.

53. "La scène de Molière et son organisation," *Le Moliériste*, June–July–August, 1887, pp. 70–71.

54. *Antiquités,* tome II, p. 161 (3000), and tome III, p. 47 (4000). Cf. Despois, op. cit. p. 33, and Holsboer, *Mise en scène*, p. 64.

55. Cf. Leclerc, *Origines*, p. 178.

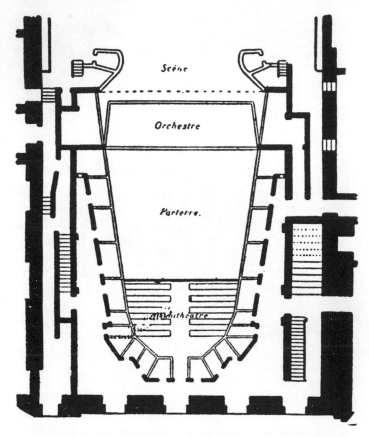

FIG. 111.—Blondel's plan of the Palais Royal auditorium.

that *Peleo e Teti*, in 1654, was originally to be staged in the Palais Royal, but was removed to the Petit Bourbon because the former house might not have held the public that was expected.[56] In 1659, when Mazarin is preparing for the festivities of the royal marriage, the Palais Royal is considered too small for them.[57] Contemporary capacity figures are in any case suspect. However this may be, the figures are reduced by Lyonnet to 1450, and by Fritsche to 1400. Lagrave, considering the house in the eighteenth century, is of the opinion that no serious internal structural modifications are brought to it during the period with which he is dealing (1715–1750) and after those of Vigarani in 1674; with the aid of plans of 1763, to which he draws attention for the first time, he reaches the following conclusion: ". . . en tout, 1270 places sans compter les 'petites loges.' Si l'on tient compte des habitudes

56. Prunières, *Opéra italien*, p. 160.
57. Ibid., p. 214.

du temps, on supposera qu'en cas d'affluence, la salle de l'opéra peut recevoir de 1300 à 1400 spectateurs, et peut-être plus.''[58]

The engraving of *Le Soir* illustrates the first form of progression caused by the two conflicting functions. That part of the auditorium which is visible suggests a single rectangular hall with galleries. The line of vision from these galleries is quite irrelevant to the stage, to which, indeed, the majority of spectators are paying very little attention. It is obviously contemporary with *Mirame*, having the same proscenium arch and steps. The rest of the details we must, like our predecessors, fill in from Sauval, and here the evidence becomes confused. The ground floor is all, or nearly all, *parterre*. Sauval's description of the house floor is nothing like the picture given to us by *Le Soir*. It is entirely, or perhaps almost entirely occupied by an *amphithéâtre*, whose length he gives as 10 or 11 *toises*, i.e. 60 to 66 feet.[59] It is composed of twenty-seven shallow stone steps between 4 and 5½ inches in height, and 23 inches deep,[60] giving a total depth of 51¾ feet. This leaves a distance of roughly 8 to 14 feet unaccounted for, and probably taken up by the "espèce de grand portique, ou trois grands arcades'' of which Sauval speaks; there seems little doubt that it could not be a miniature pit: Sauval definitely states that the whole house was filled by the amphitheater—"La scène est élevée à un des bouts, et le reste occupé par 27 degrés de pierre''—while the stone seats would be too low to permit of spectators standing in front of them. There could however have been a small unused space between the nearest (and lowest) stone bench and the stage edge.

We were forced to the conclusion that either the *Le Soir* engraver has suppressed the amphitheater to show his royalty (and the stage) or that it refers to a performance before its installation. The first of these suppositions has been echoed by Deierkauf-Holsboer. But Gaston Hall has proposed a much neater solution: the engraving is that of the *petite salle de spectacle* of the Palais Royal, since there were two, not the large theater which Molière was to alter, possibly removing, according to Deierkauf-Holsboer, the *gradins* at the stage end to make way for the boxes from the Petit Bourbon and no doubt his beloved *parterre*.[61]

The most advanced feature of this auditorium is obviously the considerable depth of this so-called *amphithéâtre*. Yet this is a function of the original exclusiveness of the house, eventually to disappear.[62] The *gradins*, in spite of Sauval's enthusiasm,

58. Sauval and Fritsche quoted by Deierkauf-Holsboer, *La mise en scène dans le théâtre français à Paris de 1600 à 1673*, Paris, 1960. Lagrave, *Le théâtre et le public à Paris de 1715 à 1750*, Paris, 1972, p. 86.

59. Tome III, p. 47.

60. Tome II, p. 162.

61. Deierkauf-Holsboer, op. cit., p. 31. Gaston Hall, review of Wadsworth, *Molière and the Italian Theatrical Tradition*, 1977, in *Oeuvres et Critiques*, 3, 1978.

62. The audience of *Mirame* seems to have been picked, both in the absolute sense and to fit and fill the theater. Cf. the Abbé de Marolles, quoted by Celler, *Décors*, p. 24: "On n'y entrait que par billets, et ces billets n'étaient donnés qu'à ceux qui se trouvèrent marqués sur le mémoire de Son Eminence, chacun selon sa condition.'' The abbé de Boisrobert, Celler goes on, was exiled at the request of the duchesse d'Aiguillon for having introduced into the house two women of doubtful virtue.

are an ill-fated venture in more ways than one. Far too low to sit on, benches were normally added to them. It may have been this unfortunate disposition that gave to the incorrigible Christina of Sweden the occasion for one of her typical public manifestations: "Etant un jour à la comédie avec la Reine Anne, mère de Louis XIV, elle s'y tint dans une posture si indécente, qu'elle avait les pieds plus hauts que la tête, ce qui faisait entrevoir ce que doit cacher la femme la moins modeste . . ."[63]

Let us note of this first French *amphithéâtre*, that there is no sign at all of its being amphitheatrical in the general sense of the term. Everything points to straight rows of steps rising backwards, particularly if we glance at Blondel's plan, which shows such an "amphitheater," though diminished. The *gradins* were constructed in stone, thus catering in solid form, at the opposite end of the theater from the stage, and as opposed to the *loges*, for the perspective line of vision. Directly behind them, was the arcade comprising three arches. This suggests to us that the back wall of the house was not yet rounded.[64]

The only real concession to the times then in this first form of the Palais Royal is the *amphithéâtre*. Its slope is very mild, though when Sauval says that the spectators on the twenty-seventh step are not above the actors, we may treat it with reserve;[65] a height for the steps of 4½ inches brings the top one to 10 feet 1½ inches, whilst 5½ inches would give us 12 feet 4½ inches, to which we must add the height of a seated spectator.

The facility with which this house is reverted to its "collective" function reminds us of the impermanence of the limited polarized disposition which had been installed. For the famous ball given after *Orfeo* in 1647, Torelli had no difficulty in throwing flooring across stage and auditorium, to reduce the whole to a level, reminiscent of a similar device by Roubo in the eighteenth century. The public ball seemed fated to attach itself to the opera, whose home the Palais Royal was to be for such a long time. Despois mentions the authorization of the "bal de l'opera" by Louis XIV on the 7th January 1713, adding that it could not be inaugurated until one Father Sebastian, Carmelite, invented a movable floor to go across the pit.[66]

What precise structural alterations Molière instigated we do not know, apart from his installation of his own *loges*. Fritsche, like Holsboer, thinks that Molière enlarged the pit.[67] This would involve shortening the amphitheater which, as we have noted, was of stone, but this does not render the modification impossible. The house was in a bad way, but modifications of such a nature would be the producer's

63. Dreux du Radier, *Récréations historiques*, 1764, tome II, p. 120.
64. Bjurström (*Giacomo Torelli and Baroque Stage Design*) suggests that Lemercier's original construction, the theater of *Mirame* in 1641, had an auditorium rounded at the back. Hélène Leclerc, in her detailed review of his work, (RHT, 1961–62, p. 185), regards this as an error propagated by Bapst.
65. Tome III, p. 47.
66. Op. cit., p. 82.
67. "La scène de Molière et son organisation," p. 72.

own responsibility; Ratabon, the *contrôleur des bâtiments*, had received orders to repair, but apparently his orders go no farther than that: "Le S. de Ratabon reçut un ordre exprès de faire les grosses réparations . . ."[68]

The 22nd February 1674 finds the Vigarani family busy with the modifications to the Palais Royal.[69] This strikes us as a more likely moment for the major changes, other than the pit, and we can now understand how Blondel's plan attests the scope of the alteration. The rectangular periphery has been ignored to some extent, and the lines of the auditorium, rounded at the back and reduced in width, now permit the former long parallel lines of the house to open out towards the stage. They do however remain straight, so that the *loges* have only a slightly improved view. Not only this, but there is a third row of *loges*. We know of their existence from the *Mercure* of June 1677, which tells us that for one performance the attendance was so numerous that the *livrée*, accustomed to frequent the third row, were debarred and the *loges* given over to people of quality.[70] The opening lines towards the stage and the rounded end are an acoustic improvement (the Vigaranis have by this time the sad lesson of the Salle des Machines from which to profit); but the *amphithéâtre* is seriously reduced to increase accommodation in the pit, and still faces the vanishing point in straight rows.

For heavy problems, timid solutions. Such is the first regular French opera house in the seventeenth century. Acoustics are its new *bête noire*, pushing its auditorium back down the centuries towards a particular form of ellipse; the perspective stage convention it has evolved is pushing it the other way: towards the retention of the rectangular evils it has, while yet seeking a solution to that relic of the enemy camp, the *loge* facing inward.

Having followed the process with some precision, we are now equipped to observe its minor variants (for they remain minor) through the other theaters.

The Gracht

In speaking of this theater we must bear in mind that we are discussing a reconstruction, and not a contemporary theater plan (Fig. 112).[71] For the same reason it is not possible to date it, as the details in the contracts on which it is based naturally range in their dating. However, if we place it in the fifth decade of the century, we shall not be far wrong. Liebrecht notes three main parts to the auditorium: *loges*, *amphithéâtre*, and *parquet* (our *parterre*), the last two separated by a barrier. Two points about the *loges* strike the eye: firstly, there is only one row of them, and that placed very low down on the wall; secondly, their partitions slope towards the stage. Both these features are clearly inspired by the desire to improve the field of view of the spectator in relation to the perspective vanishing point. The wandering Frenchmen

68. *Registre de la Grange*, tome I, p. 26.
69. Letter from Carlo to Count Graziani, Rouchès, *Inventaire*, no. 357, p. 194.
70. Quoted by Mélèse, *Le théâtre et le public à Paris sous Louis XIV*, p. 42.
71. Liebrecht, *Histoire du théâtre français à Bruxelles au XVIIe et au XVIIIe siècle*, pp. 38 et seq.

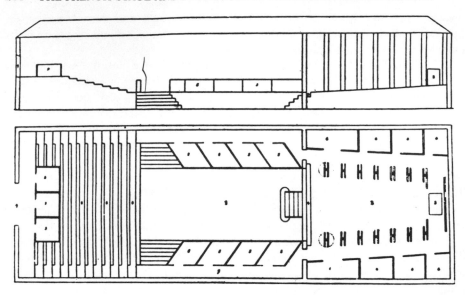

FIG. 112.—Reconstruction of the Gracht Theater in Brussels.

are in advance of their metropolitan colleagues in this. Yet we must make one serious proviso: "Une grille mobile, sur le devant, permettaient aux dames de la noblesse, auxquelles ces places étaient réservées, de se dissimuler aux regards du parterre."[72] Having, in the interests of the line of sight, improved the line of the *loges*, the troupe are compelled to pander to the demands of a differentiated society, certain elements of which wish to look at the public while enjoying privacy themselves, in what is a pale reflection of the *loggia* in the pigeon-cote house of the Venetian opera; by limiting vision itself, they permit the audience to turn in upon itself. This seems to have been a feature of the Italian theater which was borrowed by the Low Countries, witness Fransen: "L'amour se donnait carrière au théâtre comme à l'église. Devant les 'maisonnettes' (c'est ainsi que les Hollandais du XVIIe siècle appelaient les loges) il y avait des rideaux qu'on pouvait tirer. Un auteur, Tengnagel, dit dans une pièce en vers de 1639:

> Au Théâtre jadis se plaisaient les jeunes gens amoureux
> Avait-on envie de folâtrer un peu, vite on tirait les rideaux,
> Mais aujourd'hui tout est ouvert. Plus rien à faire.[73]

The *loges* are restricted in number: apart from the existence of only one row of them, only three appear at the back of the hall, above the amphitheater, which is larger

72. Ibid., p. 39.
73. *Les comédiens français en Hollande*, 1925, p. 18.

than that of Lully's opera. On the whole, except for the fact that it follows the external rectangular line of the building, and so has not yet begun to progress towards the ellipse, we may regard it as representing a similar stage, on a smaller scale, and having no acoustic problems.

The Salle des Machines

Mazarin had intended the theater at the Palais des Tuileries to be originally erected behind his own Palace. The space seemed ample, but Gaspare Vigarani "ne le trouva ni assez propre, ni assez commode." He proposed another site in the same alignment as the plans of the Louvre, which Mazarin had undertaken to finish by joining it to the Tuileries.[74] Le Vau, in executing this project, was already building the pavilions of the Louvre and extending the Tuileries buildings to the North. In this extension, the stage of the Salle des Machines was to be erected.[75]

In the contemporary and in more recent criticisms of the shape of this theater, based on its great length and lack of width, Vigarani has tended to be excused on the grounds that he neither chose the site nor built the walls.[76] We can see from the above that he was at least instrumental in choosing the site, though it is true that Le Vau had already planned the exterior edifice with which Gaspare Vigarani had hoped to be entrusted himself. Let us then admit that Vigarani was, like any other theater architect of the time, confronted with the pre-existing rectangle, although he himself chose the emplacement which carried these conditions with it. With the exception of this, a great many of the criticisms of the house are incorrectly aimed. Bernini, for instance, voiced a general criticism when he said that the hall was too narrow, and too big (Fig. 113).[77]

These charges require some qualification. Vigarani, firstly, was to blame for the overall size, which was not, as Rouchès makes out, completely conditioned by the site. The overall length of this theater is the choice of a skilled Italian constructor of theaters (he had Carpi, Mantua, Modena to his credit when he arrived) and moreover he wins this point of length in a controversy with Le Vau himself at whose door the blame for the form has been laid; Marzarin, in a letter to the abbé Buti of the 18th August 1659, reveals this fully:

"Je vois la différence d'avis qui est entre le sieur Vigarani et le sieur le Vau sur la longueur du théâtre et il me semble que si, par raison d'architecture et pour le

74. Pure, *Idée des spectacles*, p. 311.
75. Prunières, *Opéra italien*, p. 215.
76. Rouchès, *Inventaire*, no. 228, pp. 109–10.
77. Ibid., no. 230, pp. 112–13. For a cross-section of the auditorium, also by Blondel, see Leclerc, *Origines*, Pl. XXX. Complete plans of the theater also appear in Mariette, *L'Architecture française*, 1727. The plan shown illustrates the state of the theater in 1754. Jacques Heuzey (RHT, tomes I–II, 1954, pp. 60–67) throws considerable new light on the changing shape of this theater, publishing a hitherto unidentified sketch of a theater house which is undoubtedly the Salle des Machines, and which he dates between 1659 and 1662.

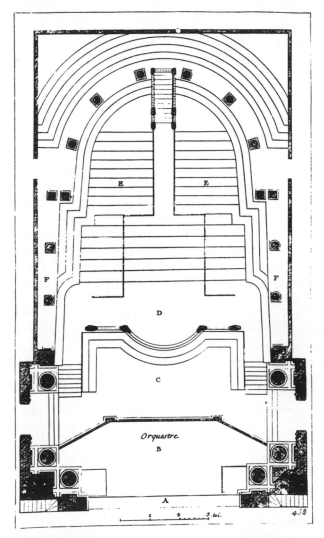

FIG. 113.—Blondel's plan of the auditorium of the Salle des Machines.

faire plus beau, il faut qu'il soit et plus long et plus large, il n'y a considération qui doive empêcher de le faire à la perfection."[78]

Now, a scrutiny of Lully's opera and this auditorium shows very little difference in comparative dimensions. Vigarani's auditorium is not itself particularly elongated. Rouchès gives its width as 51 feet.[79] Blondel's plan, with an accompanying

78. Quoted by Prunières, *Opéra italien*, p. 216.
79. *Inventaire*, p. xviii.

scale, gives us dimensions of approximately 52 feet by 94 feet 8 inches to the stage edge, a reasonable proportion. The stage, however, was 132 feet deep,[80] giving an overall dimension of 226 feet 8 inches (approximately) by 52 feet, and a deeper stage than auditorium. This it is which accounts for all the accusations of an elongated theater, yet even so the figures are not unlike those of the Petit Bourbon— 210 feet by 54. Vigarani had been given his head in the matter of baroque stage depth, which he installs *ad absurdum.* The auditorium is a mixture of the Italian court theater and a public opera house. The concept of the amphitheater has gone much farther than in previous French theaters: for the court, on the best line of sight, there is the French type of straight "amphitheater" in retreating rows of *gradins* ("E" in the figure) rising gently as at the Palais Royal; the external rectangle is ignored to a greater extent than before, for where *loges* appear in Lully's opera house around the lines of the auditorium, Vigarani has now put in further *gradins* along similar lines. The curved (and steeply rising) extension of the amphitheater at the back of the house was destined for the officers of the King's household.[81] The vertical surface of the walls is exploited by two rows of deep galleries, supported on columns.

The back curve of the house could hardly affect the bad acoustics, since the external angles of the walls are unmodified, while the deep galleries and low, heavily coffered ceiling would also have a deleterious effect.[82] Yet the line of vision is on the whole improved. Of the difficulties of hearing in the theater there can be no doubt, although the very deep stage perhaps did as much as the auditorium to achieve this. Only Brice has a good word for it: "Chacun y peut voir et entendre fort commodément."[83] His kind remark is certainly untrue: here were two masters, acoustics and optics, which could not both be served fully. Gaspare Vigarani had tried to serve them both a little too hard. In the eighteenth century, after a most desultory career, the Salle des Machines reverts to the old god with the mute spectacles of Servandoni, throwing out the other completely. Vigarani had had the misfortune to enjoy unlimited scope for the baroque stage in an edifice which was meant to act as midwife to the new opera.

In conclusion, we find that with this building again there is still in the minds of those who project it a nostalgia for the old collective forms; Vigarani kills this

80. Pure, *Idée des spectacles*, p. 314, gives a width of 49 feet between the corridors, and a length of 93 feet to the stage edge. He gives the stage length as 22 toises, i.e., 132 feet, and claims that the dimensions were given to him personally by Carlo Vigarani (pp. 312-13). The explanatory *livret* (printed in 1671) of Molière's *Psyché* gives a length of 40 toises or 240 feet "en deux parties: l'une est pour le théâtre, et l'autre pour l'assemblée."

81. Rouchès, *Inventaire*, p. xix. We assume that the tiers of seats referred to as "E" in Blondel's plan existed in the seventeenth century. They are to be found neither in his previous plan (Pl. 23 of *Architecture françoise*, attributed to Vigarani), nor in Silvestre's plan of 1668, possibly intended to show the house as it was in 1662 (see Heuzey, op. cit., Pls. IX and X). They are, however, present in Heuzey's sketch (1659-1662?), and he himself seems at a loss to explain their absence in the others, suggesting that perhaps in the first state of the theater they were movable.

82. Ibid., p. xvii, Prunières, *Opéra italien*, p. 282, Celler, *Décors*, p. 48.

83. *Description nouvelle de ce qu'il y a de plus remarquable dans la ville de Paris*, 1684, p. 30.

too: "Pour moi, après avoir examiné ledit mémoire {de Vigarani], je suis de son avis: qu'il n'est pas possible de faire dans un même lieu une salle de comédie et un lieu pour les tournois et autres exercices à cheval."[84]

With this house, theater architecture in France has reached a point where it is possible for the historian to speak of influence upon Italy. Thus, Leclerc suggests a possible relationship with Torelli's theater at Fano, since Torelli could have admired the Salle des Machines before he left France.[85] This is most unlikely. Torelli had no reason to esteem the Vigarani family or admire any of their works. They had replaced him in the favor of Mazarin, and when, in 1660, Molière removes the *loges* from the Petit Bourbon to place them in the Palais Royal, Gaspare Vigarani seizes upon the decorations which Molière had been obliged to leave behind, and burns them to destroy the memory of his rival.[86] Torelli is suspected of being the author of a libel against the Salle des Machines: *Reflessioni sopra la fabrica del nuovo teatro.*[87]

The Versailles Projects

The King and court move into Versailles for the summer of 1682. Vigarani and the architect Mansard both draw up plans for a "salle des ballets," and their interest for the theater historian has recently been underlined by Alfred Marie. The source he indicates, in the Cabinet des Estampes of the Bibliothèque Nationale, has both plans together with four other anonymous ones and one anonymous cross section.[88] Vigarani's plan is the most interesting (Fig. 114). The theater was to be smaller, more intimate, than the Salle des Machines. The curve of the seating is flatter, and more complete than with that theater, and fits more snugly into a less elongated rectangle. Like the Salle des Machines, two galleries, undivided except by the supporting pillars, are planned above the curved *amphithéâtre*. The house is clearly more "narcissistic" than Vigarani's previous structure: the King's place, marked "Haut dais," is a focal point for the majority of the seated audience to a greater extent than is the stage.[89] The whole area of the "haut dais," presumably reserved for the royal family whose seats would be brought to the theater, slopes down slightly to the pit, which is at floor level three feet below.

Thus, the proportions of the house itself are more harmonious than those of the Salle des Machines, yet there is still a deep stage, and the proportions as between house length and stage length are similar in the two structures:

84. Letter from Colbert to Mazarin, 1st September, 1659. Quoted by Rouchès, *Inventaire*, p. 17.
85. *Origines*, p. 178.
86. *Registre de la Grange*, p. 27.
87. Rouchès, *Inventaire*, no. 51, p. 14 (Lodovico to the cardinal d'Este).
88. Est. BN, Va 361 (VII), *Papiers de Robert de Cotte*. Also Archives des Bâtiments Civils. Marie, "Les théâtres du château de Versailles," RHT, vol. II, 1951.
89. See also Marie, "La salle du théâtre de Fontainebleau," RHT, vol. III, 1951.

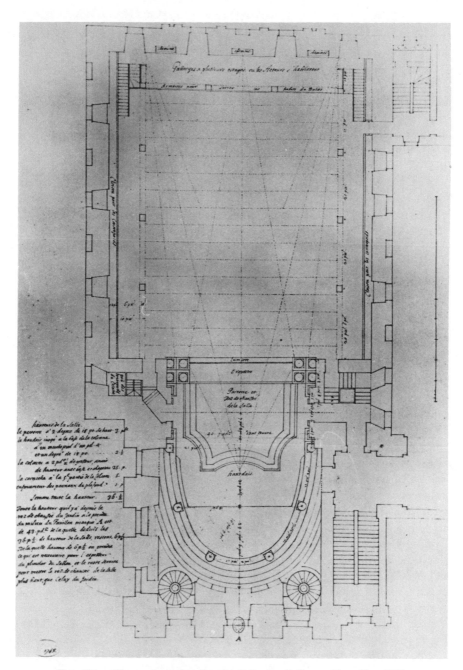

FIG. 114.—Vigarani's project for the Salle des Ballets at Versailles, 1685.

	Length of Auditorium	Width of Auditorium	Length of Stage
Salle des Machines	93 ft.	49 ft.	132 ft.
Salle des Ballets	66 ft. 10 in.	40 ft.	84 ft.

Vigarani insists on the length of the ballet stage in an explanatory note: "Il est très important de conserver les Quatorze toises de profondeur du Théâtre." He emphasizes too the depth required below stage for the machines: "La fosse aux contrepoids doit couvrir six toises de profondeur au-dessous du rez de chaussée du jardin."

An interesting divergence is the isolated position of the pit in the Salle des Ballets. The relation between the King's position and the perspective vanishing point, worked out from that position, is also excellently illustrated.

Mansard's project displays broadly the same features (Fig. 115). Again there is a small, compact, rear portion of the house for the royal family, surrounded by a curved amphitheater, and then a space no doubt for the pit (since it is there in the other plans) between the two prolonged poles of this auditorium. It is almost as though the pit is placed entirely beneath a very deep proscenium arch. The proportions of this stage and auditorium are similar to those of Vigarani. Our remaining figures (116 and 117) show simple and unimportant variations on this layout. Figure 117 is interesting in that the ends of the amphitheater part of the auditorium are turned outwards slightly in a timid attempt to cope with the problems of the "places de souffrance."

The Jeu de Paume de l'Etoile

This final home of the Comédie Française in the seventeenth century opened on the 18th April 1689.[90] It represents the biggest advance in permanent terms in the lines of the house (Fig. 118). There is still no sign of the theater's acquiring any "droit de cité" as an autonomous structure, and indeed we have seen what odyssey the players were to accomplish before they finally came to rest in precisely the same type of building as a troupe might have lighted upon in 1600. Blondel brings out well the inconvenience of the vicinity in which it is placed: the site, he says, is "fort irrégulier, sans que depuis ce temps il ait été possible à cette compagnie de pouvoir agrandir de nouveau leur Hôtel, les bâtiments particuliers entre lesquels il se trouve élevé, et ce quartier en général étant si peuplé, qu'il n'est pas possible d'espérer de pouvoir non seulement jamais rendre cette Salle plus spacieuse, mais même de procurer aux Acteurs des commodités intérieures pour leur usage personnel."[91] D'Orbay, the architect, adopts the treatment of the quadrilateral that is to be found in the Palais Royal: a rounded end farthest from the stage, and the two lines of *loges* widening towards the stage to the extent in this instance of five feet. The amphi-

90. Léris, *Dictionnaire portatif*, p. xix.
91. *Architecture françoise*, tome II, p. 30.

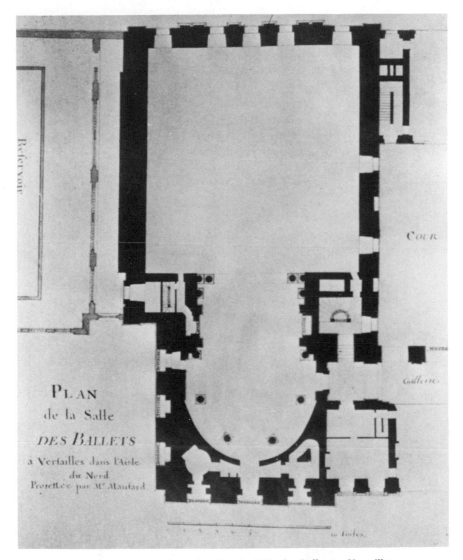

FIG. 115.—Mansard's project for the Salle des Ballets at Versailles.

theater, raked and furnished with benches, is raised six feet above the pit at its point
of juncture with this latter.[92] The *premières loges* contain the places of the King and
Queen and are nineteen in number, stretching all round the walls. The three rows
of *loges* are not in retreat, but immediately on top of one another, again typical of
the century. All the old evils of the *loges* are apparent: they continue to a point very
close to the stage, forming "places de souffrance."

92. Roubo, *Traité de la construction des théâtres*, 1777, p. 28.

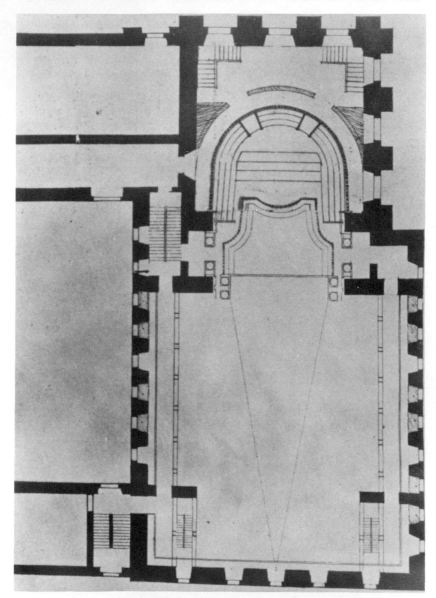

FIG. 116.—Anonymous project for the Salle des Ballets at Versailles.

The designer does however go farther than his colleagues in that not only does he ignore the external quadrilateral of the building, but he destroys its effect by building an inner complete wall which forms the line of his house; it is therefore a real line, acoustically, consolidating the ephemeral line of the Palais Royal. Some form of accommodation must have been built for an orchestra at the front of the house, for in 1716 the opera wreaks its revenge on this forward gesture, relegating

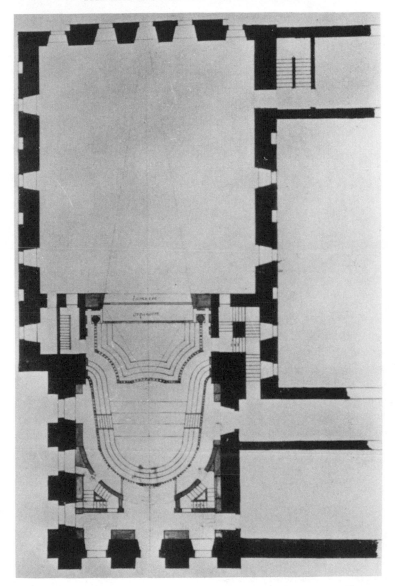

FIG. 117.—Anonymous project for the Salle des Ballets at Versailles.

the diminished number of violins to the back: "Ce faisant, faire défense auxdits Comédiens français d'avoir un Orchestre dans leur salle; Ordonner qu'ils feront détruire Celui qui y est, sauf à eux de placer leurs violons ou Instruments, qui ne pourront excéder le nombre de six dans les Troisièmes Loges du fond de ladite salle, où ils étaient ci-devant."[93]

93. Arch. Nat. 0¹ 618 (3).

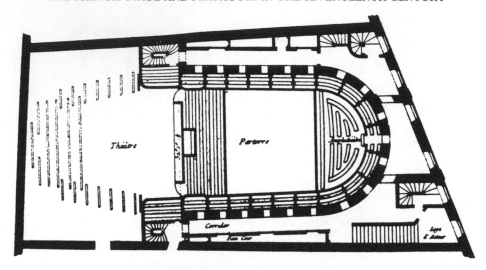

FIG. 118.—D'Orbay's Comédie Française.

This is the answer to Despois' guess as to their position in his analysis of Coypel's engraving of 1726, in which he notices the absence of musicians from the place which is nowadays the orchestra pit, and assumes that they were in one of the *loges*, as in the time of Chappuzeau.[94]

Here in this first permanent house of the Comédie Française, our study comes to a suitable end. The French seventeenth century, under the impact of the Italian Order, emerges in our view as a long dichotomy of baroque and classical. The former is destined to divorce audience and actor, stage and auditorium. Yet paradoxically the collective mass spectacle of the Royal Entry, closely allied to the mystery play, serves as a Trojan Horse in which the baroque enters the theater building. It fastens upon the larger edifices which, paradoxically again, had served till then for more collective forms of the dramatic art. The scenographer, his eyes fixed on the distances of perspective, pays no heed to the shape of the theater: it is in this century that the nondescript word "salle" is used to mean a theater auditorium. The net result, socially, is the diminution of the theater performance as a significant occasion, and dramatically, of the power of entrance.

In that theater least suited to spectacle by its unimposing proportions, the Hôtel de Bourgogne, the dramatic entrance is preserved and increases in power. Potentially, Racinian tragedy is the kernel of the theatrical occasion, the focus of an utterly homogeneous social moment. If that focus had been permitted to exert its attraction in a theater edifice worthy of its intensity, the century of Louis XIV would have been golden indeed.

94. Despois, op. cit. p. 128. Nicole Bourdel, "L'Hôtel des Comédiens Français," RHT, tome II, 1955, pp. 145 et seq., publishes some of the original plans for this theater. The article brings out well the way in which d'Orbay and the players set out to break the spell of the *jeu de paume*.

BIBLIOGRAPHY

FROM 1800 TO THE PRESENT DAY

(Dramatic works are not normally quoted)

ADHEMAR, Jean. (See LINZELER).

ALCOVER, Madeleine. 'Les lieux et les temps dans L'Illusion Comique.' *French Studies,* Vol. XXV, 1976.

ALLEN, James T. *Stage Antiquities of the Greeks and Romans and Their Influence.* London, 1927, Reprint, 1963.

——*On the Athenian Theater before 441 B.C.* California, 1937.

ANCONA, Alessandro d'. *Origini del teatro italiano.* 2 vols. Florence, 1891.

ANTI, Carlo, POLACCO, Luigi. *Nuove ricerchi su teatri greci arcaici.* Padua, 1969.

——*Teatri greci arcaici da Minosse a Pericle.* Padua, 1947.

Architecture et dramaturgie. Paris, 1950 ('notes sténographiques de la première session du Centre d'Etudes Philosophiques et Techniques du Théâtre tenue à la Sorbonne en décembre 1948 et consacrée aux rapports du lieu théâtral avec la dramaturgie présente et à venir.')

ARTAUD, Antonin. *Le théâtre et son double.* Paris, 1938.

ATTINGER, Gustave. *L'Esprit de la commedia dell'arte dans le théâtre français.* Neuchâtel, 1950.

BABEAU, Albert. 'Le Théâtre des Tuileries sous Louis XIV, Louis XV, et Louis XVI.' *Bulletin de la Société de l'Histoire de Paris et de l'Ile de France,* tome XXII, 1896.

——*Le jardin des Tuileries au XVIIe et au XVIIIe siècle.* Paris, 1902.

BAKER, Blanche M. *Dramatic Bibliography. An annotated list of books on the history and criticism of drama and the stage and on the the the allied arts of the theater.* New York, 1933.

BAPST, Germain. *Essai sur l'histoire des panoramas et des dioramas.* Paris, 1891.

——*Etudes sur les mystères au moyen âge.* Paris, 1892.

——*Essai sur l'histoire du théâtre, la mise en scène, le décor, le costume, l'architecture, l'éclairage, l'hygiène.* Paris, 1893.

BARLOW, Graham. 'The Hôtel de Bourgogne according to Sir James Thornhill.' *Theatre Research International,* Vol. I, 1976.

'BAROQUE (Le) au théâtre, et la théâtralité du baroque.' *Actes des Journées Internationales d'Etude du Baroque,* Vol. II, Montauban, 1967.

BARSACQ, André. 'Lois scéniques.' *Revue Théâtrale,* No. 5, April–May, 1947.

BASCHET, Armand. *Les comédiens italiens à la cour de France sous Charles IX, Henri III, Henri IV et Louis XIII.* Paris, 1882.

BASKERVILLE, Charles R. (ed.). *Pierre Gringore's Pageants for the Entry of Mary Tudor in Paris.* Chicago, 1934.

BATY, Gaston. *Rideau baissé.* Paris, 1949.

——and René CHAVANCE. *Vie de l'art théâtral des origines à nos jours.* Paris, 1932.

BAUCHAL, Charles. *Nouveau dictionnaire biographique et critique des architectes français.* Paris, 1887.

BEARE, William. *The Roman Stage.* London, 1968.

BEIJER, Agne. 'Vigarani et Bérain au Palais Royal.' *Revue d'Histoire du Théâtre,* Nos. 2–3, 1956.

——'Neues zum Teatro Olimpico.' *Maske und Kothurn,* I, 1955.

——'An early sixteenth-century scenic design in the National Museum, Stockholm, and its historical background.' *Theatre Research/Recherches Théâtrales,* Vol. IV, No. 2, 1962.

BERNARD, Auguste-Joseph. *Geofroy Tory, peintre et graveur, premier imprimeur royal, réformateur de l'orthographe et de la typographie sous François Ier.* Paris, 1857.

BERNARDIN, N.M. *Un précurseur de Racine: Tristan l'Hermite, sieur Du Solier (1601–1655), sa famille, sa vie, ses oeuvres,* Paris, 1895.

BERTON, R. *Les monuments romains de la cité d'Aoste.* Aosta, 1951.

BIEBER, Margarete. *The History of the Greek and Roman Theater.* Princeton, 1939, 2nd edn. London, 1961.

BJURSTRÖM, Per. *Giacomo Torelli and Baroque Stage Design.* Stockholm, 1961.

——and Bengt DAHLBACK. *Théâtres et fêtes à Paris au XVIe et XVIIe siècles. Catalogue de l'exposition du Musée Carnavalet,* Paris, 1956.

——'Servandoni, décorateur de théâtre.' *Revue d'Histoire du Théâtre,* no. 3, 1954.

——'Servandoni et la Salle des Machines.' *Revue d'Histoire du Théâtre,* no. 3, 1959.

——'Notes on Giacomo Torelli.' *Theatre Research/Recherches Théâtrales,* vol. III, No. 1, 1961.

BOLL, André. *La mise en scène contemporaine: son évolution.* Paris, 1944.

BONDINO, Francis. *Présentation des pièces à machine au XVIIe siècle: mise en scène, décors, costumes.* Centres d'Etudes Théâtrales, Université de Paris X, 1971.

BONNASSIES, Jules. *Les anciens bâtiments de la Comédie Française.* Paris, 1868.

BORCHERDT, H.H. *Das Europäische Theater im Mittelalter und in der Renaissance.* Leipzig, 1935.

BOUCHE, Jacques. 'Servandoni.' *Gazette des Beaux Arts,* tome IV, August, 1910.

BOUCHOT, Henri. *Catalogue des dessins relatifs à l'histoire du théâtre conservés au département des Estampes de la Bibliothèque Nationale.* Paris, 1896.

BOURDEL, Nicole. 'L'établissement et la construction de l'Hôtel des Comédiens Français, rue des Fossés-Saint-Germain-des-Prés (Ancienne Comédie) 1687–90.' *Revue d'Histoire du Théâtre,* no. 11, 1955.

BOYSSE, Ernest. *Le théâtre des Jésuites.* Paris, 1880.

BRAY, René. *La formation de la doctrine classique en France.* Paris, 1927.

BUNIM, M.S. 'Further notes on space in mediaeval painting and on the forerunners of perspective.' *Speculum,* no. 22, 1947.

BUTTERWECK, Georg. 'Das Dionysostheater: neue Rekonstruktion des Grundrisses des Dionysostheaters und der theatralischen Architekturdarstellungsformen in Athen im 5. Jahrhundert v. Chr.' *Maske und Kothurn,* 20th year, 1974.

CALOT, Franz. 'Les collections théâtrales de l'Arsenal.' *Bulletin du Bibliophile,* December, 1934.

CAMPARDON, Emile. *Les spectacles de la Foire.* 2 vols. Paris, 1877.

CAMPBELL, Lily B. *Scenes and Machines on the English Stage during the Renaissance.* Cambridge, 1923.

CAPPS, Edward. *Vitruvius and the Greek Stage.* Chicago, 1893.

CELLER, Ludovic (pseud. Leclerc). *Les origines de l'opéra et le ballet de la reine (1581).* Paris, 1868. Reprint, Geneva, 1970.

——*Les décors, les costumes et la mise en scène au XVIIe siècle. 1615–1680.* Paris, 1869.

CHARTROU, J. *Les entrées solennelles et triomphales à la Renaissance (1484–1551).* Paris, 1928.

CHARVET, Etienne-Léon-Gabriel. *Sébastien Serlio.* Lyons, 1869.

CHASLES, Emile. *La Comédie en France au XVIe siècle.* Paris, 1862.

CHENEY, Sheldon. *Stage Decoration.* London, 1928.

CHEVALLEY, Sylvie. 'Le Mémoire de Mahelot, Laurent et autres décorateurs.' *Comédie Française,* no. 24, 1973.

——*La Comédie Française.* Paris, 1961.

CHRISTOUT, Marie-Françoise. 'Décor d'opéras et pièces à machines au XVIIIe siècle. Servandoni illusioniste.' *Médecine de France,* no. 109.

——'Techniques et effets du merveilleux dans le ballet et les arts voisins.' *Revue d'Histoire du Théâtre,* no. 1, 1963.

——*Le ballet de cour de Louis XIV, 1643–1672, mises en scène.* Paris, 1967.

COHEN, Gustave. *Le théâtre à Paris et aux environs à la fin du XIVe siècle.* Nogent-le-Rotrou, 1910.

——*L'Evolution de la mise en scène dans le théâtre français.* Lille, 1910.

——*Le livre de conduite du régisseur.* Strasburg, 1925.

——*Histoire de la mise en scène dans le théâtre religieux français du moyen âge.* Nouvelle édition revue et augmentée. Paris, 1926.

——(preface). *La comédie latine en France au XIIe siècle.* 2 vols. Poitiers, 1931.

——*Le théâtre en France au moyen âge.* Paris, 1948.

——'Un terme de scénologie médiévale: "Lieu" ou "Mansion".' *Mélanges de Philologie et d'Histoire Littéraire offerts à Edmond Huguet.* Paris, n.d.

COLOMBIER, Pierre.   'Jean Goujon et le Vitruve de 1547.' *Gazette des Beaux Arts,* tome V, 1931.

CONTANT, Clément, and Joseph de FILIPPI. *Parallèle des principaux théâtres modernes de l'Europe et des machines théâtrales françaises, allemandes et anglaises.* Paris, 1860.

CURZON, Henri Parent de.   *Etat sommaire des pièces et documents concernant le théâtre et la musique conservés aux Archives Nationales.* Besançon, 1899.

DAINVILLE, François de.   'Décoration théâtrale dans les collèges des Jésuites au XVIIe siècle.' *Revue d'Histoire du Théâtre,* no. IV, 1951.

DEIERKAUF-HOLSBOER, S. Wilma (see also Holsboer).   'Vie d'Alexandre Hardy, Poète du roi.' *Proceedings of the American Philosophical Society,* vol. 91, no. 4, October, 1947. 2nd edn. Paris, 1972.

——'La vie théâtrale à Paris de 1612 à 1614.' *Modern Language Notes,* January, 1948.

——*Le théâtre du Marais,* tome I, *La période de gloire et de fortune. 1634 (1629) – 1648.* Paris, 1954. Tome II, *Le berceau de l'Opéra et de la Comédie Française, 1648–1675.* Paris, 1958.

——*L'histoire de la mise en scène dans le théâtre français à Paris de 1600 à 1673.* Paris, 1960.

——*Le théâtre de l'Hôtel de Bourgogne.* Tome I: *1548–1635.* Paris, 1968. Tome II: *Le théâtre de la Troupe Royale, 1635–1680.* Paris, 1970.

DESCOTES, Maurice.   *Le public de théâtre et son histoire.* Paris, 1964.

DESPOIS, Eugène.   *Le théâtre français sous Louis XIV.* Paris, 1874.

DESTRANGES, E.   *Le théâtre à Nantes depuis ses origines jusqu'à nos jours, 1430–1893.* Paris, 1893.

DIETRICH, Margret.   'Pomponius Laetus' Wiedererweckung des Antiken Theaters.' *Maske und Kothurn,* 3rd year, 1957.

——'Perspective et art scénique à l'époque baroque.' *Theatre Research/Recherches Théâtrales,* vol. III, No. 2, 1961.

——*Europäische Dramaturgie.* Vienna, 1952.

DONALDSON, J.W.   *The Theatre of the Greeks,* London, 1875. 7th edn. New York, 1973.

DONNET, Alexis, and ORGIAZZI.   *Architectonographie des théâtres de Paris ou parallèle historique et critique de ces édifices considérés sous le rapport de l'architecture et de la décoration.* 2 vols. Plates. Paris, 1821.

DÖRPFELD, Wilhelm, and E. REISCH. *Das griechische Theater.* Athens, 1896.

D'ORS, Eugenio.   *Du baroque (version française de Mme Agathe Rouardt-Valéry),* Paris, 1936.

DOUTREPONT, George. *Les acteurs masqués et enfarinés du XVIe au XVIIe siècle.* Brussels, 1928.

DUBECH, Lucien.   *Histoire générale illustrée du théâtre.* 5 vols. Paris, 1931–4.

DUCHARTRE, Pierre-Louis.   *La comédie italienne.* Paris, 1925.

——(ed.). *Recueil de plusieurs fragments des premières comédies italiennes qui ont esté représentées en France sous le règne de Henry III. Recueil dit de Fossard.* Paris, 1928.

DULAURE, J.A.   *Histoire physique, civile, et morale de Paris depuis les premiers temps historiques jusqu'à nos jours.* 10 vols. 5th edn. Paris, 1834.

DUMESNIL, René.   *L'Opéra et l'Opéra Comique.* Paris, 1947.

——*Histoire illustrée du théâtre lyrique.* Paris, 1953.

DUMON, K.   *Ad Vitruvii, V. viii* (brochure). Leyden, 1892.

DUPLESSIS, Georges.   *Inventaire de la collection d'estampes relatives à l'histoire de France.* Paris, 1877–84.

EDGERTON, Samuel Y., Jr. *The Renaissance Discovery of Linear Perspective.* New York, 1975.
ELSE, Gerald F. *The Origin and Early Form of Greek Tragedy.* Cambridge, Mass., 1967.
EVANS, Joan. *Art in Mediaeval France.* London, New York, Toronto, 1948.

FABER, Frédéric. *Histoire du théâtre français en Belgique.* 5 vols. Brussels, 1878–80.
FAGUET, Emile. *La tragédie française au XVIe sieècle (1550–1600).* Paris, 1883.
FISCHEL, Oscar. 'Art and the theatre.' *Burlington Magazine,* vol. LXVI, January-February, 1935.
FLECHSIG, E. *Die Dekoration der modernen Bühne in Italien.* Dresden, 1894.
FLEMING, M. 'Formen der Humanistenbühne.' *Maske und Kothurn,* No. 6, 1960.
FLEMING, Willi. 'Geschichte des Jesuitentheaters in den Ländern deutscher Zunge.' *Schriften der Gesellschaft für Theatergeschichte,* vol. XXXII, Berlin, 1923.
FLICKINGER, Roy. *The Greek Theater and its Drama.* Chicago, 1926.
FOGARTY, C.M. 'A reconstruction of the interior of the Hôtel de Bourgogne.' *Maske und Kothurn,* vol. XXVI, no. 1, 1980, 1–15.
——with Tom Lawrenson. 'The lessons of the reconstructed performance.' *Theatre Survey* XXII, 1981, 141–59.
FORESTIER, C.R. and DELAFOSSE. 'Marchés d'aménagement de Jeux de Paume en théâtres, au XVIIe Siècle.' *Revue d'Histoire du Théâtre,* I, no. 4, 1948–9.
FOURNEL, Victor. *Contemporains de Molière.* 3 vols. Paris, 1863–75.
FRANSEN, J. *Les comédiens français en Hollande au XVIIe et au XVIIIe siècle.* Paris, 1925.
——'Documents inédits de l'Hôtel de Bourgogne.' *Revue d'Histoire Littéraire de la France,* tome XXIV, 1927.
FRITSCHE, H. 'La scène de Molière et son organisation. Traduit en français par M. Metzger.' *Le Moliériste,* June-July-August, 1887.

GARDNER, Percy. 'The scenery of the Greek stage.' *Journal of Hellenic Studies,* 1899.
——*New Chapters in Greek Art.* Oxford, 1926.
GASTE, Armand. *La querelle du Cid.* Paris, 1898.
GEBHARD, Elizabeth K. *The Theater at Isthmia.* Chicago, 1973.
GILDER, Rosamond, and FREEDLEY, George. *Theatre Collections in Libraries and Museums.* London, 1936.
GOFFLOT, L-V. *Le théâtre au collège du moyen âge à nos jours.* Paris, 1907.
GOLDER, John. ' "L'Hypocondriaque" de Rotrou: un essai de reconstitution d'une des premières mises en scène à l'Hôtel de Bourgogne.' *Revue d'Histoire du Théâtre,* no. 3, 1979, 247–270.
——'The Théâtre du Marais in 1644: a new look at the old evidence concerning France's second public theatre.' *Theatre Survey* XXV (2) 1984.
GOSSET, Alphonse. *Traité de la construction des théâtres.* Paris, 1886.
GOUHIER, Henri. *L'Essence du théâtre.* Paris, 1943.
GREISENEGGER, Wolfgang. 'Überlegungen zum Theater der Renaissance in Italien: Serlios Typenszene als Ergebnis einer ikonographischen Tradition.' *Maske und Kothurn,* 18th year, 1972.
GREGOR, Joseph. 'The technique of stage design in its relation to theatre architecture.' *Theatre Arts Monthly,* March, 1933.
GROS, Etienne. *Philippe Quinault, sa vie et son oeuvre.* Paris, 1926.
——'Les origines de la tragédie lyrique et la place des tragédies en machines dans l'évolution du théâtre vers l'opéra.' *Revue d'Histoire Littéraire de la France,* April-June, 1928.
GUENEE, Bernard, and LEHOUS, Françoise. *Les entrées royales françaises de 1328 à 1515.* Paris, 1968.
GUIFFREY, Jules. *Comptes des bâtiments du roi sous le règne de Louis XIV. Documents inédits sur l'histoire de la France, 3e série - archéologie.* 5 vols. Paris, 1881.

HAIGH, A.E. *The Attic Theatre*, 3rd edn. Reviewed and in part re-written by A.W. Pickard-Cambridge, Oxford, 1907.

HALL, Gaston. Review of WADSWORTH, Philip A. *Molière and the Italian Theatrical Tradition,* n.p., 1977. In *Oeuvres et Critiques*, 3 (1978).

HAMMITSCHE, Martin. *Der moderne Theaterbau.* Berlin, 1906.

HARASZTI, Jules. 'La littérature dramatique au temps de la Renaissance, considérée dans ses rapports avec la scène.' *Revue d'Histoire Littéraire de la France*, tome XI, 1904.

HERZEL, Roger W. 'The Décor of Molière's Stage: the Testimony of Brissart and Chauveau.' *PMLA,* October, 1978.

HEUZEY, Jacques. 'Notes sur un dessin représentant la Salle des Machines au XVIIe siècle.' *Revue d'Histoire du Théâtre*, nos. 1–2, 1954.

——'Du costume et de la décoration tragique au XVIIe siècle,' *Revue d'Histoire du Théâtre,* no. 1, 1960.

——'Le décor de Phèdre.' *Revue d'Histoire du Théâtre,* no. 1, 1962.

——'Sur les frontispices tragiques du XVIIe siècle.' *Revue d'Histoire du Théâtre*, no. 4, 1966.

——'*Le martyre de Sainte Catherine*, tragédie en prose de M. de la Serre — étude de cinq gravures de l'édition de 1643.' *Revue d'Histoire du Théâtre*, no. 4, 1967.

——'Sur une tapisserie du style Louis XIV à sujet théâtral.' *Revue d'Histoire du Théâtre,* no. 1, 1977.

HEWITT, Barnard, (ed.). *The Renaissance Stage: Documents of Serlio, Sabbattini and Furttenbach, translated by Allardyce Nicoll, John H. McDowell and George R. Kernodle.* University of Miami, 1958.

HOLSBOER, S. Wilma. *Histoire de la mise en scène dans le théâtre français de 1600 à 1657.* Paris, 1933.

HORN-MONVAL, Madeleine. 'Le théâtre du Petit Bourbon.' *Revue d'Histoire du Théâtre,* nos. 1–2, 1948.

——'La grande machinerie théâtrale et ses origines.' *Revue d'Histoire du Théâtre,* no. 4, 1957.

HOTSON, Leslie, *Shakespeare's Wooden O.* London, 1959.

HOUDARD, Georges, *Les châteaux royaux de Saint-Germain-en-Laye, 1124–1789.* 2 vols. Saint-Germain-en-Laye, 1909–1911.

HOUSSAYE, Arsène. *La Comédie Française, 1680–1880.* Paris, 1880.

HOWARTH, William B. and THOMAS, Merlin (ed.). *Molière: Stage and Study, Essays in Honour of Will Moore.* Oxford, 1973.

ILLINGWORTH, David. 'Documents inédits et nouvelles précisions sur le théâtre de l'Hôtel de Bourgogne d'après les documents du XVIIIe siècle.' *Revue d'Histoire du Théâtre,* no. 2, 1970.

——'L'Hôtel de Bourgogne: une salle de théâtre "a l'italienne" à Paris en 1647 ?' *Revue d'Histoire du Théâtre,* no. 1, 1971.

INTERNATIONAL THEATRE INSTITUTE. *Conference on Modern Theatre Architecture.* Paris, 19–21 June 1950. (Typescript verbatim report.)

JACQUOT, Jean (ed.). *Le lieu théâtral à la Renaissance.* Paris, 1964.

——(ed.). *Les fêtes de la Renaissance.* Paris, 1956. (vols. I and III.)

JEANMAIRE, Henri. *Dionysos.* Paris, 1951.

JEFFERY, Brian. *French Renaissance Comedy, 1552–1630.* Oxford, 1969.

JONES, Leslie W. *More about the London Vitruvius.* Cambridge, Mass. 1937.

JULLEVILLE, L. Petit de. *Les mystères.* 2 vols. Paris, 1880.

JURGENS, Madeleine, and MAXFIELD-MILLER, Elizabeth. *Cent ans de recherches sur Molière, sur sa famille et sur les comédies de sa troupe.* Paris, 1963.

KERNODLE, George R. *From Art to Theatre.* Chicago, 1944.

KINDERMANN, Heinz.   *Theatergeschichte Europas.* vols. II and III. Salzburg, 1959. Revised edn. 1966.

KONIGSON, Elie.   *La représentation d'un mystère de la Passion à Valenciennes en 1547.* Paris, 1969.

——*L'Espace théâtral médiéval.* Paris, 1975.

KRAUTHEIMER, R.   'The Tragic and Comic Scenes of the Renaissance.' *Gazette des Beaux Arts,* 1948.

'La querelle du Rond', *Revue Théâtrale,* no. 29, 9e année, 1955.

LACHEZ, Théodore.   *Acoustique et optique des salles de réunion publique, théâtres et amphithéâtres, spectacles, concerts, etc.* Paris, 1848.

LACOUR, L.   'Mise en scène et représentation d'un opéra en province vers la fin du XVIe siècle.' *Revue française,* tome XII, 1858.

LACROIX, Paul (ed.).   *Ballets et mascarades de cour de Henri III à Louis XIV.* 6 vols. Geneva, 1868–70.

——*Recueil de farces, soties et moralités du XVe siècle* (par P.L. Jacob). Paris, 1859.

LAGRAVE, Henri.   *Le théâtre et le public à Paris de 1715 à 1750.* Paris, 1972.

LANCASTER, Henry Carrington.   *A History of French Dramatic Literature in the Seventeenth Century.* 5 parts. Baltimore, 1929–32.

——'Le décor de l'Arimène de Montreux.' *Revue du seizième siècle,* tome XVI, 1929.

LANSON, Gustave.   'Etudes sur les origines de la tragédie classique en France.' *Revue d'Histoire Littéraire de la France,* 1903.

——'Notes sur un passage de Vitruve et sur l'origine de la distinction des genres dans le théâtre de la Renaissance.' *Revue de la Renaissance,* 1905.

——*Esquisse d'une histoire de la tragédie française.* New York, 1920.

LAUMANN, E.-M.   *La machinerie au théâtre depuis les Grecs jusqu'à nos jours.* Paris, 1898.

LAURENCIE, L. de la.   'Les pastorales en musique au XVIIe siècle en France et leur influence sur l'opéra français.' *Report of the 4th Congress of the I.M.S.* London, 1912.

LAVEDAN, Pierre.   *Histoire de l'urbanisme, Renaissance et temps modernes.* Paris, 1941.

LAVISSE, Ernest.   *Histoire de France depuis les origines jusqu'à la Révolution.* 9 vols. Paris, 1911–26.

LAWLER, Lilian B.   *The Maenads: a contribution to the study of the dance in Ancient Greece.* Memoirs of the American Academy in Rome, VI, 1927.

LAWRENSON, Thomas E.   'The *théâtre étagé* in the seventeenth century French theatre.' *French Studies,* January, 1950.

——'La mise en scène dans l'Arimène de Nicolas de Montreux.' *Bibliothèque d'Humanisme et Renaissance,* tome XVIII, 1956.

——'Ville imaginaire, fête, et décor de théâtre: autour d'un recueil de Geoffroy Tory.' In *Fêtes de la Renaissance,* Paris, 1956.

——(with Richard Southern and Donald Roy) 'Le Mémoire de Mahelot et l'*Agarite* de Durval—vers une reconstitution pratique.' In *Le lieu théâtral à la Renaissance,* Paris, 1964.

——'Les éditions illustrées de Térence.' In *Le lieu théâtral à la Renaissance,* Paris, 1964.

——'The Contemporary Staging of Théophile's *Pyrame et Thisbé:* the open stage imprisoned.' In *Modern Miscellany - Presented to Eugène Vinaver.* Manchester, New York, 1969.

——'Les lieux du spectacle (XVIIe siècle.)' *L'Architecture d'Aujourd'hui,* no. 152, 1970.

LAWTON, Harold Walter.   'Notes sur le décor scénique au XVIe siècle.' *Revue du XVIe siècle,* tome XV, 1928.

——*Térence en France au XVIe siècle, éditions et traductions.* Paris, 1926. Reprint 1970. Tome II, *Imitations et influences.* Geneva, 1972.

LEBEGUE, Raymond. *La tragédie religieuse en France.* Paris, 1929.

——*Le théâtre baroque en France.* Bibliothèque d'Humanisme et Renaissance. Travaux et Documents, 1942, tome II, pp. 161-84.

——'Die Inszenierung im französischen Theater der Renaissance,' *Maske und Kothurn*, 5th year, 1959.

——'Unité et pluralité de lieu dans le théâtre français,' In *Le lieu théâtral à la Renaissance*, Paris, 1964.

——*Le théâtre comique en France, de Pathelin à Mélite.* Paris, 1972.

——'Le Térence de Trechsel,' In *L'Humanisme lyonnais au XVIe siècle*, Grenoble, 1974.

LECLERC, Hélène, *Les origines italiennes de l'architecture théâtrale. L'Evolution des formes en Italie de la Renaissance à la fin du XVIIe siècle.* Paris, 1946.

——'La scénographie italienne de la Renaissance à nos jours.' *Revue d'Histoire du Théâtre*, no. 1, 1951.

——'La grande machinerie théâtrale et ses origines,' *Revue d'Histoire du Théâtre*, no. 4, 1957.

——'Circé, ou le ballet comique de la royne (1581): Métaphysique du son et de la lumière.' *Theatre Research/Recherches Théâtrales*, vol. III, no. 2, 1961.

——'La scène d'illusion et l'hégémonie du théâtre à l'italienne.' In *Histoire des Spectacles*, Encyclopédie de la Pléiade, Paris, 1965.

LEMONNIER, Henry (ed.). *Procès verbaux de l'Académie Royale d'Architecture.* 8 vols. Paris, 1911-24.

LEPIK, Wilhelmina, *The Mathematical Planning of Ancient Theatres as Revealed in the Work of Vitruvius.* Wroclaw, 1949.

LE VAYER, Paul, *Les Entrées solennelles à Paris des rois et reines de France, des souverains et princes étrangers, ambassadeurs etc., bibliographie sommaire.* Paris, 1896.

LIEBRECHT, Henri. *Histoire du théâtre français à Bruxelles au XVIIe et au XVIIIe siècle.* Paris, 1923.

LINTILHAC, Eugène F. L. *Histoire générale du théâtre en France.* 4 vols. Paris, n.d.

LINZELER, André and ADHEMAR, Jean. *Inventaire du fonds français. Graveurs du seizième siècle.* (Bibliothèque Nationale, Cabinet des Estampes.) Paris, 1932-5.

LOUGH, John. *Paris Theatre Audiences in the Seventeenth and Eighteenth Centuries.* London, 1957.

LOUKOMSKI, G. J. K. *Andrea Palladio, sa vie, son oeuvre.* Paris, 1927.

——*Maestri dell'architettura classica da Vitruvio allo Scamozzi.* Milan, 1933.

——*Les théâtres anciens et modernes.* (Plates.) Paris, 1934.

McGOWAN, Margaret. *L'Art du ballet de cour en France, 1581-1643.* Paris, 1963.

MAGAGNTO, Licisco. 'The Genesis of the Teatro Olimpico.' *Journal of the Warburg and Courtauld Institutes*, vol. XIV, July–December, 1951.

——*Teatri italiani del Cinquecento.* Venice, 1954.

MAGNE, Emile. *Les plaisirs et les fêtes en France au XVIIe siècle.* Geneva, 1944.

MAGRINI, Antonio. *Il Teatro Olimpico*, Padua, 1847.

MANCINI, Franco, MURARO, Maria-Teresa, POVOLEDA, Elena. *Illusione e la practica teatrale. Guida e catalogo della mostra a cure di . . .* Vincenza, 1975.

MANGINI, Nicola. *I teatri di Venezia.* Milan, 1974.

MARCEL, Pierre. *Les influences italiennes sur la Renaissance artistique française. Un vulgarisateur, Jean Martin.* Paris, n.d.

MARIE, Alfred. 'Les théâtres du château de Versailles.' *Revue d'Histoire du Théâtre*, no. 2, 1951.

——'La salle du théâtre de Fontainebleau.' *Revue d'Histoire du Théâtre*, no. 3, 1951.

MARSAN, Jules. *La pastorale dramatique en France à la fin du XVIe et au commencement du XVIIe siècle.* Paris, 1905.

MARTIN, Henry. 'Le "Térence des Ducs" et la mise en scène au moyen âge.' *Bulletin de la Société d'Histoire du Théâtre*, no. 1, Paris, 1902.

The Mask (review). 'A design by San Gallo.' vol. XI, no. 4, October, 1925.

MEAUME, Edouard. 'Traité de perspective, manuscrit inédit de Sébastien Leclerc (vers 1680).' *Nouvelles Archives de l'Art Français*, p. 308. Paris, 1876.

MELESE, Pierre. *Le théâtre et le public sous Louis XIV.* Paris, 1934.

——*Répertoire analytique des documents contemporains d'information et de critique concernant le théâtre à Paris sous Louis XIV, 1659–1715.* Paris, 1934.

MICHEL, André-Paul-Charles. *Histoire de l'art depuis les premiers temps chrétiens jusqu'à nos jours.* 18 vols., Paris, 1905–1929.

MIGNON, Maurice. *Etudes sur le théâtre français et italien de la Renaissance.* Paris, 1923.

MONGREDIEN, Georges. *La vie quotidienne sous Louis XIV.* Paris, 1948.

MONTILLA, Robert B. 'Awnings in Roman Theatres and Amphitheatres.' *Theatre Survey,* vol. X, no. 1, 1969.

MOREL, Jacques. 'La présentation scénique du songe dans les tragédies françaises au XVIIe siècle.' *Revue d'Histoire du Théâtre,* no. 2, 1951.

MOREY, C.R. *Mediaeval Art.* New York, 1942.

MORICE, Emile. 'La mise en scène depuis les mystères jusqu'au Cid.' *Revue de Paris,* tomes XXII and XXIII, 1835.

MORTET, Victor. *Recherches critiques sur Vitruve et son oeuvre.* 6 fasc. Paris, 1902–8.

MOUREY, Gabriel. *Le livre des fêtes françaises.* Paris, 1930.

MOYNET, J. *L'envers du théâtre: machines et décorations.* Paris, 1874.

——*La machinerie théâtrale, trucs et décors.* Paris, 1893.

MUNTZ, Eugène. *La Renaissance en Italie et en France à l'époque de Charles VIII.* Paris, 1885.

NAGLER, Alois Maria. 'The Commedia drawings of the Corsini Scenari.' *Maske und Kothurn,* 15th year, 1969.

——'The Campidoglio stage of 1513.' *Maske und Kothurn,* 16th year, 1970.

——*The Medieval Religious Stage.* New Haven, 1976.

NAVARRE, Octave. *Dionysos, étude sur l'organisation matérielle du théâtre athénien.* Paris, 1895.

——*Le théâtre grec — l'édifice, l'organisation matérielle, les représentations . . .* Paris, 1925. Reprint, Paris, 1976.

——*Les représentations dramatiques en Grèce.* Paris, 1930.

NEVILLE LEES, Dorothy. 'Theatre Museums and their uses.' *Theatre Arts Monthly,* May and September, 1933.

NICOLL, Allardyce. *The Development of the Theatre.* 5th edn. London, 1966.

NIEMEYER, C. 'The Hôtel de Bourgogne', *Theatre Annual,* 1947.

NIETZSCHE, Frederick. *L'origine de la tragédie, ou hellénisme et pessimisme.* Trans. Marnold and Morland. Paris, 1901.

NOLHAC, Pierre de. *La création de Versailles.* Versailles, 1901.

NUITTER, Charles, and Ernest THOINAN. *Les origines de l'opéra français.* Paris, 1886.

PARIS, Paulin. *La mise en scène des mystères.* Paris, 1885.

PICARD, Raymond. 'Racine et Chauveau.' *Journal of the Warburg and Courtauld Institutes,* vol. XIV, nos. 3–4, 1951.

PICKARD-CAMBRIDGE, Arthur. *The Theatre of Dionysus in Athens.* Oxford, 1946.

PIFTEAU, Benjamin, and J. GOUJON. *Histoire du théâtre en France des origines au Cid, 1398–1636.* Paris, 1879.

POUGIN, F.-A.-A. *Dictionnaire historique et pittoresque du théâtre et des arts qui s'y rattachent.* Paris, 1885.

POULAIN, Roger. *Salles de spectacle et d'auditions.* Paris, 1933.

POUPE, E. *Les représentations scéniques à Cuers à la fin du XVIe siècle et au commencement du XVIIe.* Paris, 1900.

——*Documents relatifs à des représentations scéniques à Correns au XVIe et au XVIIe siècle.* Paris, 1901.

——*Documents relatifs à des représentations scéniques en Provence au XVIe siècle.* Paris, 1904.

——*Documents relatifs à des représentations scéniques en Provence du XVe au XVIIe siècle.* Paris, 1905.

PRUDENT, Henri, and P. GUADET. *Les théâtres du Palais Royal.* Orleans, n.d.

PRUNIERES, Henry. *L'Opéra italien en France avant Lulli.* Paris, 1913.

——*Le Ballet de cour en France avant Benserade et Lulli.* Paris, 1914.

PUPPI, Lionello. *Il teatro Olimpico. A cura dell'Accademia Olimpica di Vicenza.* Vicenza, 1963.

PURKIS, Helen M.C. 'The illustrations to Curzio Gonzaga's *Gli Inganni*: variations on the comic scene of Serlio.' *Letterature Moderne,* no. 3, 1957.

——'Les intermèdes à la cour de France au XVIe siècle.' *Bibliothèque d'Humanisme et Renaissance,* tome XX, 1958.

——(with LAWRENSON, Thomas Edward.) 'Les éditions illustrées de Térence dans l'histoire du théâtre. Spectacles dans un fauteuil?' in *Le Lieu théâtral à la Renaissance.* Paris, 1964.

——'Quelques observations sur les intermèdes dans le théâtre des Jésuites en France.' *Revue d'Histoire du Théâtre,* no. 2, 1966.

RASZEWSKI, Zbigniew. 'Josef Furttenbach: Scena di Comedia' *Pamietnik Teatralny,* vol. 3 (7), 1953.

REES, Kelley. 'The Significance of the Parodoi in the Greek Theater.' *American Journal of Philology,* vol. XXXII, 1911.

REISS, Timothy J. *Toward Dramatic Illusion: Theatrical Technique and Meaning from Hardy to Horace.* New Haven and London, 1971.

REY-FLAUD, Henri. *Le cercle magique, Essai sur le théâtre en rond à la fin du Moyen Age.* Paris, 1973.

RIDGEWAY, Sir William. *The Origin of Tragedy.* London, 1910.

——*Drama and the Dramatic Dances of non-European Races in Special Reference to the Origin of Greek Tragedy.* London, 1915.

RIGAL, Eugène, *Hôtel de Bourgogne et Marais, esquisse d'une histoire des théâtres de Paris, de 1548 à 1635.* Paris, 1887.

——*Alexandre Hardy et le théâtre français à la fin du XVIe et au commencement du XVIIe siècle.* Paris, 1889.

——*Le théâtre français avant la période classique.* Paris, 1901.

——'La mise en scène dans les tragédies du seizième siècle.' *Revue d'Histoire Littéraire de la France,* 1905.

——*De Jodelle à Molière: tragédie, comédie, tragi-comédie.* Paris, 1911.

ROLLAND, Joachim. *Notes pour servir à l'étude de la société et du théâtre en France au XVIIe et au XVIIIe siècle.* Paris, 1931.

ROLLAND, Romain. *Les origines du théâtre lyrique moderne. Histoire de l'opéra en Europe avant Lulli et Scarlatti.* Paris, 1895.

——*Musiciens d'autrefois.* 6th edn. Paris, 1919.

ROLLE, M.F. 'Bernard Salomon (le petit Bernard), peintre et graveur sur bois. Documents sur la part prise par lui aux travaux de l'entrée à Lyon du Cardinal d'Este, sous les ordres du peintre florentin Benedetto dal Bene, et à ceux de l'entrée de Henri II et de Catherine, dont il eut la direction (1540-1548), signature.' *Archives de l'art français,* 2e série, tome I, no. 68212. Paris, 1861.

RONDEL, Auguste. 'La bibliographie dramatique et les collections de théâtre en France.' *Bulletin de la Société d'Histoire du Théâtre,* January–March, 1918.

——*Catalogue analytique sommaire de la collection théâtrale Rondel. Suivi d'un guide pratique à travers la bibliographie théâtrale et d'une chronologie des ouvrages d'information et de critique théâtrale.* Paris, 1932.

ROUCHES, Gabriel. *Inventaire des lettres et papiers manuscrits de Gaspare, Carlo et Lodovico Vigarani, conservés aux Archives d'Etat de Modène. 1634-1688.* Paris, 1913.

ROUSSET, Jean. *La littérature de l'âge baroque en France.* Paris, 1953.

——'L'Ile enchantée — Fête et théâtre au XVIIe siècle.' *Mélanges de littérature comparée et de philologie offerts à M. Brahmer.* Warsaw, 1967.

——*L'Intérieur et l'extérieur: Essais sur la poésie et sur le théâtre au XVIIe siècle.*   Paris, 1968.
ROY, Donald.   'La scène de l'Hôtel de Bourgogne.'   *Revue d'Histoire du Théâtre,*   no. 3, 1967.
——'Mahelot's "Nights": a traditional stage effect.'   in *Gallica: Essays presented to J. Haywood Thomas by colleagues, pupils, and friends.*   Cardiff, 1969.
ROYER, Alphonse.   *Histoire de l'opéra.*   Paris, 1875.
——*Histoire universelle du théâtre.*   4 vols.   Paris, 1869–70.

SAINTE-BEUVE, C.-A.   *Tableau historique et critique de la poésie française au XVIe siècle.*   2 vols.   Paris, 1828.
SAXON, Arthur H.   'Giuseppe Galli-Bibienas architetture e prospettive.'   *Maske und Kothurn,* no. 2, 1969.
SAUTEL, Joseph.   *Le théâtre de Vaison et les théâtres romains de la vallée du Rhône.*   (Brochure).   Avignon, 1946.
SCHERER, Jacques.   *La dramaturgie classique en France.*   Paris, n.d.
SCHMIDT, Expeditus.   *Die Bühnenverhältnisse des Deutschen Schuldramas und seine volkstümlichen Ableger im sechzehnten Jahrhundert.*   Vol. 24 of *Forschungen zur neueren Literaturgeschichte.*   Berlin, 1903.
SCHMITT, Natalie Crohn.   'Was there a Mediaeval Theatre in the Round?'.   *Theatre Notebook,* vols. XXIII and XXIV, 1968–70.
SCHÖNE, Günter.   'Les traités de perspective: sources historiques du théâtre.'   *Theatre Research/Recherches Théâtrales,* vol. III, no. 3, 1961.
SCHRADE, Leo.   *La représentation d'Edipo Tiranno au Teatro Olimpico* (Vicence 1585).   Paris, 1960.
SONREL, Pierre.   *Traité de scénographie.*   Paris, 1943.
SOULIE, Eudore.   *Recherches sur Molière et sa famille.*   Paris, 1863.
SOUTHERN, Richard.   *The Mediaeval Theatre in the Round.*   London, 1957.
STATES, Bert O., Jr.   'Servandoni et la Salle des Machines.'   *Revue d'Histoire du Théâtre,* no. 1, 1961.
STUART, Donald Clive.   *Stage Decoration in France in the Middle Ages.*   New York: Columbia University Press, 1910; reprinted AMS Press, 1966.

TAPIE, Victor L.   *Baroque et classicisme.*   Paris, 1957.
Théâtre et collectivité ('Sténogrammes des secondes et troisièmes sessions du Centre d'Etudes Philosophiques et Techniques du Théâtre').   Paris, 1951.
THOMSON, George.   *Aeschylus and Athens. A study in the social origins of drama.*   2nd edn.   London, 1945.
TOLDO, Pierre.   'La comédie française de la Renaissance.'   *Revue d'Histoire Littéraire de la France,* 1897, 1898, 1899, 1900.

VANUXEM, Jacques.   'Emblèmes et devises vers 1600–1680.'   *Bulletin de la Société d'Histoire de l'Art Français,* 1954.
——'Racine, les machines et les fêtes.'   *Revue d'Histoire Littéraire de la France,* 1954.
——'Le décor de théâtre sous Louis XIV.'   *Revue d'Histoire du XVIIe Siècle,* no. 39, 1958.
——'Les entrées royales sous Louis XIII et Louis XIV.'   *Médecine de France,* April, 1959.
——'Les fêtes de Louis XIV et le baroque de la *Finta Pazza* à *Psyché* (1645–1671).'   *Actes des journées internationales des études du baroque.*   Montauban, 1967.
——'La scénographie des fêtes de Louis XIV auxquelles a participé Molière.'   *Revue d'Histoire du XVIIe siècle,* no. 99, 1973.
VEDIER, Georges.   *Origine et évolution de la dramaturgie néo-classique. L'influence des arts plastiques en Italie et en France: le rideau, la mise en scène, et les trois unités.*   Paris, 1955.
VILLIERS, André.   'Théâtre en rond aux U.S.A.'   *Revue Théâtrale,* no. 20, 7th year.

———'L'ouverture de la scène à l'Hôtel de Bourgogne.' *Revue d'Histoire du Théâtre*, no. 2, 1970.

———'Sur la pratique du rideau de scène au XVIIe siècle.' *Revue d'Histoire du Théâtre*, no. 1, 1977.

VINAVER, Eugène. *Racine et la poésie tragique.* Paris, 1951.

VITU, A. *Archéologie moliéresque. Le jeu de paume des Mestayers ou l'Illustre Théâtre.* Paris, 1883.

WEIGERT, Roger-Armand. *Inventaire du fonds français, graveurs du XVIIe siècle.* Paris, 1883.

WILEY, W.L. *The Early Public Theater in France.* Cambridge, Mass. 1960.

———'The Hôtel de Bourgogne. Another Look at France's First Public Theatre.' *Studies in Philology*, vol. LXX, December, 1973, no. 5.

YATES, Frances A. *The French Academies in the Sixteenth Century.* London, 1947.

YOUNG, Bert Edward, and G.P. YOUNG. *Le Registre de la Grange.* 2 vols. Paris, 1947.

BEFORE 1800

(Dramatic works are not normally quoted)

ACCOLTI, Pietro. *Lo Inganno de Gl'Occhi, prospettiva pratica di . . . gentihuomo fiorentino. E della Toscana Accademia del Disegno . . .* In Firenze . . . MDCXXV.

ALBERTI. *Leonis Baptistae Florentini viri clarissimi libri de re aedificatoria decem.* Parhisiis, 1512.

ALBERTI, Leone Battista. *De Re Aedificatoria libri decem . . . Recens summa diligentia capitibus distincti, et afoedis mendis repurgati, per Eberhardum Tappium Lunensem . . .* Argentorati, excudebat M. Jacobus Cammerlander Moguntinus. Anno 1541.

ALBERTI, L.-B. *D'Architecture et Art de bien bastir du seigneur Léon Baptiste Albert, Gentilhomme Florentin, divisée en dix liures, Traduicts de Latin en François, par deffunct IAN MARTIN, Parisien, nagueres Secretaire du Reuerendissime Cardinal de Lenancour.* A Paris . . . 1553.

ALBERTUS, Leo Baptista. *De Re Aedificatoria Libri Decem.* Florentiae, 1485.

ALEAUME, J. *La perspective spéculative et pratique.* Paris, 1643.

Almanach historique et raisonné des architectes, peintres, sculpteurs, graveurs et ciseleurs. Paris, 1776.

ARISTOTLE. *Aristotelis liber de Poetica, ab Antonio Riccobono, . . . latine conversa et clarissimis partitionibus ac notationibus ad oram libri positis illustrata.* Venetiis, 1584.

AUBIGNAC, d' (François Hedelin). *La pratique du théâtre, oeuvre très-nécessaire à tous ceux qui veulent s'appliquer à la composition des poèmes dramatiques . . .* Paris, 1657.

———*La pratique du théâtre.* Nouvelle édition, préface et notes de Martino. Paris, 1927.

———*Térence justifié, ou deux dissertations concernant l'art du théâtre . . . Contre les erreurs de Maistre Gilles Ménage, Advocat en Parlement.* Paris, 1656.

BARBARO, Daniel. *I DIECI LIBRI Dell'Architettura di M. Vitruvio tradutti et commentati da Monsignor Barbaro Eletto patriarca d'Aquilegia. Con due Tavole, l'una di tutto quello si contiene per i Capi nell'Opera, l'altra per dechiaratione di tutte le cose d'importanza.* In Vinegia . . . MDLVI.

BARBARO, Daniello. *La pratica della Perspettiva, di Monsignor Daniel Eletto Patriarca d'Aquilegia, opera molto profittavole a Pittori, Scultori e Architetti.* Venetia, 1559.

BEAUJOYEULX, Baltazar de. *Balet comique de la Royne, faict aux nopces de Monsieur le Duc de Joyeuse et Madamoyselle de Vaudemont sa soeur . . .* 1582. Ed. Margaret M. MC-GOWAN. Binghamton, N.Y., 1982. Renaissance Triumphs and Magnificences, IV.

BEAUCHAMPS, Pierre-François Godard de. *Recherches sur les théâtres de France, depuis l'année onze cent soixante un jusqu'à présent.* Paris, 1735.

BLONDEL, Jacques-François. *L'Architecture françois, ou Recueil des plans, élévations, coupes et profils des églises, maisons royales, palais, hôtels et édifices les plus considérables de Paris, etc. etc.* Paris, 1752–6.

BOINDIN, Nicolas. *Lettres historiques sur tous les Spectacles de Paris.* Paris, 1719.

BONTEMS (pseud.), Gérard. *Nouveau recueil de pièces comiques et facétieuses Les plus agréables et divertissantes de ce Temps.* Dernière édition augmentée. Cologne, n.d.

BOSSE, Abraham. *Manière universelle de M. Desargues, pour pratiquer la perspective par petit-pied, comme le géométral, Ensemble les places et proportions des fortes et faibles touches, teintes ou couleurs.* Paris, 1648.

——*Moyen universel de pratiquer la perspective sur les tableaux ou surfaces irrégulières, ensemble quelques particularitez concernant cet art et celui de la graveure en taille douce.* Paris, 1653.

——*Traité des pratiques géométrales et perspectives enseignées dans l'Académie royale de peinture et sculpture.* Paris, 1665.

——*Traité des manières de dessiner les ordres de l'architecture antique en toutes leurs parties . . .* Paris, 1664.

——*Des ordres de colonnes en l'architecture et plusieurs autres dépendances d'icelle.* Paris, 1664.

BRICE, Germain. *Description nouvelle de ce qu'il y a de plus remarquable dans la ville de Paris.* Paris, 1684.

BRUMOY, le Rév. Père. *Le Théâtre des Grecs.* 3 vols. Paris, 1730.

BULLANT, Jean. *Reigle génralle d'architecture des cinq manières de colonnes, à sçavoir: tuscane, dorique, ionique, corinthe et composite; et enrichi de plusieurs autres à l'exemple de l'antique; veu, recorrigé et augmenté par l'auteur de cinq autres ordres de colonnes suivant les reigles et doctrine de Vitruve . . . A Escouen, par . . .* Paris, 1568.

CASTELVETRO, Lodovico. *Poetica d'Aristotele vulgarizzata et sposta.* Vienna, 1570.

CAUS, Salomon. *Les Raisons des forces mouvantes, avec diverses machines tant utilles que plaisantes; ausquelles sont adjoints plusieurs desseings de Grotes et Fontaines . . .* Paris, MDC. XXIIII. (Also Frankfurt, 1615.)

——*La Perspective, Avec la raison des ombres et miroirs par . . . Ingénieur du Sérénissime Prince de Galles dédié à son Altesse.* A Londres . . . Anno Dom. 1612.

C'est l'ordre qui a este tenu a la nouvelle et joyeuse entree que tres-hault tresexcellent et trespuissant Prince, le Roy treschrestien Henry deuxiesme de ce nom, a faicte en sa bonne ville et cité de Paris, capitale de son Royaume le seiziesme jour de Juing. M.D.XLIX. A Paris, Par Jean Dallier.

CHANTELOU, Paul-Fréart, sieur de. *Journal du voyage du cavalier Bernin en France.* Ed. Ludovic Lalanne, Paris, 1885.

CHAPPUZEAU, Samuel. *Le théâtre françois.* Lyons, 1674.

——*Le théâtre français.* Préface de Georges Monval, artiste de l'Odéon. Paris, 1876.

CORNEILLE. *OEuvres.* Ed. Marty-Laveaux. 12 vols. Paris, 1862–68.

COUSIN, Jean. *LIVRE de Perspective de Iehan Cousin Senonois, maistre Painctre à Paris.* Paris, 1560.

DELORME, Philibert. *Architecture . . . œuvre entière.* Paris, 1626.

DESARGUES, Girard. *Exemples de l'une des manières universelles du S. G. D. L.* (Girard Desargues, Lyonnais.) Paris, 1636.

——*OEuvres, réunies et analysées par M. Poudra.* 2 vols. Paris, 1864.

DUBREUIL, Le P. Jean. *La Perspective pratique par un Parisien de la Compagnie de Jésus.* 3 vols. Paris, 1642–9.

DUCANGE, Charles Dufresne. *Dissertation des assemblées et des fêtes solennelles des Rois de France.* Paris, 1668.

DUCERCEAU, Jacques Androuet. *Livre d'Architecture de . . . contenant les plans et dessaings de cinquante bastimens tous différens . . .* Paris, 1559.

——*Second Livre d'Architecture par . . . contenant plusieurs et diverses ordonnances de cheminées, lucarnes, portes, fonteines, puis et pavillons . . .* Paris, 1561.

——*Leçons de Perspective positive.* Paris, 1576.

——*Le Premier (Second) volume des plus excellents bastiments de France* . . . Paris, 1576–9.

——*Livre des édifices antiques romains, contenant les ordonnances et desseings des plus signalez et principaux bastiments* . . . Paris, 1584.

DUMONT, Gabriel-Martin. *Parallèle des plans des plus belles salles de spectacle d'Italie et de France, avec des détails de machines théâtrales.* Paris, n.d. (Plates.) (Published fragmentarily between 1760 and 1777, according to Contant and Filippi, q.v., and between 1764 and 1777 according to Holsboer.)

DURERUS. *Albertus Nurembergensis pictor huius etatis celeberrimus, versus e Germanica lingua in Latinam, Pictoribus, Fabris, Aerariis ac lignariis, Lapicidis, Statuariis* . . . Lutetiae Anno M.D. XXXII.

ENTREES.

——*C'est la déduction du somptueux ordre, plaisantz spectacles et magnifiques théatres dressés et exhibés, par les citoiens de Rouen, ville métropolitaine du pays de Normandie, à la sacrée Majesté du très chrestien Roy de France Henry Second, leur souverain seigneur, et à très illustre Dame, Ma Dame Katherine de Médicis, la Royne son épouse, lors de leur triumphant, joyeulx et nouvel advenement en icelle ville, qui fut es jours de mercredy et jeudy premier et second jour d'octobre 1550.* Ed. Margaret M. McGowan. Amsterdam, 1974. Renaissance Triumphs and Magnificences, II.

——*La joyeuse et magnifique entrée de Mgr. François, fils de France et frère unique du Roy* . . . *en sa très renommée ville d'Anvers, 1582.* Ed. Helen M. C. Purkis. Amsterdam, 1974. Renaissance Triumphs and Magnificences, V.

——*Bref et sommaire recueil de ce qui a esté faict* . . . *à la joyeuse et triumphante entrée du très-puissant, très-magnanime et très-chrestien Prince Charles* . . . *en sa bonne ville & cité de Paris* . . . *le mardi sixiesme jour de mars MDLXXXI.* Ed. Frances A. Yates. Amsterdam, 1974. Renaissance Triumphs and Magnificences, III.

——(DU PUYS, Rémi). *La triumphante et solennelle entrée faicte sur le nouvel et joyeux advenement de très haut et très puissant prince monsr. Charles Prince des Espagnes* . . . *en sa ville de Bruges l'An Quinze Centz et Quinze le dixhuictiesme jour d'Apuril après Paches.* Ed. Sidney Anglo. Amsterdam, 1975. Renaissance Triumphs and Magnificences, I.

FELIBIEN, André. *Relation de la feste de Versailles du 18e juillet 1668 par* . . . Paris, 1668.

——*Les Divertissements de Versailles, donnez par le Roy au retour de la conquête de la Franche-Comté.* Paris, 1674.

FREART, Roland, sieur de. *Parallèle de l'architecture antique avec la moderne* . . . Paris, 1650.

FURTTENBACH, Joseph, the elder. *Architectura civilis.* Ulm, 1628.

GHERARDI, Evariste. *Le Théâtre Italien* . . . *ou Recueil général de toutes les comédies et scènes françaises jouées par les Comédiens Italiens du Roi.* Paris, 1700.

GIRAUD, Paul Émile, and U. CHEVALIER (ed.). *Le mystère des Trois Doms.* Lyons, 1887.

GODEFROY, Denis. *Le Cérémonial françois* . . . *recueilli par Théodore Godefroy* . . . *et mis en lumière par Denis Godefroy* . . . 2 vols. Paris, 1649.

GODEFROY, Théodore. *Le Cérémonial de France, ou Description des cérémonies, rangs, et séances observées aux couronnements, entrées et enterrements des roys et reynes de France.* Paris, 1619.

GREBAN, Arnoul. *Le Mystère des Actes des Apôtres représenté à Bourges en avril 1536.* Ed. Baron Auguste Théodore de Girardot. Paris, 1854.

HONDIUS, Henry. *Instruction en la Science de Perspective.* La Haye, 1625.

HURET, Grégoire. *Optique de portraiture et de Peinture* . . . Paris, 1670.

INGEGNERI, Angelo. *Della poesia rappresentativa.* *Parte seconda: Del modo di rappresentare le favole sceniche.* Ferrara, 1598.

JODE, Gérard de.   *Ruinarum variarum fabricarum delineationes.*   Antwerp, 1560 (?).

LA FONTAINE.   *Epistre à M. de Niert, sur l'opéra.*   (In *OEuvres*, ed. Régnier, tome IX, pp. 154 et seq.   Paris, 1892.)
LA GRANGE, S. de.   *Registre de . . . Précedé d'une notice biographique, par M. Edouard Thierry.*   Paris, 1876.   (See also YOUNG and YOUNG.)
LA MESNARDIERE, Jules de.   *Poétique.*   Paris, 1639.
LERIS, Antoine de.   *Dictionnaire portatif historique et littéraire des théâtres.*   2nd edn.   Paris, 1763.

Magnifica, La . . . Et triumphale entrata del Xtianigimo Re di Francia Henrico Secondo di questo nome, fatta nella nobile et antiqua città di Lyone à lui e alla serenissima consorte Chaterina, alli 21 di Septembre 1548.   Colla particolare descrizione della Commedia che fece recitare la Natione fiorentina à richiesta di sua maiestà Xtianigima.   Lyons, 1549.
Magnificence, La . . . de la superbe et triumphante entree de la noble et antique Cité de Lyon faicte au Treschrestien Roy de France Henry deuxiesme de ce Nom, Et à la Royne Catherine son Espouse le XXIII de Septembre M.D. XLVIII.   Lyons, 1549.
MAHELOT, Laurent.   *La mise en scène à Paris au XVIIe siècle, mémoire de Laurent Mahelot et Michel Laurent, publié avec une notice et des notes par Emile Dacier.* (Extract from *Mémoires de la Société d'Histoire de Paris et de l'Ile de France*, tome XXVIII, 1901.)
———(ed. Lancaster, Henry Carrington).   *Le mémoire de Mahelot, Laurent, et d'autres décorateurs de l'Hôtel de Bourgogne et de la Comédie Française au XVIIe siécle.*   Paris, 1920.
MAIRET, J. de.   *La Sylvie.*   Edition critique de Jules Marsan.   Paris, 1905.
MARIETTE, Pierre-Jean.   *L'Architecture Française, ou Recueil des plans, Elévations, coupes et profils Des Eglises, Palais, Hôtels et Maisons particulières de Paris et des Châteaux et Maisons de Campagne ou de Plaisance, et de Plusieurs autres endroits de France.*   2 vols.   Paris, 1727.
MARLIANUS, Joannes Bartholomeus.   *De origine urbis Romae.*   1554.
———*Topographia antiquae Romae.*   Lugduni, 1534.
MAROLOIS, Samuel.   *Opera Mathematica, ou OEuvres Mathématiques, traictans de Géométrie, Perspective, Architecture et fortification, par S. . . .*   Hagae-Comitis . . . MDCXIIII.
MATHIEU, Pierre.   *L'Entrée de la Reine à Lyon, le 3 décembre, 1600.*   Lyons, 1600.
MILIZIA, Fr.   *Memorie degli architetti antichi e moderni.*   Parma, 1781.
MONTENARI, Giovanni.   *Del Teatro Olimpico di Andrea Palladio in Vicenza.*   2nd edn.   Padua, 1749.
MONTJOYE.   *Le pas des armes de l'arc triumphal ou tout honneur est enclos tenu à l'entrée de la Royne à Paris en la rue Saint-Anthoine, près les Tournelles, par puissant seigneur Monseigneur le duc de Valloys et de Bretaigne ou tous les nobles hommes doivent prendre leur adresse pour acquérir loz, honneur et gloire militaire, rédigé et mis par escript par Montjoye, roy d'armes, selon les compaignies et journées ainsi comme le tout a esté faict.*   Paris, 1514.
MONTREUX, Nicolas de.   See OLLENIX.
MOUHY, Chevalier de.   *Abrégé de l'histoire du théâtre français depuis son origine justqu'au premier juin 1780.*   4 vols.   Paris, 1780.

NAVARRE, Marguerite de.   *(Les) Marguerites de la Marguerite des princesses, tres illustre royne de Navarre.*   2 vols.   Lyons, 1547.
NICERON, Jean-François.   *La Perspective curieuse ou Magie artificielle des effets merveilleux de l'optique.   Par . . . Parisien de l'Ordre des Minimes.*   Paris, 1638.

OLLENIX DU MONT-SACRE (pseud. of Nicolas de Montreux).   *L'Arimène, ou berger désespéré.*   Paris, Saugrain and Des Rues, 1597.
———. . .Paris, chez Dominique Salis, 1597.
———. . . Nantes, chez Pierre Doriou, 1597.

ORMESSON, Olivier Le Fèvre d'. *Journal . . . et extraits des mémoires d'André Lefèvre d'Ormesson. Publiés par M. Chéruel.* 2 vols. Paris, 1860-1.

OUTREMAN, Henri d'. *Histoire de la ville et comté de Valenciennes.* Douai, 1639.

PALLADIO, Andrea. *I quatro libri dell'Architettura di . . .* Venice, 1580.

PAPON, Loys. *Oeuvres du Chanoine . . . Seigneur de Marcilly, poète forésien du XVIe siècle. Imprimées pour la première fois sur les manuscrits originaux par les soins et aux frais de Mr. N. Yemeniz.* Lyons, 1857.

PARFAICT, François et Claude. *Histoire du théâtre français.* 15 vols. Amsterdam, 1735-49.

PATTE, Pierre. *Essai sur l'Architecture théâtrale ou de l'ordonnance la plus avantageuse à une salle de spectacle relativement aux principes de l'Optique et de l'Acoustique, avec un examen des principaux théâtres de l'Europe et une analyse des écrits les plus importants sur cette matière.* Paris, 1782.

PECKHAM, John. *Prospectiva communis Johannis archiepiscopi cantuarensis.* Mediolani, *circa* 1480.

PELERIN, Jean (dit Viator). *De artificiali Perspectiva.* Toul, 1505.

——*De artificiali Perspectiva, Secondo.* Toul, 1509.

——*De artificiali Perspectiva, Tertio.* Toul, 1521.

——*De artificiali Perspectiva* (2nd edn. facsimile), ed. Tross. Paris, 1860.

——*La Perspective positive de Viator, traduite de latin en françois, augmentée et illustrée par maistre Estienne Martelange, de la compagnie de Jésus, avec les figures gravées à La Fléche per Mathurin Jousse.* 1626.

PERRAULT, Charles. *Parallèle des anciens et des modernes.* 4 vols. Paris, 1688-97.

PIGANIOL DE LA FORCE, Jean-Aymar. *Nouvelle description de la France.* 6 vols. Paris, 1718.

POLLUX, Julii Pollucis. *Onomasticon.* Basileae, 1536.

——*Julii Pollucis Onomasticon . . . nunc primum Latinitate donatum, Rodolpho Gualthero Tigurino Interprete.* Basle, 1541.

POZZO, Andrea. *Perspectiva pictorum et architectorum, pars prima.* Rome, 1693.

——*La Perspective propre des peintres et des architectes, par . . . 2e partie.* Rome, 1700.

——*Prospettiva de'pittori et architetti.* (Both parts.) Rome, 1702.

Pratique nouvelle et universelle de la Perspective sur les seules parties égales du Compas de proportion, sans y ajouter aucune ligne d'optique. (Anon.) Paris, 1640.

PURE, Michel de. *Idée des spectacles anciens et nouveaux.* Paris, 1668.

RADIER, J.-F. Dreux du. *Récréations historiques.* Amsterdam, 1764.

REAUX, Tallemant des. *Historiettes.* Ed. Monmerqué and Paulin Paris. 9 vols. Paris, 1854-60.

SABBATTINI, Nicolà. *La pratica di fabricar scene e macchine ne'teatri.* 1st edn. (contains Bk. 1 only). Pesaro, 1637.

——*La pratica di fabricar scene e macchine ne'teatri.* 2nd edn. Ravenna, 1638.

——*Pratique pour fabriquer scènes et machines de théâtre.* Trad. Mlles. M. et R. Carnavaggia, avec la collaboration de Louis Jouvet. Neuchâtel, 1942.

——*Practica etc.* Ed. POVOLEDO, Elena. *Con aggiunti documenti inediti e disegni originali a cura di . . .*, Rome, 1955.

SAINT-EVREMOND, *Œuvres.* Nouvelle edn. par Des Maizeaux. London, 1711.

SAUVAL, Henri. *Histoire et recherches des antiquités de la ville de Paris.* 3 vols. Paris, 1724.

SERLIO, Sebastiano. *Il Primo libro d'Architettura, di . . . Bolognese. Le premier livre d'Architecture de Sébastien Serlio, Bolognois, mis en langue Françoyse par Iehan Martin (suivi du second livre de Perspective).* Paris, 1545.

——*Reigles Generales de l'Architecture, sur les cinq manieres d'edifices, a sçavoir Thuscane, Doricq; Ionicq; Corinthe et Composite, avec les exemples d'anticuitez, selon la doctrine de Vitruve.* Trans. (and printed) Van Aelst, Antwerp, 1545.

——*Il Secundo Libro di Perspettiva; il primo libro di Architettura.*   Paris, 1545, Venice, 1560.

SERVANDONI, J.-N.   *Description abrégée de l'Eglise de Saint-Pierre de Rome et de la Représentation de cette église donnée à Paris, dans la Salle des Machines des Tuileries aux mois de Mars et d'Avril 1738.*   Paris, 1738.

——*Description du spectacle de Pandore etc.*   Paris, 1739.

——*Description du spectacle de la Descente d'Enée aux Enfers etc.*   Paris, 1740.

——*Description du spectacle des Aventures d'Ulysse à son retour du siège de Troie jusqu'à son arrivée à Ithaque etc.*   Paris, 1741.

——*Spectacle de Héro et Léandre etc.*   Paris, 1742.

——*La Forêt enchantée, représentation tirée du poème italien de la Jerusalem délivrée, spectacle orné de machines, animé d'acteurs pantomimes et accompagné d'une musique etc.*   Paris, 1754.

——*Le Triomphe de l'Amour conjugal, spectacle orné de machines, animé d'acteurs pantomimes etc.*   Paris, 1755.

——*La Conquête du Mogol etc.*   Paris, 1756.   (Attributed to Servandoni.)

——*Description du spectacle de la Constance couronnée etc.*   Paris, 1757.

——*Description du spectacle de la Chute des Anges rebelles etc.*   Paris, 1758.

SIRIGATTI, Lorenzo.   *La practica di prospettiva del Cavaliere . . .*   2nd edn.   Venice, 1625.

SOMMI DE', Leone.   *Quattro dialoghi in matteria di rappresentazione sceniche.*   Ed. MAROTTI, Ferruchio.   Archivio del Teatro Italiano, no. 1, 1969.

TRISTAN L'HERMITE.   *La Mariane.*   Ed. Madeleine, Paris, 1917.

TROILI, Giulio.   *Paradossi per praticare la prospettiva senza saperla.*   Bologna, 1683.

UBALDUS, Guidus.   *GUIDIBALDI e marchionibus montis Perspectivae Libri Sex.*   Pisauri, MDC.

VASARI.   *Le Vite.*   Ed. Milanesi, Florence, 1878–85.

VAULEZARD, le s. de.   *Abrégé ou raccourci de la Perspective par l'Imitation . . .*   Paris, 1633.

VIGNOLA, G. Barozzi da.   *Le due Regole della Prospettiva pratica di . . .*   Rome, 1583.

VINCI DE, Léonard.   *Traité de la Peinture, donné au public et traduit d'italien en français.*   Par R.F.S.D.C. (Roland Fréart Sieur de Chambray.)   Paris, 1651.

——*Trattato della Pittura di . . . Nouamente dato in luce . . .*   In Parigi, M.DC.LI.

VITRUVIUS.   *Lucii Vitruvii Pollionis De Architectura Libri Decem.   Detta Sulpiciana da. Giov. SULPICIO DA VEROLI che un union a Pomponion Leto . . .*   Roma, 1486.

——*M. Vitruvius per JOCUNDUM solito castigatior factus cum figuris et tabula ut, iam, legi et intellegi possit.*   Venetiis, 1511.

——*V. iterum et Frontinus a iocumdo* [sic] *revisi repurgatique quantum ex collatione licuit.*   Philippi de Giunta Florentini Anno Domini 1513.

——*M. Vitruvius Pollio.   De Architectura Libri Decem, traducti de latino in vulgare.   (Cesare CESARIANO.)*   Milano, 1521.

——Photographic re-edition of the above. Bronx/London, 1968.

——*M. Vitruvii de architectura libri decem, summa diligentia decogniti . . . Additis Julii Frontini de aqueductibus libris, propter materiae affinitatem.*   1523.   (Printed at Lyons according to Brunet.)

——*Architettura con il suo Commento et Figure Vetruvio in volgar lingua raportato per M. Giambattista CAPORALI de Perugia.*   Perugia, 1536.

——*Raison d'architecture antique extraicte de Vitruve et aultres anciens Architecteurs, nouuellement traduite d'espaignol* [of D. Sagredo] *en Françoys . . .*   Paris, 1539.

——*PHILANDER, Guillaume.   In decem libros M. Vitruuii Pollionis 'de Architectura' annotationes.*   Paris, 1545.

——*Architecture, ou art de bien bastir, Romain antique: mis de Latin en Françoys, par Ian Martin.*   Paris, 1547.   (Photographic reprint, Farnborough, 1964).

——*Architecture, ou Art de bien bastir, de Marc Vitruue Pollion Autheur Romain antique: mis de Latin* en Françoys, par Iehan Martin Secretaire de Monseigneur le Cardinal de Lenoncourt.   Paris, MD. XLVII.   (Also Paris, 1572, and Geneva, 1618 and 1628.)

——De architectura libri decem . . . accesserunt G. Philandri . . . annotationes . . . adjecta est G. Agricolae de mensuris et ponderibus libros, eodem autore.   Lugduni, 1552.   (Also 1586.)

——Epitome ou extrait abrégé des dix livres d'architecture de Marc Vitruve Pollion. Enrichi des figures et pourtraits pour l'intelligence du livre.   Par Ian Gardet Bourbonnois et Dominique Bertin Parisien.   Avec les annotations sur les plus difficiles passages de l'auteur.   A Tolose, 1559.   (Also Paris, 1567 and 1568.)

——Julien MAUCLERC.   Traitté de l'Architecture suivant Vitruve . . .   Paris, 1648.

——Les Dix livres d'Architecture de Vitruve, corrigés et traduits nouvellement en français avec des Notes et des figures.   (Claude Perrault.)   Paris, 1673, with an abrégé in 1674.   (Also Amsterdam, 1681, and Paris, 1684.)

——Les dix livres d'architecture de Vitruve avec les notes de Perrault.   Nouvelle édition revue et corrigée et augmentée d'un grand nombre de planches et de notes importantes . . . par E. Tardieu et A. Coussin fils.   2 vols.   Paris, 1836.

——Traduction sous la direction de M. Nisard, Professeur d'Eloquence Latine au Collège de France.   Paris, 1846.

——Trans. Choisy.   4 vols.   Paris, 1909.

——The Loeb Translation (Granger).   Based on the oldest manuscript of Vitruvius, Harleian 2767 of the British Museum. London, 1931.

——De l'architecture.   Paris, 1969.

VOLTAIRE.   Commentaires sur Corneille.   Vols. XXXI and XXXII of the Moland edn.   Paris, 1877–85.

VRIES, Jean Vredeman de.   La très noble perspective de . . . à savoir la théorie pratique et instruction fondamentale d'icelle . . .   Amsterdam, 1619.

MANUSCRIPTS

BIBLIOTHEQUE NATIONALE

Fonds latin 10277: tenth-century manuscript of Vitruvius' De Architectura.

Nouvelles acquisitions latines 1236: Antiphonaire de l'église de Nevers.   The fly-leaf is part of an eleventh-century manuscript of Vitruvius.

Nouvelles acquisitions latines 1422: manuscript of Vitruvius in a fifteenth-century hand.

Fonds français 12345: Mémoires pour servir à l'histoire de l'Académie Royale de Peinture et de Sculpture (XVIIe siècle).

——12338: Premier livre d'Architecture de Marc-Vitruve Pollion, a César Auguste.

——7801: Papiers de l'architecte Robert de Cotte, surintendant de bâtiments du roi (1667–1739.)

——21675–21679: Collection La Mare. (Bâtiments.)

——24352–243357: Accounts of the court ballet.   A chronology of published ballets.   (Recueil de ballets, opéras, pastorales et tragédies.)

——Réserve 24330: Mémoire de Laurent Mahelot et de Michel Laurent.

——9153: Papiers de l'architecte Etienne-Louis Boullée, membre de l'Institut, mort le 17 pluviose, an VII (5 fév. 1799).

ARCHIVES NATIONALES

O^1 13: Registres du Secrétariat de la Maison du Roi.

O^1 15: Registres du Secrétariat de la Maison du Roi.

O^1 16: Registres du Secrétariat de la Maison du Roi.

O^1 613: Papiers concernant l'Académie Royale de Musique.
O^1 618: Papiers concernant l'Académie Royale de Musique.
O^1 1929–30: Verbatim reports of the Académie Royale d'Architecture.
O^1 2984: Pièces justificatives des menus plaisirs du roi.
O^1 3259: La Ferté collection. Essai sur les fêtes, réjouissances publiques etc.
O^1 3260–3265: Fêtes, cérémonies, etc.

ENGRAVINGS

CABINET DES ESTAMPES OF THE BIBLIOTHEQUE NATIONALE

Aa 5: The Petit Bourbon (Métezeau).
Ed 1a: Béatrizet's Theatre of Marcellus.
Ed 2b: Engravings by Jacques-Androuet Ducerceau.
Ed 2i: *Sur Jacques-Androuet Ducerceau et son fils Jean-Baptiste,* Callen père.
Ed 5h Réserve: Volume of engravings without title or pagination; A LION PAR IAN DE
      TOURNES M.D. LVI.
Cc 92: Pierre Perret (1555–1639) Scènes de farce française.   An engraving with a verse
      inscription ('La farce des Grecz descendue') is not in fact by Perret but by Francois
      Clouet, see Adhémar, *Inventaire,* vol. II, p. 268.
Gc 6: Lafréry: Theatre of Marcellus (after Béatrizet).
Ha 55: Drawings by Louis-Etienne Boullée.
Ob 1: The Petit Bourbon (Delamonce).   Also Ziarnko.
Va 361 VII: Versailles.   Projects for the salle des ballets in the North Wing of the château,
      by Mansard and Vigarani, together with four anonymous projects.

CABINET DES ESTAMPES OF THE MUSEE CARNAVALET

20 A: Plan des jardins du Palais des Thuilleries, de l'invention de M. le Nôtre, comme il
      est à présent à Paris, chez M. Langlois . . .   Also, Morceaux du Jardin des Thuil-
      leries, marquez des mêmes Lettres sur le Plan général.

INDEX

Dramatic works are normally listed under authors

273